DATE DUE

Learning by Doing in Markets, Firms, and Countries

A National Bureau
of Economic Research
Conference Report

Learning by Doing in Markets, Firms, and Countries

Edited by **Naomi R. Lamoreaux,
Daniel M. G. Raff,
and Peter Temin**

The University of Chicago Press

Chicago and London

NAOMI R. LAMOREAUX is professor of economics and history at the University of California, Los Angeles, and a research associate of the National Bureau of Economic Research. DANIEL M. G. RAFF is associate professor of management at the Wharton School of the University of Pennsylvania, associate professor of history at the university, and a faculty research fellow of the National Bureau of Economic Research. PETER TEMIN is the Elisha Gray II Professor of Economics at the Massachusetts Institute of Technology and a research associate of the National Bureau of Economic Research.

The University of Chicago Press, Chicago 60637
The University of Chicago Press, Ltd., London
© 1999 by the National Bureau of Economic Research
All rights reserved. Published 1999
Printed in the United States of America
08 07 06 05 04 03 02 01 00 99   1 2 3 4 5
ISBN: 0-226-46832-1 (cloth)
ISBN: 0-226-46834-8 (paper)

Library of Congress Cataloging-in-Publication Data

Learning by doing in markets, firms, and countries / Naomi R.
    Lamoreaux, Daniel M. G. Raff, and Peter Temin.
        p.   cm.—(A National Bureau of Economic Research confer-
    ence report)
    Proceedings from a conference.
    Includes bibliographical references (p.   ) and indexes.
        ISBN 0-226-46832-1 (alk. paper).—ISBN 0-226-46834-8 (pbk. :
    alk. paper)
    1. Organizational learning—Congresses.   2. Business intelli-
    gence—History—Congresses.   3. Business enterprises—History—
    Case studies—Congresses.   4. Business—History—Congresses.
    I. Lamoreaux, Naomi R.   II. Raff, Daniel M. G.   III. Temin, Peter.
    IV. Series: Conference report (National Bureau of Economic Re-
    search)
    HD58.82.L385 1999
    338.7—dc21   98-8558
                                                                      CIP

Since this volume is a record of conference proceedings, it has been exempted from the rules governing critical review of manuscripts by the Board of Directors of the National Bureau (resolution adopted 8 June 1948, as revised 21 November 1949 and 20 April 1968).

Contents

Introduction

Naomi R. Lamoreaux, Daniel M. G. Raff, and Peter Temin

Business history ought to be an interdisciplinary subject. Because businesses are first and foremost economic units that make such decisions as how much of a good to produce, how to make it, and what to charge for it, the "dismal science" of economics inevitably has a role to play in understanding their behavior. At the same time, however, businesses are organizations of people whose choices are affected by the social and cultural environment in which they live and work. Hence understanding how businesses operated in the past—and why they succeeded or failed—is also an interpretive activity that requires the tools and sensitivity of historical scholarship.

Unfortunately, there is little communication today between economists and historians or even between economic historians (who are largely economists by training) and business historians (who typically come out of history departments). The former have organized themselves into the Economic History Association; the latter into the Business History Conference. Only a small number of people attend both sets of meetings. Moreover, the two groups of scholars largely subscribe to and publish in different journals. Economic histo-

Naomi R. Lamoreaux is professor of economics and history at the University of California, Los Angeles, and a research associate of the National Bureau of Economic Research. Daniel M. G. Raff is associate professor of management at the Wharton School of the University of Pennsylvania, associate professor of history at the university, and a faculty research fellow of the National Bureau of Economic Research. Peter Temin is the Elisha Gray II Professor of Economic History and Applied Economics at the Massachusetts Institute of Technology and a research associate of the National Bureau of Economic Research.

The authors are grateful to Bruce Greenwald, Constance Helfat, Bruce Kogut, Daniel Levinthal, Jean-Laurent Rosenthal, Kenneth Sokoloff, Sidney Winter, and Mary Yeager for many helpful conversations, to all the NBER conference participants for their enthusiastic engagement, and to Martin Feldstein for his steadfast support. Participants in the Hagley Museum and Library Conference on the Future of Business History, especially the discussant Philip Scranton, gave thoughtful and, in the very best sense, provocative reactions to a related paper (Lamoreaux, Raff, and Temin 1997). The usual disclaimer applies.

rians read the *Journal of Economic History* and *Explorations in Economic History,* and business historians the *Business History Review* and the conference's annual publication, *Business and Economic History.* There are relatively few articles in either set of journals that appeal to both groups of scholars.

Although this division can be traced back to the period before World War II, recent developments in economic theory now make it possible to bring the two groups of scholars together in writing a new kind of business history. In this introduction we first detail the history of relations between economic and business historians from the early twentieth century on. We then outline some aspects of the new theory that, we believe, will further interdisciplinary research in business history and make the work of business historians more interesting to the larger community of economists and historians. This book is the third in a series. The essays collected in this volume, as in the previous two (Temin 1991; Lamoreaux and Raff 1995), were originally presented at a conference organized to bring business and economic historians together. They are concrete examples of the kind of theoretically informed business history that we are promoting. Hence we conclude our introduction by situating this volume relative to the previous two and highlighting the contributions made by the individual essays toward a more complete understanding of how businesses—and other organizations—have functioned in the past.

Economic History and Business History

The field of economic history had its formal beginning in the United States in 1892 when Harvard created a chair in the subject and appointed British scholar William J. Ashley to fill it. A number of other universities followed Harvard's example and established similar chairs during the last decade of the nineteenth century. After the First World War, a new generation of economic historians assumed positions of leadership, and the field began a period of rapid growth. One of the most important of the new scholars was Edwin F. Gay, who had replaced Ashley at Harvard and who went on to lend his prestige and energies to a major program of institution building. Among the fruits of his efforts were the National Bureau of Economic Research, the Commission on Recent Economic Changes, the Commission on Recent Social Trends, and the Social Science Research Council. Underlying all of these organizations was Gay's belief that research in economic history, particularly the careful amassing of long-term quantitative data sets, would provide a vital foundation for both historical understanding and policy making. For similar reasons, Gay believed that it was important for archives to collect business papers, and he helped to found an association devoted to this end, the Business History Society. One of his students, N. S. B. Gras, the first Strauss Professor of Business History at the Harvard Business School, became a leader of the new subfield of business history; and from 1928 to 1931, Gay and Gras co-edited the *Journal of*

Economic and Business History, which aimed to bring together work in both subject areas (Sass 1986, 15, 29–43; Cole 1968, 558–59).

This collaborative effort soon foundered, however, over the very different conceptions the two men had about the direction that scholarship in business history should take. Gay and other economic historians at the time believed that business history should contribute to the synthetic view of economic history they were seeking to construct—that it was precisely because businesses were subjected to the discipline of the market that their records could provide insight into larger economic processes. Gras, on the other hand, had little use for the type of theorizing that characterized the more established field. He was a rigidly inductive thinker who believed that business behavior should be studied for its own sake, and that new generalizations would ultimately emerge from case studies amassed by scholars doing highly focused research on particular enterprises. He and Gay disagreed vehemently about the amount of such work the journal should publish, and the two men (and their respective fields) became increasingly estranged. Gay resigned his editorial position in 1931, and the journal folded the next year (Sass 1986, 42–45; Heaton 1952, 194).

Although Gras had a number of followers, many scholars interested in the study of business history soon grew frustrated with the particularism of his approach; and for a time, it seemed as if there would be a reconciliation of business and economic history. Economists like Arthur H. Cole, whose work fell within both subdisciplines, led a new wave of organization building that culminated in the 1940s with the founding of the Economic History Association, the Council for Research in Economic History, and the Center for Research in Entrepreneurial History at Harvard (Heaton 1941, 1965; Sass 1986, 54–59). As the history of the center illustrates, however, whatever reconciliation occurred was short-lived.

Scholars at the center were interested in reinjecting theory into the study of business history. Their starting point was Joseph Schumpeter's concept of entrepreneurship as a creative act that shifted the economy's production possibility frontier outward in a discontinuous fashion (Schumpeter 1934). Entrepreneurship was an important subject to study, they argued, because this kind of creativity was the key to sustained improvements in social well-being. However, Schumpeter himself was unable to explain why some societies at some times produce disproportionate numbers of entrepreneurs. Neoclassical price theory also appeared to lack answers to such questions, and so scholars at the center turned instead to sociological (particularly Parsonian) models of human behavior in order to understand why some cultures seem to offer particularly fertile ground for entrepreneurial innovation. The work of the most important historians associated with the center—David Landes, Thomas Cochran, and Alfred D. Chandler, Jr., are good examples—consistently employed concepts and addressed debates at the heart of this sociological literature, even when they did not make extensive use of its rather arcane vocabulary and categories of analysis.[1]

Parsons's approach to the study of society was essentially an equilibrium one, and there was nothing inherently incompatible between the broad syntheses of business history developed by scholars at the center and the work of economic historians trained in economics. In recent years, indeed, economists as prominent as Oliver Williamson and David Teece have found much to admire in Chandler's model of the evolution of business organizations (Williamson 1981; Teece 1993).[2] But circumstances at the time made the differences seem more important than they actually were. During the early 1950s, concern about the causes of underdevelopment in large parts of the world led to heated debates about the role of entrepreneurship in industrialization. On the positive side, of course, were scholars at the center. The negative side was championed by Alexander Gerschenkron, also of Harvard, who in this debate stressed the role of natural-resource endowments, income levels, and the size of the domestic market (Abramovitz and David 1996, 50–57). The spirit of the negative view was essentially that of neoclassical economics, and Gerschenkron's students, along with those of the equally prominent economist Simon Kuznets, formed the vanguard of what came to be known as the New Economic History (or sometimes cliometrics), a brand of scholarship committed to the systematic application of neoclassical economic theory and formal hypothesis testing to the study of the past.[3]

The young scholars who led the cliometrics movement disparaged the importance of heroic individuals and so, ipso facto, the entire topic of entrepreneurial history. Douglass North, for example, famously downgraded the role of the entrepreneur in his *Economic Growth of the United States.* Entrepreneurs, he argued, did little more than respond to opportunities to maximize profits; their role was essentially passive. If Eli Whitney had not invented the cotton gin, someone else would have: "The growing dilemma of the South was that the demand for its traditional export staples was no longer increasing and its heavy capital investment was in slaves. . . . [I]nvention of the cotton gin can be viewed as a response to the dilemma rather than as an independent accidental development" (North 1961, 8, 52). Technological innovation was induced by changes in relative prices—that is, by market-driven opportunities for profit. There was no reason to devote time or resources to studying the entrepreneurial function in American business.

1. This search for theory often took the form of written scholarly debate in the pages of the center's in-house journal, *Explorations in Entrepreneurial History.* For a study of the process by which participants turned to Parsonian sociology, see Sass (1986, 107–223). For an analysis of the utility of this body of theory from someone associated for a time with the center, see Galambos (1969).

2. In addition, the faculty of the Graduate School of Business of the University of Chicago, well known for their orthodox economic views, awarded Chandler the Melamed Award for his book *Scale and Scope.*

3. For a more extended treatment of these opposing views, see Lamoreaux (1998).

As the cliometricians grew in strength and came increasingly to dominate the Economic History Association, business historians gradually abandoned that organization in favor of a recently formed alternative. The Business History Conference had its origin in a series of meetings, beginning at Northwestern in 1954, that brought together economic and business historians who were rebelling, again, against the atheoretical type of scholarship promoted by Gras. The group met twice in 1954, once in 1956, once in 1958, and then yearly thereafter; and in 1971 it transformed itself into a full-fledged professional association with dues, officers, a board of trustees, and a journal (albeit one that published only a single issue a year). Although many of its original members were economists and the association was initially formed to bring economists and historians together, from the 1970s on the conference increasingly served to provide historians fleeing the cliometric revolution with a new organizational base.[4]

To the present day, the Business History Conference is dominated by trained historians, whereas the Economic History Association is controlled by trained economists. Despite large areas of common interest, the professional reference groups, not to mention the norms about what constitutes interesting questions, pertinent evidence, and persuasive argument, sometimes seem alarmingly different. Moreover, in the absence of a compelling new interdisciplinary effort, this divergence seems likely to endure. The purpose of the conferences we have organized is to make such an effort and to bring business and economic historians together once again. It is our contention that recent developments in economic theory provide a historic opportunity for greater communication, and we think that the essays that resulted from these conferences show the new interdisciplinary approach to be uncommonly promising.

Beyond Traditional Neoclassical Economics

When today's business historians react negatively to the idea of using economic theory in their work, they typically have in mind a type of standard neoclassical modeling that no longer plays much of a role in advanced research. This older tradition dominated the discipline during the 1960s and 1970s, at the very time when the split between economic and business historians became embodied in rival organizations, and it is still taught in the economics courses that many budding historians take (and dislike) as undergraduates. Although the misconception is therefore understandable, the result has

4. Alfred D. Chandler, Jr., opposed the move to transform the Business History Conference into a formal organization because he did not want to abandon the Economic History Association to the cliometricians. His point of view did not prevail, however (videotape of "Heritage Session," consisting of informal remarks by Harold F. Williamson, Sr., Donald Kemmerer, Alfred D. Chandler, Jr., and Wayne Broehl [reading comments from Thomas Cochran], 34th Annual Meeting of the Business History Conference, Atlanta, 1988). We would like to thank William Hausman for providing us with a copy of this tape. We are also basing this account on the recollections of Louis Cain, communicated to Naomi Lamoreaux in an email message of 18 January 1996.

been to leave historians largely uninformed about recent work in economics, in particular the extent to which theorists have abandoned the neoclassical assumption that all economic actors make decisions on the basis of perfect information. Economists have now begun instead to reconceptualize the world as a place where information is scarce, imperfect, and costly, where bounds to the rationality of human beings affect their economic decision making, where institutional structures evolve in response to problems of imperfect information, and where economic processes can have multiple outcomes depending on both participants' past experiences and their perceptions of each other's actions. This new thinking has made economic theory much more useful for the writing of business history and vice versa.

Although traditional neoclassical economics purported to offer a "theory of the firm," in fact it was not centrally about firms. The neoclassical approach put the market at the core of the analysis and focused attention primarily on the determination of equilibrium prices and transacted quantities. Firms as such figured in the analysis only in such detail as was necessary to make the models of markets work. This treatment was no different from that which the theory accorded to other economic actors, but because firms typically are complex organizations composed of people who often have conflicting interests and goals, the effect was particularly unworldly. Neoclassical theory endowed firms with perfect knowledge of the marginal benefits and costs attached to all possible actions and with the ability to act both instantaneously and effectively. Whereas consumers were portrayed as maximizing utility, a concept that at least paid lip service to the idea that human beings may have different preferences, firms were depicted as maximizing the more objective concept of profits. Indeed, neoclassical theory treated firms as little more than equation-solving entities that, given market prices, determined output by equalizing marginal revenue and marginal cost.

Neoclassical economics' single-minded focus on markets, however, was not without its advantages. One important strength was its ability to tie the behavior of individuals and firms directly to competitive processes so as to highlight the disciplinary impact of the market. Another was the way in which it linked the actions of economic actors to a rigorously defined concept of social welfare. Competition was efficient in the sense that it led to a Pareto-optimal equilibrium—that is, to a situation where it was impossible to make any one person better off without making at least one other person worse off.[5]

More recent work has aimed at correcting some of the deficiencies of neoclassical theory's restrictive focus on market competition without losing all of

---

5. This statement is known as the fundamental theorem of welfare economics and can be found in any elementary microeconomics text. It is of more than abstract importance, as it has provided, for example, the intellectual basis for the recent deregulation movement. Critics of this view typically do not dispute the notion that competitive equilibrium is efficient in a static sense, but instead point out that Pareto efficiency is often achieved at the cost of a high degree of social inequality because there is nothing in these market processes that can correct an unequal initial distribution of income and wealth.

its advantages. The new research has progressed in a number of directions, and we summarized some of these (particularly principal-agent and transaction-cost analysis) in our previous volumes.[6] In the present essay, we focus on developments that explore the ways in which firms (and other organizations) learn: the role past experience plays in deciding what should be done in a world in which information is imperfect; how different firms, even within the same industry, can learn different things; and how the results of these varied learning processes can come to be embodied in individual firms' practices and structures, so that there is a great deal of persistent heterogeneity, even within a given industry.

The least formal and (to historians) most accessible version of this theory is the so-called evolutionary economics developed by Richard Nelson and Sidney Winter (1982). Although Nelson and Winter do not scrap the role of market discipline in their model, they place human actions, rather than relatively abstract market mechanisms, squarely at the center of their analysis. In their view, decision makers within firms want to maximize profits, but they do so by making choices in a trial-and-error and decidedly not omniscient fashion. One way of thinking about these choices is to imagine a decision maker considering what the value should be of some decision variable that he or she controls. How should the decision maker proceed? An optimizing but not omniscient actor might begin with the status quo and perform an incremental analysis. Would a small change in the value (in some particular direction) of a variable he or she controls increase profits? If the answer appears to be yes, the next step would be to repeat the exercise based on the new value. If the answer appears to be no, the decision maker would try an equally incremental change in the opposite direction. If the answer in both directions is no, the decision maker would stick with the status quo.

From the neoclassical perspective, this model of understanding decision making might appear to be little more than an explication of how firms get to equilibrium prices and quantities. But the difference in emphasis that is implicit in this focus on actions (as opposed to outcomes) has profound implications for what the student of firms ought to study. The reason is that the action-based approach immediately draws attention away from markets and market mechanisms in and of themselves and instead focuses it on such important questions as what decision makers actually know and how what they know affects what they do. The critical assumption that the evolutionary economists make—the assumption that distinguishes them most dramatically from their neoclassical predecessors—is that decision makers within firms in fact know very little about the opportunities and costs of unfamiliar or new procedures and activities. They have to feel their way along.

Because the level of uncertainty is so high, choices that yield positive out-

---

6. See the introductions to Temin (1991) and Lamoreaux and Raff (1995), and especially Raff and Temin, "Business History and Recent Economic Theory," in the former, 7–40.

comes often become embedded in the routines and organizational culture of enterprises. A business does something in a particular way and achieves good results. It then attempts to build on its success by exploiting this experience. It finds that expanding the same or similar practices to other areas in an incremental way is a profitable thing to do, in part because it has already mastered these practices. As a result, past ways of doing things gradually come to play a greater and greater role in the operations of the enterprise. This process of institutionalizing previous achievements can make it difficult for firms to respond to challenges that require them to operate in novel ways, but it can also be an important source of competitive advantage. Rivals may find a firm's success difficult to imitate because the routines in question depend to a very considerable extent on firm-specific knowledge and experiences. Successful imitation can involve replicating not only a product or production process but also the entire organizational environment that generated and sustained the innovation. It is often extremely difficult for other firms even to learn the outward details of what is required, let alone understand what underlies them.

The implications of this approach are thus very different from those of standard neoclassical theory. Under conventional assumptions, the neoclassical "theory of the firm" yields one global optimum—that is, one equilibrium level of prices and output toward which firms' incremental trial-and-error decision-making processes will inevitably push them. Competitive pressures force all enterprises to move toward the least-cost method of production—toward a technologically defined best practice. Otherwise they fail. On the other hand, the more action- and knowledge-oriented approach associated with evolutionary economics leaves open the possibility that firms' myopic decision-making processes may leave them in positions that are local, rather than global, optima. Where a firm ends up depends on where it started—on status quo ante decisions and patterns already established. From this perspective, a firm's costs are a function not only of the technology it employs but also of the organizational routines that put that technology to work. Competitive pressures still operate to keep firms on their toes, but successful firms, even within the same industry, can differ strikingly in ways that are remarkably persistent over time. Understanding the sources of such variation—and hence the nature of industrial competition itself—therefore requires both a general understanding of how economic actors are likely to behave under conditions of imperfect information and the ability to track the ways in which enterprises build up firm-specific routines and capabilities over time. In other words, it requires us to marry the time-tested methods of historical inquiry with insights from new theoretical developments in economics.

More formal versions of the new theory take as their starting point George Stigler's formulation of knowledge as an economic good (1964). Like all economic goods, knowledge has a cost, and so people and firms are only willing to acquire it if they expect its marginal benefit to exceed its marginal cost. Because it is common for the former to fall short of the latter, individuals and firms often make decisions without the full range of potentially available relevant information. Whereas the analysis described above simply assumes that almost all relevant information is costly for all actors, these more formal alternatives allow for the possibility that groups may possess varying amounts and qualities of information because the costs they face in obtaining knowledge differ.

There has been a tremendous growth in recent years in the number and types of models that aim to elucidate the implications for organizational behavior and competitive outcomes of such differences in the cost and possession of information. Economics journals are full of papers embodying new assumptions that generate novel solutions. But the richness of this literature is also its Achilles' heel, because it gives the appearance that anything can happen in the absence of good—that is, cheap—information. Of course, this impression is false—there are many constraints operating to limit the choices that actors make. At the simplest level, the desire to pay one's bills or make a profit can limit the number of actions that seem wise; similarly, competitive forces can constrain the alternatives that are reasonable to take. Nonetheless, eliminating more than the most obviously unrealistic models requires concerted scholarly effort. Economists have approached this problem by refining their theoretical apparatus, but they have also begun to analyze real-world examples—actual company histories—for insight into the nature of the information that matters both for firm and market behavior (Gibbons 1997).

Business history is an obvious place for economists to turn for assistance. But in order for business historians to provide theorists with this kind of intellectual discipline, they have to communicate the import of their findings in a way that economists can appreciate. As the essays in this volume show, there is no requirement that historians adopt formal theoretical approaches in their work or even that they weave their narratives around abstract economic models. All that is necessary is that they share with economists a few fundamental assumptions about how human beings behave. Too often, historians have reacted to the limitations of the neoclassical approach by attacking the notion of economic rationality itself—by challenging the idea that at its heart economic behavior is fundamentally a matter of weighing the expected outcomes of alternative decisions in a systematic fashion. But this is throwing out the baby with the bath water. One does not have to assume that economic actors are all-knowing to believe that they make the most advantageous choices they can on the basis of the limited information they possess. Thanks to recent theoretical developments, economists are now employing a more commonsensical notion of rationality—one that business historians should be able to embrace without doing violence to any of their deeply held beliefs about the importance of context, ideas, or culture. As a result, historians can offer economists intellectual discipline simply by focusing their efforts on what they are well-trained to do: elucidating what economic actors actually know at any given point in time, how they use their knowledge to make informed choices, and how they learn from their past decisions. In short, there is now the opportunity for renewed dialogue between those who analyze business decisions at an abstract level (economists) and those who analyze them in their individual, concrete, and idiosyncratic variety (historians)—dialogue that will not only help economists improve their modeling but will also provide stimulating new questions for historians to explore in their research.

Contents of the Current Volume

The two previous volumes in this series essentially asked the question, "What goes on inside firms?" They advanced the answer that business leaders have been centrally preoccupied with the management of information flows and asymmetries (situations where one party in a relationship has more or better information than another). The individual essays dealt with subjects as widely disparate as small watchmakers versus large automobile firms, or local mortgage banks versus investment behemoths like J. P. Morgan and Company, but they can be grouped into three broad categories. The first group traced efforts by business leaders to improve their knowledge of subordinates' activities, the second analyzed the ways in which alternative organizational arrangements could reduce informational asymmetries, and the third showed how legal and regulatory constraints could affect business's ability to cope with information problems. The collective impact of the essays was to demonstrate that many characteristic features of modern business organizations can be understood in terms of the scarcity and value of information.

Although some of the essays in the previous volumes dealt with learning processes, the present volume moves this theme to center stage by asking explicitly how firms, industries, and even nations can learn to overcome uncertainty. It shows that organizations—like people—learn different things in different ways and that this variation has implications for competitive outcomes. The essays in this volume thus mark a transition from focusing on problems that are common to a whole class of firms or industries to explaining why firms, groups, and nations can differ in important and persistent ways.

The essays in the first part of the volume explore some of the techniques that firms employ to create competitively valuable informational asymmetries and at the same time prevent unfavorable ones from arising. The starting point is the observation that the amount of information firms possess depends upon the extent to which they invest in collecting it. In "Inventors, Firms, and the Market for Technology in the Late Nineteenth and Early Twentieth Centuries," Naomi Lamoreaux and Kenneth Sokoloff argue that an active market for patented inventions developed over the course of the nineteenth century. In the "high-tech" parts of the economy in particular, firms seeking to stay on the technological cutting edge began to devote resources to building staffs of employees whose main function was acquire to knowledge about inventions developed outside the firm and decide whether the company should purchase rights to use them. In an environment where many inventions were protected by patents and where this kind of property right was vigorously enforced, investment in collecting information about new developments throughout the economy was vital to success. A wrong decision about the value of a patent could mean that a competitor gained control of vital technology.

Because investments in capabilities of this sort were expensive, some firms turned to organizational substitutes. Many small firms, for example, used patent solicitors to keep abreast of inventions related to their interests. Although initially the main purpose of these legal representatives was to shepherd applications through the Patent Office and to defend patentees in interference and infringement proceedings, over time they developed specialized technical expertise that firms could tap to keep up with developments in the rest of the economy. Another organizational substitute was the patent pool. As Steven Usselman describes in "Patents, Engineering Professionals, and the Pipelines of Innovation: The Internalization of Technical Discovery by Nineteenth-Century American Railroads," pools were employed by large firms in industries (like railroads) where there was already a significant amount of interfirm cooperation. They enabled firms to collude in the acquisition of new technology. Because pools insured that all patents would be cross-licensed to participating firms, they eliminated much of the risk that a competitor would monopolize an essential patent and kept the cost of inventions low.

Such substitutes for direct investment in information collection could work quite well so long as most of the important new technological developments occurred in the external environment. Once internal R&D grew in significance, however, firms that did not invest in building up research capabilities often found themselves at a competitive disadvantage. Moreover, once technological change moved inside firms, its character shifted in important ways. As Usselman suggests, it became focused less on the acquisition of patents and more on the overall goal of increasing efficiency through systemization and standardization. Improvements of this sort typically involved a great deal of firm-specific knowledge. Unlike patents, therefore, they could not be traded on the market.

Although the purpose of patent pools was to reduce asymmetries associated with the acquisition of new technologies, firms could also use similarly structured organizations to alleviate competitive pressures resulting from other kinds of information problems. For example, with cartels illegal in the United States after the turn of the century, it was in firms' interests to develop alternative ways of coping with price competition. One device that grew in popularity during the 1920s was the open-price association, the main purpose of which was the collection and dissemination of information about prices and output. The idea was that, if firms had better information about these magnitudes, price cutting would be easier to detect, and so the incentive to increase market share by undercutting competitors' prices would be greatly reduced. However, as David Genesove and Wallace Mullin found in their study of one such association, the Sugar Institute, firms were initially reluctant to make this kind of information available to competitors. The institute had to learn how to guarantee credibly that data on individual producers would be handled carefully and confidentially so that competitors would not gain any advantage from the exchange. Even so, firms were reluctant to share certain kinds of information, for example, detailed reports of their sales. At the root of the problem were informational asymmetries within the organization itself. Firms that were large relative to the market knew more about what their competitors were doing than firms that were small, and they were not willing to give up that advantage. This fundamental inequality in access to information proved impossible to overcome.

The second group of essays in this collection focuses on the ways in which firms built up special capabilities over time, capabilities that could be sources both of competitive advantage and of resistance to new kinds of learning. In his reconsideration of learning by doing in the production of bombers during World War II, Kazuhiro Mishina describes how Boeing's managers succeeded in effecting the enormous productivity increases needed to satisfy insistent demands from the military for additional planes. Over a period of only four years, the direct labor time it took to make a B-17 bomber at Boeing declined from seventy-one worker-years to a mere eight. Mishina shows that the prompt to productivity growth was not cumulative experience per se, but rather the dramatic increases in the flow of production that Boeing had to accommodate. Boeing's managers learned, in other words, because they were experiencing extraordinary new pressures on capacity.

Not all firms were able to respond so successfully to these pressures, however. Boeing's achievement, Mishina shows, resulted from its flexible use of space and its group assembly techniques. By contrast, Ford attempted to apply its automobile technology to aircraft production, transferring its mass-production assembly-line techniques to the manufacture of airplanes. These methods meant that space in Ford's plants was rigidly partitioned by assembly lines and dedicated to particular uses, a structure that made it difficult for Ford to increase its output rapidly in response to the skyrocketing military demand for planes.

Ford's more rigid system proved disastrous, and the firm emerged from the Great Depression and World War II nearly bankrupt. To rescue the failing enterprise, the new CEO, Henry Ford II, lured a whole team of executives away from General Motors. The GM people immediately set to work reinventing Ford along the lines of GM—that is, they set about replacing Ford's highly centralized organizational structure with the decentralized multidivisional form used at GM. As David Hounshell's chapter shows, the GM people seemed to be succeeding in restructuring Ford. In a key vote in late 1949, for example, the company's top executives approved a plan to build two new engine plants that would provide the firm with badly needed production capacity and at the same time further the process of decentralization. Less than a month later, however, the decision was reversed. Although there are no records that reveal what actually happened at that subsequent meeting, Hounshell goes to great lengths to elucidate the various possible influences shaping the decision.

Part of the explanation for the shift appears to be the difficulty of the project itself. Ford's centralized organizational structure was embodied in physical capital in the form of the huge River Rouge plant in Detroit. As the executives confronted the costs involved in dismantling the Rouge in order to transform Ford's organizational structure along GM lines, they seem to have backed away from the project. Rather than copy GM, Ford instead developed a new business strategy that made effective use of its own sunk investments in plant and in particular ways of doing things, a strategy that proved profitable in the next period.

When firms failed to exploit the capacities they had built up over the years, the results could be momentous. The case of Sears offers an instructive lesson. As the chapter by Daniel Raff and Peter Temin argues, Sears faced two important turning points during its history—the first in the mid-1920s, and the second in the late 1970s. During the first episode, Julius Rosenwald hired General Robert Wood to add retail stores to Sears's catalogue business. This expansion made good use of the expertise and goodwill that Sears had already accumulated and enabled the firm to hold onto its clientele as families became more urban, work moved from agriculture into industry, and people increasingly traveled by car. In the second episode, Sears's executives debated the firm's future path. One group wanted to follow what it thought to be General Wood's example and add new dimensions to Sears's retail activities; another group wanted to revitalize the company's stores. The first group won, and Sears expanded into financial services. But the hoped-for synergy between the sale of goods, on the one hand, and financial instruments, on the other, did not materialize. More important, the executives' misperception of the firm's special capabilities cost the firm many years in its contest with stores like Wal-Mart and The Gap, stores that increased their market share by using new information technology to lower prices and improve responsiveness to consumer demand.

The final section of the volume extends the notion of learning from the level of firms to that of nations. The idea is that nations, like firms, can make investments in specific ways of organizing economic activity—what we call institutions—that give them economic advantages in a world where information is imperfect and costly. Alfred D. Chandler, Jr., has argued that the large-scale enterprises that emerged in the United States during the early twentieth century (in large measure because cartels were illegal here) were responsible for the extraordinary performance of the U.S. economy (Chandler 1977, 1990). But Leslie Hannah's essay shows that this view will not withstand empirical scrutiny. Hannah tracks the performance of the largest firms in the United States, Great Britain, and Germany over the course of the twentieth century, and finds that large firms in general and U.S. firms in particular have not done especially well. Chandler assumed that managerial control of vertically integrated enterprises provided a coordination mechanism superior to any that could operate through the market, but this assumption has also been called increasingly into question.[7]

If large-scale enterprises do not account for the extraordinary success of the U.S. economy during the early twentieth century, what does? Hannah argues that the explanation for long-run national differences in economic performance must reside either in the nonindustrial sectors of the economy or in the achievements of small firms. Rising to the challenge that this kind of question poses, Gavin Wright has attempted to elucidate the particular "social capabilities" that allowed the United States to move into a position of world economic leadership by 1890.[8] In "Can a Nation Learn? American Technology as a Network Phenomenon," Wright focuses on the networks of people that made possible the transfer of technological knowledge throughout the nation. During the early nineteenth century this type of communication was facilitated by the high geographic mobility of labor, particularly the movement of skilled mechanics with a great deal of technological know-how. Over the course of the century, however, these networks became more formal as technological change increasingly became the work of engineers with college training and budding professional identities. The engineers organized themselves into national societies devoted to the promotion of their fields and spread their brand of specialized knowledge to like-minded people in other parts of the country.

Perhaps the most important of these networks centered on the mining industry. One common explanation for the U.S. economy's extraordinary performance by the early twentieth century was its abundant raw material resources, but Wright shows that the nation's share of resource production during this period greatly exceeded what we now know to be its share of reserves. What accounted for the superior U.S. performance, he argues, was not resources per se, but the capacity to exploit them that the nation had acquired through its network of mining engineers. The important lesson to take away from this example, then, is that nations like firms have business histories. That is, we can understand their success by studying the special organizational and institutional arrangements they developed to exploit informational asymmetries.

Conclusions

The three volumes we have published, and especially this last collection of essays, demonstrate through myriad examples that information is crucial to economic success. More than any other factor, the ability to collect and use

7. For example, Michael Enright (1995) has shown that small vertically disintegrated but geographically concentrated firms can develop coordination mechanisms that are superior to managerial hierarchies in their flexibility to respond to changes in consumer demand. Similar arguments about the advantages of clusters of small vertically disintegrated firms over large managerially directed enterprises have been made by scholars as diverse as Michael Piore and Charles Sabel (1984) and Philip Scranton (1983, 1989).

8. See also David and Wright (1992); Abramovitz and David (1996).

information effectively determines whether firms, industry groups, and even nations will succeed or fail. There are several more subtle points to underscore, however. First, although it is obviously important for firms and other organizations to learn about the external environment (for example, about market opportunities and technological developments), it is equally important that they be introspective—that is, that they devote resources to learning about the capabilities that their own ongoing operations are creating and to understanding the opportunities that are evolving as a result. Second, the outcome of these learning processes, especially the introspective ones, may well be quite firm-specific. As a result, economic organizations ranging from firms to nations may develop special capabilities that distinguish them in striking ways from the other organizations with which they compete. Finally, although the essays in these volumes have dealt with many very specific subjects and indeed have highlighted the idiosyncratic aspects of the individual firms and organizations studied, the essays nonetheless have an underlying coherence. All of the authors take the imperfect state of information as their starting point, and all aim to illuminate the ways in which this condition effects the playing out of economic life. This common preoccupation then leads to a deeper source of coherence—the structural unity behind all these various topics. The information problems that firms face in their internal operations are not so different from those that they face in dealing with the external environment or from those faced by firms and other economic actors when they interact with one another. Further, the solutions adopted in response to these information problems typically have many features in common, even though they often result in the creation of capabilities that are specific to the organization. In sharp contrast, therefore, to the case studies that characterized the Grasian tradition of business history, the essays in these volumes contribute to a coherent view of American economic development and organizational change.[9]

Fruitful exploration of these underlying ideas depends first and foremost upon genuine interaction between economists and business historians. These two groups of scholars do different things. Business historians are primarily interested in understanding changes over time in the behavior and structure of particular economic organizations. Economists are primarily concerned with building general models of economic relationships and with exploring the implications of the models they build. Despite their very different interests, however, the two groups of scholars have much to gain from intellectual exchange. As we have already suggested, business historians can turn to economic theory for intriguing new questions and for the light a coherent perspective sheds on an otherwise untidy past. On the other hand, business history can offer economists useful correctives and provocative examples that will inspire them to give their models heightened realism and greater practical significance. Business decisions, after all, are not abstract optimization exercises. They are embedded

---

9. For such a summary view, see Lamoreaux, Raff, and Temin (1997).

in contexts. Moreover, because past choices condition future ones, the study of these contexts has an important historical dimension—capabilities built up slowly over time affect firms' evaluation (and ability to take advantage) of new possibilities. Hence it is really only by marrying historical methods with insights from the new economic theory—by making business history truly interdisciplinary—that scholars can obtain a full understanding of the nature and determinants of competition and the sources of economic success.

References

Abramovitz, Moses, and Paul A. David. 1996. Convergence and Deferred Catch-up: Productivity Leadership and the Waning of American Exceptionalism. In *The Mosaic of Economic Growth,* ed. Ralph Landau, Timothy Taylor, and Gavin Wright, 21–62. Stanford, CA: Stanford University Press.

Chandler, Alfred D., Jr. 1977. *The Visible Hand: The Managerial Revolution in American Business.* Cambridge: Harvard University Press.

———. 1990. *Scale and Scope: The Dynamics of Industrial Capitalism.* Cambridge: Harvard University Press.

Cole, Arthur H. 1968. Economic History in the United States: Formative Years of a Discipline. *Journal of Economic History* 28 (December): 556–89.

David, Paul A., and Gavin Wright. 1992. Resource Abundance and American Economic Leadership. Stanford University Center for Economic Policy Research Publication 267.

Enright, Michael J. 1995. Organization and Coordination in Geographically Concentrated Industries. In *Coordination and Information: Historical Perspectives on the Organization of Enterprise,* ed. Naomi R. Lamoreaux and Daniel M. G. Raff, 103–43. Chicago: University of Chicago Press.

Galambos, Louis. 1969. Parsonian Sociology and Post-Progressive History. *Social Science Quarterly* 50 (June): 25–45.

Gibbons, Robert. 1997. An Introduction to Applicable Game Theory. *Journal of Economic Perspectives* 11 (winter): 127–49.

Heaton, Herbert. 1941. The Early History of the Economic History Association. *Journal of Economic History* 1 (December sup.): 107–9.

———. 1952. *A Scholar in Action: Edwin F. Gay.* Cambridge: Harvard University Press.

———. 1965. Twenty-Five Years of the Economic History Association: A Reflective Evaluation. *Journal of Economic History* 25 (December): 465–79.

Lamoreaux, Naomi R. Economic History and the Cliometric Revolution. In *Imagined Histories: American Historians and the Past,* ed. Anthony Molho and Gordon Wood. Princeton: Princeton University Press.

Lamoreaux, Naomi R., and Daniel M. G. Raff, eds. 1995. *Coordination and Information: Historical Perspectives on the Organization of Enterprise.* Chicago: University of Chicago Press.

Lamoreaux, Naomi R., Daniel M. G. Raff, and Peter Temin. 1997. New Economic Approaches to the Study of Business History. *Business and Economic History* 26 (fall): 57–79.

Nelson, Richard R., and Sydney G. Winter. 1982. *An Evolutionary Theory of Economic Change.* Cambridge: Harvard University Press.

North, Douglass C. 1961. *The Economic Growth of the United States, 1790–1860.* Englewood Cliffs, NJ: Prentice Hall.

Piore, Michael J., and Charles F. Sabel. 1984. *The Second Industrial Divide.* New York: Basic.

Raff, Daniel M. G., and Peter Temin. 1991. Business History and Recent Economic Theory: Imperfect Information, Incentives, and the Internal Organization of Firms. In *Inside the Business Enterprise,* ed. Peter Temin, 7–35. Chicago: University of Chicago Press.

Sass, Steven A. 1986. *Entrepreneurial Historians and History: Leadership and Rationality in American Economic Historiography, 1940–1960.* New York: Garland.

Schumpeter, Joseph A. 1934. *The Theory of Economic Development: An Inquiry into Profits, Capital, Credit, Interest, and the Business Cycle.* Cambridge: Harvard University Press.

Scranton, Philip. 1983. *Proprietary Capitalism: The Textile Manufacture at Philadelphia, 1800–1885.* New York: Cambridge University Press.

———. 1989. *Figured Tapestry: Production, Markets, and Power in Philadelphia Textiles, 1885–1941.* New York: Cambridge University Press.

Stigler, George. 1964. A Theory of Oligopoly. *Journal of Political Economy* 72 (February): 44–61.

Teece, David J. 1993. The Dynamics of Industrial Capitalism, Perspectives on Alfred Chandler's *Scale and Scope. Journal of Economic Literature* 31 (March): 199–225.

Temin, Peter, ed. 1991. *Inside the Business Enterprise: Historical Perspectives on the Use of Information.* Chicago: University of Chicago Press.

Williamson, Oliver E. 1981. The Modern Corporation: Origins, Evolution, Attributes. *Journal of Economic Literature* 19 (December): 1537–68.

1 Inventors, Firms, and the Market for Technology in the Late Nineteenth and Early Twentieth Centuries

Naomi R. Lamoreaux and Kenneth L. Sokoloff

Recent economic theory suggests that large firms invest in building their own R&D facilities because there are significant problems associated with contracting for new technological developments in the market. In the first place, the uncertainties associated with valuing technological information are sufficiently great that even if such knowledge could be "displayed on a shelf," sellers would have difficulty pricing it and buyers would have trouble deciding whether to purchase it. Technological information is unlikely to be displayed in this manner, however, because sellers are concerned not to reveal too much about their discoveries. As a result, trade in technological information is diffi-

Naomi R. Lamoreaux is professor of economics and history at the University of California, Los Angeles, and a research associate of the National Bureau of Economic Research. Kenneth L. Sokoloff is professor of economics at the University of California, Los Angeles, and a research associate of the National Bureau of Economic Research.

The authors would like to express their appreciation to their research assistants Marigee Bacolod, Dalit Baranoff, Lisa Boehmer, Nancy Cole, Yael Elad, Svjetlana Gacinovic, Anna Maria Lagiss, Huagang Li, Catherine Truong Ly, Elizabeth Cluff, Homan Dayani, Gina Franco, Brian Houghton, Charles Kaljian, Kristina Khona, David Madero Suarez, John Majewski, Yolanda McDonough, Heidi Pack, Carolyn Richardson, Edward Saldana, and Gabrielle Stanley. Without their able help the authors would not have been able to write this article. They also thank Marjorie Ciarlante and Carolyn Cooper for teaching them how to access the Patent Office's assignment records in the National Archives, Sheldon Hochheiser for his assistance at the AT&T Archives, Jonathan Liebowitz for introducing them to the collections at the Center for Lowell History, and the many helpful librarians and archivists they encountered at these institutions, as well as at the Harvard Graduate School of Business Administration's Baker Library, the Newberry Library, and the Rhode Island Historical Society Library. They have also benefited from the suggestions of Cameron Campbell, Stanley Engerman, Louis Galambos, David Hounshell, Adam Jaffe, Zorina Khan, Margaret Levenstein, Christine MacLeod, Lisa Marovich, Rebecca Menes, Daniel Raff, Jean-Laurent Rosenthal, Jonathan Skinner, William Summerhill, Peter Temin, Ross Thomson, Steven Usselman, Mary Yeager, and participants in economic history seminars at Stanford University, the University of Toronto, and the University of California, Berkeley, the Business History Conference, and the NBER conference that generated this volume. Financial support for this research was provided by the National Science Foundation and the Academic Senate of the University of California, Los Angeles.

19

cult to conduct. Firms may hesitate to purchase new technologies without full information about how they work, but inventors may balk at providing this level of detail for fear of losing control of their intellectual property. At the same time, scholars argue, there are informational advantages to be gained from moving R&D in house. Many innovations are stimulated by knowledge gained in production and marketing activities. This kind of knowledge is largely firm-specific. It can be readily communicated through interactions among personnel responsible for different functions within a firm, but it is much less easily transmitted across organizational boundaries. According to this view, then, in-house R&D laboratories triumphed over market exchanges of technology because they made superior use of information generated within the firm and minimized the transaction costs associated with increasingly complex and expensive forms of technological change (Teece 1988; Mowery 1983, 1995; Zeckhauser 1996; Arrow 1962).

In this essay, we offer an alternative view based on our assessment of the information and contracting problems that firms actually faced at the time they began to build their R&D capabilities. In particular, we argue that scholars have overemphasized the information problems associated with contracting for new technological developments in the market. Contrary to what one might expect from the literature, the data show that an extensive trade in new technological ideas did develop over the course of the nineteenth century, supported by the patent system and by the emergence of information channels and intermediaries that facilitated the sale of patents at arm's length.

The growth of this market for technology had important implications, we suggest, for the extent to which invention was integrated with development. Early inventors, of course, typically engaged in both sets of activities—either commercializing their ideas themselves or joining with outside investors to form enterprises to exploit their patents. This combination of activities certainly continued and, indeed, even thrived where the growth of the market made it easier to gain financial backing. But the expansion of trade in technology also made possible a new division of labor, as inventors increasingly took advantage of the greater returns to specialization that accompanied this growth and focused their energies and resources on invention itself. Firms in turn responded to the expansion of this trade by developing capabilities that enabled them to learn about and assess externally generated inventions. In an environment where many inventions were protected by patents and where this kind of property right was vigorously enforced, maintaining one's competitive position often meant purchasing (or at least contracting for the right to use) patented technology. Indeed, a wrong decision about the value of a patent could mean that a competitor gained control of vital technology.[1]

---

1. As Steven Usselman's essay (chap. 2 in this volume) shows, well-organized industries like railroads sometimes formed patent pools to lower the risks of making wrong decisions and to prevent technological blackmail.

During the late nineteenth and early twentieth centuries, firms devoted a considerable part of their energies and resources to keeping on top of technological ideas originating outside their bounds. This strategy was particularly important for firms in the "high-tech" industries of the time—industries like electricity and telecommunications, where technologies were complex and undergoing rapid change. As time went on, however, firms in these industries increasingly turned their attention to developing their own internal inventive capabilities. The reasons for this shift are beyond the scope of this essay, but they include such developments as the rising cost of the human and physical capital required for invention (which made it difficult for inventors to continue to operate independently) and the emergence of large firms with significant market power (which made patents an increasingly important factor in oligopolistic competition).

What we can and do argue in this essay, however, is that the shift was unlikely to have been driven by firms' desire to take advantage of the lower transaction costs associated with in-house R&D compared to market purchases of technology. During the late nineteenth and early twentieth centuries there already existed a well-functioning market for invention. By contrast, when firms decided to invest in internal R&D facilities, they faced significant new information and contracting problems—problems that scholars have failed to appreciate. In order, for example, to reap the fruits that might be derived from bringing inventors within the enterprise, firms had to learn how to manage creative individuals so as to elicit their loyalty and enhance their productivity. Entrepreneurially oriented inventors initially moved in and out of employment positions and, even worse from the standpoint of firms, often tried to exploit personally inventions that they devised on company time. Before firms could capture the gains from their investments in R&D, therefore, they had to learn how to tighten up their contractual relations with employee inventors and how to convince such personnel that advancement within the enterprise was an attractive alternative to self-employment. These were not easy lessons to master. It took twenty or thirty years just for firms to work out standard employment contracts giving them property rights to inventions developed in their facilities; other problems associated with managing creative people were never completely resolved. Hence where recent scholarship has emphasized the difficulties of contracting for technology in the market and the relative ease of integrating invention and production within the firm, we reverse the story. During the late nineteenth and early twentieth centuries there was a well-functioning market for invention, but significant organizational learning had to occur before firms could productively focus on in-house R&D.

1.1   The Patent System and the Market for Technology

The patent system provided the institutional framework within which trade in technology evolved over the course of the nineteenth century. Consciously

designed with the aim of encouraging inventive activity—and thus technological progress—the U.S. system provided the first and true inventor of a device
with an exclusive property right for a fixed term of years. One important feature of the law was that inventors had to be individual men or women; firms
could not receive patents directly for ideas developed in their shops. These individual inventors then had the option of exploiting their property rights themselves, or they could sell (assign) or lease (license) them to others, whether
individuals or firms. Of course, inventors' ability to find buyers or licensees
for their patents depended on the security of these property rights. From the
beginning, responsibility for enforcing patent rights was left to the federal
courts, and as Zorina Khan has shown, judges quickly evolved an effective set
of principles for protecting the rights of patentees and of those who purchased
or licensed patented technologies. As a result, not only did thousands of inventors pay rather substantial fees to obtain patents, but large numbers of individuals and firms paid even greater amounts to purchase or license patent rights
(Khan 1995).

Although one purpose of the patent system was to stimulate invention by
granting creative individuals secure rights to their intellectual property, another
was to promote the diffusion of technological knowledge. The law required
all patentees to provide the Patent Office with detailed specifications for their
inventions (including, where appropriate, working models), and the result was
a central storehouse of information that was open to all. Anyone could journey
to Washington and research others' inventions in the Patent Office files. In
addition, more convenient means of tapping this rich source of information
soon developed. The Patent Office itself published an annual list of patents
issued, and private journals, many of them issued by the leading patent agencies of the day, emerged by the middle of the nineteenth century to improve
upon this service. One of the most important was *Scientific American,* published by Munn and Company, the largest patent agency of the nineteenth century. Others included the *American Artisan,* published by Brown, Coombs and
Company; the *American Inventor,* by the American Patent Agency; and the
Patent Right Gazette, by the United States Patent Right Association (which,
despite its name, functioned as a general patent agency). Aimed at national
readerships, these journals featured articles about major technological improvements, printed complete lists of patents issued sometimes on a weekly
basis, and offered to provide readers with copies of full patent specifications
for a small fee. They also included a variety of advertisements that disseminated information about inventions (or how to profit from them), placed by patent agents and lawyers soliciting clients, detective agencies specializing in patent issues, inventors seeking partners with capital to invest, patent holders
hoping to sell or license rights to their technologies, and producers of patented
products trying to increase their sales. Over time, moreover, specialized trade
journals also emerged in industry after industry to keep producers informed

about patents of interest. The *Journal of the Society of Glass Technology,* for example, provided detailed descriptions of all patents taken out in the United States and Britain that were relevant to the manufacture of glass.

As individuals, patent agents and lawyers also became important channels through which people and firms far from Washington could exploit the information in Patent Office files. Their numbers began to mushroom in the 1840s, first in the vicinity of Washington and then in other urban centers, especially in the Northeast. By the mid-1880s, there were about 550 such agents registered to practice before the Patent Office, with almost a quarter located in the District of Columbia, slightly more than half in New England and the Middle Atlantic states, another fifth in the Midwest, and the rest scattered among a few southern and western locations. Solicitors in different cities linked themselves in chains of correspondent relations (similar to those that characterized the banking system at the same time), thereby providing their local clients with access to agents in Washington and information on patenting activity across the country.[2]

There is plenty of anecdotal evidence to suggest that all these channels of information made possible by the patent system worked effectively to diffuse technological knowledge. Inventors scanned patent lists in search of developments in their fields and subscribed to periodicals relevant to their interests. For example, Elias E. Reis reported that, when he read in the *Official Gazette of the United States Patent Office* in 1886 about a patent issued to Elihu Thomson for a method of electrical welding, there "immediately opened up to my mind a field of new applications to which I saw I could apply my system of producing heat in large quantities."[3] Charles H. Roth, an inventor of bicycle tires, subscribed to two papers, *Bicycling World* and *Bearings,* in order to keep abreast of technological developments related to cycling. He also "read other papers at the bicycle stores and at the Crescent Wheel Club Rooms, of which club I was a member."[4] To give a different kind of example, the journals of Wright, Brown, Quinby and May, patent solicitors, were filled with notations of payments received from clients for searches of Patent Office records. For instance, when the officers of the Waltham Watch Company decided to explore the possibility of producing self-winding clocks and watches, they asked Wright, Brown, Quinby and May to conduct a search for them so they could

2. The growth and geographic spread of patent agents and solicitors can be followed through city directories and through the U.S. Patent Office's *Roster of Registered Attorneys Entitled to Practice before the United States Patent Office.* For insight into the correspondent relations of these agents, see Wright, Brown, Quinby & May Correspondence Files, Waltham Watch Company, 1854–1929, MSS 598, case 2, Baker Library, Harvard Graduate School of Business Administration.

3. See "Record of Elias E. Reis," 8, *Thomson v. Reis,* case 13,971, box 1,845, Interference Case Files, 1836–1905, Records of the Patent Office, Record Group 241, National Archives.

4. "Record of Roth," 6, *Roth v. Brown & Stillman,* case 17,930, box 2,488, Interference Case Files, 1836–1905.

learn about techniques already in use and reduce the risk of being sued for infringement.[5]

Even more interesting for our purposes, these various channels of information were also used by patentees to market their inventions. Advice manuals recommended that, "if the inventor can afford it, it is well to have the invention illustrated and described in one or more of the scientific and mechanical publications of the day." This announcement might then, if necessary (and the manuals claimed that further advertisement often would not be necessary), "be followed up by ordinary advertising . . . in the paper or papers which are designed to meet the eye of the class or classes of persons to whom the invention is of special interest." Advertisements in trade papers in turn might be followed by personal solicitations to potential buyers, whose names could be obtained from "men in New York and other large cities, who make it their business to furnish, for a reasonable consideration, full and complete lists of all parties engaged in any particular trade, occupation, profession, or manufacture throughout the country" (Simonds 1871, 19, 24–26).

Patentees who did not feel able or willing to devote so much of their time to marketing their inventions could turn to intermediaries for assistance. Virtually any businessman could perform this function, as records of patents offered for sale to important firms show.[6] But it was common for patent solicitors and agents to play the role of middleman. Although the original function of these specialists was to shepherd applications for patents through the official review process and (in the case of the lawyers) to defend previously issued patents in interference and infringement proceedings, as time went on they acquired additional functions and often began to serve as intermediaries in the sale of technology. There appears to have been some disagreement among solicitors about whether such activity was proper, but many moved in this direction, advertising their willingness to sell patents on commission.[7] Some solicitors, in

---

5. The example is from a letter from the Waltham Watch Company to Wright, Brown, Quinby & May, 25 January 1915, Wright, Brown, Quinby & May Correspondence Files, Waltham Watch Company, 1854–1929, case 2. For numerous other instances, see Journal 1, Wright, Brown, Quinby & May, 1881–1950, MSS 831, Baker Library, Harvard Graduate School of Business Administration.

6. For example, the Nicholson File Company was offered the opportunity to buy a patent for a rasp by a manufacturer of engine governors who had acquired it for resale. Similarly, intermediaries with main businesses as diverse as textile manufacturing and engineering consulting submitted inventions for sale to AT&T. See correspondence between the Nicholson File Company and Stillman B. Allen, 1873–75, Patent Records from Trunk, Nicholson File Co., MSS 587, Rhode Island Historical Society Manuscript Collections; and T. D. Lockwood, Reports of Inventions (Not Approved), 1904–8, box 1383, AT&T Corporate Archives.

7. H. W. Boardman and Company (1869, 13), solicitors of American and European patents, stated unequivocally that the firm rigidly adhered to a rule "never to take contingent interests in applications for Patents, nor to negotiate sales of Patent rights, or become the owners in whole or in part of them. We deem all such to be deviations from that rigid professional course necessary to insure the strictest honor and integrity toward a client." Simonds (1871, 7–9) took a similar position, advising patentees to sell their inventions themselves and not be seduced by the promises of such agents. See also Hutchinson and Criswell (1899, 161–62); Cresee (1907, 41–43).

fact, became known for this service, and inventors would seek them out to find buyers for their patents. For example, a party with an interest in a "Patent Self Oiler" for railroad cars wrote an agent named Lemuel Jenks to solicit his assistance in marketing their device: "We intend to sell it to one person for the six New England States and I therefore wish you would give me your opinion in that matter: to viz what price you think we should ask; what would we have to pay you for your assistance in carrying and effecting a sale."[8] The records of important concerns such as the American Telephone and Telegraph Company (AT&T) contain numerous letters from inventors offering their own patents for sale, but also a nearly equivalent number of approaches from patent agents and solicitors marketing inventions on behalf of their patentee clients.[9]

1.2   A Quantitative Picture of the Market

The extent to which the market for patented technology was already well established by 1870, especially in the northeastern regions of the country, can be seen from table 1.1, which reports descriptive statistics for a sample of assignment contracts.[10] In order for the sale of a patent to be legally binding, a copy of the contract had to be deposited with the Patent Office in Washington. These contracts are now stored at the National Archives, and our sample consists of all the approximately 4,600 contracts filed during the months of January 1871, January 1891, and January 1911. Although the number of assignment contracts increased dramatically over this period, more than doubling between 1871 and 1911, the number of patents filed increased even more rapidly. As a result, the ratio of assignments in our sample to the total number of patents issued actually peaked by the beginning of our period, declining from 0.83 in 1870–71 to 0.71 in 1890–91 and 1910–11.[11]

The high volume by 1870 of contracts relative to patents is a strong indication that trade in rights to patented technology was already well developed. In addition, the high proportion early on of what we are calling "geographic assignments"—that is, sales of patent rights that were restricted to some (often distant) subregion of the United States—suggests that a significant amount of arm's-length trading was already occurring by midcentury. Although the

8. Letter of 30 April 1870 from Aug. H. Fick (last name not completely legible) to Jenks, Lemuel Jenks, 1844–1879, MSS 867, box 3, folder 59, Baker Library, Harvard Graduate School of Business Administration.

9. See T. D. Lockwood, Reports of Inventions (Not Approved), 1904–8.

10. In this paper we focus on national aggregates. In other work (Lamoreaux and Sokoloff 1996) we deal with the issue of why the market for technology did not develop uniformly across the nation.

11. It is important to note that these ratios are not measures of the proportion of patents that were ever assigned, which we cannot calculate, but instead are estimates of the volume of assignment activity relative to patenting activity. One cannot infer from the fall in these ratios that the proportion of patents ever assigned also declined after 1870–71. The drop over time in the proportion of secondary and geographic assignments might have reduced the estimated ratios, even if the overall proportion of patents ever assigned continued to rise.

Table 1.1 **Descriptive Statistics on Assignments Made before and after Issue of Patents**

	1870–71	1890–91	1910–11
New England			
Assignment to patenting index	115.1	109.5	132.4
% assigned after issue	70.4	31.2	30.1
% secondary assignments	26.6	14.8	12.0
% geographic assignments	17.1	0.8	0.0
Middle Atlantic			
Assignment to patenting index	100.7	94.8	116.3
% assigned after issue	70.9	44.4	37.9
% secondary assignments	33.3	16.4	11.0
% geographic assignments	19.1	1.9	0.7
East North Central			
Assignment to patenting index	96.3	118.1	104.9
% assigned after issue	77.7	48.5	32.8
% secondary assignments	18.1	18.4	11.8
% geographic assignments	34.3	5.7	1.8
West North Central			
Assignment to patenting index	90.7	110.1	73.5
% assigned after issue	77.4	48.6	42.6
% secondary assignments	32.3	19.2	11.0
% geographic assignments	41.9	13.0	2.6
South			
Assignment to patenting index	60.0	68.9	68.0
% assigned after issue	74.4	42.3	48.2
% secondary assignments	27.9	11.3	19.1
% geographic assignments	20.9	6.2	2.5
West			
Assignment to patenting index	150.0	67.2	81.5
% assigned after issue	59.1	57.4	36.0
% secondary assignments	22.7	11.4	10.4
% geographic assignments	18.2	7.4	1.2
Total domestic			
Assignment to patenting index	100.0	100.0	100.0
% assigned after issue	72.3	44.1	36.5
% secondary assignments	27.8	16.4	12.0
% geographic assignments	22.8	4.6	1.2
Assignments to patents ratio	0.83	0.71	0.71
Number of contracts	794	1,373	1,869

Source: Our sample consists of all assignment contracts filed with the Patent Office during the months of January 1871, January 1891, and January 1911. These contracts are recorded in "Liber" volumes stored at the National Archives.

Notes: There are a total of about 4,600 contracts in our sample. Only those involving assignors that resided in the United States are included in this table. The assignment-to-patenting index is based on the ratio of assignments originating in the respective regions (given by the residence of the assignor) to the number of patents filed from that region in 1870, 1890, and 1910 respectively. In each year the index has been set so that the national average equals 100. The percentage of secondary assignments refers to the proportion of assignments where the assignor was neither the patentee nor a relative of the patentee. The percentage of geographic patent assignments refers to the proportion of assignments where the right transferred was for a geographic unit smaller than the nation.

proportion of geographic assignments dropped dramatically between 1870–71 and 1910–11, this change did not mean that market trade in technology was falling off. Rather the decline should be seen as a consequence of the growth of national product markets. Once manufacturers in a single location could retail their products nationally, it made less sense to try to sell geographically exclusive rights to producers in different parts of the country. Producers were now more interested in purchasing full national rights that would give them a competitive edge over rivals elsewhere.[12]

Two related changes are also apparent in the table. In 1870–71, secondary assignments—that is, sales of patents where the assigner was neither the patentee nor a relative of the patentee—accounted for more than a quarter of total sales. By 1910–11, the figure had fallen to 12 percent. In other words, there was less reselling of patents as time went on; an increasingly large proportion of sales were being made directly by the patentee.[13] More important, the proportion of assignments that occurred after the date the patent was issued dropped from 72.3 percent of the total in 1870–71 to 36.5 percent in 1910–11. That is, as time went on patentees were able to sell their inventions earlier and earlier—often before their patents were actually issued.[14]

For the subset of inventions assigned at or before the date the patent was issued, we can get a more precise sense of the magnitude and direction of change over time. Table 1.2 is based on three random cross-sectional samples of patents drawn from the *Annual Report of the Commissioner of Patents* for the years 1870–71, 1890–91, and 1910–11. These documents report for all patents issued during the year the names of the patentees as well as the names of any assignees who were granted property rights to the patents at the time of

12. In addition, the marketing of geographic assignments had always posed information problems that could be avoided once it became possible to dispose of national rights in one fell swoop. For example, the relationship between inventors and the itinerant agents who sometimes marketed their patents in other parts of the country was open to opportunism and even outright fraud, and disreputable agents were accused of a variety of crimes—from misrepresenting the value of patents, to collecting commissions on bogus sales, to embezzling funds rightfully due inventors. Further, contemporary writers claimed that patentees who disposed of their rights piecemeal risked the possibility that familiarity with the device would stimulate some other inventor to patent a substitute or an improvement that would reduce the value of the original patent and therefore the proceeds from later sales. For this reason they advised inventors to dispose of a patent in its entirety "as soon as possible after its issue" (Simonds 1871, 28–29; An Experienced and Successful Inventor 1901, 58–59; Cresee 1907, 26–27, 61).

13. Although assignment contracts had to be filed with the Patent Office in order to be legally binding, there was no similar legal requirement to file licensing agreements. Our sample of assignment contracts does contain some licensing agreements, but they are very few in number, and anecdotal evidence suggests that those recorded in this manner were a declining proportion of the total of such agreements over time. It is likely, therefore, that the decrease in secondary assignments was more than compensated for by an increase in licenses, and that our figures understate this important (and growing) dimension of the market for patented technology.

14. At least part of the rise in the fraction of assignments that occurred before issue resulted from an increase in the length of time consumed by the application process. In order to get a rough idea of the extent of the increase, we compared two samples of 125 patents each drawn from the October 1874 and October 1911 issues of the *Official Gazette of the United States Patent Office.* In 1874, the median time between application and issue was 4 months and the mean 5.8 months. In 1911, the median was 12 months and the mean 18.2 months.

Table 1.2   **Assignment of Patents at Issue, 1870–1911**

	1870–71	1890–91	1910–11
Number of patents	1,563	2,031	2,512
% of patents assigned	18.4	29.3	31.1
% of assignments to group including patentee	52.1	41.5	25.4
% of assignments in which patentee assigned away all rights to unrelated individuals	24.7	11.1	10.4
% of assignments in which patentee assigned away all rights to a company	23.6	47.1	64.2
% of assignments in which patentee assigned away all rights to a company with the same name as the patentee	5.6	11.8	9.2
% of patents in which patentee maintained stake (did not assign or assigned to group including patentee or assigned to company with the same name)	92.2	86.3	79.7

Sources: The table is based on three random cross-sectional samples of patents drawn from the *Annual Report of the Commissioner of Patents* for the years 1870–71, 1890–91, 1910–11.

Notes: The three samples total slightly under 6,600 patents, including those granted to foreigners. The table includes only patents awarded to residents of the United States. The category "% of assignments to group including patentee" consists of patents assigned to one or more individuals including the patentee, an individual with the same family name as the patentee, or an individual specifically designated as an agent for the patentee. Patents assigned to companies with the same last name as the patentee were included in the general category of patents assigned to companies, as well as in the particular category of companies with the same name as the patentee. It is, of course, also possible that patentees had an ownership stake in companies that did not bear their name.

issue. Table 1.2 reports the frequency with which patents in these samples were assigned at issue, as well as the frequency of various types of assignments, including the proportion that went to companies. The table also provides a summary measure of the extent to which patentees retained a stake in their inventions—that is, the total number of patents not assigned at the time of issue plus the number of those assigned that went to groups including the patentee or to companies with the same name as the patentee.

When combined with the information from table 1.1, the figures in table 1.2 suggest a progression over time. Initially, inventors not only came up with new technological ideas but also developed and commercialized them, sometimes by starting their own businesses, sometimes by selling partial rights to their ideas to producers in different geographic markets, and sometimes by doing both. As the market for technology expanded and matured, inventors seem to have employed it to facilitate these kinds of business activities. For example, during the early 1870s assignments at issue typically involved the sale of shares of patent rights to groups of individuals who were not coinventors, but who generally resided in the vicinity of the patentee, and it is likely that these partial assignments compensated local partners for advances of capital to support the development and commercialization of the inventions. Over time, however, a

Table 1.3   **Distribution of Patents by Patentee Commitment to Patenting, 1790–1930**

	Number of "Career" Patents by Patentee (%)					
	1 Patent	2 Patents	3 Patents	4–5 Patents	6–9 Patents	10+ Patents
1790–1811	51.0	19.0	12.0	7.6	7.0	3.5
1812–29	57.5	17.4	7.1	7.6	5.5	4.9
1830–42	57.4	16.5	8.1	8.0	5.6	4.4
1870–71	21.1	12.5	9.9	15.8	11.8	28.9
1890–91	19.5	10.3	10.3	10.3	13.8	35.9
1910–11	33.2	14.3	8.2	9.8	9.4	25.0

Sources: The figures from 1790 to 1842 are from Sokoloff and Khan 1990, 363–78. The figures for the later years were computed from a longitudinal data set constructed by selecting all the patentees in the cross-sectional samples (see table 1.2 for a description) whose family names began with the letter *B* and collecting information on the patents they received during the twenty-five years before and after they appeared in the samples. This data contains information of 6,057 patents granted to the 561 *B* inventors.

second pattern emerged as patentees increasingly relinquished all property rights to their inventions by the time of issue, assigning their rights in particular to companies. The shift can be seen as a drop in the proportion of patents in which the patentee retained a direct stake—from 92.2 percent in 1870–71 to 79.7 percent in 1910–11. Because many of the patents not assigned at issue were probably of limited economic value, however, the change can be seen more clearly in the fall in the proportion of assignments that went to groups that included the patentee—from 52.1 percent in 1870–71 to 25.4 percent in 1910–11.[15]

The growth of trade in patented technologies was accompanied by dramatic increases in the degree to which patentees specialized in inventive activity. This development is reflected in table 1.3, which presents estimates of how the share of patents awarded to inventors with long-term commitments to patenting changed over the course of the nineteenth century. We obtained the estimates for 1870–71, 1890–91, and 1910–11 by selecting from our three cross-sectional samples inventors whose last names began with the letter *B* and collecting information on all the patents these inventors received in the twenty-five years before and after they appeared in the respective sample. We then grouped the inventors according to the total number of patents they obtained over the fifty-year period and calculated how all the patents in each cross-section were distributed across these groups. Finally, we compared our results with data on career patenting for the period 1790–1842 compiled by Kenneth Sokoloff and Zorina Khan (1990).

The figures indicate a major shift, with the proportion of patents awarded to

15. As we will show below, however, a significant proportion of the assignments to companies involved firms in which the patentees were officers.

Table 1.4   **Average Number of Patents Awarded to Various Types of Patentees, 1870–1911**

	1870–71	1890–91	1910–11
Year total of patents for all patentees	1.92	2.29	2.00
	(1,563)	(2,031)	(2,512)
Year total of patents for patentees who did not assign	1.67	1.99	1.61
	(1,275)	(1,436)	(1,730)
Year total of patents for patentees who assigned	3.03	3.00	2.87
	(288)	(595)	(782)
Year total of patents for patentees who assigned to a group including themselves	1.75	1.79	1.60
	(150)	(247)	(199)
Year total of patents for patentees who assigned away all their rights to unrelated individuals	3.85	2.95	2.51
	(71)	(66)	(81)
Year total of patents for patentees who assigned away all their rights to companies	4.97	4.10	3.43
	(68)	(280)	(502)
Year total of patents for patentees who assigned away all their rights to companies with the same name as the patentee	3.31	5.41	4.35
	(16)	(70)	(72)

Sources: The table is based on three cross-sectional samples drawn from the *Annual Report of the Commissioner of Patents* for the years 1870–71, 1890–91, 1910–11.

Notes: For each patent in the sample, we counted all of the other patents received by that patentee in the same year. For additional information on these samples and on the definitions of the categories, see table 1.2. The number of sample observations for each cell is reported within parentheses.

individuals who received ten or more patents over their careers increasing from below 5 percent in the three early cross-sections to 25 percent or more in the three cross-sections between 1870 and 1911. The early 1800s were a relatively democratic era of invention, when a broad segment of the population was acquainted with the basic elements of the technology in use, and the typical inventor filed only one or two patents over his or her lifetime. The rapid expansion of the market for patents that occurred during the second third of the nineteenth century made it easier to extract returns from technological discoveries by selling off patent rights, and seems to have coincided with the emergence of a class of inventors who were relatively specialized at inventive activity. Occasional inventors, whose efforts at technological creativity were only one aspect of their work, continued to be significant contributors to technological change, but their share of patents fell sharply. From over 70 percent as late as the 1830s, the share of patents accounted for by individuals with only one or two career patents declined to less than 35 percent by the 1870s.

Another, perhaps more direct, indication of the relationship between specialization at invention and the practice of selling off patent rights is the higher productivity of patentees who assigned to companies. In table 1.4, we report for our three cross-sectional samples from 1870–71, 1890–91, and 1910–11 the average number of patents received by individual patentees in a single year, grouped by whether the patentee had assigned away his or her rights (and to whom) before the date of issue of the patent. As is clear, patentees who assigned their patents at issue were more productive (in terms of the number of patents they received in a given year) than those who did not assign. Moreover, inventors who assigned their full patent rights to unrelated individuals or to companies were more productive than those who retained a share of their patents. The patentees who consistently received the most patents per year were those who assigned at issue to companies, and it is interesting to note that the relatively small but growing number of patentees who assigned away all rights to companies that bore their last name were by 1890–91 the most productive of all.

1.3   Inventors and Firms

Both the growing tendency of inventors to assign all rights to their patents at issue to companies and the greater productivity at invention of patentees who disposed of their patents in this way, raise questions about the identity of these inventors and the nature of their relationship with the companies to which they assigned. There are three main possibilities: first, that the inventors were independent agents who sold their patents in arm's-length transactions; second, that they were principals (for example, officers or proprietors) of the firms to which they assigned; and third, that they were employees of their assignees. These three possibilities have different implications for the extent to which invention was integrated with development. The first case, of course, implies a clear division of labor between those who invented and those who developed the inventions commercially. The second case is more ambiguous, because we cannot tell from this kind of information alone whether the patentees formed companies in order to integrate invention with commercial development or whether they were seeking to provide themselves with a better vehicle to support their specialization in inventive activity. The third case is the one most favorable to those who would argue for an increased integration of invention and development within large firms. However, to the extent that inventors who assigned to their employers obtained more patents than those who did not, the difference may not have resulted from efficiency gains deriving from integration, but instead from inventors' greater ability to specialize within large-scale enterprises or from cost savings derived from economies of scale in carrying out invention or in filing patent applications.

Unfortunately, because assignments of patents typically take the same contractual form whether they involve arm's-length sales, grants of patent rights by principals to their associated firms, or the acquisition by firms of employees' inventions, it is difficult to get a sense of the relative importance of these different kinds of transactions over time. We have, however, devised a number of alternative ways to approach the problem. Although these alternatives are individually partial and imperfect, collectively they allow us to conclude with reasonable confidence that the acquisition by firms of employees' inventions

Table 1.5   **Relative Numbers of Patents Assigned after and at Issue to Individuals and Companies**

	After Issue		At Issue		
	No.	%	No.	%	Total
1871					
To individuals	454	73.2	166	26.8	620
To companies	112	68.3	52	31.7	164
Total	566	72.2	218	27.8	784
1891					
To individuals	370	45.6	441	54.4	811
To companies	230	41.8	320	58.2	550
Total	600	44.1	761	55.9	1,361
1911					
To individuals	307	40.4	453	59.6	760
To companies	369	33.6	728	66.4	1,097
Total	676	36.4	1,181	63.6	1,857

Source: For a description of the sample, see table 1.1.

cannot account either for the general trend in assignments in favor of companies or the greater productivity at invention of patentees who assigned away their patent rights.

Our first, and least direct, approach is based on the assumption that assignments that occurred in the context of the employment relationship were more likely to occur at the time the patent was issued for the simple reason that, in such cases, the company commonly assumed responsibility for patenting the invention, paying all the necessary fees and providing legal counsel, in exchange for an immediate assignment. Table 1.5 (which is based on the January 1871, 1891, and 1911 samples of assignment contracts) shows that there was nothing remarkable about the propensity of companies to obtain assignments at issue. Although the proportion of assignments to companies that took place before issue always exceeded that of assignments to individuals, the difference was relatively small and showed only a slight tendency to widen over time. More important, the proportion of assignments that occurred at issue increased dramatically over time for both types of assignees, suggesting that the change resulted more from improvements in the general market for technology than from the movement of inventors within firms.[16]

A second approach uses the longitudinal data on our *B* patentees to explore the extent to which there were stable, ongoing relationships between patentees and assignees. In table 1.6, we present, for different classes of patentees, a measure of the degree of "contractual mobility," where contractual mobility is defined as the number of different assignees over time to which a patentee

16. Once again, however, it is important to note that the time interval between application for a patent and issue by the Patent Office also increased over this period.

Table 1.6   Contractual Mobility among Patentees, by Their Productivity at Patenting

Number of Patents Received by Patentee over Career	% Assigned	% Assigned to Companies	Did Not Assign Any Patents		1		2–3		4–5		6+		Total	
			No.	%	No.	%	No.	%	No.	%	No.	%	No.	%
							Distribution of Patentees							
1	19.2	5.3	122	80.8	29	19.2	—	—	—	—	—	—	151	26.9
2–5	18.5	7.2	121	62.1	62	31.8	11	5.6	1	0.5	—	—	195	34.8
6–10	26.3	16.3	31	38.8	17	21.3	25	31.3	7	8.8	—	—	80	14.3
11–19	31.7	21.7	10	16.7	22	36.7	15	25.0	11	18.3	2	3.3	60	10.7
20+	49.3	41.3	4	5.3	9	12.0	29	38.7	15	20.0	18	24.0	75	13.4
Total			288	51.3	139	24.8	80	14.3	34	6.1	20	3.6	561	100.0
							Distribution of Patents							
1	19.2	5.3	122	80.8	29	19.2	—	—	—	—	—	—	151	2.5
2–5	19.5	6.2	352	57.8	209	34.3	43	7.1	5	0.8	—	—	609	10.1
6–10	28.8	15.2	238	38.5	129	20.9	194	31.4	57	9.2	—	—	618	10.2
11–19	35.0	23.3	138	15.8	330	37.8	214	24.5	157	18.0	33	3.8	872	14.4
20+	58.0	47.2	117	3.1	466	12.2	1,361	35.8	864	22.7	999	26.2	3,807	62.9
Total			967	16.0	1,163	19.2	1,812	29.9	1,083	17.9	1,032	17.0	6,057	100.0

Source: The estimates were computed from the *B* data set described in the note to table 1.3.

Notes: The top panel presents the distribution of the 561 inventors in the data set, broken down by the total number of patents the inventor received over his "career" (defined as the twenty-five years before and after he appeared in the sample) and by the number of different assignees to whom he assigned patents at the time of issue. Where the inventor assigned a patent to a group of individuals, that group was treated as one assignee. In the top panel, the estimates of "% Assigned" and "% Assigned to Companies" were calculated from a subset of patents consisting of one randomly drawn patent for each of the 561 patentees. The distribution in the lower panel pertains to all of the 6,057 patents received by the 561 inventors over their careers. The figures for "% Assigned" and "% Assigned to Companies" are accordingly based on all of the patents received by the patentees in the respective categories.

transferred patent rights at issue. The upper panel reports the distribution for the individual *B* patentees, broken down by the total number of patents received over their careers and by the number of different assignees to which they transferred patent rights. The lower panel reports the analogous distribution for all of the patents received by the *B* patentees. This distribution is equivalent to a weighted version of the distribution in the upper panel, where the weights are the numbers of patents received by the patentees over their careers.

As the figures in table 1.6 indicate, the most highly productive patentees (those with twenty or more career patents) were not generally tied to single assignees. Only 12 percent of the patentees in this class relied on one assignee throughout their careers. By contrast, 44 percent contracted with four or more different assignees over time. (The analogous figures for the number of patents associated with this group were 12.2 and 48.9 percent respectively.) These results make it difficult to believe that stable employment relationships were responsible for the high productivity at patenting we observe among inventors who assigned away their patent rights. If these inventors were in fact employees, then they were employees who often either moved restlessly from job to job or who, despite their positions, behaved entrepreneurially and assigned their patents to buyers other than their employers. This conclusion appears even stronger when one recognizes that the percentages in the table pertain only to patents that were actually assigned at issue. The highly productive patentees in this group chose to retain control at issue of the rights to more than 40 percent of the patents they received, reserving for themselves the ability to sell or license their inventions in the future. It is likely that if we had information on subsequent assignments or licensing agreements, our estimates of the extent of contractual mobility would only increase.

In order to get a more direct understanding of the relationship between patentees and their assignees, we traced the inventors in our *B* sample through city directories and, wherever possible, recorded their occupations and/or places of employment for the years in which they were issued patents.[17] The resulting subset is certainly not representative of the general population of patentees. In the first place, it is more urban.[18] In the second, it is biased in favor of those who were more occupationally settled and therefore more likely to be picked up in the directories. As a consequence of this bias in favor of stability, one

17. For this exercise we used an earlier version of the longitudinal *B* sample that included data on most but not all of the fifty years surrounding each patentee's appearance in a cross-sectional sample. The effect of using the incomplete sample was to reduce the average number of assignees per patentee and thus to increase the likelihood of finding apparently stable relationships between patentees and assignees. Although the period of time for which we have data ranged from 1843 to 1935, 96 percent of the observations fell between 1867 and 1930.

18. Patentees in the subsample came from more than fifty cities, but more than 50 percent of the observations in each of our three subperiods came from the same six cities (Baltimore, Boston, Chicago, Cleveland, New York, and Philadelphia). One potential problem: the post-1910 subsample is very different from the others in the limited representation of New York and the large fraction of observations from Chicago (over 30 percent).

might expect that assignments made to companies by patentees in long-term employment relationships would be more prominent in this subset of the data than in the B sample as a whole.[19] As we will show, however, employees who assigned their patents to their companies still played only a minor role.

In table 1.7, we summarize the information collected for this subsample of urban patentees by presenting for each of three time periods descriptive statistics on the distribution of patentees (based on one randomly selected patent per patentee) and on the distribution of all their patents. The distributions are broken down in the upper panel of the table by occupational class and, in the bottom panel, by type of relationship between patentee and assignee. Caution in generalizing from this data is warranted because the subsample is clearly not representative of the entire population of patentees and because we were not able to determine the employment status of all of the inventors. Nevertheless, the results strongly suggest that, until well into the twentieth century, when inventors transferred the rights to their patented technologies to others, their assignees were unlikely to be their employers. The proportion of patentees in the subsample who were employees averaged only 28 percent over the entire period, and the fraction of patents they accounted for was even less (20.7 percent on average). Moreover, the share of assignments at issue made by employees to employers hovered around the modest level of 10 percent.[20]

Although the relatively small role played by employee patentees was an enduring feature of this era, several major changes in the market for technology are evident in the patterns of assignments at issue. First, as we have already documented using other data sets, patentees became increasingly likely over time to assign away all rights to their patents at the time of issue. This trend is reflected in table 1.7 in the sharp decline in the fraction of patents not assigned at issue (from 75.1 percent before 1890 to 29.7 percent after 1910). Second, there was also a significant increase over time in the proportion of patents transferred at issue to assignees who had a formal association with the patentee—that is, to patentees' employers or to firms in which patentees were principals or officers. This total rose from a mere 6.6 percent of patents before 1890, when arm's-length exchanges were more common, to 43.6 percent after 1910. Virtually all of the increase resulted from the dramatic growth both in the proportion of patents accounted for by principals and officers in firms and in the tendency of such individuals to assign their patents to their companies. The share of patents awarded to principals and officers rose steadily from 37.2

19. Comparison of the patenting and assignment data for individuals from the B sample whom we could locate in city directories with similar information for individuals whom we could not suggests that such a bias is probably present.

20. Because there is a significant group of patent assignments for which we were unable to determine the association (or lack thereof) between the patentee and the assignee, the actual figures for assignments by employees to employers were likely somewhat higher. However, the qualitative result that patentees assigning to their employers did not account for a large share of the assignments of patented technologies seems firm. The bias owing to measurement error would almost certainly be offset by that attributable to our relying here on assignments at issue.

Table 1.7   **Occupations of Patentees and Relationships to Assignees as Indicated by City Directories**

		Before 1890	1890–1910	After 1910	All Years
Occupations					
Principals and officers of	% of patentees	20.6	33.9	40.4	30.8
firms	% of patents	37.2	46.5	60.5	49.0
Employees	% of patentees	20.6	36.9	19.2	28.0
	% of patents	18.1	25.9	17.3	20.7
Unknown or independent	% of patentees	58.8	29.2	40.4	43.2
	% of patents	44.7	27.6	22.2	30.3
Total	No. of patentees	68	65	52	185
	No. of patents	454	641	603	1,698
Relationship between patentee and assignee					
No assignment	% of patentees	77.9	53.9	51.9	62.2
	% of patents	75.1	49.0	29.7	49.1
Patentee to employer	% of patentees	1.5	6.2	5.8	4.3
	% of patents	2.0	8.9	6.6	6.2
Patentee is principal or	% of patentees	2.9	9.2	13.5	8.1
officer in assignee firm	% of patents	4.6	19.2	37.0	21.6
Patentee and assignee are	% of patentees	0.0	4.6	0.0	1.6
related by name	% of patents	1.3	1.4	0.5	1.1
Unknown relation	% of patentees	5.9	10.8	23.1	12.4
	% of patents	7.5	7.2	21.1	12.2
Patentee has no relation	% of patentees	11.8	15.4	5.8	11.4
to assignee	% of patents	9.5	14.4	5.1	9.8

Notes: The data on which this table is based were constructed by searching the available city directories for information on the occupation and place of work of the patentees in our *B* sample (described in the note to table 1.3). This search was conducted on an earlier, incomplete version of the sample, which did not include all of the career patents issued to each of the 561 patentees. The effort yielded information on 185 patentees, who were responsible for 1,698 patents according to our partial listing. The information retrieved from the city directories was then used to classify each of the patentees we found, at the time of each of his patents in our partial sample, by occupation and by relationship to the assignee of the patent (if the patent was assigned at issue). Three occupational classes were defined. A patentee was classified as a "principal" if listed in the respective directory as an officer of a firm (president, vice president, treasurer, secretary, or general manager), or with an occupation that seemed to indicate proprietorship (for example, manufacturer or inventor). A patentee was classified as an "employee" if listed in the respective directory with an occupation that suggested a subordinate position in a firm (for example, manager, super-intendent, salesman, clerk, chief engineer, or foreman). A patentee was classified in the "independent" or "unknown" category if it was unclear from the occupation whether the individual was a principal or employee (for example, agent, engineer, machinist, brewer, chemist, or printer), and if no firm was listed as a place of work. As for the classification of the relationship between the patentee and the assignee, six categories were defined, the first being those cases where the patent was not assigned at issue. An assign-ment was classified as being from a patentee to an employer if the patentee was an employee and the assignee had the same or a similar name as the firm listed as the place of work. A patent assignment was classified as from a principal to his firm if the patentee was a principal in the firm to which the patent was assigned. An assignment was classified as one that involved no relationship between the patentee and the assignee if a place of work was listed that was different from the name of the assignee, or if the assignee was an individual with a different surname. An assignment was classified as a case of a patentee assigning to a family member if the patentee and the assignee had the same surname. The classification "unknown relation" was used when there was no report of a place of work and the patentee was classified in the unknown or independent category. It was also used in miscellaneous cases where it was unclear whether the patentee and assignee had a formal relationship.

percent in the years before 1890 to 60.5 percent after 1910, and the fraction of patents that were assigned to a firm in which the patentee was a principal or officer increased from 4.6 percent before 1890 to 37 percent (more than half of all assignments at issue) after 1910. The increased prominence in the subsample of patentees who were principals and officers of firms was to some degree paralleled by a decrease in the proportion of patentees who were independent inventors. The difficulty of establishing that a patentee was an independent inventor means that there is greater uncertainty about trends in this category of patentees, but we know that the share of patents granted to patentees of independent or unknown status declined from 44.7 percent before 1890 to 22.2 percent after 1910. One possible explanation for these parallel patterns may have been an increase in the propensity of independent inventors to incorporate their enterprises (perhaps as an aid in raising capital). If this was indeed the case, then part of the growth in the proportion of patents issued to principals and officers of firms (as well as in the proportion of assignments at issue that went from such individuals to their companies) may have owed to a change in industrial organization rather than to a decrease in the extent of arm's-length transactions.[21]

We continue to explore changes over time in the pattern of assignments with the help of table 1.8, which reports the same distributions of patents and patentees as table 1.7, but now broken down first by categories of association and then by occupational class and time period. As is apparent from the lower percentages of patents not assigned in the distribution of patents compared to that of patentees, inventors who assigned their patents at issue received more patents on average than those who did not, across all occupational classes and time periods. Although the difference is not very large in the independent or unknown class during the two earlier subperiods, the result suggests that the higher productivity of patentees who assigned their patents at issue is not an artifact generated by a particular occupational group or type of patentee/assignee relationship. The secular trend toward higher rates of assignment at issue was likewise not specific to a single occupational class; nor did it result from a change in the occupational composition of patentees.

The advantage of the distributions presented in table 1.8 is that they allow us to explore trends in assignment behavior within each occupational class. Once again, the most important changes were the growing share of patents awarded to patentees who were principals or officers in firms and the increasing propensity of patentees in this group to assign to the companies with which they were associated. Although the employee category was the occupational

---

21. Two developments were probably at work here. The first was a general shift in the preferred form of organization for small firms away from proprietorships and partnerships to corporations. The second was a concomitant shift in the propensity to assign patent rights to the firm. The peculiarities of partnership law and the short time horizon of most firms that were organized as partnerships may have discouraged inventors from assigning their patents to their companies. Corporations, on the other hand, may have found it difficult to raise share capital unless the firm acquired title to its principals' important patents.

Table 1.8 Distribution of Patents and Patentees by Occupational Class and Relationship to Assignee, Based on Information from City Directories

		Before 1890			1890–1910			After 1910			All Years		
		Principal or Officer	Employee	Unknown or Independent	Principal or Officer	Employee	Unknown or Independent	Principal or Officer	Employee	Unknown or Independent	Principal or Officer	Employee	Unknown or Independent
No assignment	% patentees	85.7	78.6	75.0	50.0	50.0	63.2	61.9	30.0	52.4	63.2	54.2	66.3
	% patents	78.7	64.6	76.4	46.1	40.4	61.6	33.1	14.4	31.3	47.2	38.4	59.5
Patentee to employer	% patentees	—	7.1	—	—	16.7	—	—	30.0	—	—	16.7	—
	% patents	—	11.0	—	—	33.7	—	—	38.5	—	—	29.8	—
Patentee a principal or officer in assignee	% patentees	14.3	—	—	27.3	—	—	33.3	—	—	26.3	—	—
	% patents	12.4	—	—	41.3	—	—	61.1	—	—	44.1	—	—
Patentee and assignee related by name	% patentees	—	—	—	9.1	—	5.3	—	—	—	3.5	—	1.3
	% patents	0.6	3.7	1.0	2.0	—	1.7	0.8	—	—	1.2	0.9	1.0
Unknown relation	% patentees	—	7.1	7.5	—	12.5	21.1	—	30.0	42.9	—	14.6	20.0
	% patents	—	11.0	12.3	2.7	11.5	10.7	0.3	39.4	63.4	1.1	19.6	25.1
Patentee no relation to assignee	% patentees	—	7.1	17.5	13.6	20.8	10.5	4.8	10.0	4.8	7.0	14.6	12.5
	% patents	8.3	9.8	10.3	7.4	14.5	26.0	4.4	7.7	5.2	6.3	11.4	14.4

Note: See table 1.7.

class with the highest rates of assignment at issue, the estimates in table 1.8 provide further support for the idea that the transfer of patent rights by this group of patentees to their employers was not the major force behind the rise in assignment rates. Not only was the proportion of patents registered to employees relatively constant over time at a modest level, but when employees sold their patents, they appear to have been more inclined than principals and officers to assign to parties with whom they had no formal association. This inclination decreased over time. By our estimates, half or more of the patents (depending on the weighting scheme) assigned by employee patentees before 1890 went to parties other than the employer, with this percentage dropping into the 15 to 20 percent range after 1910. Nevertheless, given that the share of patentees we can identify as employees had by then shrunk below 20 percent, and that employee inventors still had relatively low rates of assignment to parties with whom they had formal associations, it is clear that the behavior of this group was not accounting for the aggregate patterns.

The evidence we obtained by tracing patentees through city directories thus leads to several generalizations about the evolution of patent assignments in the late nineteenth and early twentieth centuries. First, assignments were extensive and growing in overall volume and, at least until late in the nineteenth century, seem to have most often involved arm's-length transactions. Second, all groups of patentees increased the proportion of patents they assigned over time and exhibited an empirical association at the individual level between rates of assignment and productivity at patenting. Third, a major change in the patterns of assignment began to be apparent between 1890 and 1910, and was even more pronounced afterward. Patentees who were principals and officers or employees became more inclined to assign their patents to the firms with which they were associated, and the relative share of principals and officers among the population of patentees grew substantially. Moreover, inventors who were principals or officers in the firms to which they assigned were the most prolific patentees of any group.[22] Whether they were like the classic inventors who commercially exploited their inventions themselves (through firms that integrated invention with development and other general business activities) or whether they had organized firms that were specialized at generating new technologies remains unclear. Further research is required to determine whether this structural break reflects a renewed emphasis on integrating invention with other business activities or an extension to the level of firms of the trend toward division of labor between those concerned with invention and those concerned with commercial exploitation.[23]

22. Here again we should remind the reader that the greater difficulty of locating mobile individuals in city directories may have resulted in an overrepresentation of patentees who had stable long-term relationships with firms. However, the problem should have affected our proportions of employees as well as of principals and officers in firms.

23. It should be noted that Thomas P. Hughes (1989) has argued that this period was the golden age of the independent inventor. Our work could be interpreted as providing a quantitative basis for his assertion.

Table 1.9   Distribution of Assigned Patents by the Number of Assignments Received by the Assignee in the Year

	1 Assignment	2–3 Assignments	4–5 Assignments	6–10 Assignments	>10 Assignments
1870	63.4%	19.9%	5.4%	2.6%	8.7%
	(795)	(250)	(68)	(32)	(109)
1891	54.8%	23.5%	8.1%	8.3%	5.3%
	(2,097)	(898)	(310)	(316)	(203)
1911	41.5%	19.0%	7.3%	6.5%	25.7%
	(2,536)	(1,160)	(446)	(396)	(1,572)

Sources: These estimates of the distribution of assigned patents were calculated from a data set constructed by collecting the number of assignments received by the assignee in the respective year for all patent assignments appearing on every other page of the *Annual Report of the Commissioner of Patents* for 1870, 1891, and 1911 (assignees, like patentees, were listed in alphabetical order).

Notes: Because we ran over to the off pages in order to get a complete accounting of all the patent assignments received by the assignees sampled, our procedure is likely to overstate the concentration of patent assignments across assignees. Numbers of observations are in parentheses.

Finally, the results of our analysis of this urban subset of patentees is consistent with the notion that trade in the rights to patented technologies involved broad segments of the industrial sector and that the growing proportion of patents that were assigned to companies did not simply result from employees in the R&D departments of large firms transferring their inventions to their companies. Further evidence for this view is provided by table 1.9, which reports evidence on the frequency distribution of assignments among samples of assignees drawn from the *Annual Report of the Commissioner of Patents* for the years 1870, 1891, and 1911. These results, which were calculated in such a way as to provide upwardly biased estimates of the degree of concentration, suggest that the assignment of patents was extremely unconcentrated during the first two of these years, though much less so by the third. Over 60 percent of patent assignments in 1870 went to assignees who received only one assignment in that year, and more than 80 percent went to those with three or less.[24] In 1891 the proportion of those with three or less assignments was still nearly 80 percent. By 1911, however, the figure had dropped close to 60 percent, and there is evidence of a substantial shift toward greater concentration. In particular, the increase in the proportion of assignments to firms with more than ten assignments from under 10 percent in 1870 and 1891 to over 25 percent in 1911 (when General Electric alone received over 300 patent assignments) is an indication that the character and organization of trade in patented technologies had begun to change during the intervening years.

24. In 1870, the fraction that went to assignees that received more than ten assignments was 8.7 percent, a rather modest proportion but one that would have been even lower (below 3 percent) if it had not been for one outlier, the Erwin Russell Manufacturing Company in Middlesex County, Massachusetts. This company, which produced doors, door knobs, and related products, had nearly thirty patents (over half of which were design patents) assigned to it in 1870 by a single patentee.

1.4   Firms and the Market for Technology

We can get a better idea of what was accounting for this shift by looking at the behavior of the firms themselves. The case of the American Bell Telephone Company, one of the "high-tech" enterprises of the period, offers an instructive example. Bell's patent department issued annual reports detailing the number of patents it evaluated from both inside and outside sources. For example, in 1894, it investigated seventy-three patents submitted "by the public" and twelve brought to its attention by employees.[25] The company filed patent applications for virtually all of its employees' inventions—not apparently because the patent department found the ideas particularly valuable, but for morale reasons and because the cost of obtaining patents in this way was low (typically the company paid bonuses of $50 to employees whose inventions it patented).[26] The asking price for outside inventions was often thousands of dollars, and the department recommended against purchasing almost all of them. Consequently, if one were to divide the company's patents into two categories—those purchased from outsiders and those that originated within the firm—the latter would be numerically preponderant. Nonetheless, it is clear that, during this early period, it was on the assessment of outside inventions that the department spent most of its energies and resources. Company records contain numerous reports evaluating the novelty and importance of inventions offered by the public for sale. These reports were by no means pro forma; rather they included a great deal of technical detail that was specific to the invention at hand. Moreover, the company seems to have devoted the same painstaking attention to the messy, handwritten submissions of unknown inventors as it did to the more polished presentations of high-priced patent solicitors.[27] It seems, in other words, that the company was determined not to overlook any possible source of technological advantage that might be obtained by purchasing the patents of independent inventors, even though it found most of the inventions it reviewed not worth pursuing.

Indeed, documents extant in the company's records suggest that American Bell attached much greater importance in its early years to assessing inventions that originated in the external environment than it did to promoting inventive

25. It also investigated twenty-six inventions originating with employees of the local phone companies to which American Bell licensed its technology (Annual Report of the Patent Department, 1894, 7, American Bell Telephone Co., box 1302, AT&T Corporate Archives).

26. As the director of the patent department, T. D. Lockwood, wrote in his 1894 annual report (1–2), "So far as concerns the devices gotten up by our own employees . . . , the practice of the year has been, in a general way, to file an application for patent on nearly every device presented for consideration; . . . and to keep all questions of merit, and the presence, or extent of invention, largely in the background." See also Lockwood's "Statements of Objectives and Practices of AT&T Patent Department, 1877–1937," extracted in "Memorandum for Messrs. Root, Ballantine, Harlan, Bushby & Palmer," 22 November 1949, 15, Divestiture Collection, location 451 01 01, folder 17, AT&T Corporate Archives.

27. See T. D. Lockwood, Reports of Inventions (Not Approved), 1904–8. These evaluations became especially important after 1894, when the patents that had given American Bell an effective monopoly of the telephone business expired (Galambos 1992, 99).

activity within the firm. The architect of this policy was T. D. Lockwood, long-time head of the company's patent department and a vigorous opponent of what we would now call investment in R&D. As Lockwood wrote in an 1885 letter to the company's general manager, "I am fully convinced that it has never, is not now, and never will pay commercially, to keep an establishment of profes-sional inventors, or of men whose chief business it is to invent; or a corps of electricians who are assumed or expected as a part of their duty, to invent new and valuable telephones or telephonic appliances, in their employ."[28] Lock-wood's vision, as embodied in his summary later that same year of the duties of the patent department (and in the department's actual practice), placed em-phasis first and foremost on examining "patents or inventions submitted by the public for consideration" and second on examining "descriptions of inventions forwarded by the company's employees." Only at the end of the report, seventh in a list of miscellaneous duties appended after a lengthy discussion of the department's library, did he include the responsibility for suggesting "special and suitable lines of experimentation" within the firm. Much more important in his mind was the duty to "receive copies of electrical patents from Patent Office . . . , bringing to the attention of the company, such as may commend themselves for novel or striking features," "to constantly acquire information upon all classes of electrical patents," and to maintain a well-stocked library. In other words, Lockwood was mainly concerned with building American Bell's capacity to learn about and assess the merits of inventions generated elsewhere in the economy. The central mission of the company's patent department, as he saw it, was to collect information from a wide variety of sources so as to main-tain familiarity with (and be in a better position to evaluate) technological de-velopments occurring throughout the economy. Not until Theodore N. Vail be-came president in 1907 would the company shift resources to internal R&D.[29]

Bell's policy, as articulated by Lockwood, was extreme, but George Wise

---

28. The text of the letter is included in an 11 September 1952 memo by Lloyd Espenschied, "Early Company Inventing—A Revealing Letter," Western Electric Collection, location 91 05 140, folder 6, AT&T Corporate Archives. Lockwood was not completely consistent, however. He brought Stephen D. Field into his department in 1897 after the company bought some of Field's patents: "I engaged his services in 1897 or thereabouts, to make other inventions of the same kind. . . . Prior to that time he had been for a long time a sort of guerilla inventor on his own hook" (Testimony of Lockwood in *Read v. Central Union Telephone Company,* abstracted in "Memoran-dum for Messrs. Root, Ballantine, Harlan, Bushby & Palmer," 68).

29. T. D. Lockwood, "Duties of Patent Department," 23 November 1885, AT&T Collection, box 1302, AT&T Corporate Archives. Lockwood's sense of his own duties was confirmed by Vail in testimony given in 1908: "Mr. Lockwood's duties were, first to examine every patent that was issued—I mean connected with the telephone or electricity—to see whether it had any bearing on our business, and if so we tried to get some rights under it and possession of it. Next he was to examine all the devices in the carrying on of the business. . . . Of course new devices in the new business were all the time occurring to the people. Those were submitted to us from our licensees, and Mr. Lockwood would examine them as to the patentability and as to the value, and whether they had been gone over before, and all that sort of thing" (extracted in "Memorandum for Messrs. Root, Ballantine, Harlan, Bushby & Palmer," 30). On Vail's own support for internal R&D, see Galambos (1992).

has argued that Westinghouse and Edison Electric/General Electric (two other high-tech firms of the period) followed a similar strategy in the late nineteenth century of "purchas[ing] patents and short-term consulting services from independent inventors" rather than developing their own R&D facilities (Wise 1985, 69–70). We have found much the same story for firms that used older mechanical technologies as well. For example, Channing Whitaker built up the patent department and library at the Lowell Machine Shop, arguing that it was essential to keep track of patents issued to outside inventors so that the company did not waste resources reinventing what had already been developed elsewhere. He also argued that the purchase of outside patents should be considered "not a net expense, but a net saving" because it enabled managers to solve technical problems more cheaply than they could if they relied exclusively on internal resources.[30] Two decades into the twentieth century, the giant Standard Oil of New Jersey was still struggling to build up this kind of general tracking capacity. As George S. Gibb and Evelyn H. Knowlton argued in their study, *The Resurgent Years, 1911–1927,* the company had long shown little interest in promoting R&D internally and had been lax as well in building the capacity to assess and gain control of technological ideas originating in the external environment. In 1918, E. M. Clark, the new general manager of the company's Bayway refinery, began a campaign to improve the company's knowledge of outside technologies. His first step was to arrange for its patent work to be shifted to the Chicago firm of Dyrenforth, Lee, Chritton and Wiles, patent solicitors, a firm that had a great deal of expertise in petroleum-refining technology.[31] He then, in consultation with Frank A. Howard, a member of this firm, planned and promoted the creation within Standard of a development department whose purpose was to collect information about and assess new technologies originating outside the firm. According to Gibb and Knowlton, the new department was founded on the principle that "new ideas and inven-

---

30. "How the Patent Library Came into Existence," box 1, file 8; "The Value of a Patent Department to a Manufacturing Concern," box 2, file 17; both in Channing Whitaker Papers, Lambert Collection, Center for Lowell History.

31. It was common for firms without their own capabilities for assessing externally generated technology to achieve the same ends in a vertically disintegrated way by establishing a long-term relationship with a firm of patent solicitors. The Waltham Watch Company, for example, had such a relationship with the firm of Wright, Brown, Quinby and May. The solicitors' detailed, highly technical reports assessing the patentability of inventions (generated both inside and outside the company) are evidence that they were providing technological as well as legal services. In addition, the firm performed a variety of other functions for its manufacturer client: it brought new inventions to the attention of the company, compiled lists of all patents in force on particular subjects, searched out inventors in other parts of the country, and negotiated assignments with inventors both inside and outside the company. See, for example, Arthur H. Brown's 27 July 1912 report on the patentability of an instrument invented by George H. Lang and manufactured by the Stover and Lang Speedometer Company. See also the 3 March, 30 March, and 6 May 1905 letters from Wright, Brown, Quinby and May to the American Waltham Watch Company, and the 31 March 1913 letter from Olaf Ohlson, the 16 November 1914 letter from George T. May, Jr., and the 25 January 1915 letter from the Waltham Watch Company to the solicitors (Wright, Brown, Quinby & May Correspondence Files, Waltham Watch Company, 1854–1929, case 2).

tions . . . would arise in the main from external sources, and that [its] primary job . . . would be to uncover these ideas, test them out, and carry them forward to some practical end. . . . [T]he new plan was not aimed at fostering creative research." What Standard did, in essence, when it created this department was to internalize the services of its patent solicitors (Howard himself was brought in as manager) so as to acquire capabilities (similar to those developed much earlier at American Bell) for keeping abreast of outside inventions. Only in the next decade would Standard make a serious effort to promote internal R&D (Gibb and Knowlton 1956, 113–14, 122–23, 522–25).[32] Nor was Standard particularly slow in moving to this next level. Although a small number of large firms—Du Pont is the prime example—built in-house R&D facilities before World War I, Standard's experience was more typical.[33]

1.5   Inventors within Firms

The extensive efforts made by firms, including those in high-tech industries, to gain information about and evaluate inventions originating outside their bounds are strong evidence against the notion that information problems made it difficult to contract for technology at arm's length. As we shall see, the evidence suggests to the contrary that contracting problems were if anything worse within the firm than without during this period of time. Indeed, it took many firms quite a long while to work out employment relationships that enabled them to gain title to inventions developed in their shops and labs. Here, however, American Bell was an exception on the progressive side. As early as the 1880s, Bell required its employees to sign contracts giving it first right of refusal on their inventions. Such contracts were relatively rare until the period following World War I, and we have found only a few examples from the last two decades of the nineteenth century. William R. Baker, a foreman at McCormick Harvester, had this type of employment contract in the 1880s; so, in the 1890s, did William T. Smith, a foreman at William Knabe and Company's piano works.[34] According to testimony by Lockwood in 1916, even within the

32. We are indebted to David Mowery for suggesting this reference. Despite Mowery's emphasis on the difficulties of contracting for technology in the market, he recognized that one of the most important functions of early R&D facilities was to assess externally generated inventions (Mowery 1995).

33. For an overview of the development of industrial research in the United States, see Mowery and Rosenberg (1989, 35–97). On Du Pont, see Hounshell and Smith (1988). ·

34. "Record of William R. Baker," 10, *Baker v. Miller,* case 9,957, box 1,402, Interference Case Files, 1836–1905; "Record in Behalf of William T. Smith," 20, *Smith v. Perry v. Keidel,* case 16,028, box 2,212, Interference Case Files, 1836–1905. The earliest example we have been able to find of such an employment agreement was the hiring of mechanic Allan Pollock by the Boston Manufacturing Company in 1820. However, the preoccupation of Channing Whitaker (head of the patent office at the Lowell Machine Shop during the late nineteenth and early twentieth centuries) with the problem of obtaining title to employees' patents suggests that the Boston Associates did not continue to insist upon this condition of employment. See Gregory (1975, 156–57) and Whitaker's notes on court cases involving employee patent rights in box 7, file 4, Channing Whitaker Papers.

telephone industry the practice was limited to a few firms: the New England, Chicago, and Central Union telephone companies, in addition to American Bell. New York Telephone did not have such an arrangement with its employees, and as a result, American Bell was able to purchase an invention patented by one of its men.[35]

Some employment contracts explicitly mentioned patents, but gave the employing firms the right only to use—not own—inventions devised by their employees. For example, inventors in the employ of the Waltham Watch Company typically agreed only to grant the company an exclusive right to the use of their patents during the term of their employment. When the company was reorganized in 1907, it tried without much success to acquire property rights to the patents it was using, but could do little more than ask its solicitors to write polite notes inquiring whether the inventors would now be willing to make assignments.[36] At least some key employees flatly refused to assign their patents to the watch company. For example, the firm's general superintendent responded that "he has an agreement with the Company, providing for the use of his inventions, but that he does not expect to make formal assignments relating to them."[37]

Inventors at many other firms had no contractual obligations whatsoever to provide their technology to their employers and, indeed, felt little compunction about exploiting their inventions themselves, even if they came up with the ideas while working in their employers' shops. August Markert, who worked as a carpenter for A. P. Lorillard and Company (a tobacco manufacturer),

35. Testimony of T. D. Lockwood in *Read v. Central Union Telephone Company,* abstracted in "Memorandum for Messrs. Root, Ballantine, Harlan, Bushby & Palmer," 69, 71. Even American Bell was willing to acquiesce in the entrepreneurial independence of some of its employees. As late as the 1930s, for example, AT&T (American Bell's successor) negotiated special agreements with employees who preferred "to retain the license [themselves], especially for operating in further than the telephone field" and with employees who claim their "rights are so valuable that they should be paid more than a mere bonus." Similarly, at least in the early years the university scientists it kept on retainer were not required to give the company "first call" on their inventions (testimony of G. E. Folk, General Patent Attorney, before the FCC, abstracted in the "Memorandum," 125–26; testimony of T. D. Lockwood in *Read v. Central Union Telephone Company,* abstracted in the "Memorandum," 68).

36. Wright, Brown, Quinby & May to Ezra C. Fitch, 29 January 1907, Wright, Brown, Quinby & May Correspondence Files, Waltham Watch Company, 1854–1929, case 2. See also the letter from the same parties to Edward A. March, 23 January 1907.

37. Wright, Brown, Quinby & May to Matthews, Thompson & Spring, 28 February 1907, Wright, Brown, Quinby & May Correspondence Files, Waltham Watch Company, 1854–1929, case 2. Apparently, some of the Waltham Watch Company's contracts required employees to assign their patents to the firm, but these agreements do not seem to have been well enforced. So much is clear from a 1906 letter written by patent solicitors for the Waltham Watch Company to the widow of one of the firm's employees: "You are doubtless aware that under an agreement entered into between your late husband and the American Waltham Watch Company, several patents now standing in his name are to be assigned to the Company, the agreement providing that all his inventions made during a period which has not yet expired, relating in any way to Watches or to the Manufacture of Watches, shall be assigned to the Company. A large number of the patents have already been assigned; but those that have been granted since 1896 have not yet been assigned" (Wright, Brown, Quinby & May to Mrs. Duane H. Church, 24 January 1906).

reasoned that the company had a right to his inventions when its managers instructed him to work on a particular problem and told him how to go about it, but that things were different "when I got it out of my own head." Markert claimed that he had invented a device for tagging plug tobacco. When the foreman to whom he showed the machine attempted to take credit for the invention and applied for a patent for the benefit of the company, Markert filed his own application, triggering interference proceedings by the Patent Office.[38] Another inventor, M. V. Smith, testified in an interference suit that he came up with an idea for a new furnace while working as superintendent for the National Rolling Mill Company in McKeesport, Pennsylvania: "I regarded it to my best interest to keep the employees of the National Tube Works as much as possible from knowing anything about my improvement on that furnace, and resigned my position with said company, as superintendent, before I ordered the Patent Office drawings made."[39] Two employees of the American Sheet and Tin Plate Company invented a catcher for tinning machines, building the device on company time with company resources and testing it in the company's Gas City, Indiana, plant. When the machine proved promising, they quit their jobs, reasoning that "if we ever got together again in an independent plant we would have a better opportunity of obtaining suitable remuneration for the patent." The two men subsequently accepted employment with the Carnahan Tin Plate and Sheet Company, one of American's competitors. The Carnahan company promised to bear the expense of patenting the machine in exchange for a license to use it, with the inventors retaining ownership of the patent.[40] Even high-tech firms of the period experienced similar problems. Westinghouse, for example, hired William Stanley to develop a transformer, only to have him claim that a new type of lighting he invented while working on the project was his sole property. Similarly, the manager of the Edison Machine Works in

38. "Testimony on Behalf of Markert," 10, 12, *Hieatt and Hearn v. Markert,* case 8,290, box 2,854, Interference Case Files, 1836–1905. In an interference proceeding, the Patent Office held a hearing to determine which of the conflicting patentees was the first and true inventor and should be awarded the patent. The Patent Office's interference files contain numerous cases where applications for letters patent were filed both by an employee and his employer, with the former challenging the latter's claim to an invention developed while he worked for the firm. For example, S. T. Schofield contested with H. C. Cragg over which of the two men actually invented a screw feed mechanism developed while he was in the employ of the H. C. Cragg Manufacturing Company. Elmer A. Sperry found himself tied up in an interference proceeding with a draftsman he had formerly employed in his factory, and Charles A. Lindstrom had a similar experience with a draftsman he hired. See "Testimony on Behalf of S. T. Schofield," *Cragg v. Schofield,* case 25,592, PF box 3,319, ROPO Interference Case Files, 1900–1925 (the ROPO Interference Case Files are still under the control of the Patent Office but are stored at the National Archives and Record Center); "Sperry's Record," 41–42, *Sperry v. Eickemeyer v. Morgan,* case 16,498, box 2,269–72, and "Testimony on Behalf of Lindstrom," *Lindstrom v. Larson,* case 20,284/20,293, box 2,744, both in Interference Case Files, 1836–1905.

39. "Testimony in Chief of M. V. Smith in the Matter of the Interference of John Pedder vs. Martin V. Smith," 25–26, *Pedder v. Smith,* case 9,448, box 3,077, Interference Case Files, 1836–1905.

40. "Lewis & Williams Record," 4–8, *Lewis and Williams v. Cronemeyer,* case 24,270, PF box 3,133, ROPO Interference Case Files, 1900–1925.

Schenectady, New York, complained to the company's lawyers in 1890 that employees were obtaining patents but refusing to assign them to the firm.[41]

It is important to note that firms' lax policies with respect to their employees' inventions cannot simply be explained as a function of their belief that they owned title to the patents as a matter of common sense or common law. Inventors hotly contested firms' assertions that they deserved such ownership rights, and the courts typically backed inventors over their employers. Indeed, by the turn of the century, it was well established that the mere fact of an employment relationship did not entitle a firm to an employee's inventions, even if the invention was developed at company expense. If the inventor was hired for the specific purpose of building a particular machine or improving a particular product, then the employer had a right to the invention (the reason being that the employee had "only produced that which he was employed to invent. His invention [was] the precise subject of the contract of employment"). More generally, however, the courts refused to hold that a contract of employment, "albeit [one that] covers a field of labor and effort in the performance of which the employee conceived the invention," entitled the firm to an assignment of the patent.[42] This latter rule applied even to cases where a firm had employed someone with technical skills "to take charge of its works, and to devote his time and services to devising and making improvements in articles there manufactured." As the majority of the Supreme Court decided in the 1893 case *Allen C. Dalzell et al. v. Dueber Watch Case Manufacturing Company,* "in the absence of an express agreement" by which the employee promised to assign all his patents to the firm, the company could not claim ownership of the patents.[43] In other words, by their very laxness in not requiring or enforcing such "express agreements," firms jeopardized their rights to inventions developed in their shops.

Firms, however, might still obtain a use right, or shop right, to these inventions. As a principle of equity, the courts often granted firms a nonexclusive,

41. These last two examples are from Wise (1985, 70–72). By 1900, General Electric required its employees to sign contracts promising to assign their inventions to the company. In the only attempt at explaining this phenomenon that we have found in the literature, Wise argues that such contracts were a "social invention" made possible by the growth of large, centrally controlled firms. According to Wise, smaller firms "lacked the legal skills to write such a contract. And even if they hired lawyers to do the writing, enforcing the contract might require too much of the time of the owner and his few assistants." Although it is undoubtedly the case that the cost of such contractual arrangements fell over time as both firms and employees gained experience with them, it is unlikely that, even early on, these kinds of expenses were as prohibitive as Wise suggests. As we saw above, moreover, small firms were among those pioneering in the use of such contracts.

42. *United States of America v. Dubilier Condenser Corporation, United States Supreme Court Reports,* 77 *Lawyers' Edition* 1114. This 1933 case contains an excellent summary of the case law. See also 16 *American Law Reports, Annotated* (hereafter *ALR*) 1177; 32 *ALR* 1037; 44 *ALR* 593; 85 *ALR* 1512; 153 *ALR* 983; 61 *ALR* 2d 356; Prindle (1908, 84–102); Fisk (1997). Employees could not, however, claim ownership of inventions for which they had merely made suggestions that did not amount "to a new method or arrangement which in itself is a complete invention" (Johnson 1913, 189).

43. *United States Supreme Court Reports,* 37 *Lawyers' Edition* 749.

nontransferable license to use, without payment of royalty, inventions developed by their employees on company time with company resources.[44] Even here, however, the courts found it easier to enforce the principle in the presence of an express agreement with the employee, a circumstance that inspired at least one firm (the Pullman Company) to rethink its employment contracts. After learning about one such case in the fall of 1912, executives of the company began to worry that inventions developed by employees were being patented on the outside and that rights to these devices were being assigned or licensed to the firm's competitors. The executives commenced an investigation into the extent of the problem and, at the same time, began to formulate a policy about inventions patented by employees. Interestingly, in the earliest drafts of the policy, the company claimed no ownership rights to its employees' inventions, seeking only to insure its legal "license to use devices on our own cars without royalty." In these early drafts, the company even planned to pay employee inventors half of any royalties it collected on cars constructed for outside companies and acknowledged that "other outside arrangements" could "be made direct by the inventor."[45] Only after several months and several drafts had gone by did the company decide on a policy to require employees to "give the Company preference in disposing of the title to such invention and the patent therefor, in addition to the shop-right which the law implies." In exchange, the company offered to pay a bonus of $250 for any invention which it decided should be patented.[46] There is no evidence that the articulation of this policy was accompanied by any new R&D initiatives; it was simply an attempt to insure the company control of inventions produced by its employees. The final draft differed from the initial versions mainly in the company's decision to claim full property rights to employees' inventions and thus deny competitors' access to this technology.[47]

The Pullman Company's attempt to gain control of the inventions of its employees was part of a more general move to improve its ability to assess the value of new technologies. The centerpiece of this policy was the creation of a new Committee on Standards in 1912. The committee consisted of senior managers with considerable technical expertise, and was charged with evaluating

44. Key cases included the 1886 *Charles H. Hapgood et al. v. Horace L. Hewitt, United States Supreme Court Reports*, 30 *Lawyers' Edition* 369, and the 1896 *Jabez H. Gill v. United States*, 40 *Lawyers' Edition* 480. For a summary of the case law, see *United States of America v. Dubilier Condenser Corporation*; 61 *ALR* 2d 356.

45. See the minutes of the 22 October 1912 and 7 January 1913 meetings of the Committee on Standards, Operating Department, Chief Engineer, Equipment Standards and Testing Records, 1889–1956, box 2, folder 4, Pullman Company Archives, Newberry Library.

46. "Policy and Procedure in Patent Matters," 21 November 1913, Secretary & Treasurer, Office of the Secretary & Treasurer, box 1, folder 2, Pullman Company Archives.

47. The new policy was articulated in part as an effort to encourage improvements by employees, but this language was mainly an attempt to make more palatable what was really a radical and unilateral change in the nature of the employment contract. The circumstances under which the policy was formulated—and the bulk of the document's provisions—make it clear that the purpose of the policy was to impose restrictions on employees' behavior.

the inventions of employees and deciding which ones were worth attempting to patent. The committee was further charged with responsibility for deciding which outside patents the company should purchase: "no letter recommending a particular invention should be written by an official in this Company without the approval of the Committee on Standards."[48] The committee had additional duties (for example, testing the properties of inputs into the firm's production process and setting and enforcing quality standards for its products) but in other respects functioned much like the patent department that AT&T had set up earlier. It was part of the process by which the firm learned to improve its ability to tap new technologies, whether they were generated inside the enterprise or out.

Although the evidence suggests that employment contracts giving a company ownership of its employees' inventions were not yet routine during the first two decades of the twentieth century, by the 1930s such agreements appear to have been commonplace. The Committee on Patents of the U.S. House of Representatives held hearings in 1936 about proposed revisions to the patent law. As part of its investigation, the committee sent inquiries to a number of companies that included a question about employees' contractual obligation to assign inventions to the firm. Fourteen of the responses (ranging from giant enterprises such as Standard Oil and International Harvester to a number of small aviation companies) were reprinted as appendixes to the hearings. In almost all cases the firms reported that the great majority of the patents they owned originated with their own employees who had contractual obligations to assign their inventions to the company. There thus seems to have been a pronounced shift toward reliance on internally generated technologies in the period after the First World War.[49]

1.6 Learning by Firms

The sources of this shift are complex and involve developments, such as the growth of oligopolistic competition, that are beyond the bounds of our research. But the change can also to some extent be understood as the outcome of the processes we have been describing. In the first place, as firms tightened up their internal affairs, they were in a better position to exploit the inventive talent already present in their organizations. In the second, the capabilities they had built up to assess externally generated inventions could also be put to other uses within the firm—could be employed, for example, to pinpoint fruitful

48. Policy and Procedure in Patent Matters, 8.
49. U.S. Congress, House, *Hearings before the Committee on Patents . . . on H.R. 4523, a Bill Providing for the Recording of Patent Pooling Agreements and Contracts with the Commissioner of Patents* (Washington, DC: Government Printing Office, 1936), parts 2–4. The firms reporting were Beech-Nut Packing, Curtis Aeroplane and Motor, Douglas Aircraft, Great Lakes Aircraft, Hercules Powder, Ingersoll Rand, International Business Machines, International Harvester, North American Aviation, Socony-Vacuum Oil, Standard Oil, Sun Oil Company, Western Union, and Wright Aeronautical Corporation.

areas of research in which the company might itself engage. Moreover, firms that invested in such expertise had to invest as well in facilities to develop and commercialize the inventions they purchased, facilities that could be turned to the development of internally generated inventions and then expanded into departments devoted more broadly to R&D. Indeed, this was the sequence of events that occurred at Standard Oil.

Perhaps more important, as the complexity of technology increased by the end of the nineteenth and especially by the early twentieth century, it became more and more difficult for inventors to maintain their independence. Even though the growth of the market for technology had made it easier for patentees to sell off their property rights at an early date and to form corporations to exploit their inventions, they still faced a great deal of financial uncertainty—especially in those sectors of the economy where the costs of invention, in terms of both human and physical capital, were likely to be greatest. In the electrical field, for example, Elias E. Reis was unable to patent (let alone develop) all his inventions for exploiting the heat generated by electrical currents, because even the preliminary expenses of building models and applying for patents for all of them were too much for his backer to bear. Although Reis "repeatedly" explained "that not only was their filing of great importance, but that unless we did so . . . the applications that have already been filed . . . would suffer very materially, and, perhaps, to an irretrievable extent," his patron would not put up additional money until revenues from the earlier patents he had financed began to materialize. "Had I the means available to enable me to file some of these applications," Reis claimed, "I should certainly have done so long since, but as matters stand, and have stood, I . . . do not find myself at liberty to seek the assistance of others." Desperate for funds, Reis had assigned his backer rights to all his inventions in exchange for financial help. Support of this kind was hard to get, Reis felt, and he was not willing to jeopardize the relationship by seeking other sources of aid.[50]

It is, of course, possible that Reis had difficulty obtaining financing for his inventions because they were not thought to be very valuable, but other inventors whose ideas had proven worth experienced similar difficulties.[51] A good illustration is Charles J. Van Depoele, developer of electrical motive systems for trolleys. Van Depoele was perennially short of the capital he needed to commercialize his inventions, and he repeatedly signed away his rights for what appear in retrospect to be paltry sums. In 1880, for example, he assigned the Canadian patents for all his inventions and any additional ones he would devise over the next thirty years to one Reuben G. Lunt, in exchange for a cash

---

50. "Record of Elias E. Reis," 26–30, 52, *Thomson v. Reis,* case 13,971, box 1,845, Interference Case Files, 1836–1905.

51. Moreover, the infringement suit between Reis and Elihu Thomson shows that Reis's ideas were similar to those developed and exploited commercially by Thomson. See "Testimony on Behalf of Elihu Thomson," case 13,418, box 1,845, Interference Case Files, 1836–1905.

payment of $5,000 (much of it conditional on the success of Lunt's enterprise). When the cash was not forthcoming, he was forced to take 10 percent of the company's stock as payment. Earlier that same year he tried to form a joint-stock company capitalized at $100,000 to exploit his American patents. The agreement allocated $70,000 of the stock to George N. Chase "for Services rendered in organizing Said Company & to be sold for Working Capital." The aim of this manipulation was to acquire a working capital of a mere $10,000. Whether this company ever got off the ground is not clear, but in 1885 Van Depoele formed a partnership with William A. Stiles and Albert L. Sweet, to each of whom he assigned a one-third interest in his inventions. The partnership's capital consisted of little more than his patents, though Sweet was to advance the firm $1,000 to get the business started. Finally, in 1888 Van Depoele gave up trying to exploit his inventions himself and took a job with the Thomson-Houston Electric Company, the predecessor of General Electric, accepting in exchange for assignments of his past and future inventions a salary of $5,000 a year, plus a royalty of $5 for every railroad car the company equipped with electrical motive power during the life of his patents. Thomson-Houston had the capital and access to financing that Van Depoele was unable to obtain on his own, despite the undoubted value of his patents.[52]

Few inventors, of course, were able to obtain such lucrative contracts, and as a result few were willing to agree, as Van Depoele did, to assign all past and future inventions to the company. When the Edison Machine Works' manager complained in 1890 that employees were refusing to turn over their patents to the firm, the company's lawyers had responded that the solution was to institute contracts requiring employees to make such assignments as a matter of course. The lawyers hastened to add, however, "We fear our suggestion is somewhat impracticable" (Wise 1985, 71). It is likely that the problem they had in mind was resistance by employees. That at least is the implication as well of a 1908 book on patents written by Edwin J. Prindle and published by *Engineering Magazine,* one of the earliest trade journals to address managers' concerns. Concluding a chapter, "The Patent Relations of Employer and Employee," Prindle urged manufacturers to follow the example of some leading firms and require that "every employee who is at all likely to make inventions" sign contracts providing for the assignment of patents to the company. Prindle admitted

---

52. Articles of agreement between Charles Joseph Van Depoele, Electrician, and Albert Wahl, both of Detroit, and Reuben Greenliff Lunt of Toronto, 27 November 1880; agreement dated 4 March 1880; agreement between Charles J. Van Depoele, William A. Stiles, and Albert L. Sweet, 6 June 1885; agreement between Charles J. Van Depoele and the Thomson-Houston Electric Co., 1888; all in folder labeled "Business Papers—Agreements, etc. 1877–89," Charles J. Van Depoele, 1877–92, MSS 867, Unbound Papers, Baker Library, Harvard University Graduate School of Business Administration. The folder also includes several other propositions aimed at raising capital, none of which seem to have been successful. According to W. Bernard Carlson (1991, 216) the Thomson-Houston Electric Company, as part of the deal, acquired the Van Depoele Electric Manufacturing Company, which was purchased for its "railway and motor patents."

that it was often difficult to induce employees to sign such agreements, but he argued that the resistance might be overcome if officers set good examples by binding themselves in the same way (Prindle 1908, 101).

A 1912 letter from a consulting engineer named William Wright to Pullman's president, J. S. Runnells, makes a related point in arguing that personnel issues were at the heart of employee resistance to this type of contract. According to Wright, in "recent years many of the large manufacturing industries in this country have established systems for . . . receiving new ideas from employees." Without such systems in place, employee inventors typically acted on their own: "If one of them thinks of an invention, he is afraid to let it be known to anyone else because of the danger of his ideas being appropriated, and so he works them out in secret and sends them to the Patent Office and if successful in obtaining a patent he generally finds himself in possession of something that is impossible for him to handle to advantage, or he disposes of it to some outside concern for a consideration."[53] Thus, in order to induce employees to assign their patents to their employers as a matter of course, firms had to assuage workers' fears that superiors would steal their ideas. They also had to develop ways of rewarding employees for their inventions and of convincing them that these rewards were superior to those that could be earned on the outside.

Even if resistance to this type of employment contract was overcome, however, such agreements were really only meaningful if inventors stayed with the same firm for an extended period of time. Otherwise, it would be difficult for the company to demonstrate that a particular invention was devised during the patentee's term of employment. High rates of turnover by technologically knowledgeable people were a significant problem for firms during the late nineteenth and early twentieth centuries, even though it was increasingly difficult for inventors to establish themselves in independent businesses. As the case of Rollin Abell illustrates, inventors were entrepreneurially oriented and constantly moved in and out of employment positions in response to perceived opportunities and financial exigencies. Abell clearly thought of himself as an independent inventor, but from time to time he found it desirable to seek employment within firms. In 1899 he worked for the General Electric Company in Lynn, Massachusetts, but he left the firm in order to go into a partnership with a Dr. Beard to develop a "coaster break" he had invented. A year later he opened his own office in Boston "to make drawings and design machinery." Apparently, this business was not successful enough to pay the office rent, and after attempting to continue it out of his home, he gave up and took a job with the Sub-Marine Signal Company of Boston. After a short stint at that firm, he testified, "[I] resumed working for myself on patent drawings and designing

---

53. William Wright to J. S. Runnells, 21 October 1912, Operating Department, Chief Engineer, Equipment Standards and Testing Records, 1889–1956, box 3, folder 21, Pullman Company Archives.

machinery," spending several months in 1903 developing a carpet loom in Worcester, Massachusetts. A couple of years earlier, he had met some businessmen at an automobile show in New York who were interested in steam vehicles. Subsequent conversations led in 1903 to his employment by a Mr. Newcomb to design a steam touring car in New Jersey. Later that same year he was in Boston, again designing a car for someone named Barlow. The task completed, he returned to the "business of making drawings and designing machinery as before," and there our knowledge of him ends.[54] The Patent Office's interference records contain a wealth of examples of inventors with similarly high turnover rates. To give a few examples, William E. Forster, an inventor of sole-leveling machines for the shoe industry, worked for at least five different firms between 1887 and 1894; Arthur F. Randall, an inventor of steam motor vehicles, worked independently and for at least three firms (including a patent solicitor) between 1897 and 1899; and William W. Wilson, an inventor of adding machines, worked for five different companies in that industry between 1901 and 1906.[55]

We can get a more comprehensive idea of what firms were up against by returning to the subsample of B patentees whom we were able to track through city directories. The reader will recall that, compared to the full B sample, the smaller data set is biased toward patentees with stable careers. Even so, if we focus on the most productive of these patentees (the fifty-one inventors who had at least ten patents for which we were able to find corresponding city directory entries), we find that only seven (14 percent) finished their careers in stable employment positions. By contrast, twenty-eight (55 percent) ended up as long-time principals in businesses. The rest either bounced around from one category to another, or could not readily be classified as either employees or principals. The implication is that productive inventors preferred to end their careers as independent proprietors. If they could not achieve this goal, then they often continued to move restlessly from position to position.

As both the anecdotal and the quantitative evidence suggests, before firms could reap the fruits that might be obtained from internalizing the process of invention, they had to learn to solve a number of important personnel problems. In particular, they had to reduce both employee turnover and inventors' resistance to signing over the fruits of their creativity to their employers. That is, they had to learn how to convince inventors, who had long regarded independent entrepreneurship as the key to upward mobility, that steady employment offered both rewards and opportunities for advancement. In addition, firms had to learn how to tighten up their managerial hierarchies so that they

---

54. Deposition of Rollin Abell, "Testimony on Behalf of Randall & Bates," 78–82, *Lemp v. Randall & Bates,* case 24,587, PF box 3,309, ROPO Interference Case Files, 1900–1925.

55. "Preliminary Statement and Record in Behalf of William E. Forster," 1–2, 65, *Forster v. Judd,* case 16,542, box 2,279, Interference Case Files, 1836–1905; "Testimony on Behalf of Randall & Bates," 4, 31, 33; "Wilson's Record," 5–7, *Putnam v. Wilson,* case 27,129, PF box 3,255, ROPO Interference Case Files, 1900–1925.

could credibly guarantee inventors that no one else in the firm would steal their ideas.[56]

Although it is beyond the scope of this essay to describe the manner in which these tasks were accomplished, we conclude this discussion by emphasizing how much learning had to be done. In order, for example, to overcome employees' resistance and reduce the negative effect that the requirement to assign patents might have on their incentive to invent, firms typically offered employees monetary rewards for inventions that led to patents. Such bonuses, however, could themselves be a source of difficulty. As one of Western Electric's executives later testified, such a system "put a tremendous incentive" on employees to work "at counterpoints to their own associates," creating a situation where "men would not work with each other, they would not confide with each other, yet the problem which was before us was a problem which required team action." Even worse, bonuses encouraged employees to "work for themselves at the expense of their employer."

> The incentive was to get out as many patents that would pass the Patent Office as possible. An invention was made. It could be covered by one strong patent or it could be covered by a dozen minor patents. It was to the company's advantage to have it one strong patent, but it was to the employee's advantage to have a dozen minor patents, because he profited in a monetary sense. . . . Then, in addition to that, it is only a small fraction of the things which are done in a research and development laboratory that come within the purview of the patent law. It is only those things which are new and novel, and which have not been practiced before, which come within the things which the law says can be patented.[57]

In order to encourage its employees to work together, to build cases for single strong patents rather than multiple weak ones, and to work assiduously on problems that were not likely to lead to patentable solutions (problems that, as Steven Usselman tells us in chapter 2 in this volume, were an increasingly important part of the work of large firms), Western Electric, its parent company AT&T, General Electric, and similar firms stopped awarding their research employees bonuses for patents. Instead, employees in the relevant departments received straight salaries by way of compensation. Patents became only one of the factors that was taken into account in promotion decisions, and firms now faced new difficulties both in measuring the output of their research employees and creating credible incentives to encourage their productivity.[58]

---

56. This process paralleled in important ways the more general learning about how to manage large numbers of employees that became embodied in personnel departments during the early twentieth century. See, for example, Jacoby (1985).

57. Testimony of Dr. Frank Baldwin Jewett, U.S. Congress, House, *Hearings before the Committee on Patents,* part 1, 276–77.

58. Ibid. and testimony of Gerard Swope, 324.

1.7 Conclusions

Recent scholarly literature explains the spread of in-house research laboratories during the early twentieth century by pointing to the information problems involved in contracting for technology. We have argued, by contrast, that
these difficulties have been overemphasized—that in fact a substantial trade in
patented inventions did develop over the course of the nineteenth century,
much of it taking the form of transactions conducted at arm's length through
the market. In the middle of the century, assignments of patent rights tended to
occur after the patent was issued and were often partial in character, restricted
to some (perhaps distant) geographic subdivision of the United States. As the
century progressed, however, it became increasingly common for patentees to
sell full national rights to their inventions and to dispose of these rights more
and more quickly—often by the time the patent was officially issued. These
trends cannot be accounted for by the movement of inventors within firms or
by the growing tendency of employee inventors to assign their patents to the
firms for which they worked. Rather the changes seem to have resulted from
improvements in the efficiency of the market for technology—from increases
in the flow and quality of information about new technological developments,
from a growth in the number of patent agents and solicitors willing to serve as
intermediaries in this market, and from firms' own investments in the capacity
to track technological developments around the country. As we have seen, enterprises as diverse as the American Bell Telephone Company and the Lowell
Machine Shop put great stock during this period in their ability to evaluate
externally generated inventions.

Toward the end of the century, however, the nature of the market for technology began to change as the proportion of apparently arm's-length transactions
declined in favor of assignments made at issue by patentees who were formally
associated with their assignees in some way.[59] Although this change may have
betokened a reintegration of inventive and developmental activities within the
firm, possibly driven by the kind of information problems discussed in the
recent literature, this interpretation is by no means certain. In the first place,
the change was largely accounted for by the increasing tendency of inventors
who were principals in companies to assign their inventions to their firms. In
the second, it is possible that the growing number of patentees who behaved in
this manner were forming companies mainly to facilitate their specialization
in invention. Once again, the one thing we can say with some certainty is that
the pattern was not accounted for by the rising tendency of employees to assign
their inventions to their employers. Although the proportion of employee inven-

---

59. Although the relationship is unclear, it is interesting to note that the beginning of this change
in the market for technology coincided with the beginning of a long-term decline in rates of patenting per capita. This latter development occurred first in geographic areas, like New England, that
were long-time leaders in invention, and then spread to the national level (Lamoreaux and Sokoloff
1996, 12688; Griliches 1994).

tors who transferred patent rights to their companies increased after 1890, the numbers of these patentees were still too small to account for the aggregate patterns.

Moreover, when large firms began during the early twentieth century to invest in developing their internal inventive capabilities, they faced a number of significant difficulties. Most important, they had to insure that they obtained property rights to inventions conceived on company time with company resources. The solution to this problem was to require employees to sign contracts that obligated them to assign their patents to the firm. Before such contracts could become routine, however, a number of nontrivial difficulties had to be resolved. Firms had to overcome employee resistance, and they had to reduce the high turnover rates that made such requirements effectively unenforceable. In other words, entrepreneurially oriented inventors had to be convinced that loyal service to a firm offered a combination of security and opportunities for advancement superior to that likely to come from self-employment. The increased costs of inventive activity and the resulting greater risks borne by independent inventors by the early twentieth century helped firms to make their case. But there was still a lot of learning involved. Hence, in important ways, the story we tell for the early twentieth century turns the recent literature on its head. Economic actors at that time had a great deal of experience contracting for new technological ideas in the market; what they did not know, and had to spend a great deal of time and energy learning, was how to manage creative individuals within the firm.

References

Arrow, Kenneth J. 1962. Economic Welfare and the Allocation of Resources for Invention. In *The Rate and Direction of Inventive Activity,* 609–25. Princeton: Princeton University Press.

Boardman, H. W., and Co. 1869. *Hints to Inventors and Others Interested in Patent Matters.* Boston: privately printed.

Carlson, W. Bernard. 1991. *Innovation as a Social Process: Elihu Thomson and the Rise of General Electric, 1870–1900.* New York: Cambridge University Press.

Cresee, F. A. 1907. *Practical Pointers for Patentees, Containing Valuable Information and Advice on the Sale of Patents.* New York: Munn & Co.

An Experienced and Successful Inventor. 1901. *Inventor's Manual: How to Work a Patent to Make It Pay.* New York: Norman W. Henley & Co.

Fisk, Catherine L. 1997. Removing "the Fuel of Interest" from "the Fire of Genius": Law and the Employee Inventor, 1830–1930. Unpublished paper.

Galambos, Louis. 1992. Theodore N. Vail and the Role of Innovation in the Modern Bell System. *Business History Review* 66 (spring): 95–126.

Gibb, George Sweet, and Evelyn H. Knowlton. 1956. *The Resurgent Years, 1911–1927: History of Standard Oil Company (New Jersey).* New York: Harper & Brothers.

Gregory, Frances W. 1975. *Nathan Appleton: Merchant and Entrepreneur, 1779–1861.* Charlottesville: University Press of Virginia.

Griliches, Zvi. 1994. Productivity, R&D, and the Data Constraint. *American Economic Review* 84 (March): 1–23.

Hounshell, David A., and John Kenly Smith, Jr. 1988. *Science and Corporate Strategy: Du Pont R&D, 1902–1980.* New York: Cambridge University Press.

Hughes, Thomas P. 1989. *American Genesis: A Century of Invention and Technological Enthusiasm.* New York: Viking Penguin.

Hutchinson, W. B., and J. A. E. Criswell. 1899. *Patents and How to Make Money out of Them.* New York: D. Van Nostrand Co.

Jacoby, Sanford M. 1985. *Employing Bureaucracy: Managers, Unions, and the Transformation of Work in American Industry, 1900–1945.* New York: Columbia University Press.

Johnson, Nathan C. 1913. Patent Law and the Nature of Patents. *Sibley Journal of Engineering* 27 (January): 186–94.

Khan, B. Zorina. 1995. Property Rights and Patent Litigation in Early Nineteenth-Century America. *Journal of Economic History* 55 (March): 58–97.

Lamoreaux, Naomi R., and Kenneth L. Sokoloff. 1996. Long-Term Change in the Organization of Inventive Activity. *Proceedings of the National Academy of Sciences* 93 (November): 12686–92.

Mowery, David C. 1983. The Relationship between Intrafirm and Contractual Forms of Industrial Research in American Manufacturing, 1900–1940. *Explorations in Economic History* 20 (October): 351–74.

———. 1995. The Boundaries of the U.S. Firm in R&D. In *Coordination and Information: Historical Perspectives on the Organization of Enterprise,* ed. Naomi R. Lamoreaux and Daniel M. G. Raff, 147–76. Chicago: University of Chicago Press.

Mowery, David C., and Nathan Rosenberg. 1989. *Technology and the Pursuit of Economic Growth.* New York: Cambridge University Press.

Prindle, Edwin J. 1908. *Patents as a Factor in Manufacturing.* New York: Engineering Magazine.

Simonds, William Edgar. 1871. *Practical Suggestions on the Sale of Patents.* Hartford, CT: privately printed.

Sokoloff, Kenneth L., and B. Zorina Khan. 1990. The Democratization of Invention during Early Industrialization: Evidence from the United States, 1790–1846. *Journal of Economic History* 50 (June): 363–78.

Teece, David J. 1988. Technological Change and the Nature of the Firm. In *Technical Change and Economic Theory,* ed. Giovanni Dosi, Christopher Freeman, Richard Nelson, Gerard Silverberg, and Luc Soete, 256–81. London: Pinter.

Wise, George. 1985. *Willis R. Whitney, General Electric, and the Origins of U.S. Industrial Research.* New York: Columbia University Press.

Zeckhauser, Richard. 1996. The Challenge of Contracting for Technological Information. *Proceedings of the National Academy of Sciences* 93 (November): 12743–48.

Comment   Adam B. Jaffe

This paper provides a fascinating statistical snapshot of invention during the early phases of the transition to organized industrial research from the era of individual invention and entrepreneurship. It demonstrates that, at the turn of

Adam B. Jaffe is professor of economics at Brandeis University and a research associate of the National Bureau of Economic Research.

the century, there was an active market in apparently arm's-length sales of inventions from individual inventors to firms who were not the inventor's employer, apparently commonly including inventors employed by one firm selling patents to another firm. Further, this technology market was economically significant, representing both a significant source of new technology for major firms and a significant destination for the patents of important inventors. This picture raises a number of interesting issues for our understanding of the nature of the invention process and its relationship to organizations.

The long period of time after the emergence of large industrial enterprises during which employees were not typically contractually bound to assign their inventions to their employers demonstrates the danger of the practice, common among organizational theorists, of assuming that observed organizational forms must be optimal. Despite the incentive problems that exist when an employee's ideas become the property of her employer, it cannot be optimal to pay someone full-time, and provide them with equipment on which to experiment, while permitting them to retain residual rights in inventions developed on company time and equipment. Further, it does not appear that lack of knowledge or specific legal impediment prevented the adoption of the more efficient employment contracts, as some firms did adopt this policy, and no apparent change in the law occurred before the practice eventually became widespread. Lamoreaux and Sokoloff's evidence suggests that strong organizational inertia was at work. Companies found it difficult to institute the policy unilaterally; what is less clear from the paper is why they were unwilling to compensate employees sufficiently to induce them to accept what was surely a potentially Pareto-improving regime change. In any event, this story confirms the applicability to the organizational realm of Keynes's observation about the elapsed time before we see "long-run" equilibrium.

The implications for current thinking about technology and organizations of the finding of a robust technology market are more subtle and, ultimately, less clear. The authors accurately represent the current conventional wisdom, that is, that widespread vertical integration between invention and production is inevitable, because of complementarity among the processes of production, marketing, and research, and because of difficulties in contracting over "knowledge" as a commodity. That a robust arm's-length technology market existed for so long, that it grew rather than shrinking during the initial rise of large corporations, and that it was heavily relied upon by the most technologically sophisticated firms of the period does seem to call this conventional wisdom into question. I will devote the remainder of this comment to the discussion of possibilities for reconciliation of the paper's evidence with the conventional view.

One conceptual possibility is that, of the two reasons typically given for vertical integration (complementarity and contracting difficulties in knowledge), it is really the first that is most important, and such complementarity is much more important today than it was at the turn of the century. Besides being excessively convenient, this explanation is not compelling. The invention of the early period was largely mechanical, and focused on the manufacturing process. It is hard to see how it was a process *less* complementary with manufacturing than today's science-based research.

A second possibility is that interpreting this evidence as contradicting the optimality of vertical integration is falling prey to the fallacy of assuming that observed organizational forms are optimal. Current theory doesn't say that selling technology is impossible, just that it is costly. Perhaps the arm's-length technology market of the early 1900s was a distinctly second-best situation that persisted only because it took a long time to get the superior form of vertical integration going. Indeed, since to really make vertical integration pay firms would have to own their employees' inventions, the inertia that prevented the more rapid adoption of this innovation also thereby limited the effectiveness of integration and perhaps preserved the vitality of the arm's-length market. One can visualize a negative feedback loop, in which the vitality of the arm's-length market makes employees resistant to relinquishing their rights to their inventions, while employers' inability to control their employees' inventions limits the effectiveness of integration and thereby forces them to rely on the arm's-length market. Seen through this lens, this aspect of the paper provides further evidence for the slowness with which superior forms take over, rather than undermining the conventional wisdom about the sources of superiority of the integrated form.

Finally, the evidence of the paper regarding the viability of a market for technology relates only to patented, and hence patentable, inventions. It is well understood that much of industrial technology is not patented and is probably not patentable. Clearly, the lack of an explicit property right such as a patent greatly aggravates the difficulty of selling technology at arm's length. Thus even if it were true that all currently patentable inventions are easily amenable to arm's-length trade, it could still be the case that much if not most of modern technology is not amenable. Further, one of the reasons for inventions not being patentable is the difficulty of reducing them to the kind of explicit description necessary for the patent application. Thus technologies that are not patentable are likely to be inherently harder to contract on.

It is well known that the "propensity to patent," which can be thought of as the ratio of the number of patent applications to the number of inventions, has been falling throughout this century. Thus it is possible that arm's-length trade was feasible for much or most of industrial technology at the turn of the century, but is infeasible or at least inefficient for most of industrial technology today.

While the thrust of these comments is that I remain reasonably convinced that arm's-length purchase of inventions is today expensive and inefficient for much of modern technology, it is interesting to note that "outsourcing" of R&D

is generally believed to be increasing. This takes several forms. Some firms are relying increasingly on grants and contracts to universities rather than performing relatively "basic" research in-house. Firms also seem increasingly to acquire access to technology through a variety of alliances with other firms; these alliances constitute a sort of halfway house between arm's-length purchase and vertical integration. Thus the questions of how efficiently markets and organizations handle inventions, and of what properties of different kinds of technologies affect the relative efficiency of different organizational and contractual forms, remain open and important. The authors have made a very interesting and useful contribution to this discussion.

2 Patents, Engineering Professionals, and the Pipelines of Innovation: The Internalization of Technical Discovery by Nineteenth-Century American Railroads

Steven W. Usselman

What are the sources of technological change? Why and how do people create new techniques, and why and how do they or others choose to employ them? In designing the American patent system, the revolutionary generation provided answers to these deceptively simple questions. The founders conceived of innovation as occurring through a set of discrete exchanges in a market for novelty. A group of creators—we'll call them inventors—responds to incentives held forth by that market. The value of any particular novelty is set by the supply of alternatives and by the demand of consumers—many of whom are themselves producers—who draw upon the techniques available in the market for novelty in order to obtain perceived advantages. Government underwrites this market by providing temporary monopolies, without which the returns to invention would drop to zero and the incentive to innovate would evaporate. The patent system thus exhibits the same genius as the larger document of which it is a part: it provides a mechanism or structure that operates independently of the particulars involved.

But does that mechanism characterize all innovation? Does it apply equally well to all fields of technical knowledge, including those with highly organized communities of expertise focused on vast technical systems? And what happens as institutions such as corporations and trade associations alter market structures? In such circumstances can we detect alternative paths of innovation, and are those alternatives compatible with the mechanisms outlined in the patent system?

These questions are no mere abstractions. They are practical issues that first arose, perhaps not surprisingly, in the context of American railroading. This highly concentrated and technically sophisticated industry challenged the

Steven W. Usselman is associate professor of history in the School of History, Technology, and Society at the Georgia Institute of Technology.

patent system, as it did so many other areas of law, with unprecedented and unanticipated conditions. By the middle of the nineteenth century, claims by patent holders that conditions in the railroad industry interfered with the presumed free market exchange of patented inventions began to find sympathetic hearings in court. Convinced that inventors were not reaping a just return, several federal judges improvised a remedy known as the "doctrine of savings." This principle required infringers to compensate patent holders by paying three times the savings they had derived from using the invention, rather than merely three times the prevailing license fee. Railroads, suddenly exposed to far greater financial liabilities for patent infringement than they had ever anticipated, objected strenuously to the new doctrine. In one of the earliest examples of interfirm collective action, leading carriers formed trade associations to coordinate legal appeals and share the cost of litigation in key cases. As these disputes dragged on in court, not to be resolved fully until the 1880s, the associations carried the fight for relief from patent liability to Congress. Their proposed series of reforms to the patent laws attracted the attention of virtually everyone connected with the patent system and occupied both the House and Senate for critical weeks during successive terms in the late 1870s.

The doctrine of savings sparked such extraordinary measures not simply because it exposed railroads to significant financial liabilities in a few notable patent cases, but because it raised fundamental questions about the paths of technical change in the nineteenth-century American economy. In the eyes of railroads, the largest and most complex enterprises in that economy, the doctrine threatened to disrupt emerging conduits of innovation. For reasons having to do with the competitive structure of the industry and the evolving nature of its technology, railroads over the course of the nineteenth century increasingly sought to bypass the market for patented technologies. They hoped instead to internalize the process of technical discovery by incorporating it within a sustained, cooperative effort at steady improvement pursued by engineers and other salaried personnel employed by firms throughout the industry. Judges applying the doctrine of savings in effect called for railroads to pass the fruits of that widespread technical effort back to creative individuals, rather than permitting railroads to absorb the benefits of new techniques directly into the cost structures of transportation services. To no one's surprise, inventors supported the courts in this effort, but so too did many consumers of new technology who still viewed the patent system as an effective conduit of innovation in their industries.[1] Few areas of the economy had yet acquired the characteristics of railroading, and advocates of patent reform thus faced a daunting task in seeking changes in general statutes that would accommodate their special concerns while leaving the system intact.

---

1. As Naomi Lamoreaux and Kenneth Sokoloff (chap. 1 in this volume) suggest, consumers had good reason to believe the market for patented technologies had come to function as an especially effective conduit of innovation in the latter half of the nineteenth century.

In the end, Congress could not find a way to address conditions in the railroad industry without alienating the many inventors and innovators who saw no reason to disrupt the established rules governing patents, and the proposed reforms died in conference committee. Yet the story does not end there. Railroads ultimately found relief in the hands of a legal system that proved more capable than Congress of tailoring remedies to particular circumstances. Even with legislation still pending, railroad fury over the doctrine of savings subsided as the Supreme Court embraced a model of innovation that varied considerably from the form idealized by the patent system. In effect, justices accepted the arguments of American railroads that technical creativity in their industry typically resulted from the efforts of ordinary mechanics and engineers, not through discrete acts of patentable invention. The shifting legal climate at once legitimated customary practices by railroads regarding patents and new technology and provided them with incentives to internalize the process of technical discovery more thoroughly and more formally. By keeping closer watch over technical activities taking place in their own facilities and by utilizing patent associations and various technical and engineering societies to exchange information about new technology, railroads monitored technical progress in ways that enabled them to find favor in a justice system increasingly sympathetic to the idea that much innovation originated and diffused through channels independent of the patent system.

This paper examines that internalization of discovery by American railroads and reflects upon its broader significance for our understanding of technical innovation in the emergent corporate economy of nineteenth-century America. It begins by tracing the competitive forces and technical factors that prompted railroads by midcentury to take a proactive role in the process of technical change. Under these conditions railroads and inventors alike had good reason to suspect that the model of innovation presumed under the patent system did not correspond to the actual conditions prevailing in the railroad industry. A close look at the cases that prompted railroads to pursue patent reform reveals the extent of the discrepancy and the enormity of the stakes involved. After discussing the patent cases in some detail, the paper describes the ways in which railroads further internalized the process of technical change in light of the shifting legal climate. In order to situate those developments more broadly, the paper then introduces a dual-pipeline schematic of innovation flows and discusses its relevance to railroads and to the economy as a whole. A brief comparative conclusion suggests that, though the passage from inventive marketplace to administered innovation may have set railroads apart from most other businesses during the nineteenth century, the internalization of technical change in the railroad industry may have anticipated similar developments in other systems-based industries of a later day.

2.1 Insider Innovation: Patterns of Change in Early Railroad Technology

What, then, were the particular circumstances that brought railroads into conflict with the patent system? More specifically, why by the third quarter of the nineteenth century did so many informed observers agree that the railroad industry did not facilitate the exchanges of technical novelties necessary to establish a market value of a patented innovation?

To some extent, the answers to these questions must be traced back to the earliest days of the railroad industry and to the nature of the competition it fostered. American railroading began as a series of localized experiments with an unproven technology of revolutionary potential. During their early decades, most railroads enjoyed a local monopoly in the market for railroad services. They functioned as semipublic ventures whose purpose was not so much to race westward to a common destination and compete for the same pool of traffic as other lines, but to build an infrastructure that would lure capital and human resources away from other locales. The vastness of the North American landscape helped sustain this developmental function for many decades.[2]

In some respects this pool of isolated enterprises constituted an ideal market for enterprising inventors. The records of the patent office reveal that railroads accounted for a disproportionate share of patents during the antebellum period. Every year the list of new patents published in the annual report of the commissioner of patents contained more and more devices under the headings "Civil Engineering and Architecture" and "Land Conveyance." Most of these pertained to railroads. Between 1852 and 1865 the number of patents granted for inventions pertaining directly to railroads increased from about 50 to over 500 per year.[3] Some inventions, such as the Howe truss and the Westinghouse air brake (patented in 1869), earned their creators renown and some fortune.

Some evidence suggests, moreover, that patentees and railroads engaged in market transactions very much like those we would envision under the patent

2. This paragraph and many of my subsequent generalizations about technological innovation in the railroad industry lean heavily on my forthcoming study, "Regulating Innovation: The Business and Politics of Technical Change on American Railroads, 1846–1916." Some of the material in this study appeared originally in "Running the Machine: The Management of Technical Change on American Railroads, 1860–1910" (Ph.D. diss., University of Delaware, 1985). The literature on early railroad development in the United States is vast. For a recent treatment, see Colleen A. Dunlavy, *Politics and Industrialization: Early Railroads in the United States and Prussia* (Princeton: Princeton University Press, 1994).

3. Statistics on patents come from reports of the commissioner of patents, which appear annually in the collected documents of the U.S. House of Representatives and the U.S. Senate. For the years discussed here, these reports contain only sketchy information on the number of patents granted for railroad inventions. The commissioner provided itemized tabulations of patents sporadically, and the categories used often did not identify clearly those patents that served the railroads. The figure cited for 1852 comes from the "Report of the Commissioner of Patents for 1852," U.S. Senate, 32d Cong., 2d sess., Executive Document 55, p. 438. That for 1865 appears in the "Report of the Commissioner of Patents for 1865," U.S. House of Representatives, 39th Cong., 1st sess., Executive Document 52, p. 18.

system. Circulars describing patented devices flowed into the offices of railroad executives, and at least some managers paid them serious attention. Robert Harris, chief operating officer of the Chicago, Burlington, and Quincy during the 1860s and much of the 1870s, regularly passed the circulars on to his subordinates and solicited their opinions. An admitted enthusiast for new technology, Harris corresponded frequently with inventors.[4] In addition to providing testimonials for their advertisements, Harris sometimes offered hints about how best to promote an invention he particularly liked, such as the Miller platform.[5] When Burlington employees wrote to their chief about an idea, he gave them a considered judgment on its technical merits and coached them on marketing strategies, including patents. On two occasions during the early 1870s, Harris personally set inventors up in the Burlington's facilities and encouraged them to develop patentable inventions.[6] Once, in a fit of exasperation caused by one insistent inventor, Harris scrawled to a subordinate, "Patents and passes will be the death of me!"[7] This was no idle complaint; Harris did devote much of his energies to the subject. Perhaps not surprisingly, he would come to play a major role in railroad efforts to reform the patent system.

No other top executive left behind a record of such thorough involvement with patents as Harris, but many of his contemporaries at other lines certainly gave the subject close attention. The board of directors at the Pennsylvania Railroad frequently considered questions pertaining to innovation, and its Committee on Supplies negotiated licensing agreements with several inventors.[8] The Pennsylvania's famed president, J. Edgar Thomson, personally investigated new technologies such as steel rails and negotiated contracts with individuals such as George Westinghouse, inventor of the air brake.[9] Thomson's counterpart at the rival Baltimore and Ohio, John Work Garrett, seldom exhibited the same perceptive attention to technical detail (much to the detri-

4. Robert Harris's letterbooks and many other of his papers can be found in the papers of the Chicago, Burlington, and Quincy Railroad at the Newberry Library in Chicago (hereafter, CBQ Papers). Much of his correspondence pertaining to inventions can be found in the subject file 33 1870 2.5. On one occasion, Harris advised an inventor not to rest his hopes on the testimonial "of one who is known to be so ready to entertain novelties as I am" (R. Harris to J. A. Sleeper, 8 August 1872, CBQ Papers, 3H4.1, 28:116–18.

5. Harris to W. W. Wilcox, 18 October 1867, 11:22; to Col. Miller, 2 May 1868, and 7 May 1868, 12:302, 327; to J. F. Joy, 11 May 1868, 12:338–340; to Thomas Swingard, 22 March 1869, 15:259; to P. S. Henning, 4 June 1869, 16:239; to Col. C. G. Hammond, 15 November 1869, 18:92; to C. E. Perkins, 16 November 1869, 18:104–7; all in CBQ Papers, 3H4.1.

6. R. Harris to F. H. Tubbs, 17 June 1868, and 1 June 1870, CBQ Papers, 3H4.1, 12:501, 20:287–88; to W. W. Wilcox, 7 May 1869, CBQ Papers, 3H4.1, 16:38; to J. Q. A. Bean, 20 June 1870, CBQ Papers, 3H4.1, 20:378.

7. R. Harris to Mr. Hitchcock, 23 December 1868, CBQ Papers, 3H4.1.

8. Pennsylvania Railroad, Minutes of the Committee on Supplies, accompanying Minutes of the Meetings of the Board of Directors. These are available at the Hagley Museum and Library, Wilmington, DE, Acc. 1807 (hereafter Board Papers, PRR Papers).

9. On steel rails, see *Annual Report of the Pennsylvania Railroad* 17 (1863): 13–14, and 20 (1866): 26–27, 63–64. On air brakes, see Minutes of the Meeting of the Road Committee, 22 December 1869, 12 January 1870, 21 January 1870, 9 February 1870; David H. Williams to J. Edgar Thomson, 12 December 1869, all in Board Papers, PRR Papers.

ment of his company), but Garrett and his personal assistant maintained active correspondences on technical affairs and patents.[10] Top management at another eastern railroad, the Philadelphia and Reading, followed an arrangement typical of many lines. They trusted almost all technical questions to a single individual, master mechanic John E. Wootten, who monitored railroad technology and patents with a verve that surpassed even that of Harris at the Burlington.[11] At most railroads, it seems, the development and acquisition of new technology formed a routine subject of discussion in the highest echelons of management. Frequently, the discussion involved patents.

Yet even in this early period, some features of the railroad industry tended to work against the model of technical change embedded in the patent system. Because railroads operated their own machine shops and foundries for purposes of maintenance and repair, they often possessed skills that enabled them to develop their own solutions to technical problems. Individuals such as Wootten considered it something of a badge of honor that he could devise his own solutions to any technical challenge.[12] As an institution, the Pennsylvania Railroad exhibited a similar bravado, with considerable justification. Roads such as the Burlington, itself much admired among western roads for its technical competence, routinely looked to the Pennsylvania for guidance on technical matters.[13] In 1867, to cite one example of the Pennsylvania's attitude, the railroad had one of its mechanics investigate ways of ventilating cars, a problem that had long attracted the attention of many inventors. The mechanic concluded that given six months' time the Pennsylvania could develop a better ventilator than any then available.[14] Other railroads acted similarly. When the Baltimore and Ohio grew irritated at paying a supplier for its journal boxes, it asked one of its own mechanics to devise an alternative. Within weeks, the railroad had negotiated a much more favorable agreement with the supplier.[15] As these examples suggest, inventors and suppliers of railroad technology operated in a world of extraordinarily well-educated customers who could easily fend for themselves if provoked.

The personnel who worked in the railroad shops, as well as the engineers

---

10. See especially the Patents and Inventions File in the archives of the Baltimore and Ohio Railroad, MS 1925, Maryland Historical Society, Baltimore (hereafter B&O Papers); the letters of John Work Garrett, MS 2003, Maryland Historical Society (hereafter Garrett Papers).

11. Wootten's letters are in the archives of the Philadelphia and Reading Railroad, Hagley Museum and Library, Wilmington, DE, Acc. 1451 (hereafter Reading Papers).

12. Letterbooks of John E. Wootten, Reading Papers. See also James L. Holton, "John Wootten: Locomotive Pioneer," *Historical Review of Berks County* (summer 1978): 97–107.

13. When discussing technology, managers at the Burlington frequently inquired about practices on the Pennsylvania, and on several occasions they referred outside inventors to that line. By the same token, lines to the west of Chicago frequently consulted the Burlington on technical matters. See CBQ Papers.

14. Minutes of the Meetings of the Board of Directors, 18 April 1866, 5:47; 2 May 1866, 5:50; 19 April 1866, 5:67; 6 March 1867, 5:108, Board Papers, PRR Papers.

15. Patents and Invention File, B&O Papers, contains many letters pertaining to the innovation, known as the Lightner journal box. J. C. Davis to John King, Jr., n.d., provides a useful summary of the case.

who operated the locomotives, occupied an ambiguous position between employee and independent expert. Sometimes railroads encouraged these men to patent devices; other times they expressed the idea that modification and experiment were essential parts of the job. In 1850 James Millholland, master mechanic at the Philadelphia and Reading prior to Wootten, received $1,000 from his employer in payment for rights to all of his inventions. But by no means had this become a standard condition of employment at the Reading or elsewhere in the industry.[16] Robert Harris of the Burlington told a mechanic who asked for compensation that "one in the employ of a railroad company has no rightful claim upon that company for a patent fee upon an article introduced or invented in the prosecution of his ordinary duties," and that "to the performance of the duties of any position one's best efforts and ingenuity should be given."[17] Harris's bark, however, proved louder than his bite. He later awarded the mechanic $350, and on occasion paid similar premiums to other creative employees. In general, Harris seems to have assumed a gentleman's agreement would prevail in such circumstances, with the railroad paying for the patent application and the inventor granting his employer unlimited use of the device. When his successor, Charles Perkins, neglected to pay the fees for one employee, a close subordinate corrected the oversight and told Perkins that "our practice in this matter has been uniform for a number of years back, and several patents have been taken out under it."[18]

The nature of competition in the railroad industry further blurred distinctions between producers and consumers of railroad technology. Because railroads during their early lives did not see themselves as being engaged in direct competition with one another over technical performance, they saw little purpose in monopolizing a technique developed in-house. Sensing that in this experimental stage they had more to gain by openness than secrecy, railroads generally exchanged technical information quite freely. The various lines operated almost as a set of concurrent experiments taking place in a number of different laboratories, with managers applying the same basic technique to a variety of conditions and discovering innumerable useful adaptations in the process.

The developmental function of railroad enterprise during this formative period could also draw railroads into unusually close relationships with suppliers. As providers of an essential utility, railroads seldom restricted their business transactions with suppliers to the purchase of a commodity. The two parties also exchanged transportation services and traffic volume. In many cases, moreover, railroads provided capital to their suppliers. These sorts of exchanges were embedded within the development policies of the railroads, and they often dovetailed comfortably with the personal interests of managers.

16. Managers Minutes, 15 March 1850, Board of Directors Minute Book, book C, p. 9, Reading Papers.
17. R. Harris to C. M. Higginson, 6 November 1875, CBQ Papers, 3H4.1.
18. Henry B. Strong to C. E. Perkins, 1 November 1888, CBQ Papers, 3P4.57.

Andrew Carnegie and his fellow officers at the Pennsylvania made fortunes by investing in supply firms with which the Pennsylvania did business.[19] The Baldwin Locomotive Works, located near the Pennsylvania's main offices on Broad Street in Philadelphia, rose to prominence when a loose consortium of lines with ties to the Pennsylvania funneled large orders and vital working capital its way.[20] One cannot begin to comprehend the operations of the nineteenth-century steel industry without taking such factors into account.[21]

These unusual characteristics of relations between railroads and suppliers of technology, combined with the special nature of railroad technology and the distinctive aspects of competition among railroads, produced an environment in which innovation can hardly be described as flowing from free competition among inventors seeking to meet the demands of a broad market. Rather, the process of technical discovery might best be characterized, to borrow a phrase from Naomi Lamoreaux, as "Insider Innovation."[22] Information about railroad technology flowed among a network of interested and unequal parties whose perspectives and decisions regarding technical innovations involved a complex mix of motives. Though the railroad industry fostered a climate of experiment and trial that put new technologies through a rigorous market test, success often came to those with advantages that went beyond mere technical accomplishment.

The essential medium of exchange in this complex network of exchange was the patent license. Virtually all railroads preferred to obtain licenses rather than buying patented products on the open market. The Pennsylvania, especially, exhibited this tendency early and pursued it relentlessly, and other railroads followed suit.[23] Licenses enabled railroads to take advantage of the manufacturing abilities of their own shops and those of the major shops and foundries along their lines with whom they subcontracted. More important, they helped railroads absorb new techniques into the pool of inside knowledge that resided within those technical facilities. Railroads clearly expected that techniques covered by licenses would soon be modified in ways that rendered them generic. Only by retaining exclusive control of their patents and integrating for-

19. Harold C. Livesay, *Andrew Carnegie and the Rise of Big Business* (Boston: Little, Brown, 1975), 45–75.

20. John K. Brown, *The Baldwin Locomotive Works, 1831–1915: A Study in American Industrial Practice* (Baltimore: Johns Hopkins University Press, 1995).

21. Elting E. Morison, *Men, Machines, and Modern Times* (Cambridge: MIT Press, 1966), 123–205; Usselman, "Running the Machine," 81–133; Glenn Porter and Harold C. Livesay, *Merchants and Manufacturers: Studies in the Changing Structure of Nineteenth Century Manufacturing* (Baltimore: Johns Hopkins University Press, 1971), 79–115, 131–53; Thomas J. Misa, *A Nation of Steel* (Baltimore: Johns Hopkins University Press, 1995).

22. The phrase comes from her recent study, *Insider Lending: Banks, Personal Connections, and Economic Development in Industrial New England* (Cambridge: Cambridge University Press, 1996), which emphasizes the importance of kinship ties and other close relations in the early-nineteenth-century economy.

23. Minutes of the Meetings of the Board of Directors and Associated Reports, Board Papers, PRR Papers.

ward into production could inventors avoid that fate. So great was the desire to internalize new techniques that the Pennsylvania even pressed to obtain a license from George Westinghouse, an inventor who had located his manufacturing facilities along its tracks and who had received funding from several of the railroad's Pittsburgh executives.[24]

The ultimate intent of railroads was apparent as well in their willingness to forgo paying any fee and to risk infringement. Latecomers to an innovation were especially prone to flaunt claims of patentees. This behavior derived in part from trends in price. Though they might debate whether the phenomenon resulted from trial discounts granted at the beginning of the monopoly period or from extortionist rates demanded later on, most people involved with railroad technology agreed that license fees increased during the life of a patent.[25] Higher prices of course discouraged payment in their own right. Perhaps more importantly, they increased the effective penalty for infringement, because courts awarded damages totaling three times the amount a patent holder would have earned from the established license fee. Instead of paying an inflated fee, railroads would infringe and claim the lower fee as the established one if taken to court. With each passing year in a patent's life, moreover, the possibility arose that another patent covering a similar principle would come to light. If this happened, railroads stopped paying fees and left the inventors to battle over the question of priority. This practice had become so routine by 1872 that Harris told an employee who had invented a new grain door, "You should buy [another inventor] out before selling your door to other railroads; otherwise, with two claims, roads will use doors and pay for neither."[26]

2.2   Outside Liabilities: The Doctrine of Savings and Patent Law

Robert Harris's advice to inventors attains a heightened significance when considered in light of a series of important legal cases pending at the time in the federal courts. The cases involved a new legal doctrine known as the doctrine of savings. Articulated by judges in a series of cases involving railroads, this doctrine established a novel method of assessing damages for infringement. Traditionally, courts had arrived at a damage figure by determining the profits patent holders made through sales of their inventions to consumers who had not infringed. Those convicted of infringement paid three times the profits lost. (In situations where the patent holder sold licenses instead of finished

24. Minutes of the Meeting of the Road Committee, 22 December 1869, 12 January 1870, 21 January 1870, 9 February 1870; George Westinghouse, Jr., to D. H. Williams, 13 November 1869; David H. Williams to J. Edgar Thomson, 12 December 1869; all in Board Papers, PRR Papers.

25. U.S. Senate, "Arguments before the Committees on Patents of the Senate and the House of Representatives in Support of and Suggesting Amendments to Bills (S. 300 and H.R. 1612) to Amend the Statutes in Relation to Patents, and for Other Purposes," 45th Cong., 2d sess., Miscellaneous Document no. 50.

26. Robert Harris to Bassler, 4 April 1872, CBQ Papers, 3H4.1, 26:498.

products, damages totaled three times the established license fee.) This method of assessing damages presumed that enough transactions had taken place to establish a market price for either the patented item or the license. Over time, however, several patent holders convinced the courts that in industries such as railroading the market never established a fair value for an invention. Because they possessed extensive technical expertise in their repair facilities and could generally manufacture and refine any new technology, railroads almost always preferred to obtain licenses rather than purchase patented devices. With a few firms controlling the bulk of the mileage, the market did not have sufficient consumers to establish a fair price for the license. A few railroads bought licenses (often at a discount before a device had proven its worth), then others infringed, figuring they would at worst pay three times an artificially discounted price. Once courts accepted this argument, as they had good reason to do, judges searched for alternative means of calculating damages. They settled on asking infringers to pay three times the savings they had obtained by employing the patented technology.[27]

The doctrine of savings posed a severe threat to railroads. Under the doctrine their cavalier practices regarding licenses could be turned back against them with damages far greater than they had ever imagined. The threat was all the more alarming because, by dealing with innovators on an ad hoc basis, railroad managers had never defined a coherent set of patent policies. Until 1872, for example, Harris did not even maintain a centralized list of all licensing agreements.[28] Such lax procedures had served the railroads well under the regime of insider innovation. Now, under the doctrine of savings, they left railroads exposed to vast liabilities and threatened to disrupt permanently the established routines of technical discovery.

As railroads wasted no time in pointing out, the doctrine of savings left much to be desired. On a strictly practical level it asked courts to account for a firm's costs more closely than many firms could themselves. But railroads also objected on more philosophical grounds. The doctrine presumed that the economic benefits of new technologies resulted entirely from the inventive act and not at all from the innovative efforts of the companies that employed them. Even the best accounting of savings, moreover, failed to account for benefits such as improved safety and comfort, whose value could not easily be expressed in terms of expenses saved. Yet for all its limitations, the doctrine of savings marked a serious and carefully reasoned effort by the judicial system to take a system of patent law that had been conceived for a market economy

27. In addition to U.S. Senate, "Arguments before the Committees on Patents," this summary and my subsequent discussion of cases and legislation involving the doctrine of savings is based largely on U.S. House of Representatives, "Report of the Committee on Patents," 2 March 1875, 43d Cong., 2d sess., Rept. 274; and U.S. Senate, "Reports of the Committee on Patents," 4 February 1873, 42d Cong., 3d sess., Rept. 369; 2 June 1874, 43d Cong., 1st sess., Rept. 471; 5 March 1878, 45th Cong., 2d sess., Rept. 116.

28. A list of licenses, prepared at Harris's request when he discovered the lapse, can be found in the CBQ Papers, f32.4.

and apply it to an environment characterized by limited or nonexistent markets. Railroads would find it very difficult to overcome.

Of the several cases that led to the doctrine of savings, by far the most important involved two patents covering "double-acting" brakes for railroad cars. Holders of these patents, which were initially issued in the early 1850s and were reissued by Congress two decades later, claimed that the devices had saved railroads substantial sums in wages by enabling brakeman to set two brakes at once. In one case, known as the Stevens patent, the Supreme Court twice concurred. Following its favorable decisions in 1868 and 1882, owners of the patent secured settlements with many railroads for $25 per car for each year of infringement.[29] Liabilities in the second case, known as the Tanner patent, threatened to run considerably higher. In the early 1870s, federal courts in Illinois twice affixed damages of several hundred dollars per car for each year of service.[30]

Railroads sought to counter these rulings through coordinated action. Early in 1867 the major Chicago roads and other western lines agreed to join the Western Railroad Association (WRA), which would conduct common defenses in patent suits and monitor all issues relating to patents in the industry.[31] About a dozen major eastern roads agreed to form an identical organization the same year.[32] Lines would pay annual fees, assessed in proportion to earnings, and in return receive full legal services, including consultation on the legal status of all inventions. The railroad patent associations thus constituted

29. James R. Doolittle to J. W. Garrett, 16 May 1870, B&O Papers. The Baltimore and Ohio balked at these terms and conducted its own suit against the Stevens claim, but in 1882 the Supreme Court again ruled against the railroads. At that point the Western Railroad Association advised the Pennsylvania to settle for a fixed fee of $25,000 (George Harding to Wayne McVeagh, 4 December 1882; A. McCallum to Hon. James A. Logan, 3 January 1883; John Scott to Geo. Roberts, 9 January 1883; all in Board Papers, PRR Papers).

30. The first judgment, based on savings in wheel wear as well as brakemen's wages, assessed damages at $455 per car per year. They totaled nearly $64,000 on the Chicago and North Western Railroad alone. Other lines had incurred substantially larger liability. Two years later the court reduced the allowance for wheel wear, but damages remained over $300 per car per year (*Railway Company v. Sayles, U.S. Reports,* 97 [October 1878]: 556–57; U.S. House of Representatives, "Report of the Committee on Patents").

31. U.S. Senate, "Arguments before the Committees on Patents," 191–92.

32. Isaac Hinckley to J. W. Garrett, 1 April 1867, Garrett Papers, box 86, subject 9614; John J. Harrower, *History of the Eastern Railroad Association* (Eastern Railroad Association, 1905), 22–30. Some plans for the two associations were laid in October 1866 at the meeting of the National Railway Convention, whose proceedings of May 1867 reported that constitutions for the proposed organizations were still being circulated among prospective members. Those proceedings noted that in early 1866 New England railroads had organized for common defense in a suit involving the brake patent of C. B. Turner. Impetus for the associations came from the brake cases, and the efforts under way to create a national organization devoted to railroad interests certainly contributed to their rapid formulation (*Proceedings of the National Railroad Convention* [New York, 1867], 20–22). I am indebted to Professor Colleen Dunlavy of the University of Wisconsin for this reference. On the efforts to form national railroad organizations, see Dunlavy, *Politics and Industrialization,* chap. 4 (145–201); Colleen A. Dunlavy, "Organizing Railroad Interests: The Creation of National Railroad Associations in the United States and Prussia," *Business and Economic History,* 2d series, 19 (1990): 133–42.

an effort to formalize and preserve the internalization of technical discovery that had always been a significant component of innovation in the industry.

The key to the associations was collective, unified action. Members agreed to provide any information regarding disputed technologies and to inform the associations of inventions developed in their own shops. Such knowledge would help lawyers prepare their appeals. More importantly, railroads hoped to prevent patent holders in the future from quietly negotiating agreements with a few lines, then later using those agreements to gain legitimacy in the eyes of the courts and extract large settlements from other lines that had accumulated significant liabilities under the doctrine of savings. Any member who reached a settlement with an individual currently bringing suit against another member would sacrifice its rights to defense by the association.[33]

As association lawyers prepared their appeals to the Supreme Court, the nervous railroads quietly approached their friends on the congressional judiciary committees with proposals to reform the patent laws. To their delight, association lobbyists found themselves in the unlikely company of the Grangers, whose farm constituency had been plagued by lawsuits claiming infringement of patents for the driven well (basically, a pipe sunk in the ground until it tapped water) and the swing gate (a common device used to sort livestock and keep it penned). Unable to travel to federal courts to meet the accusations, outraged farmers had petitioned Congress for relief. Decrying the patent system as yet another conspiracy between capitalists and government to create exploitative monopoly power, the petitioners asked to be exempted from liability under so-called innocent-purchaser provisions. (If such provisions became law, one skeptical Congressman later quipped, the best patent adviser would be the one who knew the least.) The revisions supported by the railroads appeared temperate in comparison yet still moved the patent laws toward the goals Grangers desired. The bill sailed through committee and onto the floor of both houses. Only the last-minute intervention of powerful New York senator Roscoe Conkling, who revealed the backroom machinations of the railroads, scuttled the proposed reforms.[34]

Patent reform remained a hot issue when Congress reconvened. Now, however, the proposed changes would have to pass through the standing committees on patents. In the Senate, this committee was dominated by liberal Republican and mugwump New Englanders who practiced law in the federal courts at Boston, which because of the preponderance of patents granted in the region were generally regarded as the most sophisticated and influential venue for patent litigation in the country. These men treated the patent system with the sense of benevolent stewardship that characterized their approach to most political issues. (Their chair was a New Hampshirite by the name of Bainbridge

---

33. Eastern Railroad Association, "Constitution," 6 February 1867, copy in Garrett Papers, box 86, subject 9614. On the assessment of fees, see also Harrower, *History,* 31.

34. This brief summary of the efforts to reform the patent law is based on U.S. Senate, "Arguments before the Committees on Patents"; U.S. Senate, "Reports of the Committee on Patents"; and a thorough reading of the *Congressional Record* for the period of debate, 1876–84.

Wadleigh.) With reverential tones they guarded it from radical reforms such as those proposed by the Grangers, while claiming for themselves the responsibility of adjusting the patent laws in light of the serious concerns raised by railroads. Fearful that the amendments proposed by railroads themselves would gut the system, they sought to orchestrate a compromise. They proposed implementing a statute of limitations on lawsuits and requiring patent holders to renew their rights every few years or forfeit the right to sue. Most importantly for railroads, committee members acknowledged the difficulty of accounting for the savings derived from new techniques and called for courts to focus instead on establishing an appropriate license fee.[35]

As befit its stewardship role, the committee proceeded in a highly deliberate and open fashion. It invited patent experts representing a variety of manufacturing interests to testify at hearings on the bill, including those from the shoe industry who bought patented equipment and those from the machining firms who supplied them, and distributed published transcripts widely. When the bill at last came before the full Senate in December 1878, Wadleigh presented it as a technical measure requiring little debate. But the Senate refused to entrust the experts. To the chagrin of the moderate reformers, westerners immediately resumed the call for innocent-purchaser provisions, while Conkling and his allies again denigrated the bill as the handiwork of railroads. Astoundingly, the debate stretched on for weeks, occupying much of the brief but critical lame-duck session which for Republicans marked a last gasp before they relinquished their eighteen-year stranglehold on the House and Senate. The measures eventually passed, but not in time for conference with the House, which had approved a more radical set of reforms. Responsibility for reforming the patent system would remain with the courts.[36]

There, the railroads finally found relief. In October 1878, with the patent legislation pending and the Senate debate still two months away, the Supreme Court at last handed down its decision in the Tanner case. Rather than confront the issue of the doctrine of savings directly, the justices based their decision on WRA and Eastern Railroad Association arguments that the railroads had easily found alternatives to the Tanner method of linking the brakes. Some lines, they claimed, had tried out several arrangements for linking brakes on an experimental basis prior to the time Tanner obtained his patent. These experiments, in the opinion of the railroads, demonstrated that the idea of linking brakes was "in the air" at the time and thus did not deserve broad coverage in a patent. The court agreed. Though the experimental devices were "not so perfect as that of [Tanner]" and though railroads had never actually patented them, noted

---

35. This characterization of the Senate Committee on Patents is based primarily upon U.S. Senate, "Report of the Committee on Patents," 5 March 1878, 45th Cong., 2d sess., Rept. 116; on profiles obtained from standard congressional biographical references; and on coverage and editorials pertaining to the political dispute in the *New York Times, Scientific American,* and other periodicals.

36. This brief summary of the legislative debate is based on a close reading of the *Congressional Record.*

the justices in reversing a series of rulings by lower courts, their use invalidated Tanner's claim to have achieved a basic principle. "Like almost all other inventions," confidently wrote Justice Bradley of an innovation that had occurred three decades earlier, "that of double brakes came when, in the progress of mechanical improvement, it was needed; and being sought by many minds, it is not wonderful that it was developed in different and independent forms." Expressing a philosophy of technical change in which the railroads and others who employed patented technologies could find great comfort, he continued, "[I]f the advance towards the thing desired is gradual, and proceeds step by step, so that no one can claim the complete whole, then each is entitled only to the specific form of device which he produces.[37]

As Bradley's telling reference to "almost all other inventions" suggests, this ruling held a significance far beyond the case of double-acting brakes. A few years later, the justices elaborated on the theory of innovation they had advanced in the Tanner case.

> The process of development in manufactures creates a constant demand for new appliances, which the skill of the ordinary head-workmen and engineers is generally adequate to devise, and which, indeed, are the natural and proper outgrowth of such development. Each step forward prepares the way for the next, and each is usually taken by spontaneous trials in a hundred different places. To grant a single party a monopoly of every slight advance made, except where the exercise of invention somewhat above ordinary mechanical or engineering skill is distinctly shown, is unjust in principle and injurious in its consequences. . . .
>
> It was never the object of [the patent] laws to grant a monopoly for every trifling device, every shadow of a shade of an idea, which would naturally and spontaneously occur to any skilled mechanic or operator in the ordinary progress of manufacturers. Such an indiscriminate creation of exclusive privileges tends rather to obstruct than to stimulate invention.
>
> It creates a class of speculative schemers, who make it their business to watch the advancing wave of improvement and gather its foam in the form of patented monopolies, which enable them to lay a heavy tax upon the industry of the country without contributing anything to the real advancement of the art. It embarrasses the honest pursuit of business with fears and apprehensions of concealed liens and unknown liabilities to law suits and vexatious accountings for profits made in good faith.[38]

With this rationale the Supreme Court effectively sanctioned the sorts of legal arguments that the railroad associations would almost always be capable of advancing. With access to nearly all companies and with individual firms taking great care to document their technical activities, the lawyers at the ERA and the WRA could readily establish precedence and undermine broad claims

37. *Railway Co. v. Sayles, U.S. Reports* 97 (October 1878): 556–57.
38. The case was *Atlantic Works v. Brady,* decided 5 March 1883, and quoted in *Annual Report of the Executive Committee of the Eastern Railroad Association* 19 (1885): 16 (hereafter *ERA Annual Reports*).

pertaining to virtually any aspect of technology.[39] Since courts retained the right to review questions pertaining to originality at every stage of appeal, the railroads stood an excellent chance of escaping liability at some point in the judicial process. With courts willing to consider techniques that had not been patented as evidence of priority, moreover, the associations or their members would not have to take out patents themselves in order to accomplish their goal. (Though as a precaution they often did so, making sure that the individuals holding the rights turned them over to an association member.) Railroads needed only to pool information and to keep a united front in their dealings with patent holders.[40]

Perhaps the surest testimony to the effectiveness of the patent associations—and to the diminished importance of patented devices—was in the reduced frequency of litigation. "During the last three years," reported the secretary of the ERA in 1887, "only four suits for infringement of patents have been brought against our members," and all but one was "unimportant, commenced by the patentees themselves, and of a local nature.[41] Frustrated inventors, unable or unwilling to pursue their claims individually, channeled their fight into collective assaults on the associations themselves. In a rare display of concerted action, they banded together under the auspices of the Inventors Protective Agency, which lobbied Congress and sued the patent associations for restraint of trade.[42] But these efforts went for naught. Courts upheld the rights of railroads to combine in their defenses in patent cases, and Congress twice rejected petitions that would have declared the ERA and WRA in violation of the antitrust laws.[43]

Ironically, the biggest threat to the associations came ultimately from their own success. With virtually no litigation afoot, some railroad executives began to question their utility. Association secretaries, in a classic illustration of the bureaucratic propensity for self-preservation, subtly began to redefine their mission. Newsletters and reports increasingly provided advice of a narrowly technical nature, with little or no reference to legal issues.[44] One WRA secre-

39. By 1876 the WRA already included eighty-one lines operating 32,000 miles of track (U.S. Senate, "Arguments before the Committees on Patents," 191–92). Within a year of the Tanner decision, nearly every major line in the east belonged to the ERA (Isaac Hinckley to J. W. Garrett, 24 July 1879, Garrett Papers, box 86, subject 9614).

40. In 1878 the ERA amended its constitution to provide stronger sanctions against firms that negotiated their own agreements with holders of disputed patents. The secretary of the association complained that such deals lent credence to the claims of inventors and hurt the chances for success in court. "To obtain the best results," he cautioned, "the members of the Association must act as a unit, and it is believed that this unity of action has been the true cause of our success heretofore" (*ERA Annual Report* 12 [1878–79]: 8–9).

41. *ERA Annual Report* 21 (1887): 26.

42. *New York Times,* 21 October 1883, 3; 23 October 1883, 8; 24 October 1883, 4.

43. *ERA Annual Reports; New York Times,* 8 May 1892, 20; *Scientific American* 3 May 1890, 176; 12 March 1892, 160–61; William K. Tubman, *Petition to the Congress of the United States* (New York, 1894, printed circular).

44. The files of the Baltimore and Ohio and the Chicago, Burlington, and Quincy contain numerous examples of WRA and ERA work in this regard. On these activities at the Burlington, see especially the letterbooks of Robert Harris, CBQ Papers, 3H4.1, 9W5.2; the letterbooks of C. E.

tary even went so far as to suggest he organize a bureau of inventions that would serve as a clearinghouse for information about railroad technology. The idea went nowhere, for it ran counter to the whole objective of internalizing the paths of innovation and minimizing the prominence of patents. Another enterprising secretary was fired after he allowed a patent holder (and, events later revealed, business partner) to advertise an invention as having the imprimatur of the WRA. Like the proposed bureau, this stunt managed to invert the essential function of the associations. Railroads were not in the business of certifying patents.

2.3   Engineered Innovation: Learning within Limits

It is tempting, perhaps, to interpret the story of the brake cases and the rise of the patent associations as merely an attempt by powerful business organizations to escape a rightful obligation. The backroom lobbying by railroad lawyers certainly lends some credence to the idea. The fact that railroads ultimately found redress in the courts, which so often provided them with safe haven in the hostile political climate of the late nineteenth century, perhaps furthers the suspicion. Others contemplating the cases may take an opposite approach and dismiss the dispute as little more than an anomaly created by those unscrupulous speculators, the "patent sharks."

Neither of these interpretations strikes me as persuasive. Without question, the brake patents were owned by business agents who were far removed from the actual inventors of the double-acting arrangements. But this hardly distinguishes them from thousands of other patents at the time. As Lamoreaux and Sokoloff (chap. 1 in this volume) amply demonstrate, agents routinely took possession of patents; their relentless efforts to collect compensation are testimony to the growing vibrancy of the market mechanisms that lay at the foundation of the patent system. The claims those agents made under the doctrine of savings, moreover, constituted something much more threatening to railroads than a mere nuisance that could readily be sidestepped by resort to political clout or judicial sympathy. The brake cases posed a threat so fundamental to the economic vitality of the railroads that some of their most respected executives personally led the drive to form the first national trade organizations in an effort to combat it. The concerns these men raised merited serious consideration from a panel of the country's most respected patent attorneys, from the entire U.S. Congress, and from the nation's highest courts. That the courts ultimately proved the source of relief had less to do with conspiracy than with the historic difficulties of legislating changes in a system that purports to govern a single, universal process of technical discovery. Quite simply, Congress could not accommodate the special concerns of railroads without sacrificing essential

---

Perkins, CBQ Papers, 3P4.4; and the in-letters of T. J. Potter, CBQ Papers, 3P6.21. At the Baltimore and Ohio, see Patents and Inventions File, B&O Papers.

features of a patent system that still functioned quite capably in most segments of the economy. Courts provided a forum of greater flexibility. As has so often been the case in the history of the patent system and in other areas of American law, judges found it possible to tailor a reform that would suit the particular circumstances, while legislatures foundered on the necessity of writing comprehensive provisions.

The fervency of the arguments and prestige of the participants provide more than ample evidence that the dispute mattered a great deal. Yet to fully appreciate why it mattered, we need to step back from the details and situate the conflict in the larger context of American railroading and the shifting patterns of innovation in the late nineteenth century.

The brake cases broke at a moment of transition for American railroading. The grand developmental epic had reached its denouement with the extraordinary postbellum boom of the northern and western economy. The ensuing financial collapse of the midseventies ushered in a dramatically different era. No longer able to reap the easy bonanza initially made possible by the marriage of railroad technology to virgin land and resources, railroads faced increasingly intense competition for traffic that might travel over any of several highly capitalized routes. Government, which had long been a source of subsidy for railroads, now threatened them with regulation that would further intensify the pressures to cut fares and shave costs. Though new frontiers would open during the 1880s in the Pacific Northwest and to a lesser extent in the Gulf Coast region, the paramount concern at many of the most influential carriers was now to utilize existing facilities fully and keep costs low. Managers at these established lines tried to attract a large and steady volume of traffic and push it through their network of tracks as smoothly as possible. In the words of Burlington president Charles Perkins, they focused on "running the machine."[45]

The passage from expansive development to operational stewardship dramatically altered the paths of technical change in the railroad industry. The new objectives imparted an emphasis on standardization and routine that often bordered on the obsessive. Managers sought to diminish the degree of personal autonomy that had long characterized railroad innovation and to impose order over their technical affairs through bureaucratic control. They withdrew from direct investments in their suppliers and turned responsibility for technology over to salaried engineers who appreciated the importance of uniformity and happily pursued incremental change that functioned within the existing system. Through laboratory experiment and controlled study of actual practice, these academically trained professionals substituted sustained analysis for the hit-and-miss approach of inventors and mechanics. Cooperation in technical affairs grew more formalized and extensive, as lines exchanged equipment and

---

45. The phrase comes from C. E. Perkins, "Memorandum on Organization," ca. 1890, CBQ Papers, 3P6.36. This paragraph and the remainder of this section are derived largely from Usselman, *Regulating Innovation*.

forged alliances that facilitated uninterrupted long-distance transport. Engineers from competing lines, together with representatives from major suppliers, negotiated technical specifications through trade associations and professional organizations that soon came to function as the centers of technical knowledge in the industry. Interestingly, the constitutions of these organizations expressly prohibited the advocacy of specific, patented articles in their specifications and standards.[46]

The rise of engineers to prominence in American railroading during the last quarter of the nineteenth century produced a situation rife with paradox. On the surface, railroading seemed to lack the technical vitality and spirit of experimentation that had characterized its first half century. Yet in reality the pace of innovation quickened. Though railroads now seldom provided Americans with the spectacular bursts of productive efficiency made possible by the initial substitution of rails and engines for roads and horses or canals and flatboats, the railroad industry itself attained far more impressive improvements in productivity than ever before.[47]

Railroads achieved this success, moreover, precisely *because* they constricted the realm of technical possibilities and pursued one grand objective with single-minded purpose. In order to simplify operations and reduce the possibility of accidents, for example, managers dictated that trains be run as slowly as possible, even if it meant purchasing additional cars. No one knew for sure whether this was the optimal mode of operation, but everyone appreciated that the choice brought an essential measure of order to what might have otherwise become a hopelessly complex balancing act. Railroads laid down another simplifying ground rule when they elected to maintain a reliable, trained workforce rather than press forward with labor-saving devices. Wary of disruptive strikes and of the growing strength of the brotherhoods, railroads kept workers in the system.[48] The technologies of steel rails and larger cars and locomotives enabled them to increase labor productivity without significantly altering work routines. The few new devices railroads willingly introduced, such as automatic signals, were intended to serve the ideal of ordered, regular movement of trains through the system.[49]

By laying down clear ground rules about operations and shunning innova-

---

46. Usselman, *Regulating Innovation.*

47. Albert Fishlow, "Productivity and Technological Change in the Railroad Sector, 1840–1910," in *Output, Employment, and Productivity in the United States after 1800,* ed. National Bureau of Economic Research (New York: Cambridge University Press, 1966), 583–646.

48. On workers and technological change in railroading, see Walter Licht, *Working for the Railroad: The Organization of Work in the Nineteenth Century* (Princeton: Princeton University Press, 1983); Shelton Stomquist, *A Generation of Boomers: The Pattern of Railroad Labor Conflict in Nineteenth Century America* (Champaign-Urbana: University of Illinois Press, 1987); James H. Drucker, *Men of the Steel Rails: Workers on the Atchison, Topeka, and Santa Fe Railroad, 1869–1900* (Lincoln: University of Nebraska Press, 1983); Steven W. Usselman, "Mixed Signals: The Annoying Allure of Automatic Train Control for American Railroads," paper presented at the annual meeting of the Society for the History of Technology, Washington, DC, 15 October 1993.

49. On railroad attitudes toward automatic signals, see Steven W. Usselman, "Changing Embedded Systems: The Economics and Politics of Innovation in American Railroad Signaling, 1876–1914," in *Changing Large Technical Systems,* ed. Jane Summerton (Boulder: Westview Press,

tions that threatened to disrupt them, railroads channeled the collective energies of mechanics, engineers, and suppliers into a few vital areas. They provided clear objectives around which a broad, impersonal technical community could organize. Virtually everyone connected with the railroad industry understood what was to be done and, more importantly, what should not be tried. They were immersed in what the historian Reese Jenkins has termed a "business-technological mindset."[50] Or, to draw on language that has recently informed much work in the economics of innovation, they functioned within a particular technical paradigm, in which the basic technology seemed to be following a natural trajectory.[51]

Engineers thrived in such a well-defined environment. With so much already decided upon and worked out, they could readily draw upon their abilities to optimize performance and apply those skills across a realm far vaster than any other of the day. In railroading, which had experienced a sustained and chaotic building boom for nearly half a century, engineers encountered a system with lots of "slack." Its outlines were clearly determined, but its details were largely unrefined. Engineers could readily identify ways to derive increased efficiency without disrupting the basic contours of the system. Indeed, they could accomplish a great deal simply by imposing a degree of order and routine on what already existed. Within the firm, managers organized procedures that channeled all improvements up to a central clearinghouse in the staff offices, where they were evaluated in departments headed by college-trained engineers and chemists. Often the explicit goal of superintendents of motive power and other staff officers was to limit experimentation taking place in shops and elsewhere along the lines.[52] Eventually railroads consolidated the design and test of locomotives, rails, and other essential equipment in these offices.[53]

1994), 93–116; Steven W. Usselman, "The Lure of Technology and the Appeal of Order: Railroad Safety Regulation in Nineteenth Century America," *Business and Economic History,* 2d series, 21 (1992): 290–99.

50. Reese V. Jenkins, *Images and Enterprise: Technology and the American Photographic Industry, 1839–1925* (Baltimore: Johns Hopkins University Press, 1975).

51. Giovanni Dosi, "Technological Paradigms and Technological Trajectories," *Research Policy* 11 (1982): 147–62. See also Edward W. Constant II, *The Origins of the Turbojet Revolution* (Baltimore: Johns Hopkins University Press, 1980).

52. When the Pennsylvania Railroad established the central office of superintendent of motive power, it stipulated that "he shall furnish others with standards and instructions required to insure a perfect uniformity in construction and repairs of all the company's rolling stock and machinery" (Minutes of the Meetings of the Board of Directors, 13 September 1882, 10:68, Board Papers, PRR Papers). His counterpart at the Burlington implemented a program of biannual meetings with master mechanics in order to extract information about experiments taking place along the line. The purpose was not to encourage experimentation, but to curtail it. The absence of such monitoring mechanisms, he warned, would "certainly bring about unlimited experimenting and [make it] exceedingly difficult . . . to maintain even a pretense of standards" (G. W. Rhodes to Besler, 22 November 1887, CBQ Papers, 3P4.51). Rhodes's boss, Burlington president Charles Perkins, had previously issued an edict expressly prohibiting employees from working on new technology on company time in the railroad's shops (memorandum from C. E. Perkins, 27 March 1880, CBQ Papers, 3P6.36). These documents indicate that the primary purpose of bureaucratizing railroad technical affairs was to encourage standardization rather than innovation.

53. The Pennsylvania Railroad founded chemical and mechanical laboratories in 1876. By the early twentieth century they had grown into some of the largest analytical testing facilities in the

Railroads also reached out to their major suppliers, such as the steel companies who rolled the rails and the builders who assembled the cars and locomotives. Both the capital-intensive process of manufacturing steel and the labor-intensive assembly work of the equipment builders held out enormous potential for learning by doing. Railroads facilitated the learning process by concentrating their purchases in a few major suppliers. These favored suppliers could capture economies of scale and rapidly accumulate knowledge, reaping benefits they supposedly passed on to the railroads in the form of lower prices and higher performance. To ensure they did, railroads insisted in their purchasing agreements on the right to examine procedures at the manufacturing sites and to set technical specifications that dictated details of production as well as design. The drafting of specifications, which was done through engineering organizations and by individual lines in negotiation with their suppliers, became an important medium for passing lessons learned in actual service and in the railroad's laboratories back to the manufacturers. Railroad test departments asserted a powerful influence over rail manufacture, dictating specifics such as the temperature at rolling and the amount of waste to be sheared from ingots at various stages of production, and their drawing rooms became the source of most locomotive design. In addition to providing such influence over the process of innovation, this close give-and-take with a limited number of suppliers also helped railroads maintain the uniformity they so valued.[54]

These new departures in the internalization of discovery did not, of course, obviate the need for policies regarding patents. Indeed, the growing emphasis on standardization and uniformity lent additional urgency to questions about licenses and liabilities raised by the brake cases. Outside suppliers who retained control of their patents might gain enormous leverage if their devices became standard equipment on cars that railroads now exchanged freely among themselves. Not surprisingly, railroads went to great lengths to avoid making commitments in their official standards to patented technologies that were available from only a single supplier. The patent associations played an essential role in that effort by alerting railroads to potential liabilities and by helping ensure that most innovations entered the pool of generic techniques. By enabling railroads to act in concert, moreover, the associations helped keep them from driving up the price of licenses.

None of the measures discussed here—the pooling of technical expertise and close linkages with technical experts at key suppliers, the channeling of innovation upward to standardizing bodies within the firm and across the in-

---

United States, and many other railroads had followed the Pennsylvania's lead. The experience of labs at the Pennsylvania can be traced through the files of the Association of Transportation Officers and those of the Motive Power Department, PRR Papers. Material on similar facilities can be found in the CBQ Papers and the Reading Papers. See also Usselman, *Regulating Innovation.*

54. Misa, *Nation of Steel.*

dustry, the growing reliance on engineers and the universal methods and language of scientific analysis—fits easily within a model of innovation that emphasizes the selection mechanisms of the market. In each case, railroads intervened in the marketplace and broke down the barrier between the creation of new technology and its use. Railroads also sought consciously to limit the number of participants in the market for innovation. They narrowed the potential sources of innovation by cultivating relationships with a few suppliers, and by cooperating with other lines to set uniform standards they restricted the number of selectors as well. Ultimately, railroads blurred the distinction between invention and selection so thoroughly that one could hardly detect the extraordinary innovation taking place.

Yet though the paths of innovation made possible by engineering studies and coordinated specifications often involved a conscious restructuring of market mechanisms, they by no means closed the process of technical change off from the forces of market competition. Engineers were creatures of capital who tied their work more closely to cost objectives than did most mechanics and inventors. They more readily situated their work within the larger context of the overarching system or paradigm and the competitive environment that encompassed them. Because engineers never ventured far from established, measured routines, they never lost sight of the potential economic returns of their activities. In their hands, innovation occurred as a routine by-product of the ongoing pursuit of operational efficiency, which in turn was driven by the competition to provide transportation services. The incentives to innovate thus were felt not through a market for novelty, but directly through the market for the ultimate, standardized product of low-cost transportation.

2.4   Parallel Pipelines, Persistent Patenters

In stressing the importance and accomplishments of engineered innovation to American railroading during the last quarter of the nineteenth century, I do not mean to imply that this approach to technical change entirely supplanted the patent system and the market for inventive novelty. As Lamoreaux and Sokoloff suggest (chap. 1 in this volume), the patent system provided an increasingly vibrant conduit of new technology in many segments of the economy during the very same period. Even in the railroad industry itself, a few conspicuous individual inventors such as George Westinghouse and George Pullman managed to retain control of patented technologies and build commercial empires around them. During the opening decades of the twentieth century, moreover, railroads would discover certain limitations of an approach to technical change grounded in engineering study and refinement. Faced with an extraordinary surge in traffic, they struggled with mixed success to relieve congestion by pursuing further incremental improvements. Their inability to respond more creatively may have resulted in part from uncertainty surrounding government regulation, but even in the absence of regulation, railroads clearly faced a tall order in attempting to reorient their technical efforts and encourage more radical departures from routine.[55]

Rather than hold up railroads of the late nineteenth century as exemplars of a "better" or "more efficient" approach to technical change, then, I would suggest instead that we conceive of technical innovation as flowing through two parallel and overlapping pipelines. The first operates through the patent system and the market for inventive novelty. This pipeline carries discrete, patented technologies suspended in air, water, or some other inert medium. It is fed by the creative acts of individuals. The second pipeline conveys a steady stream of incremental improvements, refinements, and analyses that blend into a somewhat homogeneous fluid. At its source this conduit taps a pool of expertise residing in salaried employees and other technical personnel, engineering societies, and colleges and universities. These pipelines are highly idealized, of course. In reality, innovation flows in neither the wholly atomized nor the seamlessly synthesized fashion I have suggested. Indeed, even my stylized formulation emphasizes that the pipelines of innovation overlap, creating a third channel in which particles of invention float within a fluid of steady refinement. Still, I think we can easily recognize these two distinct conduits in the ways we traditionally have characterized and investigated technical change. In this volume, for instance, we can readily identify the inventive pipeline in the study of Lamoreaux and Sokoloff (chap. 1), while it seems fair to say that the essay by Gavin Wright (chap. 8) explores matters largely encompassed by the engineering pipeline.

As those chapters suggest, the pipelines of innovation are by no means static entities. They are created and altered by a variety of institutional innovations and by the changing sources of supply that feed them. The patent system, for instance, operated more effectively over the late nineteenth century as intermediaries such as patent agents facilitated the flow of information about patents across a larger area. In assuming this role, agents not only distributed the fruits of inventive creativity more broadly; they also increased the pool of available new technologies by enabling creative individuals to concentrate their efforts on invention. Similarly, Gavin Wright describes how a variety of institutional developments, especially the rise of engineering education and the emergence of institutions devoted to the study of metallurgy and minerals, at once increased the supply of technical knowledge and facilitated its diffusion through the United States in the decades around the turn of the twentieth century.

American railroads, like firms in all industries seeking to innovate, attempted to tap these broadening streams of invention and knowledge by building a set of parallel pipelines dedicated to their own specific needs. Constructing these feeder lines to specific firms and industries necessarily involved

---

55. The changing course of technical change in early-twentieth-century railroading is discussed in the closing chapters of Usselman, *Regulating Innovation*. On government regulation, see Albro Martin, *Enterprise Denied: Origins of the Decline of American Railroads, 1897–1917* (New York: Columbia University Press, 1971).

a narrowing of the broader pipelines, as railroads tried to siphon off only the inventions and knowledge that appeared most promising to their particular needs. In the case of the patent pipeline, new instruments such as trade journals and patent agents helped railroads focus their inquiries and identify techniques of particular interest. (As Lamoreaux and Sokoloff demonstrate, the trends in patent assignments over time indicate that agents perhaps facilitated specialization as well as diffusion.) As the correspondence of Robert Harris and the history of the railroad patent associations suggest, such winnowing was motivated as much by a desire to extricate railroads from a mushrooming morass of patented alternatives as by a fervent desire to identify inventions they might otherwise have missed. The insider relationships railroads cultivated with chosen suppliers likewise served to simplify choices from a dizzying array of options. Later, some of those same relationships helped railroads construct a pipeline of engineered innovation. That pipeline took better shape with the development of engineering societies and trade associations, which linked railroads with one another and to the institutions described by Wright. Indeed, railroads were so prominent in early professional engineering circles that one can hardly separate the larger developments Wright chronicles from the ones discussed above in connection with railroads. Over time, however, a set of engineering organizations dedicated exclusively to railroading emerged.[56]

In constructing these dedicated, industry-specific pipelines and specifying more clearly the range of viable technical alternatives, railroads did not necessarily slow the pace of innovation. For as any student of fluid dynamics can attest, narrowing a pipe without reducing the volume of input will increase the rate of flow. This, I would argue, is precisely what happened in the late nineteenth century. By defining their technical objectives quite specifically, railroads accelerated the flow of knowledge into their industry from the rapidly expanding pipeline of expertise described by Wright. Metallurgists and materials scientists focused their efforts relentlessly on producing cars and locomotives of greater size and fuel efficiency, heavier and more durable rails, and superior lubricants. Together these innovations drove down costs in an industry dedicated to carrying a high volume of bulk commodities across long distances.[57]

With the pipeline analogy in mind, we can perhaps better comprehend the importance of the brake cases and the doctrine of savings. This dispute involved a fundamental issue in the construction of the engineering pipeline. In attempting to place an economic value on what railroads viewed as a generic improvement (i.e., a product of the engineering pipeline) and in threatening to

---

56. For excellent histories of two general engineering societies, see Daniel H. Calhoun, *The American Civil Engineer: Origins and Conflict* (Cambridge: MIT Press, 1960); Bruce Sinclair, *A Centennial History of the American Society of Mechanical Engineers, 1880–1980* (Toronto: University of Toronto Press, 1980). On engineering societies more specifically oriented toward railroading, see Usselman, "Running the Machine."

57. This analysis follows that of Fishlow, "Productivity."

return that amount to inventors, judges in the brake cases were in effect seeking to preserve the inventive pipeline as the primary source of innovation in railroading. If courts could identify hidden liabilities in the case of an innovation involving brakes, railroads wondered, what would keep them from acting similarly in vital areas such as rail design and car construction? Would courts always deem the inventive pipeline predominant? Later, the justices of the Supreme Court moved in precisely the opposite direction. Their notion that technical change proceeded across a broad front through the collective efforts of many anonymous practitioners effectively attributed the lion's share of innovation to the engineering pipeline. The Court's thinking did not compel railroads to pursue the engineering approach, but it did remove a potential blockage that may have prevented them from doing so.

The fact that these shifting judicial doctrines involved brakes is no mere coincidence, for braking was precisely the sort of technology that characteristically occupied the interstitial space where the two pipelines overlapped. Like most of the technologies that clearly fell into the inventive pipeline, braking technology usually involved mechanical parts. In contrast to many mechanical appliances that might be integrated into the design of a locomotive, moreover, brakes could easily be viewed and treated in isolation from the rest of the technological system in which they functioned. Applying double-acting brake rigging to a car did not involve any further alterations to that car or to the trains in which it traveled. In these respects, braking lent itself to a patent system that conceived of technology as discrete and particular, one that initially had required prospective patenters to submit working models with their applications. Techniques that fit most readily into the engineering pipeline, by contrast, often involved new processes or craft knowledge gained through experience or study.

While braking exhibited the physical attributes characteristic of much technology flowing through the inventive pipeline, it served purposes that placed it more in the realm of engineered innovation. In general, techniques that emerged from the engineering conduit served primarily to lower the costs of transportation rather than to provide qualitative changes in service. Such innovation was aimed at the concerns of railroad management and not at the experience of railroad customers, who usually encountered its effects indirectly in the form of lower rates rather than directly in the form of increased comfort or novel services. It was a rare passenger or shipper who could muster much excitement over the changing size and shape of the rails, no matter how strenuously railroads sought to persuade them that such changes were the ultimate source of falling rates and improved safety. A patented new folding bed in a Pullman car, by contrast, could evoke raves of enthusiasm from the traveling public while leaving railroad management unimpressed. Passengers did take some interest in the matter of brakes, of course, at least to the extent they perceived their safety and comfort were at stake. But an innovation such as the double-acting mechanisms constituted more of a refinement in existing techniques than a novel departure offering dramatically increased safety. Its greatest benefits were lower labor costs and reduced wheel wear, not shorter stopping distances, and railroads deployed it more extensively in freight service than on passenger cars.

One reason railroads shunned the double-acting mechanism in passenger service was the availability of an alternative, the continuous air brake. Patented in 1869 by George Westinghouse, the air brake rapidly became standard equipment on passenger trains and late in the century became a common feature of freight service as well.[58] Westinghouse used the air brake as a springboard into an astounding career as an inventor and manufacturer. His list of accomplishments included a second railroad-supply firm, the Union Switch and Signal Company, which at the turn of the twentieth century was far and away the largest provider of electric and pneumatic switching and signaling installations to American railroads.

On the surface Westinghouse's career seems to fly in the face of the notion that technical innovation in railroading flowed increasingly from a pipeline of generic incremental improvements. Upon closer inspection, however, we can see that in many respects Westinghouse is the exception who proves the rule. For his triumphs differed in two substantial respects from other innovations that occupied a middle position between inventive and engineered innovation.[59]

In the first place, both his braking and signaling technologies possessed technical attributes that distinguished them from many railroad innovations of the period. Each employed a novel technology—compressed air in the case of brakes, electricity in that of signals—that fell outside the established mechanical expertise of railroads. As a consequence, Westinghouse's railroad customers could not so easily absorb his designs into the reservoir of knowledge residing in their shops. With their arrays of interconnected compressors, valves, wires, motors, and other devices, moreover, Westinghouse's products appeared to function as complex, integrated systems that needed to be deployed wholesale or not at all. These qualities enabled Westinghouse to establish and maintain proprietary control much more readily than most other inventors. By patenting the essential hose coupling that connected brakes on each car with the air cylinder located on the locomotive, for instance, Westinghouse blocked railroads from mixing in brakes of alternative design. Deemed insurmountable by the WRA, the patent forced lines either to make a wholesale change to his devices or to maintain trains in multiple and incompatible formats, at severe cost to uniformity. Westinghouse thus leveraged the growing emphasis on standardization in precisely the way railroads hoped to prevent.

The second distinctive feature of Westinghouse's inventive enterprises was that he appealed past the railroads and pitched his products directly to consumers who rode the trains. This was especially true in the case of the air brake,

58. Steven W. Usselman, "Air Brakes for Freight Trains: Technological Innovation in the American Railroad Industry, 1869–1900," *Business History Review* 58 (spring 1984): 30–50.

59. Steven W. Usselman, "From Novelty to Utility: George Westinghouse and the Business of Innovation during the Age of Edison," *Business History Review* 66 (summer 1992): 251–304.

which he publicized masterfully by staging trials in the wake of a deadly accident at Revere, Massachusetts, that had attracted widespread attention from the public and from the state railroad commission. Though railroad executives were skeptical that automatic brakes would truly provide improved safety, they felt powerless to resist the overwhelming demand. "I have no doubt that [the air brake] will be made a subject of reference in advertisements," the Burlington's Harris wrote to a subordinate who resisted deploying the new device, "and that whether the traveling public would really be more safe or not, they would *think* so."[60]

In the case of freight operations, which occurred outside of public purview and involved extensive interchange of equipment among companies, railroads were willing to wait Westinghouse out. They employed air brakes only in especially demanding conditions such as fast freight and long mountainous descents, where increased control provided substantial economic benefits in the form of reduced wear and tear. Meanwhile, railroads laid plans to hold extensive trials of freight brakes upon expiration of Westinghouse's patents. To their chagrin, trials held at Burlington in 1886 and 1887 revealed severe limitations in all continuous brakes when they were deployed suddenly on long trains. Westinghouse seized the opportunity and introduced revised, "quick-action" equipment featuring valve work covered by new patents. Though these patents did not provide quite the ironclad protection he had enjoyed previously under the coupling patent, his threats of legal action kept all but the most steadfast competitors at bay. Railroads then resumed their holding pattern. Most did not place air brakes on freight equipment until after Congress passed legislation compelling them to do so. Government had done what railroads had expressly avoided—enshrined a proprietary technique in a standard—with Westinghouse again the beneficiary.[61]

---

60. R. Harris to C. E. Perkins, 25 April 1870, CBQ Papers, 3H4.1, 20:26–27, emphasis in original.

61. Westinghouse attempted to repeat his triumph in the area of railroad signaling—a technology that again appealed primarily to a sense of safety and that utilized the unfamiliar technology of electricity. In the 1880s he bought a fundamental patent covering the type of circuit required to make automatic signals operate in a fail-safe fashion. Most railroads, however, found they could do without his products, in large part because the public never mobilized a movement for automatic circuits. The few railroads that chose to deploy Westinghouse's signaling appliances did so on their own terms. They used them only in the most congested areas, where the automatic equipment could space traffic more effectively and keep it flowing more smoothly than any other means, thus saving vast capital expenditures on new track and reducing labor costs. Railroads tended to purchase signaling systems on a contract basis, with Westinghouse and his suppliers bidding to install customized plants at particular locations rather than sending lots of standardized components. Competitive advantages in the signaling business resulted in large measure from the knowledge acquired by engineers who designed custom configurations in the field and by skilled mechanics who translated those plans into unique devices. But patents also proved to be an important strategic tool in signaling. They enabled Westinghouse to build a stockpile of proprietary techniques that kept his competitors at bay, much as he and General Electric did in the field of electrical power. See Usselman, "From Novelty to Utility."

The annals of late-nineteenth-century invention contain a few other names associated with railroads, men such as Pullman with his palace cars and Swift and Armour with their fleets of refrigerated equipment. Like Westinghouse, these exceptional figures offered not operational efficiencies yielding lower rates and reduced fares (indeed, in the eyes of railroads these innovations threatened to complicate operations in ways that ran counter to the objectives of standardization and efficiency), but creature comforts such as greater safety and stylish service for which customers would pay a premium. Most technologies of this ilk appeared first in the passenger branch of the industry and diffused slowly if at all to the much larger and more lucrative freight side. (The refrigerated freight car—probably the most conspicuous possible exception— functioned as a component in a specialized branch of trade that catered to upper-class urbanites who wanted fresh dressed meat.)[62] The upscale consumers who traveled the rails and purchased the specialties railroads made available thus sustained markets for genuine novelty. Within those niches, the patent system still came into play.

But figures such as Westinghouse and Pullman remained conspicuous exceptions in the railroad industry of the late nineteenth century. Their devices, moreover, seldom contributed significant operating economies to the railroads themselves. Such benefits flowed instead from the pipeline of engineered innovation. By limiting their horizons and channeling their efforts, railroads discovered an enormous potential for improved performance. For them, less innovation was more.

2.5 Lessons

How typical were the nineteenth-century railroads? What does their experience suggest about the process of learning and discovery in other industries or at other times?

There is good reason to be cautious in drawing generalizations from the railroad experience. The conditions that gave rise to the patent associations resulted in large measure from characteristics peculiar to the railroad industry. Few other areas of enterprise offered the rich opportunities for technical exchange among seeming competitors. Few consumers of innovation possessed as much knowledge and expertise as railroads, and few had the sort of leverage over suppliers railroads obtained from their role as transportation providers. The fact that the brake cases were ultimately resolved through a flexible legal doctrine rather than through blanket legislative reform suggests that very different conditions prevailed elsewhere in the economy. As the career of George Westinghouse suggests, the patent system certainly remained central to the

---

62. On railroad resistance to refrigerator cars, see Mary Yeager, *Competition and Regulation: The Development of Oligopoly in the Meat Packing Industry* (Greenwich, CT: Greenwood, 1981).

course of innovation in emergent industries such as electric power and even retained a vital role within railroading itself in niches where novelty assumed special value.

The further internalization of discovery that followed the judgments in the brake cases likewise owed a great deal to the peculiar internal dynamics of the railroad industry. By the 1870s, American railroading had reached a point in its evolution that called above all for systemization and standardization. Owing to a combination of public policies and private incentives, the industry had grown heavily capitalized without having undergone intensive development and refinement. As many railroads stopped infiltrating new territory and turned their attention to moving commodities as efficiently as possible across long distances, the engineers took over. But engineers did not attain anything approaching such prominence in any other industry until the twentieth century. By then, moreover, railroads had begun to discover that the engineering approach to innovation had limits of its own. Under the stress of larger and more diverse traffic, the technical paradigm that had served railroads so effectively during the last quarter of the nineteenth century no longer yielded the anticipated benefits. Railroads found themselves groping for solutions that demanded more radical departures from routine and greater novelty than engineers could readily provide.

While considerations such as these suggest that the internalization of technical discovery described in this paper should not be taken as a normal state of affairs, we can nevertheless detect certain parallels between railroading and other industries. Some useful comparison, for instance, can be drawn between railroads and steel producers of the same period.[63] The distinguished Harvard economist F. W. Taussig noted these common trends in a 1901 essay for the *Quarterly Journal of Economics*. Entitled simply "The Iron Industry of the United States," the essay in reality sought to portray the recent growth of the entire American economy as largely a product of the pursuit of "routine and system." Taussig reserved especially high praise for "the wonderful growth of scientific and technical education" that had "[promoted] the rapid spread and complete utilization of the best processes." "They have been largely instrumental in enabling prompt advantage to be taken of chemical, metallurgical, and mechanical improvements in the iron and steel works," he went on. "Their influence has shown itself no less in the railways, the great buildings, the textile works, the manufacturing establishments at large."[64] Significantly, Taussig tied the spread of scientific expertise to the massive investment in machinery that had preceded it and to the organizational revolution that accompanied it. His contemporaneous analysis, like the more recent historical one of Alfred Chandler and that by Gavin Wright in this volume, thus suggests that condi-

---

63. Misa, *Nation of Steel.*
64. F. W. Taussig, "The Iron Industry of the United States," *Quarterly Journal of Economics* 14 (1900): 143–70, 475–508, quote from 488.

tions prevailing in the railroad industry reflected larger changes in the patterns of investment, the structure of markets, and the organization of technical knowledge. The shifting paths of technical change apparent in railroad patent policies thus may very well foreshadow emergent trends throughout the economy.[65]

Perhaps still more fruitful insights can be gleaned if we do not restrict our focus to the nineteenth century and concentrate instead on finding industries that passed through a series of transitions similar to those traced by the railroads. During the early twentieth century, for instance, the electrical industry entered a phase quite similar to that of railroading in the late nineteenth—a fact Thomas Edison perceived perhaps a bit prematurely when he opted out of the industry in the 1880s with the whining complaint that "working day and night to increase efficiency from 80 to 85 percent is an absurdity."[66] Electrical engineers in the early twentieth century, employing terms and concepts uncannily like those of their railroad counterparts a decade earlier, steered the industry toward procedures that would employ capital more intensively. Interestingly, the utility industry could pursue its relentless focus on lowering long-distance transmission costs and driving down the costs of production in large part because the two principal suppliers of electrical equipment—Westinghouse and General Electric—had pooled their patents.[67]

At about the same time, the automobile industry passed through a similar experience. For two decades, this infant industry had supported a vibrant competition among small firms offering products of novel design. Investors looking to impose some standardization and regularity on the chaotic new field hoped a key patent issued to Henry Selden might be used to block entry into the industry. When Henry Ford successfully challenged the Selden patent in court, however, auto manufacturers turned tail and agreed to pool all of their patents. The move skewed competition away from product differentiation sustained by patented technologies and toward economies of production achieved through relentless pursuit of incremental improvement by experts.[68] The great beneficiary, of course, was Ford himself. His synthesis of generic production technologies propelled him to the forefront of the industry.[69]

The experience of the postwar computer industry offers a third example. In its infancy, firms such as Sperry sought to establish dominant positions by

---

65. Alfred D. Chandler, Jr., *The Visible Hand: The Managerial Revolution in American Business* (Cambridge: Harvard University Press, 1977). The aggregate data of Ken Sokoloff and Naomi Lamoreaux (chap. 1 in this volume) lend some additional support to this idea.

66. Quoted in Harold C. Passer, *The Electrical Manufacturers, 1875–1900: A Study in Competition, Technical Change, and Economic Growth* (Cambridge: Harvard University Press, 1953), 104.

67. The basic sources here are Passer, *Electrical Manufacturers,* and Thomas P. Hughes, *Networks of Power: Electrification in Western Society, 1880–1930* (Baltimore: Johns Hopkins University Press, 1983). For further elaboration, see Usselman, "From Novelty to Utility."

68. See James Flink, *The Automobile Age* (Cambridge: MIT Press, 1988), 51–55.

69. David A. Hounshell, *From the American System to Mass Production, 1800–1932: The Development of Manufacturing Technology in the United States* (Baltimore: Johns Hopkins University Press, 1984).

designing and patenting basic approaches to computing.[70] Despite consistent efforts to the contrary, however, control of proprietary novelties seldom proved instrumental to success in this dynamic field. Technical change occurred so rapidly and across such a broad front that patents and licensing agreements often grew obsolete before their owners secured significant returns.[71] IBM's success in the industry ultimately owed more to its capabilities in maintenance, service, and production than to particular breakthrough inventions. The firm's most risky technical venture, its backward integration into semiconductor-component production, was more in the nature of a sustained exercise in learning by doing than a one-time inventive act.[72]

In drawing attention to these examples, I do not mean to suggest that technical innovation has always proceeded more rapidly or effectively in conditions where the patent system has been suspended and responsibility for innovation has passed to salaried experts and a tightly linked technical community. Rather, these cases may point to a stage theory of technical change. In every example a period of technical creativity sustained through mechanisms close to those idealized under the patent system gave way to a shaking-out period in which experts pursued sustained refinement through more internalized means. But the process did not stop there. As in the case of the railroads, which by the early twentieth century faced a crisis of congestion that called for more radical departures from existing practice, each of the episodes discussed above culminated in a resurgence of innovation flowing more clearly from the marketplace for novelty. During the 1920s, for instance, General Motors and other automobile makers turned the frontiers of competition back to product innovation with novelties such as the automatic starter and bright lacquer finishes. Similarly, profit centers in the electrical industries shifted toward consumer appliances during the 1920s. More recently, even the staid field of electrical generating equipment has been rocked by dramatic new technical departures, while in the contemporary computer business Microsoft thrives by marketing copyrighted programs. Still other examples of such passages might be found in telecommunications and in pharmaceuticals and other branches of chemicals, where innovation frequently appears to come in waves characterized by bursts of novelty followed by long periods of consolidation and refinement.[73]

70. Kenneth Flamm, *Creating the Computer: Government, Industry, and High Technology* (Washington, DC: Brookings Institution, 1988); Nancy Stern, *From ENIAC to UNIVAC: An Appraisal of the Eckert-Mauchly Computers* (Boston: Beacon Press, 1981).

71. Flamm, *Creating the Computer;* Richard C. Lewin, "The Semiconductor Industry," in *Government and Technical Progress: A Cross-Industry Analysis,* ed. Richard R. Nelson (New York: Cambridge University Press, 1982); David C. Mowery, "Innovation, Market Structure, and Government Policy in the American Semiconductor Industry: A Survey," *Research Policy* 12 (1983): 183–97.

72. This assessment is based largely on my essay "IBM and Its Imitators: Organizational Capabilities and the Emergence of the International Computer Industry," *Business and Economic History,* 2d series, 22 (winter 1993): 1–35.

73. Louis Galambos with Jane Eliot Sewell, *Networks of Innovation* (New York: Cambridge University Press, 1995); Louis Galambos and Jeffrey L. Sturchio, "The Pharmaceutical Industry

In his 1901 essay Taussig crowed that "American industry has shown not only the inventiveness and elasticity characteristic of the Yankee from early days, but that orderly and systematic utilization of applied science in which the Germans have hitherto been—perhaps still are—most successful."[74] Whether he accurately captured the direction of change or was correct in ascribing certain attributes to a particular culture may be open to question. But the distinction he drew remains useful. For it appears a recurrent feature of modern firms, industries, and economies that they must continually balance the fruits of "inventiveness and elasticity" with the benefits of the "orderly and systematic." It follows that the process of learning and discovery will trace no single course, and that innovation will continue to flow through multiple pipelines.

Comment   Jeremy Atack

Steven Usselman's paper provides many insights into the relationship between patenting activity and the processes of innovation in large, technologically complex and capable organizations, but it also raises a number of fundamental questions. My purpose in this comment is threefold. First, I seek to set this work in the broader context of the interaction of patent law, economics and politics in the late nineteenth century—commentary that is also relevant to the paper by Lamoreaux and Sokoloff (chap. 1 in this volume). Second, I offer some additional evidence that is supportive of, and consistent with, the basic premises of both of these patents papers. Third, I discuss Usselman's interpretation of railroad behavior with respect to patents and patent case law.

While the market for inventions is usually modeled through the interaction of inventor-suppliers whose property rights are secured by the government through the patent system and a demand for improved devices and processes from users operating in a perfectly competitive environment, this is not the paradigm studied by Usselman. In his implicit model, inventions are interrelated rather than separable, the demanders are monopsonists in the input market for inventions and monopolists in the output market, demanders may also appear as suppliers and suppliers may produce no product of intrinsic merit and may not actually produce the product themselves. Not surprisingly, the resulting market works quite differently from the idealized market for inventions.

---

in the Twentieth Century: A Reappraisal of the Sources of Innovation," *History and Technology* 13 (1996): 83–100.

74. Taussig, "Iron Industry," 488.

Jeremy Atack is professor in and chair of the department of economics and business administration at Vanderbilt University and a research associate of the National Bureau of Economic Research. His research relies heavily upon the use of the manuscripts of nineteenth-century federal censuses of agriculture, manufactures, and population.

A Very Brief Primer on Patent Law

Congress was specifically granted the power "to promote . . . useful arts, by securing for limited times, to . . . inventors, the exclusive rights to their . . . discoveries" by the U.S. Constitution and was quick to act upon this authority, passing a number of different patent laws beginning with the law of 10 April 1790.[1] This law provided for up to fourteen years of protection for "any useful art, manufacture, engine, machine or device, or any improvement thereon not before known." Minor procedural revisions were made to the law in 1793 and 1800, but a more far-reaching change was made in 1819 when U.S. circuit courts were granted jurisdiction in equity of actions for patent infringements.

A major revision to the law was passed in 1836, creating a permanent experienced bureaucracy to review applications and grant patent protection. Subsequently, a number of other important changes were made to the law. In particular, as the law was originally written, a patent could not claim more than that to which it was entitled and, if void in *any* part, was void in whole. In 1837 these rules were eased where there was good faith by the patentee. In 1839 the law was amended to preserve the right to a patent within two years of discovery and allowing for the perfection of the invention possibly through public trials rather than requiring development in secret as the means of guaranteeing primacy.

Further minor modifications were made to the law as, for example, in 1861 when the patent duration was fixed at a single seventeen-year term, but the basics of the 1836 law survived into the twentieth century.

What is notable about this account of the evolution of patent law is the absence of major legislative action on patent law after the Civil War despite the fact that patent reform became the common goal of two powerful and otherwise successful lobbying groups—the National Grange and the railroads—which usually had opposing objectives. As Smith put it: "there has been, and doubtless still is in some parts of the country, a widespread hostility to the patent law. This feeling was, not many years since, very prevalent among the farmers of the West, and may still be so, though they are a class to whom the inventions of recent years have been of incalculable value. It may have been entertained and stimulated by the railroad companies, which have found it inconvenient to dispense with or pay for patented inventions."[2] Individually, the Grangers had been instrumental in securing the passage of laws regulating railroad rates while railroads had succeeded in winning federal land grants. However, their joint efforts to reform the patent system failed.

One possible explanation for this failure is that they were able to secure their

---

1. See U.S. Constitution, article I, section 8, paragraph 8. The description and chronology of patent law that follows is based upon Chauncey Smith, "A Century of Patent Law," *Quarterly Journal of Economics* 5 (1890): 44–69, especially 45–54.
2. Ibid., 58.

goals more easily through other channels. This was certainly not true for the Grange, for whom the profusion of patent infringement claims against farmers using driven (i.e., piped artesian) wells was of the greatest concern.[3] Railroads, however, may have been more successful in finding an alternative solution—the patent pool that lies at the heart of Usselman's story.

Patents and American Railroads

By the early 1850s, patents for devices to be used in railroading were being granted at a rate of about fifty per year. By the mid-1860s, the rate had increased tenfold—far faster than the railroad network had expanded.[4] Each of the dozens of railroads—some local, others regional or national—picked from the resulting menu of thousands of possible patented devices on the advice by their engineers informed by advertisements and demonstrations and governed only by personal prejudice. Those devices both large (such as steel rails, the telegraph, better signals, air brakes, and automatic couplers) and small (such as journal boxes, flues, and fireboxes) that made it through these filters were incorporated into railroad operations. Once embodied in the railroad's capital stock, innovations, taken collectively, had a major impact upon productivity which grew more than threefold or at an average annual rate of about 3 percent per year between the Civil War and 1900.[5]

However, despite the importance of innovation to railroad productivity growth, the managerial response to these inventions has not been well documented and much of what we do know is somewhat contradictory. For example, although J. Edgar Thomson, the president of the Pennsylvania Railroad, was an early and ardent champion of the steel rail and railroads consumed the majority of the nation's steel production before 1880, the railroads (including the Pennsylvania) seem to have been relatively slow to switch from iron rails to steel despite the technical and economic advantages of steel.[6] Similarly, what are probably the two most widely regarded railroad innovations (though

3. The case of the driven well has been extensively studied. See, for example, Earl W. Hayter, "The Western Farmers and the Drivewell Patent Controversy," *Agricultural History* 16 (January 1942): 16–28.

4. "Report of the Commissioner of Patents for 1852," U.S. Senate, 32d Cong., 2d sess., Executive Doc. 55, 438; "Report of the Commissioner of Patents for 1865," U.S. House of Representatives, 39th Cong., 1st sess., Executive Doc. 52, 18.

5. Albert Fishlow, "Productivity and Technological Change in the Railroad Sector, 1840–1910," in *Output, Employment, and Productivity in the United States after 1800* (New York: Columbia University Press, 1966), 583–646, especially 626.

6. For statistics on the growth of the steel industry see Peter Temin, *Iron and Steel in Nineteenth-Century America* (Cambridge: MIT Press, 1964). For a discussion of the laggard rate of adoption of steel rails, see Jeremy Atack and Jan Brueckner, "Steel Rails and American Railroads, 1867–1880," *Explorations in Economic History* 19, no. 4 (1982): 339–59; C. Knick Harley, "Steel Rails and American Railroads, 1867–1880: Cost Minimizing Choice: A Comment on the Analysis of Atack and Brueckner," *Explorations in Economic History* 20, no. 3 (1983): 248–57; Jeremy Atack and Jan Brueckner, "Steel Rails and American Railroads, 1867–1880: Reply to Harley," *Explorations in Economic History* 20, no. 3 (1983): 258–62.

ultimately of far less economic significance than the steel rail)[7]—air brakes and automatic couplers—were not fully adopted until Congress in 1893 mandated their use in all interstate commerce effective August 1900.[8]

Early on, some of this reluctance might be explained by the efforts of individual railroads to preserve their own distinctiveness as part of their grand designs to monopolize traffic along a particular route. Many of these idiosyncrasies probably originated in and manifested themselves through isolated adoptions of particular patented devices and processes that all too often became indispensable to the smooth functioning of day-to-day operations of the individual railroad.

Most of these specific innovations are undocumented, but we do know a great deal about one obvious example—the adoption and persistence of different track gauges. These not only effectively prevented shippers from taking advantage of the arbitrage opportunities afforded by small freight-rate differences between destinations but also essentially isolated communities one from another if they were located on tracks of different gauge. In 1861, for example, while most of the eastern seaboard railroads had adopted the English 4' 8½" gauge, the Cleveland and Pittsburgh used 4' 10" (still useable by "standard" locomotives and rolling stock though perhaps with some increase in risk of derailment and additional wear and tear), while the Grand Trunk used 5' 6" and the New York and Erie had a 6' gauge.[9] So long as this situation persisted, extensive trade between, say, Binghamton (on the New York and Erie) and most of Pennsylvania (where the standard gauge predominated) was unlikely, and communities could be held hostage.

As the advantages of cooperation became clearer to the railroads, barriers to exchange and interchange came down, but before the full benefits of an integrated rail system could be realized, there had to be a greater degree of uniformity across the different rail networks. This would potentially encompass almost all aspects of system operation from track design to rolling stock to shipment billing and tracking. The marketplace for ideas, while rich, was also full of confusion, particularly for a new technology. Vested interests and competing claims—some true, some false, some exaggerated, some modest, some from insiders, others from outsiders—vied for attention. How was one to choose which standard to adopt?

7. Fishlow, "Productivity and Technological Change," 639, asserts that steel rails were at least three times as important as the air brake and the automatic coupler.

8. Interestingly, railroads made two contradictory arguments. On the one hand they claimed that the devices were unproven and ineffective. On the other they asserted that adoption was proceeding as quickly as possible. See Interstate Commerce Commission, *Annual Report on the Statistics of Railways in the United States for 1891* (Washington, DC: Government Printing Office, 1892), 45; U.S. Senate Interstate Commerce Committee, *Hearings in Relation to Safety Couplers and Power Brakes in Freight Cars,* 51st Cong., 1st sess, 30 April and 14–16 May 1890. See Fishlow, "Productivity and Technological Change" 634–35.

9. George R. Taylor and Irene Neu, *The American Railroad Network, 1861–1890* (Cambridge: Harvard University Press, 1956).

The Railroad Machine and Repair Shop

The nature of railroading further complicated the situation. As extremely complex, integrated technical systems, the railroads found it difficult, if not impossible, to determine the precise contribution of each device or process to their cost savings, revenues, or profits. Outside inventors would thus have been at an even greater disadvantage in pricing the products of their ingenuity. But, even if a dollar figure could be attached to specific savings or additional earnings from individual patented devices, the railroads questioned whether their inventors were entitled to the full amount of the benefits, since parts of these at least arose from the railroad's market power and success. The number of outside inventor-suppliers was large; the number of railroad demanders relatively small and getting smaller as railroads consolidated and cooperated.

In the absence of a well-developed pool of outsider suppliers throughout much of the nineteenth century, the railroads built much of their own equipment and facilities and maintained large repair facilities to keep this capital in good working order. This was especially important given the high ratio of fixed to total costs for railroads. Although relatively little is known about these railroad machine shops and repair facilities, many of them were large whether measured in terms of employment or in terms of value of their output. Indeed, many would have ranked among the largest industrial enterprises of the time had they been separate firms. Some idea of their importance can be gauged from the data presented in table 2C.1, which lists some statistics about a few of the larger repair facilities taken from the manuscripts of the censuses of manufactures.

Based upon these data it seems obvious that railroad repair shops were major employers. Most employed hundreds of workers in a single facility. Some employed thousands. Many of these individuals must have been relatively skilled mechanics and machinists. With 643 employees in 1850, the Philadelphia and Reading Railroad machine shop, for example, accounted for 13 percent of machinists and millwrights in Pennsylvania and more than 2 percent of the national total reported by the 1850 census. It also seems reasonable, based upon the statistics in table 2C.1, to infer that these repair facilities proliferated and grew over time.

By virtue of their size and the complexity of the systems that they built, repaired, and maintained, these machine and repair shops must have served as informal schools for engineering practice, as repositories of engineering expertise, as storehouses of knowledge about what worked, what didn't, and why, and as test facilities for prospective innovations. These facilities were thus uniquely positioned to advise railroad management on which inventions worked and which didn't.

Given the complexity of the systems that they were called upon to build and repair and the interdependence between these systems, the railroad machine and repair shops found it expedient to license the right to manufacture patented

Table 2C.1   **Partial Listing of Large Railroad Repair Facilities, 1850–80**

Year	Railroad	Capital Invested ($)	Employees	Value of Output ($)	Repairs as % of Output
1850	Philadelphia & Reading	800,000	643	250,000	100
	Vermont Central	30,000	95	136,000	100
1860	Alabama & Tennessee	na	50	75,000	na
	Central Ohio	100,000	155	150,000	na
	Louisville & Nashville	165,000	250	225,000	na
	Marietta & Cincinnati	28,000	100	60,000	na
	Michigan Central	400,000	90	150,000	na
	Mississippi	6,000,000[a]	54	54,438	79
	North Carolina	400,000	60	52,950	76
	South Side	20,000	30	133,000	100
	Southern	na	60	100,000	na
	Vermont Central	750,000	144	268,300	na
	Western & Atlantic	7,500	70	207,500	na
1870	A.G.	100,000	95	72,850	77
	Burlington	75,000	278	730,989	56
	Central of New Jersey	700,000	300	97,000	43
	Cleveland & Pittsburgh	150,000	160	337,070	39
	Connecticut & Passumpsic	350,000	106	175,592	47
	Erie	400,000	547	1,301,277	39
	S.S.M.S.	399,038	193	459,158	na
	Vicksburg & Meridian	210,000	150	339,800	83
	Vermont Central & Canada	115,000	374	513,260	48
1880	Chicago & Northwestern	1,642,662	1,120	2,799,474	na
	Chicago, Burlington & Quincy	250,000	750	625,000	na
	Chicago, Burlington & Quincy	na	455	652,275	na
	Chicago, Rock Island & Pacific	750,000	799	990,665	na
	Chicago, Rock Island & Pacific	350,000	822	600,000	na
	Decatur Division of Louisville & Nashville	30,000	59	66,870	na
	Illinois Central	1,000,000	922	912,686	na
	Missouri Pacific	100,000	350	650,000	na
	Nashville, Chattanooga & St. Louis	130,000	200	185,887	na
	P.C. & S.L.	100,000	351	346,571	na
	Pennsylvania	1,525,463	1,334	2,427,043	na
	Pennsylvania	1,914,669	2,069	2,531,277	na
	Pennsylvania	na	764	1,305,000	na
	Philadelphia & Reading	120,000	130	303,000	na
	Philadelphia & Reading	360,000	551	501,000	na
	Philadelphia & Reading	350,000	400	475,000	na
	Union Pacific	35,000	11	140,000	na
	Wabash, St. Louis & Pacific	na	250	309,107	na

Source: Unpublished data from the manuscript censuses of manufactures collected by Fred Bateman and Thomas Weiss (1850, 1860, and 1870) and by Jeremy Atack and Fred Bateman (1880). These facilities are those that, fortuitously (as a result of their relative size measured by gross ouput), happened to be included in the Bateman-Weiss and Atack-Bateman large-firm samples.

Note: na = not available.

[a]Almost certainly the capital invested in the railroad, not just the machine shops.

products rather than purchase them from outside suppliers. Indeed, over time, these data from the largest machine shops show that, where repairs were separately identified, the share of repairs as opposed to production of new locomotives, rolling stock, and other railroad equipment declined over time. This finding is consistent with Usselman's story of growing railroad involvement in producing their own equipment rather than buying from outside sources.

By producing patented devices "in house" under license, railroad repair shops eliminated the possibility of being held hostage to external supply uncertainties with respect to price, quality, and delivery. At the same time they gained engineering expertise that should have proved useful not only in the production and repair of the product in question but that might also have led to the design and creation of new and improved models, possibly of a sufficiently radically new design to not be covered by the original patent. That engineering expertise and experimentation, if properly documented, could also serve as a basis for successful challenges (known as "interferences") to the grant of a patent or its enforcement on the grounds that the device lacked originality.

At what point these modified devices became entirely new products and what the economic contribution of the original idea was became matters of heated debate both inside and outside the courtroom. From the standpoint of the railroads, they had committed substantial resources to guarantee the success of a particular device, and they saw little or no reason to share those benefits or the profits of their monopoly power with outsiders.

Here lay a bone of contention between outside inventors and insider innovators. The successful outside inventors, such as George Westinghouse, resisted railroad pressure to license their technology for insider manufacture. The less successful, such as Henry Tanner, assignee of the Thompson and Bachelder patent on double-acting brakes, eventually lost control of their invention. This latter case is one to which Usselman refers in his paper. It eventually reached the Supreme Court before being resolved in favor of the railroads.

Railroad Patents, the Courts, and Patent Pools

Elsewhere, Usselman has dealt at length with the issues in the case of the *Chicago and Northwestern Railway Company V. Thomas Sayles* (97 U.S. 554)—otherwise known as the Tanner brake case—but it is worthwhile repeating some of the details here to illustrate the problems confronting the railroads given the nature of American patent law at the time.[10] The Chicago and Northwestern Railway Company was only one of many railroads sued by Sayles for patent infringement.[11] Moreover, Sayles was an active litigant in at

---

10. Steven W. Usselman, "Organizing a Market for Technological Innovation: Patent Pools and Patent Politics of American Railroads, 1860–1900," *Business and Economic History,* 2d series, 19 (1990): 203–22.

11. Sayles also appears as plaintiff in patent litigation against the Chicago, Burlington, and Quincy Railroad (case 12,416), the Dubuque and Sioux City Railroad Company (case 12,417), the Erie Railway Company (case 12,418), the Grand Trunk Railway Company (case 12,419), the

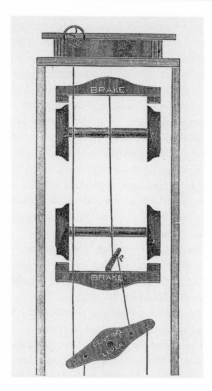

Fig. 2C.1   The Tanner double-acting brake
Source: Chicago and Northwestern Railway Company v. Thomas Sayles, 97 U.S. 554, 1053.

least one other patent case that was totally unrelated to railroads and braking systems.[12]

At issue in *Chicago and Northwestern Railway Company V. Thomas Sayles* was a patent covering so-called double-acting brakes. These operated simultaneously on a pair of wheels in the trucks at each end of a railroad car and, by an ingenious arrangement of pivots, arms, and operating rods, were equally efficient in braking regardless of the direction of travel (see figs. 2C.1 and 2C.2).

A number of patents were issued by the Patent Office covering these devices, the first in November 1848 to Charles Turner, another in October 1849 to Nehemiah Hodge, a third to Francis Stevens in November 1851, while the patent under which suit was filed was not granted until July 1852. Although the latter patent was the last of the series to be granted, it claimed primacy as a correction

---

Oregon Central Railway Company (case 12,423), the Richmond, Fredericksburg, and Potomac Railroad Company (case 12,424), and the South Carolina Railroad Company (case 12,425). See 21 *Fed. Cas.* 597–617.

12. See *Sayles v. Hapgood et al.,* case 12,420, 21 *Fed. Cas.* 605.

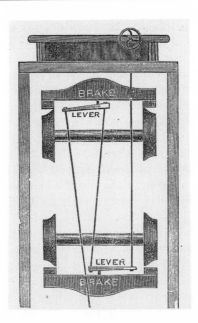

Fig. 2C.2   The Stevens double-acting brake
Source: Chicago and Northwestern Railway Company v. Thomas Sayles, 97 U.S. 554, 1054.

of an earlier, rejected patent originally filed in June 1847 by Lafayette Thompson and Asahel Bachelder. Some issues at stake in the case were additions and modifications to the patent between the date of initial filing and acceptance.

The case on appeal was one of several filed beginning in the early 1860s against individual railroads claiming for patent infringement. Specifically, Henry Tanner, assignee of the Thompson-Bachelder patent, alleged that Chicago and Northwestern Railway had infringed upon his patent rights from 1 June 1859 by their use of this device without payment, while the railroad defended itself on grounds of prior invention and preexisting use and by denying that their double-acting braking system infringed on the Tanner patent.

The circuit court had found for the plaintiff and after various legal wrangles and maneuverings had awarded damages in the amount of $63,638.40 "being $41,280 for savings in wages of brakemen, and $22,358.40 for savings in car wheels" (97 U.S. 554, 1054).

The illustrations incorporated into the Supreme Court decision (figs. 2C.1 and 2C.2) demonstrate part of the problem facing railroads: it is hard to distinguish fundamentally different principles between these two patented braking devices, thus making it impossible to determine to whom payment should be made unless the brakes that one was using corresponded exactly with one of these descriptions.

In rendering the Supreme Court's decision, Justice Bradley touched on the question of novelty, declaring "[l]ike almost all other inventions . . . [it] came when, in the progress of mechanical improvement, it was needed; and being sought by many minds, it is not wonderful that it was developed in different and independent forms, all original, and yet all bearing a somewhat general resemblance to each other. In such cases, if one inventor precedes all the rest, and strikes out something which includes and underlies all that they produce, he acquires a monopoly, and subjects them to tribute. But if the advance toward the thing desired is gradual, and proceeds step by step, so that no one can claim the complete whole, then each is entitled only to the specific form of device which he produces." On the question of primacy, Justice Bradley noted that "in 1847, when Thompson and Bachelder filed their application . . . and in 1846, when it is said that they completed their invention, double brakes were already in existence, formed as theirs was . . . in 1842 or 1843." If so, these fell well outside the two-year window of opportunity attending first public use prior to patent application, even though none of these earlier examples was available for examination. Lastly, the justices addressed the issue of overlap between the Stevens brake (fig. 2C.2) and the Tanner brake (fig. 2C.1), finding that the central feature of the Tanner brake—the central lever—had no analog in the Stevens brake, ruling therefore that it was "essentially different" and that "the two are to be regarded as independent inventions, each being limited and confined to the particular contrivance which constitutes its peculiarity." As a result the circuit court decision was vacated, but only after some sixteen-plus years of litigation. Little wonder, railroads wanted to find a different answer to their patent problem.

That solution, according to Usselman, lay in the establishment of patent pools that would eliminate the "divide and conquer" strategy for the outside inventor while strengthening the railroads' hand by pooling information about prior experiments that might usurp outsider claims to primacy and novelty in their inventions. The New England railroads were the first to organize, agreeing upon a common defense against a patent infringement suit in 1866. The following year, many of the nation's railroads joined either the Eastern Railroad Association or the Western Railroad Association, agreeing to pool information regarding their own experimentation and a common defense against patent infringement suits. These patent pools predate the collusive pools that the railroads eventually established to allocate market shares or eliminate price competition and price volatility.[13] Missing from Usselman's discussion is any evidence regarding their success, particularly the extent to which the pooled notes of insider experiments were used successfully to challenge the primacy and novelty of an outside invention.

The impetus behind the organization of patent pools came, according to

13. There was at least one earlier trade organization, the National Railway Convention, but this does not seem to have had patents or the adoption of standards as its principal concern. See Colleen A. Dunlavy, "Organizing Railroad Interests: The Creation of National Railroad Associations in the United States and Prussia," *Business and Economic History*, series 2, 19 (1990): 133–42.

Usselman, from the adoption by the courts of a new measure of the losses to inventors from patent infringement known as the doctrine of savings, which favored inventors over innovators. The problem with this interpretation, however, is one of timing (whether with the Tanner brake case or others, which assessed damages for patent infringement). The timing is tight to rest the *entire* argument on a new, untested legal ruling. The initial decision in the Tanner case in favor of the plaintiff was rendered in February 1865. The first railroad patent pool was established the following year. The Tanner case was subsequently reopened on the basis of new evidence (uncovered, perhaps, as a result of information pooling, although the Supreme Court record does not say when or precisely why) and the original decision was reaffirmed in 1871, only to be set aside by the Supreme Court in 1878. The basis of the damage calculation in the Tanner case was, however, substantially modified in December 1871 to the disadvantage of patentees in *Mowry v. Whitney* (14 Wallace 620), in which the plaintiffs had originally been awarded the *entire* profits from the manufacture and sale of annealed railroad wheels. On appeal the Supreme Court ruled that the plaintiff was "not entitled to receive more than the profits actually made in consequence of the use of [his] process" and directed that "what advantage did the defendant derive from using the complainant's invention over what he had in using other processes then open to the public . . . are his profits. They are all the benefits he derived."[14] The railroad patent pools, however, endured much longer than the legal rulings that allegedly stimulated their creation.

If adverse court decisions were not the sole or even the dominant source of the drive to organize patent pools, what was? My answer is a simple one: the creation of railroad patent pools slowed the pace of technical change from both within and without. For outside inventors, the pooling of information among the railroads reduced the expected return from invention by lowering the likelihood of novelty and by diminishing the probability of adoption by any subset of railroads. On the inside, collusion stilled the winds of "creative destruction" that jeopardized the value of existing investment. This is what abstract theory suggests.[15] It is what the casual evidence suggests. But it is not what Usselman concludes and that, I think, is cause for a second look.

14. Ibid., 649, 651.
15. Partha Dasgupta and Joseph Stiglitz, "Uncertainty, Market Structure, and the Speed of R&D," *Bell Journal of Economics* 11 (1980): 1–28.

3   The Sugar Institute Learns to Organize Information Exchange

David Genesove and Wallace P. Mullin

3.1   Introduction

One of the central tasks of a trade association is to facilitate the exchange of information among firms. Such information may involve production and sale data, or more direct information on demand conditions. Although this function has attracted some attention in the economic literature, the models treat the trade association as a "black box" that neutrally transmits verifiable information that has been submitted by the firms. In practice, a workable information-exchange agreement involves critical, concrete choices of institutional design. We consider the difficulties involved in constructing and carrying out such agreements by examining the case of the Sugar Institute, the trade association of U.S. cane sugar refiners from 1928 to 1936.

A trade association is a peculiar type of "governance structure," to use Oliver Williamson's phrase, that lies on the border between the market and the firm. While member firms cooperate in certain dimensions, they retain independence over both pricing and production decisions and internal information and accounting systems. This division of authority inevitably gives rise to a conflict between the *collective* interest of firms to share information and the *individual* interest of each firm to withhold it. For example, if firms are colluding on

David Genesove is associate professor of economics at the Massachusetts Institute of Technology and a faculty research fellow of the National Bureau of Economic Research. Wallace P. Mullin is assistant professor of economics at Michigan State University and a faculty research fellow of the National Bureau of Economic Research.

Mullin's research was supported by an MSU AURIG grant, which is gratefully acknowledged. David Burnstein provided excellent research assistance. The authors thank Ken Boyer, Margaret Levenstein, Naomi Lamoreaux, Dan Raff, Peter Temin, seminar participants at Michigan State University and the University of Michigan, and participants in the NBER preconference and conference for helpful comments. Special thanks are due to Carl Van Ness, archivist at the University of Florida, Gainesville, for his assistance in using the Braga Brothers collection. The authors also thank Fred Romanski and Gregory Plunges of the National Archives and Records Administration.

prices, then there is a collective interest in having information available to monitor and maintain collusion. But it remains in the individual firm's interest to undercut the collusive price and cheat if it can do so undetected. This tension animated the Sugar Institute in both its design and implementation, and, shortly after its formation, threatened to render impotent if not destroy the institute. Nevertheless, the members of the institute, operating through its established framework, were gradually able to exchange information cooperatively and to modify, with mixed success, industry practices.

The organization and operation of a trade association therefore involves incentive problems that are muted if not absent when information is internal to the firm.[1] First, firms must be induced to join. If nonparticipation is too attractive, the association will unravel. Second, member firms must give truthful reports of their information. A firm could violate the information-sharing agreement either by nonreporting (failing to file a report), or misreporting (filing a false report). Lacking the coercive powers of a firm over its divisions, a trade association must find other ways to induce the desired behavior of its constituent firms. Finally, the association must protect the confidentiality of any reported information not intended to be shared. These incentive problems are difficult enough when firms are identical; they become more severe when firms are heterogeneous, because that sharpens the divergence between the firms' collective and individual interests.

The Sugar Institute was organized in a period of decreased demand for sugar and substantial excess refining capacity. Similar circumstances fifty years earlier had led to the consolidation of the industry, an option foreclosed in the intervening years by the emergence of antitrust policy. Instead, the refiners chose to form a trade association, a type of industrial cooperation then in its heyday. As a substitute for a merger, a trade association is clearly inferior. Indeed, throughout the life of the institute there were continual, though vague and ineffectual, calls for real consolidations among the refiners to produce a tighter oligopoly. Nevertheless, the institute did succeed in raising price, and within a year had doubled the Lerner price index. But it soon ran afoul of the antitrust laws. The Department of Justice filed suit in March 1931. The District Court for the Southern District of New York ruled against the Sugar Institute in 1934, and the Supreme Court concurred in 1936.[2]

Information exchange served two roles for the Sugar Institute. The institute's primary objective was collusion, and information exchange helped enforce the institute's rules. The Sugar Institute never fixed prices or set either production quotas or market shares. Its methods were more indirect. Through its Code of

---

1. There are of course important incentive problems in managing information inside firms. For example, if the performance of a division will affect the compensation of its managers, then the general office may face problems in eliciting indications of poor performance. But the general office still retains greater authority over information systems and greater auditing ability than a trade association would possess over member firms.

2. *United States v. Sugar Institute,* 15 Fed. Sup. 817 (1934), 297 U.S. 553 (1936).

Ethics, it promulgated and enforced rules of trade whose purpose was to make price cuts more transparent, and so detectable, as we discuss in a companion paper (Genesove and Mullin 1997a). First among those rules was "open pricing"—the requirement that firms offer no secret price discounts. Other rules standardized contractual terms.

Some means of ensuring adherence to these rules was needed. The direct monitoring of compliance through private investigation and auditing downstream firms' records and refiners' stocks was one route taken. Another was information exchange. For example, refiners submitted production and delivery figures, and, for a time, sales figures, which the institute staff aggregated. A firm could use these aggregate figures to monitor its share of industry demand, and so infer secret price cutting if its market share fell.

But information exchange was also an end in itself. Several refiners testified at trial that the prospects of obtaining credible industry statistical information played an important role in their decision to join the institute, and the private correspondence of the vice president of one firm shows his use of institute data to benchmark his own firm's performance. The institute undertook other collective actions, such as an industry-wide advertising campaign, and standardization of sugar grades. However, such activities were secondary, and when the Supreme Court ruled against the Sugar Institute's primary actions, its members chose to dissolve it.

The broader historical context for the Sugar Institute is found in the changing political and legal environment of the 1920s and 1930s, which saw the rise and fall of trade associations, information-exchange agreements, and "open price associations." With an initial impetus provided by Arthur Jerome Eddy's 1912 book *The New Competition,* 150 open price associations were operating by 1921.[3]

From 1921 to 1928 Secretary of Commerce Herbert Hoover played a pivotal role in promoting a variety of cooperative, associational activities, including industry trade associations. As documented by Hawley (1974, 1981), Hoover promoted trade associations both directly, through the Department of Commerce's expanded jurisdiction, and indirectly, by influencing and persuading other government entities to look favorably upon such organizations.

The greatest threat to these trade associations was posed by antitrust law. Two Supreme Court decisions in 1921 and 1923 outlawed the information-exchange activities of the hardwood-lumber and linseed-oil industries, and this threatened to curtail significantly the number and activities of trade associations.[4] In *American Column and Lumber Co.,* the Supreme Court found illegal an information-exchange agreement in which members were required to submit weekly the details of individual sale transactions, including the price and

---

3. Federal Trade Commission Survey, cited in Whitney 1935, 40.
4. *American Column and Lumber Co. et al. v. United States,* 257 U.S. 377 (1921); *United States v. American Linseed Oil Co. et al.,* 262 U.S. 371 (1923).

buyer for each sale, which the trade association then reported in full to all its members.

In 1922 the Commerce Department countered this ruling by substituting its own activities for those outlawed for trade associations. It collected more data about individual industries than before, and for a period essentially acted as a clearinghouse for data provided by private trade associations. Since under both sets of arrangements the statistics were at least nominally collected by Commerce, compliant firms could not be prosecuted for an antitrust violation. Hoover also tried to convince the Department of Justice to accept the legality of trade associations that engaged solely in the exchange of statistics. Attorney General Harry M. Daugherty was resistant to this suggestion, but his departure in 1924 paved the way for successors more sympathetic to Hoover's viewpoint (Hawley 1974, 126, 136; Galambos 1966, 93).

Moreover, the Supreme Court soon adopted a friendlier attitude. The *Maple Flooring* and *Cement Manufacturers* cases of June 1925, while not directly overturning *American Column and Lumber Co.,* did significantly narrow the scope of that earlier case's prohibitions.[5] There were some important differences of fact that distinguished these latter cases from the earlier precedent. In *Maple Flooring,* for example, individual members' reports to the trade association on quantity sold, production costs, past prices received, and inventory were first summarized or masked before being distributed to other members. Also, the summary statistics were disseminated to the trade generally, and were not limited to the members, as in the earlier case. But the Supreme Court's more favorable treatment certainly reflected a changed economic and political sentiment. The Court itself acknowledged in *Maple Flooring,* "It is the consensus of opinion of economists and many of the most important agencies of Government that the public interest is served by the gathering and dissemination, in the widest possible manner, of information with respect to the production and distribution, cost and prices in actual sales, of market commodities, because the making available of such information tends to stabilize trade and industry, to produce fairer price levels and to avoid waste which inevitably attends the unintelligent conduct of economic enterprise" (582–83).

So by the time the U.S. cane sugar refiners met in 1927 to establish their trade association, they had reason to expect a generally friendly reception from the legal authorities.

Our study of the Sugar Institute complements other contributions to this conference volume. We conceive of three objects of firm learning: technology, production techniques, and organizations and incentives. Usselman (chap. 2) and Lamoreaux and Sokoloff (chap. 1) have examined learning about both technique and technology. Mishina (chap. 4) documents how knowledge about a production process was created and implemented. In contrast, we study a technologically stagnant industry. The sugar refining industry did not introduce

---

5. *Maple Flooring Manufacturers' Association et al. v. United States,* 268 U.S. 563 (1925); *Cement Manufacturers' Protective Association et al. v. United States,* 268 U.S. 588 (1925).

new production technologies in the decades surrounding the formation of the Sugar Trust.[6] Sugar-industry members did learn during the period of the Sugar Institute, but it was learning about extrafirm organizational design and the management of incentives. Organizational innovation and its application is as noteworthy as the introduction of new technologies and techniques. Charles and Frank Duryea built and operated the first automobile in the United States, Henry Ford introduced mass production, but it is Alfred Sloan whom Chandler (1962) and Williamson (1975) celebrate for successfully addressing General Motors' incentive problems through the multidivisional or M-form organizational design.

Much of our information about the internal workings of the Sugar Institute comes from the papers of Louis V. Placé, Jr., vice president of McCahan Sugar Refining, and that firm's representative as a director of the Sugar Institute. He prepared notes on meetings of the Sugar Institute's Executive Committee, board of directors, and Enforcement Committee, and these notes are available from January 1929 to July 1930.[7] They were prepared to circulate only within a circle of about six McCahan executives, so they represent a fairly candid account of the institute's motivations and activities. Placé offered strong views to his McCahan colleagues as to how the institute should operate, so he was far from a disinterested observer. We also have some correspondence to and from Placé.[8] We also use testimony from the trial record.

We highlight our findings as we foreshadow the organization of this paper. In section 3.2 we discuss more fully the incentive issues involved in organizing and maintaining a trade association. Section 3.3 addresses the Sugar Institute's formation and early development.

Section 3.4 is the core of this chapter. It discusses how the institute learned and evolved as it attempted to effect firm information exchange. The organizational design of the Sugar Institute was fairly decentralized yet created a structure for collective decision making. There were disagreements among the firms over what information should be shared. Production and delivery statistics

6. A 1945 sugar handbook's list of the apparatus used in cane sugar manufacturing contains nothing introduced beyond the nineteenth century (Spencer and Meade 1945, 72), and Yano (1982, 54) states, "It is generally agreed that the basic technologies in sugar refining were evolved in the late 19th century and no major innovations have occurred since then." Most telling is that the amount of raw sugar (whose standard grade was 96 percent pure sugar, or sucrose, and 4 percent water and impurities) required to produce 100 pounds of refined sugar (which is 100 percent sucrose) remained unchanged for decades. Because there is some loss of sucrose in the refining process, 100 pounds of raw sugar will produce less than 96 pounds of refined sugar. To produce 100 pounds of refined sugar took between 107 and 107.5 pounds of raw at the turn of the century (U.S. Industrial Commission 1900, vol. 1, part 2), 107 pounds of raw in the Sugar Institute period (U.S. Tariff Commission 1934, 109), and still 107 pounds by 1971 (Robert R. Nathan Associates 1971, 5).

7. The bibliographic citation is Placé, W. J. McCahan Sugar Refining and Molasses Company, box 11, Sugar Institute, memoranda and notes of meetings. We will cite these records herein as Placé Memoranda. A few stray memoranda up through June 1931 are also included.

8. The bibliographic citation is Placé Records, W. J. McCahan Sugar Refining and Molasses Company, box 1, M. E. Rionda Correspondence, boxes 2–3, General Correspondence. We will cite these records herein as Placé Correspondence.

were circulated with minimal difficulty, but sales statistics were shared for only a short period. The largest firms were the least willing to share information, particularly sales information. Heterogeneity among firms, of which the two salient characteristics were size and location, also played a critical role in determining membership in the institute. Some divergent interests were reconciled within the structure of the institute, while others remained outside.

Section 3.5 compares the institute to the sugar refiners' proposed code under the Agricultural Adjustment Act of 1933. Comparing the two codes reveals what lessons about organizing information exchange the industry assimilated. Section 3.6 concludes by showing how one firm used the information provided by the institute, and evaluates the overall success of the institute.

3.2 Incentive Issues in Information-Exchange Agreements

Collusive agreements are constantly in danger of being undermined by secret price cuts. Since a collusive agreement results in a price above marginal cost, participant firms have an individual incentive to undercut this price slightly and receive a larger share of industry demand and profits. A firm cheating on the collusive arrangement in this way will want to do so secretly in order to avoid retaliation from other producers.[9] Anything that makes detection of a secret price cut more likely therefore serves to enhance collusion. The Sugar Institute's Code of Ethics had as its first requirement that "sugar should be sold only upon open prices and terms publicly announced." Adherence to this requirement and the truthful provision of prices and production levels would clearly make cheating more evident.

Although we find this collusion explanation for the Sugar Institute the most compelling, we do not dismiss the possibility that efficiency concerns may have also played a role in the institute's information exchange. A number of theoretical papers have shown that there are nonstrategic incentives for firms to agree to information exchange. If each firm receives only a noisy signal of aggregate market demand, then exchanging signals will result in a more precise signal for all participants, allowing them to make better-informed production and inventory decisions, thereby reducing expected production costs. Information sharing also increases the correlation of firm strategies, precisely because this allows firms to base their decisions on commonly shared information. The combination of these effects can be both privately and socially beneficial as illustrated by Kirby (1988).

The collusion and efficiency explanations should not be viewed as mutually exclusive, however. It is possible that the exchange of production information both supported collusion and generated more precise demand information and hence more efficient planning by firms. Also, the promise of information exchange may have induced firms to join the collusive undertaking who would

9. This idea was first expressed by Stigler (1964). Its most successful formalization is Green and Porter's (1984).

have otherwise free ridden on it. In any case, ascertaining the ultimate aims of the Sugar Institute is not our primary focus here, since the problems of institutional design and evolution are present regardless of the ultimate aim.

A potentially very serious problem is that parties to an information-exchange agreement, whatever its purpose, may wish to misreport their price or production information. That is obviously true when the goal is to prevent price cutting, but it is also true if the parties are brought together by other goals. In the language of mechanism design, the trade association faces a problem of "incentive compatibility." More colloquially, it is a problem of "truth telling"—will firms be willing to report their true information, given the auditing and sanctioning technology at the disposal of the trade association?

There are two ways in which a firm might violate an information-sharing arrangement. First, it might simply refuse to report its information. Enforcement against this violation requires some sanction for nonreporting. Second, the firm might misreport its information. Enforcement against this requires not only sanction but also detection of the violation, creating a need for auditing or monitoring of firm activity and/or records.

Surprisingly, and with the exception of reports on undelivered contracts, which we discuss later, there is no indication of misreporting of *statistics* by institute members. There are several reasons why firms might not misreport. Individuals may be averse to lying for ethical or moral reasons, and thus make a distinction between the refusal to file a report and falsifying one. Also, it may be important for individuals and firms to develop a reputation for truth telling, both in their dealings inside the institute and outside it. Of course, this reputation is jeopardized only if there's a chance that the truth will out. But that was a risk in this environment, since there were other sources of information, such as brokers, customers, and the observations of purchases of raw sugar, the key input. These other sources did not enable outsiders to observe the firm's private information perfectly, but they may have allowed a sufficiently accurate assessment to deter lying. The possibility of an ex post audit by the institute (although none was ever conducted) would have a been a further deterrent. In sum, it may be too difficult to construct a credible, systematic lie, since a variety of bits of information, both internal and external to the firm, have to be made consistent with any false report.

Another enforcement problem is how to exclude nonparticipants or violators from receiving the shared information. If all participants in the agreement receive the same information from the institute, then there may be an incentive for a nonparticipant to purchase the information from a cooperative participant. This in turn would affect the incentives for participation, and in the extreme case the entire agreement would unravel. Vives (1990) addresses this issue in a setting in which no single firm is large enough to influence aggregate market outcomes, an assumption not matched in the sugar refining industry. Nevertheless his results are instructive. Under an exclusionary disclosure rule, in which only members receive shared information, information sharing is an equilibrium, provided that the costs of joining the trade association are not too high. Under a nonexclusionary disclosure, in which the information is made available to nonmembers and the public as well, the free-rider problem prevents information sharing from being an equilibrium.

A more subtle issue is how to ensure credibly the *non*sharing of information. The Sugar Institute aggregated the individual member statistical reports before distributing that aggregate information to the members and/or the trade. The central office of the Sugar Institute was more than a simple adding machine, since it had to assure members that their individual reports would not be shared with anyone else. A firm might be willing to submit its information to a central organization yet not want to share that individual information with its competitors. Failure to preserve the confidentiality of this private information could destroy the information-exchange agreement. Paradoxically, tight controls on the sharing of information could create more equilibrium sharing of information.[10]

3.3   Formation of the Sugar Institute

3.3.1   Environment and Origins

The U.S. cane sugar refiners faced serious difficulties in 1927. The combination of the revival of European beet sugar production after the war, worldwide government subsidization of beet production, and a new "slimness craze" had left the industry with substantial excess capacity. Although the industry was still relatively concentrated, with the three largest firms responsible for almost 60 percent of production, this was a far cry from the prewar years, in which a single firm had dominated the production of this homogeneous good. The result was fierce competition by way of secret price cuts and other concessions to selected customers, and so falling profit margins.

To a sugar man with a long enough memory, these conditions must have recalled the situation in the 1880s, when excess capacity was even greater and price wars prevailed. Then the solution was a grand merger of firms. This first took the form of the Sugar Trust, a combination of eighteen independent firms representing 80 percent of industry capacity. When in 1891 that form was no longer legally available, the Sugar Trust became the American Sugar Refining Company (ASRC).

---

10. The models of information sharing suggest that the crucial issue is the nature of the private information. Information could be private-valued (like the idiosyncratic costs of an individual firm), common-valued (like an individual-firm signal of industry demand), or some combination of the two. If information is completely common-valued, no firm would be willing to pay for the report of any individual firm, nor would any individual firm care about such a disclosure. With common-valued information, the aggregate report contains the only useful information; the aggregate statistic is a sufficient statistic. In the presence of private-valued information, however, there could be concerns about unauthorized disclosure.

Creane (1998) categorizes the previous literature on information sharing and advances a framework for establishing more general results.

Consolidation was the industry's continual response to similar problems throughout its early history. Over the next twenty years or so, ASRC's strategy for dealing with entry was to acquire entrants, at times after a fierce price war. The long-run success of that strategy is subject to dispute—contrast Zerbe's Chicago school skepticism (1969) of its viability with Eichner's account (1969), or consult Genesove and Mullin (1997b) for an intermediate viewpoint—but the repeated attempts to repeat the success of 1887 are evident.

In part because the buyout attempts were not completely successful, in part because of the loss of ASRC's founder, Henry Havemeyer, in 1907, and in part due to restrictions imposed by the Department of Justice's 1910 monopolization suit, ASRC shrank in size. Its market share had peaked at 91 percent in 1892, and it declined to 43 percent in 1914 (*Weekly Statistical Sugar Trade Journal*). The impact of this decline on competition, however, was masked by the government controls implemented for the war and the immediate postwar period.

By 1927 there were fifteen firms in the industry. Most were located along the Atlantic seaboard, especially between Boston and Baltimore, and refined Cuban raw (cane) sugar, although there were a few small refiners in Louisiana and Texas that refined domestic cane, and two large ones on the West Coast that refined Hawaiian raw sugar. ASRC was still the largest firm, but with only a 25 percent market share (and a quarter ownership of the next largest firm, National). As table 3.1 shows, ASRC and National were the only multiplant firms, and ASRC the only one to have plants in more than one city. The cane sugar refining industry accounted for 82.5 percent of U.S. sugar consumption. Domestic beet sugar production, concentrated in the Midwest and California, was responsible for most of the remainder (14.4 percent). A small quantity of sugar was refined "offshore," in the cane-producing islands, and imported into the United States (2.8 percent).[11]

The solution of 1887 was unavailable in 1927. The interpretation and enforcement of the Sherman Act, and its particular application to the sugar industry in the 1910 monopolization suit, had seen to that. Instead, the refiners formed a trade association, the Sugar Institute. Although preliminary discussions about forming a sugar trade association had taken place as early as 1925, significant progress was not made until a June 1927 conferral between the attorney Wilbur Cummings and the presidents of five refineries—Foster of ASRC, Lowry of Pennsylvania Sugar, Post of National, Rionda of McCahan, and Spreckels of Federal Sugar.[12] After a second meeting, Cummings con-

11. The figures are from United States Temporary National Economic Committee 1941, 112.

12. Transcript of Record, *The Sugar Institute, Inc., v. the United States,* Supreme Court of the United States, October term, 1935, 2:603–4. Although this document was prepared for the appeal to the Supreme Court, it is the transcript of the district court record. This is a condensed version of the verbatim testimony from the district court trial. Such narrative statements of evidence are produced by turning a series of questions and answers into a statement by the witness. The Transcript of Record documents can be found in the National Archives as part of the *district court* record: *United States v. Sugar Institute,* box 504274A, henceforth cited as District Court Record.

Table 3.1   U.S. Cane Sugar Refiners

Firm	Market Share in 1927	Location of Plant(s)
American Sugar Refining Co.	25.06	5 plants: Boston, New York, Philadelphia, Baltimore, New Orleans
National Sugar Refining Co.	22.07	3 plants: New York City area
California & Hawaiian	10.84	Crockett, CA
Pennsylvania Sugar Co.	6.73	Philadelphia
Arbuckle Brothers	5.80	Brooklyn, NY
Western Sugar Refinery	4.46	San Francisco
Godchaux Sugars, Inc.	4.02	Reserve, LA
W. J. McCahan Sugar Refining & Molasses Co.	3.60	Philadelphia
Savannah Sugar Refining Corp.	3.26	Savannah
Revere Sugar Refinery	3.20	Charlestown, MA
Imperial Sugar Co.	3.00	Sugar Lands, TX
Federal Sugar Refining (Spreckels Sugar) Co.[a]	2.66	Yonkers, NY
Colonial Sugars Co.	2.33	Gramercy, LA
Texas Sugar Refining Corp.	1.84	Texas City, TX
William Henderson	1.13	New Orleans

Sources: United States Temporary National Economic Committee 1941, 112. Plant locations from Palmer 1927, C-33.

[a]Federal Sugar Refining entered receivership and was reorganized as the Spreckels Sugar Company in 1929. The Spreckels company was liquidated in 1930.

ferred with officials of Secretary Hoover's Commerce Department, the Department of Justice, and the Federal Trade Commission (FTC) about the proposed trade association and its activities. By then, the political and legal environment had become conducive to the formation of trade associations and industry codes of ethics. William Donovan, who had become the head of the Antitrust Division of the Department of Justice, was willing to guide firms seeking to form trade associations that would remain within the law (Hawley 1974, 136). Donovan indicated that he had no objection to the proposed association, although he warned that such a statement did not foreclose the possibility of future prosecution. With this tentative approval in place, the five organizing refiners or "Institute Founders" suggested that Cummings write each of the other U.S. cane sugar refiners, outlining a proposed sugar trade association and inviting them to comment on the proposal and to participate in the organization of this association.[13]

This invitation, in turn, led to a meeting of all the U.S. cane sugar refiners in New York City over 12–16 December 1927. Although a representative from the firm California and Hawaiian (C&H) attended this meeting, that firm had

13. Transcript of Record, 2:606–8, District Court Record, box 504274A. Cummings's 2 September 1927 letter of invitation is in the correspondence files of Manuel Rionda y Polledo (Rionda y Polledo, Papers and Financial Records, subject file W. Cummings, 1921–43).

already indicated its intention to remain outside the association.[14] The result of this meeting was crystallized in a proposed industry Code of Ethics, which was slightly modified after a further consultation with the attorney general's office. The institute's bylaws and Code of Ethics were adopted at a meeting of member refiners 7 January 1928.[15] Of the fifteen U.S. cane sugar refiners, all but C&H joined in forming the institute.[16]

3.3.2   Goals and Structure

Although the industry Code of Ethics (see appendix) was detailed, its first and underlying principle was that "[a]ll discriminations between customers should be abolished," and open prices and publicly announced terms should therefore prevail. For example, the code prohibited quantity discounts to customers, so that a large customer such as Kroger or Coca-Cola would have to pay the same price as a small local grocer. It directly forbade special allowances for customers via rebates or transportation charges.

The code also discouraged practices that, while not discriminatory on their face, created the opportunity for secret concessions. For example, the code required that brokers selling refined sugar not be affiliated with any warehouses that stored sugar, nor any buyer be affiliated with a public, commercial warehouse that stored sugar. Combining these activities in the hands of a single party gave too large a scope for discrimination between buyers, as a broker could give a price concession to a buyer by not charging for storage services rendered.

The institute attempted to limit sales contracts to thirty days as another mechanism to ensure contractual uniformity and thereby avoid discrimination. Refined sugar was sold, both before and after the institute, on a system of price "moves." Any price increase would become effective the day after it was announced, enabling customers to make purchases at the previous, lower price. Customers would not have to take delivery immediately, but could spread out withdrawals (deliveries) against these contracts over thirty or more days. For the thirty-day limit to be effective under the institute, refiners had to "enforce" their contracts, forcing customers to take delivery.

Information exchange was an express aim of the institute's articles of incorporation.[17] Moreover, testimony at trial suggests that the prospects of obtaining

14. Transcript of Record, 2:608, District Court Record, box 504274A.

15. Ibid., 611.

16. This counts Western Sugar Refinery as an original member, although that classification is uncertain. Frank Sullivan of Western testified that his company did not initially join the institute because of pending discussions about purchase of the Spreckels interests, including Western. When those discussions fell through, however, Western joined the institute in October 1928 (ibid., 882). However, Sullivan was reported as one of the fifteen original directors of the institute (*Weekly Statistical Sugar Trade Journal,* 12 January 1928, 31), perhaps because Western cooperated in submitting statistics and received statistical reports even before it joined the institute.

17. Certificate of incorporation of the Sugar Institute, Inc., in Answer of the Defendants, *United States of America, Petitioner, v. The Sugar Institute, et al., Defendants,* in the District Court of the United States for the Southern District of New York, filed 1 August 1931, 66–67.

credible industry information played an important role in the decision of some refiners to join the institute. The testimony of W. Edward Foster, president of ASRC and one of the institute's organizers, is typical in this respect: "We . . . were rather cranks on the question of statistics. I could not see how any industry could operate successfully without knowing what was going on in the industry, because we were always moving around in the dark and we thoroughly believed that if the industry itself knew what was going on in the way of meltings [production] and deliveries, and had some knowledge of stocks, that we would have guiding posts which would enable us to better carry on our business.[18]

The macroeconomic environment, foremost the Great Depression, makes no appearance in the primary sources' discussions of the institute's formation and operation. This is in part because these sources relate to the early years of the Sugar Institute, that is, the two years before the stock market crash and the early, least severe, years of the Depression itself. But, in part, this is also due to the relatively good performance of the sugar refining industry in the early stages of the Depression. Compared to total industrial production, which declined 24 percent from December 1929 to December 1930 (Romer 1990), U.S. sugar consumption in 1930 declined by only 3.6 percent from the previous year.[19] Such relative stability is consistent with Romer's finding (1990) that the onset of the Great Depression was associated with much sharper cutbacks in purchases of durables than of nondurables, seasonally adjusted sales of which actually rose in the last months of 1929 before decreasing only slightly in early 1930. Sugar is a staple good and, although storable, in purchase decisions is more like a perishable good. As the macroeconomy continued to tumble over the next several years, sugar consumption was affected, but less than industrial production as a whole. The *Weekly Statistical Sugar Trade Journal* (4 January 1932, 18) remarked that U.S. sugar consumption in 1931 "held up remarkably well," with a decrease from 1930 of only 2 percent. Consumption fell a further 5 percent in 1932, but leveled off in 1933–35.[20] The sugar *refining* firms were somewhat sheltered from the full effects of the Depression because contemporaneous economic and political developments brought low prices for raw sugar, the chief cost component in refined sugar.[21]

Any effect of the Great Depression was probably to strengthen the incentives of firms to cooperate within the Sugar Institute. First, the reduction of industry demand, and with it the exacerbation of conditions of excess capacity, made

18. Testimony of W. Edward Foster, R. 9206, quoted in Brief for the Defendants on the Facts, 20, District Court Record, box 504270A.

19. *Weekly Statistical Sugar Trade Journal,* 15 January 1931, 18, 9 January 1930, 18.

20. *Weekly Statistical Sugar Trade Journal,* 11 January 1934, 18. Consumption increased 1 percent in 1933 over 1932, fell 2.6 percent in 1934, and rose 4 percent in 1935.

21. World raw sugar production continued to rise in the 1930s, even as raw sugar prices reached record lows (Albert and Graves 1988, introduction).

competition less profitable and hence cooperation and collusion a more attractive alternative. Financial difficulties pushed two of the smaller refiners into receivership, Spreckels in 1930 and Texas Sugar in 1931. Second, information sharing may have had particular value in the new, more uncertain environment brought on by the Great Depression. The Depression brought about not only reduced economic activity, but also greater firm and consumer *uncertainty*. Thus the knowledge refiners had accumulated from their years of business experience had become partially obsolete. As a result, the gain from sharing demand information with competitors was heightened.

Turning from goals to initial structure, the Sugar Institute was organized as a membership corporation, that is, a corporation composed of and owned by member firms. The structural details of this organization illustrate the very decentralized nature of the institute. Each member firm was represented on the institute's board of directors by one, and later two, directors, and institute counsel Wilbur Cummings served as an additional director.[22] The board of directors was authorized to elect a subset of directors to serve as an executive committee, which operated the day-to-day business affairs of the institute. Geographic proximity to New York City, where the Sugar Institute was located, of course favored the East Coast firms. Major decisions were reserved to the board.[23]

Firms could be elected members of the Sugar Institute by a majority vote of the directors present, along with the payment of an initiation fee of $500. Members could be expelled for nonpayment of dues or assessments by a majority vote of the directors present. Moreover, members could be expelled "for any conduct which, in the opinion of the Board of Directors, is prejudicial to the purposes, principles or interests of the corporation or for any other cause deemed sufficient by the Board" (By-Laws, 74–75). But expulsion was an unlikely punishment as it required a vote of at least *two-thirds* of directors present "at a meeting of the Board duly called and held for the purpose of taking such action" (75). So the institute itself had little punitive power.

The board of directors was authorized to appoint a statistics committee to "submit to the Board of Directors a detailed plan of reports to be made by the members to the [Sugar Institute]" (By-Laws, 81). Upon approval of the board, this plan was to be submitted for approval by the members, adoption or any modification requiring a four-fifths vote. At the December 1927 meeting it was initially suggested that members be required to submit any reports that the

22. The number of directors was increased to twenty-eight by a vote at the annual meeting of members on 17 January 1929 (Answer of the Defendants, 79). Placé's memo on the 14 March 1929 meeting of the board refers to the election of "additional Directors from each of the members." Also, the election for the board in 1930 brought each of the then fifteen members two representatives (*Weekly Statistical Sugar Trade Journal*, 23 January 1930, 55).

23. The bylaws stipulated that the "Executive Committee shall not be empowered to elect or expel members, to amend these By-Laws or to change the Code of Ethics" (By-Laws of the Sugar Institute, Inc., in Answer of the Defendants, 79).

institute or the Statistics Committee demanded of them. But Arbuckle Brothers refused,[24] and the agreed-upon rule became that "no plan requiring reports from members shall be binding upon any member without it shall have been approved by such member" (81).

As this example illustrates, the institute's institutional design was both cause and consequence of the institute's problems in attaining its professed goals. Many of the provisions that weakened the institute were deliberately incorporated into the original design. That, in turn, reflected an unwillingness of (some) refiners to cede discretion to a central industry organization. It is this unwillingness, coupled with the structural weaknesses, that undermined the institute's efficacy.

3.3.3   An Initial Assessment

Despite these weaknesses, however, the industry did come to exchange information previously unavailable to the refiners. This included weekly total meltings (production), total stocks on hand, and total deliveries. In addition, information as to deliveries and stocks by state were distributed weekly and monthly. The institute's statistical services were a point of pride in the refiners' defense at trial, and the Defendants' Fact Brief devotes a section to it. These particular defense claims are supported both by the public record and the private accounts of Placé.

The refiners claimed that this information "collected by the Institute could not have been obtained by the trade *through any other source*."[25] This claim is somewhat exaggerated. Accurate raw sugar imports were available from the Customs House, and the premier trade publication of the period, the *Weekly Statistical Sugar Trade Journal* (see fig. 3.1), had been reporting them for years. However, although there were no uses for raw sugar other than refined sugar, at high frequencies these figures could be used only to guess the aggregate level of production given the variable length of time for which raw sugar was stored. The journal did report production at the regional level, but, again, at high frequencies the reported figures were in part estimates; the journal's publisher and chief statistician testified that he received reports from the refiners "[w]eekly, monthly, semi-annually or, at least, yearly." The journal also published figures on deliveries, although only Western and C&H actually reported theirs. The deliveries of the other refiners were estimated on the basis of their production and estimates of their refined sugar stocks.[26] The journal published no information on the location or level of consignment stocks, or state-level sales. Thus, trade statistics were available before the Sugar Institute, but they were inaccurate, especially at high frequencies and the farther downstream the stage of activity.

---

24. Testimony of Goetzinger, in Transcript of Record, 2:680, District Court Record, box 504274A.

25. Defendants' Fact Brief, 69, District Court Record, box 504274A.

26. Gardiner, in Transcript of Record, 1:362, 369, District Court Record.

49TH Year, No. 5.   (Copyright by WILLETT & GRAY, 1925)   FEBRUARY 5, 1925

WEEKLY STATISTICAL SUGAR TRADE JOURNAL
(REG. U. S. PAT. OFF.)

RECEIPTS, DELIVERIES and IMPORTERS' STOCK

	1925 Feb. 4	1924 Feb. 6	1923 Feb. 7	1922 Feb. 8
	Tons	Tons	Tons	Tons
Receipts—Past Week				
NEW YORK	37894	26856	34769	68488
BOSTON	9133	13023	8315	19771
PHILADELPHIA	12404	38352	23801	37506
BALTIMORE	7105	4611	3810	.....
TOTAL RECEIPTS	66536	82842	70695	125765
Total since February 1	23451	78368	49548	125765
Total since January 1	245273	242902	282430	381554
Balance Year	.....	2796202	2592934	3246394
Entire Year	.....	3039104	2875364	3627948

	Tons	Tons	Tons	Tons
Importers' Stock				
NEW YORK	6460	.....	.....	.....
BOSTON	.....	.....	.....	.....
PHILADELPHIA	.....	.....	.....	.....
BALTIMORE	.....	.....	.....	.....
TOTAL IMPORTERS' STOCK	6460	None	None	None

RAW SUGAR QUOTATIONS—At New York, duty paid

	1925	1924		
	Feb. 5	Feb. 7	Inc.	Dec.
Cuba Centrifugals—				
96 Degrees	4.590	7.280	....	2.690
Highest during year†	4.770	7.410	....	2.640
Lowest during year††	4.520	4.590	....	0.070
PRICES DURING WEEK	High 4.65c	Low 4.59c		

†Jan. 5, 1925   ††Feb. 13, 1924   ††Jan. 9, 1925   ††Dec. 27, 1924

REFINED SUGAR QUOTATIONS
Basis Fine Granulated—Barrels or 100 lb. Bags
Latest quotations received by us, subject to change without notice
Terms—Cash in 7 days, less 2 per cent.

REFINERY	F. O. B.	
American	New York	6.10c
National	New York	6.10c
Arbuckle	New York	6.00c
Federal	New York	6.00c
Warner	New York	6.10c
American	Boston	6.10c
Revere	Boston	6.00c
Franklin	Philadelphia	6.10c
E. Atkins & Co.	Philadelphia	6.10c
McCahan	Philadelphia	6.10c
American	Baltimore	6.10c
Savannah	Savannah, Ga.	6.10c
American	New Orleans, La.	6.10c
Colonial	New Orleans, La.	6.00c
Henderson	New Orleans, La.	6.00c
Godchaux	New Orleans, La.	6.00c
Imperial	Sugar Land, Texas	6.00c
Texas Sugar Ref. Co.	Texas City, Tex.	6.00c
C. & H. (Basis 100 lb. bags)	S. F. Cal. (Chicago 6.00c)	6.25c
Western	S. F. Cal. (Chicago 6.00c)	6.25c

GRANULATED.—Highest and Lowest Prices.—Quotations at New York for Cane Granulated Sugar, in cents per pound less 2% for cash. The below table shows the range of prices from the first of the year to date of publication for the current year, compared with similar prices for the whole of the preceding year.

1925		1924	
HIGHEST—Jan. 1 to date—Jan. 2.	6.75	Entire Year Feb. 11	8.90
LOWEST—Jan. 1 to date—Jan. 28	6.00	Entire Year June 5	6.35

All tons in this Sugar Journal are 2,240 pounds each

U. S. ATLANTIC PORTS SUMMARY to Feb. 4, 1925, in tons,
(including NEW YORK, BOSTON, PHILADELPHIA and BALTIMORE)
THE NEW ORLEANS AND OTHER PORTS STATISTICS GIVEN ELSEWHERE

	1925 Feb. 4	1924 Feb. 6	Inc.	Dec.
Receipts for week—				
From Cuba	53550	71698	.....	18148
Porto Rico	12986	11144	1842	.....
Other W. I. Islands	.....	.....	.....	.....
Brazil	.....	.....	.....	.....
Philippine Islands	.....	.....	.....	.....
St. Croix	.....	.....	.....	.....
Java	.....	.....	.....	.....
Hawaii	.....	.....	.....	.....
Other Foreign Countries.	.....	.....	.....	.....
Domestic	.....	.....	.....	.....
TOTAL TONS	66536	82842	.....	16306
Increased since last week	18250	.....	.....	.....
To Importers	.....	.....	.....	.....
To Refiners and Consumers	66536	82842	.....	16306
Receipts since January 1—				
From Cuba	220773	228035	.....	7262
Porto Rico	20824	11922	8902	.....
Other W. I. Islands	.....	.....	.....	.....
Brazil	.....	.....	.....	.....
Philippine Islands	3676	.....	3676	.....
St. Croix	.....	.....	.....	.....
Java	.....	.....	.....	.....
Hawaii	.....	.....	.....	.....
Other Foreign Countries.	.....	2945	.....	2945
Domestic	.....	.....	.....	.....
TOTAL TONS	245273	242902	2371	.....
To Trade included above	350	770	.....	420
Deliveries—				
For Week	67075	82842	.....	15767
Increased since last week	18789	.....	.....	.....
Since January 1	238813	243696	.....	4883
Meltings by Refiners—				
For week, partly estimated	51000	64000	.....	13000
Decreased since last week..	6850	.....	.....	.....
Since January 1	217650	200230	17420	.....
Receipts to Trade considered as Meltings—				
For Week	.....	.....	.....	.....
Since January 1	350	770	.....	420
Total Meltings—				
Refiners and Trade week	51000	64000	.....	13000
Since January 1	218000	201000	17000	.....
Exports since January 1—				
Of Refined	1700	2500	.....	800
Importers' Stock—				
This week	6460	None	6460	.....
Decreased since last week..	539	.....	.....	.....
At highest point	6999	71009	.....	64010
At lowest point	None	None	.....	.....
Refiners' Stock—				
New York	29307	19686	9621	.....
Boston	3843	12426	.....	8583
Philadelphia and Baltimore.	16090	36113	.....	20023
Increased since last week	16075	.....	.....	.....
Total Stock—				
Partly estimated	55700	68225	.....	12525
Increased since last week	15536	.....	.....	.....
In all hands on January 1..	28427	26323	2104	.....
At highest point in year*..	55700	249142	.....	193442
At lowest point in year**..	28427	· 15956	12471	.....

*February 4, 1925   ** January 1, 1925
· June 11, 1924   ** December 31, 1924

Consumption—U. S. through all ports, including all sugar, Foreign and Domestic; year 1924, 4,854,479 tons; year 1923, 4,780,684 tons.

Fig. 3.1   Trade-publication statistics before the Sugar Institute

The institute's provision of state-level data may have been of greatest value to the firms. Prior to the Sugar Institute, individual refiners knew little beyond their own figures about the consumption and distribution of sugar in specific portions of the country. Because each operated only in particular geographic markets, this information was much more important than national aggregates. Campiglia of C&H testified that "the distribution by States . . . gave us a comparison with distribution of former years by States, and it gave us the quantity of stock of raw sugars and refined sugars on hand; and permitted us to determine whether stocks were piling up and accumulating or moving out freely to the trade; and many things which we considered valuable to us." [27]

The institute achieved only temporary success in exchanging sales statistics. In light of the consensus to report meltings and deliveries, what additional information would sales statistics provide? Most sugar was sold on one of the price "moves." With the knowledge of a firm's meltings and deliveries in the aftermath of a move, one could eventually estimate its sales. However, recall that the reported weekly deliveries and meltings were aggregated before being distributed to institute members. In the aftermath of a price move, these figures would help refiners estimate total sales, but not the sales of any individual refiner.

Aggregate sales statistics would therefore provide more immediate information on the level of demand. Individual sales statistics could help indicate whether a given refiner was offering secret concessions. Assuming truthful reporting, if a refiner obtained unusually large sales on a given price movement, its rivals might infer that it had offered a secret concession. In practice, the refiners agreed to circulate aggregate sales statistics, and then only temporarily.

3.4   Evolution: Inducing Information Exchange

We are faced with a puzzle. If the Sugar Institute was such a weak organization, lacking much central authority, how was it able to attain any of its goals? At an initial reading, the provision that no report would be mandatory upon a member unless approved by that member would seem to guarantee that the Sugar Institute would effect no improvement in information exchange. But the organization of the institute, along with this provision, created a framework in which members could debate and bargain over what reports would be binding. In this section we examine the learning process, and analyze the factors contributing to the institute's successes and failures in overcoming the incentive problems involved in organizing information exchange.

3.4.1   Agreeing on Shared Statistics

Arbuckle Brothers objected to the original demand that the Statistics Committee have a claim on *all* statistics because the claim was unspecified. "I stated

---

27. Quoted in Defendants' Fact Brief, 19–20, District Court Record.

that we would not agree in advance to give anybody all the information they asked for concerning our business," its representative at the early meeting later testified. It is entirely reasonable that firms would not want to surrender control over their proprietary information on an ex ante, carte-blanche basis. At this initial stage of organizing the Sugar Institute, potential members could not possibly anticipate what information might be sought in the future. But that concern need not translate into a resistance to all information exchange. Rather, the adopted provision allowed firms to determine what information would be required, after the agreement was signed. Thus was the legitimate fear of an overly inquisitive Sugar Institute structurally allayed. This ex post veto gave each firm a bargaining chip in the ex post negotiation over what information was to be required.

Since reporting was not mandatory, attempts were made to induce "voluntary" reporting of statistics, especially sales statistics. One approach was to use the Sugar Institute as a forum for moral suasion, or as a "bully pulpit." This was an initial tack taken by Judge Ballou, executive secretary of the Sugar Institute. Ballou repeatedly emphasized the collective and, by implication, individual interest in having sales statistics available. At the 14 March 1929 meeting of the directors, Ballou indicated that C&H suspected that it had received inferior sales volume on the previous buying movement because of the failure of eastern refiners to enforce the thirty-day limit on contracts. Rolph of C&H further indicated his intention to "investigate upon his return to San Francisco the amount of sugar that they sold in various parts of the country and if he arrives at the conclusion that the C. & H. proportion of sales were smaller than the share to which they were entitled he indicates that it will be his intention to break the price to the 4.75 cents basis again. Judge Ballou seized upon this opportunity to again express to all refiners present the desirability of having statistics on sales available for the Institute. Such statistics would make it impossible for anyone to arrive at an imaginary grievance regarding the amount of sugar sold by any one refiner."[28]

Ballou's statement is noteworthy for several reasons. First, exchange of sales

---

28. Placé Memoranda, Board of Directors meeting, 14 March 1929. Taken out of context, one might view Rolph's reference to the market "share to which they were entitled" as an indication that the Sugar Institute was administering an explicit price-fixing or market-allocation agreement. But the entire private and public record strongly indicates otherwise. Certainly, individual members at times spoke, almost wistfully, about using production quotas, but such matters were never acted upon. Typical is the following entry in Placé: "Mr. Babst submitted a formula for the self-regulation of meltings of individual refiners. He suggested that proper percentages of total melt must be arrived at by individual refiners taking the capacities of all refiners reported to the U.S. Government during War-time 'control' plus 50% of any subsequent increase in capacity. . . . This question of 'self-regulation' was discussed at great length but no decision was arrived at. No one expressed any opinion regarding Mr. Babst's proposed formula (11 April 1929, 1). Almost a year later, Bartlett complained "that, in spite of all the pretty speeches which have been made on this subject, there is no evidence of this principle being put into practice. Mr. Foster replied that, unfortunately, the Institute's attorney does not allow discussion of this subject on a basis which could bring actual results" (6 February 1930, 1).

information was linked to contract enforcement and homogeneity of contractual terms, at least in C&H's mind. Second, Ballou suggests that information exchange was meant, in part, to avoid price wars that would otherwise be triggered by outside factors, such as shocks to industry demand. Third, he tried to show why it was in the *individual* interest of firms to supply this information. If the absence of complete sales information triggered a price war, all firms in the industry would be harmed, including those that had chosen to keep their sales statistics private.

Moral suasion was insufficient, at least for some refiners. At this same meeting, ASRC's Foster "very emphatically stated that in his opinion it was no one's business how much business [ASRC] or any other refiner booked on any one buying movement. He stated that [ASRC] would refuse to give any statistics on sales. This had been the position of [ASRC] from the very start." ASRC was the largest of all the cane refiners, with a market share of about 25 percent. Its sales statistics would therefore be very informative about industry-wide fluctuations. This indicates the seriousness of ASRC's refusal to provide statistics, and suggests a possible source of that refusal—ASRC may have been large enough to infer industry trends on its own. Moreover, ASRC operated several plants and was active in a number of markets throughout the country, which may also have given ASRC a greater ability to assess market trends independently. ASRC's nonreporting led other firms to do the same. National, Pennsylvania, and Federal, respectively the second, third, and eleventh largest members of the institute, stopped reporting sales.[29] This suggests a domino effect ordered by firm size, since the largest firm reporting its sales may provide more information than it receives in return. Of course, this does not account for why the smaller Federal halted its reports.

With information exchange breaking down, the Sugar Institute switched to an exclusionary disclosure rule. In the 28 March 1929 meeting, Ballou "reported that he had issued (only to those refiners who were reporting sales) some interesting statistics regarding the last buying movement. He is to follow this up with further statistics regarding the rate of withdrawal of these contracts. Any refiner not now receiving these statistics can secure them by reporting his own sales records.[30]

Placé advocated a more radical change. In early April 1929 a memo that he authored was presented by McCahan's president at a special Institute Founders' meeting. The memo, which framed a sizable portion of the meeting's agenda, characterizes the early structure of the institute as suffering from nearly fatal flaws. "The conception (generally), the discussion, the wording, the approval or the rejection, and finally, the enforcement of the Institute's 'resolutions' are all dictated, not by an impartial, well-considered and comprehensive plan for the benefit of the Industry as a whole, but by the self-interest of the individual

29. Placé Memoranda, Board of Directors meeting, 14 March 1929, C&H, the third largest firm in the industry, was not a member of the institute at this time.
30. Placé Memoranda, Executive Committee meeting, 28 March 1929.

members on each separate issue. This fundamental defect in the Institute's organization has manifested itself in numerous issues," including the provision of statistics. On this issue "[d]ifferent members have arbitrarily assumed the right to refuse to furnish to the Institute any statistics which they, individually, do not care to reveal, irrespective of whether or not the Institute believes such statistics to be important in preventing serious misunderstandings." After surveying other problems attributed to the Sugar Institute's decentralized structure, the memo proposes "delegating positive power to some central authority," specifically an executive officer with binding authority.

The assembled Institute Founders referred the issue to the Statistics Committee to decide on the statistics required. The decision of that committee was "to be binding on all members." Nevertheless, no additional penalties were authorized for noncompliance with requests for statistics. At the 2 May 1929 directors' meeting, considerable discussion about enforcement resulted in the creation of an Enforcement Committee "with the power to issue regulations for the enforcement of the resolution passed today and with the authority to pass judgment on any disputed case involving brokers, warehousemen or merchants." This did not mark the end of the institute's enforcement problems, but it did set up a more explicit institutional structure for addressing those issues. By August 1929 at the latest the Enforcement Committee was successfully requesting refiner reports on undelivered contracts to assist in contract enforcement.[31]

Compliance with the request for statistics increased thereafter, although it was not accomplished immediately or uniformly. But as we have noted, the refiners came to agree to furnish weekly reports on meltings, deliveries, total stocks, and deliveries by state.

Despite these areas of agreement, there was still the highly sensitive issue of sharing of sales statistics. The major objections against furnishing sales statistics came from ASRC, National, and Arbuckle Brothers (United States Temporary National Economic Committee 1941, 121). These were the first, second, and fifth largest firms in the industry, and so they may have felt that their individual sales statistics were sufficiently informative that sharing these numbers would not be a fair trade. Another laggard in providing sales statistics was Colonial, one of the smallest refiners but also one accused of engaging in unethical practices during the institute.[32] Colonial's refusal was probably an attempt to hide its violations, however much its refusal might have been tantamount to an admission of guilt.

Since the institute was unable to make sales statistics mandatory, it reverted

---

31. Placé Memoranda, Enforcement Committee meetings, 8 August 1929, 22 August 1929, Placé was placed on the Enforcement Committee only on 1 August 1929, which therefore marks the beginning of his memoranda on the Enforcement Committee. It is possible that refiner reports to the Enforcement Committee on undelivered contracts might have been occurring for several months previously.

32. Colonial eventually acknowledged some of these violations (Placé Memoranda, Enforcement Committee meeting, 3 October 1929.

to use of an exclusionary disclosure rule; only those members making sales reports would receive sales statistics. This tactic was successful for a time in encouraging some participation, but it ultimately unraveled. C&H, which had become a member of the institute in September 1929, stopped reporting its sales statistics in February 1930, because five other refiners were not reporting.[33] Although not identified, these firms presumably included ASRC, Arbuckle Brothers, and National, whose opposition to supplying sales statistics was unconditional. If so, then C&H would have been the largest firm supplying sales statistics before halting its cooperation. C&H may have felt that cooperation on those terms was an unfair trade, since it was providing a relatively precise signal of West Coast demand in exchange for a relatively imprecise indication of East Coast demand. This precipitated a renewed discussion by the institute board. ASRC, Arbuckle Brothers, and National declared themselves "unalterably opposed" to reporting sales. Colonial, Spreckels, C&H, and McCahan refused to make sales reports unless all did. It was decided that "[t]he other eight refiners are to continue to make [these] reports and, in turn, they (and only they) will receive from the Institute a report on the total 'Sales'. . . made by the eight refiners involved."[34] But the handwriting was on the wall, and two months later, by which time only Savannah, Henderson, Imperial, and Texas, all southern refiners, were reporting sales, the collection of sales statistics was abandoned.[35] As the number of cooperating firms declined, the "aggregate" sales statistics became less informative about general market trends and more revealing about the business patterns of the cooperating firms, information that those firms might wish to remain private.

So while the attempts to exchange data on meltings and deliveries were successful, the attempt to exchange sales information was ultimately not. Interestingly, although the *Weekly Statistical Sugar Trade Journal* had been reporting weekly (estimated) meltings and deliveries since the 1880s (indeed, the credibility of these published statistics may be supported by the journal's longevity), the journal never published sales statistics. One interpretation of the difference between meltings/deliveries and sales is that the former statistics were nearly common knowledge without the institute, and the institute exchange merely made the public information more accurate. As noted earlier, independent information was available on those series from raw sugar purchases. On the other hand, perhaps that information (in part provided to the journal by the refiners themselves) was more publicly available precisely because it was less sensitive than sales information.

Since it was the larger firms that were the most reluctant to provide sales statistics, why did the larger firms participate at all? They participated because of their interest in facilitating collusion. A firm that does not intend to cheat on the collusive understanding has an incentive to share credibly its own infor-

33. Placé Memoranda, Board of Directors meeting, 14 February 1930.
34. Ibid., 13 March 1930.
35. Placé Memoranda, Executive Committee meeting, 15 May 1930.

mation, since that establishes to other firms in the industry that, in fact, it did not cheat. The alternative to information exchange might have been either continued cutthroat competition or intermittently successful collusion, with adverse industry-wide demand shocks resulting in periodic price wars. The larger firms, precisely because they controlled a greater share of industry output, had a larger incentive to make collusion workable than did the smaller firms. But the larger firms may have thought that shared meltings and delivery information would be sufficient to detect and absolve cheating, and that individual sales statistics would reveal too much about an individual refiner's business strategy.

Moreover, even if collusion motivated the formation of the Sugar Institute, it need not have embraced all the firms in the industry. In particular, the five Institute Founders may have organized the institute with an eye toward monitoring the fringe competitors. They might have doubted these fringe firms' willingness to stick with a collusive agreement, or they might have had uncertainty over these firms' supply functions. Under this view, the institute attempted to gather and disseminate aggregate industry statistics so that the larger firms could subtract out their own figures and thereby infer the supply (functions) of the fringe. This knowledge could then be used in future pricing decisions, much the same way as a dominant firm would set a price anticipating the supply response of the competitive fringe. Conversely, the promise of demand information, more valuable to the small than to the large firm, may have been the carrot that induced the small firms to participate. Unfortunately, we have uncovered no narrative evidence in support of either interpretation.

3.4.2 Audits and Investigations

Auditing and direct investigation of refiner or affiliated businesses' records provided another source of shared information. These were intended to enforce the Code of Ethics, rather than facilitate information exchange narrowly construed. There is no indication of any audit of a refiner report concerning its own meltings, deliveries, or sales, although refiner consignment stocks were audited.

The Enforcement Committee investigated and ruled on affiliations between brokers and warehouses, and between customers and warehouses. To that end, it was authorized on 9 May 1929 to retain investigators' firms to follow up on complaints, and it subsequently retained the firms Proudfoot-Chinal and the Bishop Agency. Although the authorization for these investigations nominally concerned only the separation of brokerage and storage activities, the implicit scope was much broader. At the 29 May 1929 meeting of the institute board, Colonial indicated "that refiners should be willing to throw their books open for the investigation of *any* violation of the Code of Ethics." Other firms agreed, although they found no need to adopt a resolution "because no refiner had ever failed to supply full information on any subject requiring investigation."[36]

---

36. Placé Memoranda, Board of Directors meeting, 29 May 1929.

Investigations of brokers and warehouses proceeded, many times without incident. But conflicts sometimes arose when a buyer or broker who had a close relationship with a single refiner was involved. When an investigation by an institute employee, Patterson, revealed that the Webster Grocery Company was affiliated with warehouses, Godchaux, which supplied Webster, objected to the findings, and the Enforcement Committee agreed to a new investigation by Proudfoot-Chinal.[37] When shortly thereafter the institute board authorized an investigation of warehouses and it was suggested that Patterson conduct it, the Godchaux representative "stated very emphatically that he . . . will not allow Mr. Patterson to enter the Godchaux offices again as he considers him inefficient, biased, and liable to make unsupported accusations."[38] Other board members spoke in Patterson's defense, but it was decided that the investigation of warehouses throughout the nation required a national agency, and so an outside firm was retained instead.[39]

These episodes suggest the hazards the institute faced in choosing its investigators and auditors. The institute typically decided upon an outside firm, rather than rely on member refiners themselves or use an institute employee. As the Patterson example illustrates, the neutrality of an institute employee might be challenged and thereby undermine the employee's effectiveness in other tasks. Retaining outside firms was costly in its own way. For example, the auditing firm of Haskins and Sells, retained to audit the stocks refiners were storing in consignment markets, acknowledged at the outset that it did not have experience conducting that type of audit.[40] The refiners themselves had employees with the requisite experience, but they were not used by the institute, presumably because their independence would be in doubt.[41]

The level of consignment stocks was the only area in which refiners themselves were audited. There is a single recorded incident in which a refiner withdrew its permission for such an audit. Godchaux refused permission on the grounds that its original agreement "was given with the provision that Colonial also submit to a similar audit. [But since] the Institute lacks knowledge of the warehouses in which Colonial is storing, this proviso has not been lived up to."[42] Though a single incident, this points up a weakness in the blanket authorization for the institute to conduct audits, namely, that the authorization was not binding. Just as firms were required to file statistical reports yet could fail

37. Placé Memoranda, Enforcement Committee meeting, 15 August 1929.
38. Ibid., 12 September 1929.
39. Proudfoot-Chinal was too small a firm to undertake this investigation.
40. Placé Memoranda, Board of Directors meeting, 28 February 1929.
41. Williamson's discussion (1975) of the auditing capabilities of a firm may be relevant here. He argues that an audit conducted by an internal agent, such as a representative of the general office, will be more successful than an outside audit. In addition to the greater legal rights that an internal auditor will possess, the internal auditor will receive greater cooperation from the audited unit. Similar cooperation with an outside auditor could be viewed as disloyal. In this setting, however, the need for independence and neutrality was paramount.
42. Placé Memoranda, Executive Committee meeting, 7 November 1929.

to file a report in any given week, firms could be required to open their books to the institute yet rescind that authorization in any particular case. These issues are intimately connected with the hybrid organizational design of the Sugar Institute. Just as a firm retains residual control over its information, it controls the residual right to refuse an audit by an outside agency. Even under the institute, that right was retained by the individual firms, and was waived only on a case-by-case basis.

3.4.3 Confidentiality

The Sugar Institute revealed less information to its members than it knew. It received the complete vector of reports from its members, but in most cases aggregated it before distributing it to them. In this, the institute may have been steering its way between the 1921 and 1925 Supreme Court decisions discussed in the introduction. On the other hand, aggregation may have been a requirement of incentive compatibility. A firm might not want to reveal to its competitors its own information, but might be willing to reveal that to a third party who would aggregate it first. Either reason supports the need for an intermediary.

The incentive-compatibility reason also suggests the importance of the procedures that an intermediary adopts to ensure confidentiality. Clearly, this was a concern of refiners. The institute reporting system was designed to protect confidentiality. Individual member reports were received by the institute staff, and a letter code assigned each refiner. The individual statistics were then transferred onto standard institute forms identified by code letter, without reference to the refiner's name.[43] Clearly, these efforts depended upon the integrity of the institute staff. There is no indication of any leakage of individual refiner reports. An aggregate, annual report of Sugar Institute statistics did find its way into the hands of an economics professor, and members were sufficiently upset to bring the matter to the Executive Committee.[44] The importance of the staff was highlighted after the district court decision against the Sugar Institute. Several refiners spoke of replacing the Sugar Institute with a newly organized united sugar association, which would gather, aggregate, and disseminate statistics on past prices and terms under the legal restrictions imposed by the court. An unsigned memorandum advancing this proposal noted, "Naturally, the integrity of the Association staff must be above suspicion so that no member need fear that the intimate details of his business shall be divulged."[45]

43. Minutes of the Executive Committee meeting, 30 November 1936, in Placé, W. J. McCahan Sugar Refining and Molasses Company, Sugar Institute: Reorganization and Closing, subject group 3, box 11.

44. Placé Memoranda, Executive Committee meeting, 7 November 1929.

45. Although unsigned, it is likely that the memorandum was drafted by Louis Placé and/or William Tyler of C&H (Placé, Sugar Institute: Reorganization and Closing).

3.4.4   Contract Enforcement and Misreporting

Statistical exchange advanced adherence to the Code of Ethics, as exemplified by the enforcement of delivery on thirty-day contracts.[46] Recall that refined sugar was purchased on a price move, and that the customer thereby purchased the right to take delivery gradually over the following period, which prior to the institute was thirty days or more. The Institute tried to restrict contracts to exactly thirty days, and in order to monitor compliance, the Enforcement Committee requested and received reports from refiners.

A standard contract stipulated only the quantity of sugar and the basis price, the price for standard granulated. Details such as the grades of sugar the customer wished to receive did not have to be specified until shortly before delivery.[47] If a customer had not yet furnished these instructions, that contract remained unspecified. All unspecified or undelivered contracts were supposed to be reported to the institute for each price move. These reports were not aggregated across refiners before dissemination. These figures were of interest as the contract due date approached since a firm carrying a large balance of undelivered or unspecified contracts was unlikely to meet the due date, either because of capacity constraints in production or transportation, or because the high balances signaled an unwillingness to pressure customers to take delivery. This information allowed other refiners to adjust their contract enforcement, and threaten to do so. This in turn could provide incentives for the uncooperative refiner to strengthen its own contract-enforcement efforts.

In most instances, this information was reported accurately. Some firms initially refused to supply contract figures, but this was met successfully by the actual and threatened retaliation of nonreporting by other firms. In a few other instances irregularities in reported numbers arose, apparently due to sincere misunderstandings as to how contracts should be classified.[48]

There appears to have been only a single case of intentional misreporting. Before a meeting of the Enforcement Committee in January 1930, National's representative confided to Placé and an institute staff member that he had definite evidence that other refiners had "failed to receive specifications for some contracts which they have reported to the Enforcement Committee as being specified." Consequently, National would refuse to continue reporting contract-enforcement figures, and would not undertake to force deliveries. Placé responded that he had heard similar rumors and so he "thought a 'showdown' was necessary."[49]

---

46. The institute gathered other statistics that played a role in code compliance. These were "the amount of sugar on consignment by states (weekly), the amount of sugar stored in transit by states (weekly) and the amount of sugar moved by eastern and southern differential routes for refiners' account and for customers' account. This information (being of little or no interest to the trade generally) was ordinarily sent only to members and to the importers" (Defendants' Fact Brief, 69–70, District Court Record).

47. An example of a grade is powdered sugar, which results from crushing granulated sugar.

48. Placé Memoranda, Enforcement Committee meeting, 9 January 1930.

49. Ibid., 23 January 1930.

When the meeting opened, the representatives of ASRC and Spreckels admitted that they had large balances of undelivered contracts with A&P, a major sugar customer. In both cases, they had received "dummy" instructions from A&P, meant to be canceled later, but they had classified these contracts as "specified" for institute reporting purposes. National had received and refused similar instructions from A&P, and had therefore classified its A&P contracts as unspecified. National repeated its intention to withhold contract-enforcement figures.[50] Nevertheless, the next week National agreed to return to supplying contract-enforcement figures on the understanding that all refiners would make "honest" reports.[51]

Although this is a case where misreporting occurred, it illustrates the factors that prevented it from completely undermining the agreement. First, information was available from other sources to detect possible misreporting, and this information was sufficiently credible to be used as a basis for retaliation. Second, retaliatory nonreporting was apparently sufficient to deter additional problems. Finally, the detail that Placé accords this incident suggests that misreporting was rare.

3.4.5 Participation: Members and Nonmembers

The Sugar Institute did not encompass all sugar producers, nor even all cane sugar refiners. Both technological and geographic differences limited the association's expanse. The largest California refiner was not initially a member of the institute. Offshore refiners always remained outside the institute. And beet sugar producers were organized in a separate trade association, the Domestic Sugar Bureau. Even among members themselves, there were important geographic differences. Refiners differed in the cost of shipping their sugars to consumption centers. The distance and the transportation mode (rail versus water) varied by the refiners' location. Nevertheless, over time, the institute acknowledged and accommodated these heterogeneous interests, if not through membership, then through cooperation.

C&H was the third largest U.S. cane sugar refiner, and the largest in California. Its primary marketing area was the western states, although it did compete directly with New Orleans and East Coast refiners for sales in the Midwest, including Chicago. The West was the center of the beet sugar industry, and so C&H's main competition came from there. While the Sugar Institute was being formed, similar discussions were being held among beet and Louisiana cane firms about forming the Domestic Sugar Bureau. These groups considered their interests to be opposed to those of the cane sugar refiners, and so to foster good relations with its beet sugar rivals, C&H initially chose to join their association and remain outside the other (United States Temporary National Economic Committee 1941, 115–16). Moreover, President Rolph of C&H, who desired a single trade association encompassing all sugar producers, thought

50. Ibid.
51. Ibid., 30 January 1930.

that remaining outside the institute gave him the opportunity to persuade beet sugar interests of the desirability of union.[52] If C&H failed to merge the associations within two years, Rolph intended to apply for institute membership.

To the eastern refiners C&H was the scourge of the industry. Rudolph Spreckels testified at tariff hearings in June 1929 that while "C&H has not alway precipitated the cut in refined . . . I have found their fine Italian hand back of every refiner's cut that has been made."[53] The eastern refiners' private assessments were no kinder.[54] Underlying this eastern pique was a genuine divergence of interests born of geography. Since Hawaiian raw sugar faced a lower tariff than Cuban, C&H's refining costs were lower than the eastern refiners. On the other hand, in the Midwest, where C&H and the eastern refiners actively competed, the latter were advantaged by the shorter distance to the East Coast and the cheap water transportation over the Great Lakes. C&H's absorption of this freight cost differential reduced the prices eastern refiners could command not only in the Midwest, but also within their own territories, because they could not completely price discriminate between the two regions. These differences, particularly C&H's need to absorb transportation costs, were at the heart of the C&H participation issue. Differences in costs across refiners made collusion more difficult to achieve.

Despite these differences, there were also shared interests, which helps accounts for the consultation between C&H and the institute. That Ballou had formerly served as C&H's counsel aided this interaction. Nevertheless, there were limits to what could be accomplished while C&H remained a nonmember, and by September 1929, C&H was prepared to join the Sugar Institute. Having concluded that a merger of the beet sugar and cane sugar trade associations was not imminent, Rolph carried out his initial plan to join the institute roughly two years after its formation. Nevertheless, C&H insisted on retaining its membership in the Domestic Sugar Bureau. Its application for Sugar Institute membership included the proviso that in any situation in which institute requirements conflicted with those of the bureau, the C&H would not be responsible for adhering to the institute requirement.[55] This term was accepted. There were not many conflicts between the two associations' requirements, yet this was still a considerable concession by the Sugar Institute. The willingness of incumbent members to accept a separate set of rules for C&H indicates that they had decided to address the differences with C&H within the institute rather than outside it. For C&H, membership gave a voice and vote in shaping ongoing institute resolutions; each had value precisely because the Sugar Institute was an evolving, learning organization. Correspondingly, the institute preferred C&H as a member because that made enforcing adherence to resolutions easier. Moreover, membership facilitated communication among refiners.

52. Placé Memoranda, Executive Committee meeting, 19 September 1929.
53. Spreckels testimony, U.S. Senate 1929, 167.
54. Placé Memoranda, Executive Committee meeting, 8 March 1929.
55. Placé Memoranda, Executive Committee meeting, 19 September 1929.

The Sugar Institute did not absorb all relevant interests under its tent. One example was Hershey, an "offshore" refiner operating in Cuba. Although a nonmember, Hershey intermittently supplied statistics on contract enforcement.[56] When C&H joined the institute, Ballou suggested that eventually the institute might extend Hershey at least associate membership.[57] Later, a group of southern refiners proposed that the institute either force Hershey to discontinue its "unethical" business practices in Florida or invite it to join the institute. But Spreckels and C&H, who, unlike the southern refiners, did not compete with the offshore refiners, objected to extending cooperation to membership, because offshore and domestic refiners had diametrically opposed interests on the tariff on imported refined sugar. It was felt that membership for Hershey might undermine the institute's efforts to lobby for a higher refined tariff.[58]

Tariff matters also played a role in keeping the beet sugar producers and the cane sugar refiners apart. As documented in Ellison and Mullin (1995), the domestic cane sugar refiners wanted a high tariff on refined sugar and a low tariff on their input, raw (cane) sugar. The beet sugar manufacturers, on the other hand, wanted a high tariff on imported raw cane sugar, the essential input of a near perfect substitute. Moreover, beet sugar was produced by dozens of small, price-taking firms (the price of sugar in western states equaled the San Francisco base price plus freight from San Francisco, where the West Coast cane sugar refiners were located). As a result, no individual firm had the incentive to join the institute. If the institute advanced collusion, each beet firm would prefer to free ride on the higher price.

Nevertheless, there were common interests among all sugar producers, and these were advanced through consultation between the respective trade associations.[59] The institute and the Domestic Sugar Bureau exchanged figures on the deliveries of all sugar, cane sugar, and beet sugar, by state, on a monthly basis.[60] Since beet sugar accounted for over 14 percent of U.S. consumption, such information was essential for estimating demand at both the national and regional level. Since each cane refiner had particular territories, the regional decompositions were particularly valuable. A second, less benign use would be for a division of markets between the beet and cane interests,

56. Placé Memoranda, Executive Committee meeting, 24 October 1929, indicates that Hershey was supplying its figures on undelivered contracts through its broker, Pike, and that Pike was requesting that the institute reciprocate. Hershey statistics on undelivered contracts are reported in the next week.

57. Ibid., 19 September 1929.

58. Placé Memoranda, Board of Directors meeting, 24 July 1930.

59. The Domestic Sugar Bureau had its own concerns in terms of securing membership and adherence, which is beyond the scope of this paper. "The Bureau represented 80 to 90 percent of total beet sugar production and about 30 percent of Louisiana cane production. Although none of the beet companies east of Chicago was included in the membership, the only important nonmember was the Michigan Sugar Co." (United States Temporary National Economic Committee 1941, 116).

60. Defendants' Fact Brief, 70, District Court Record.

although there is no indication that a formal or informal division of markets ever took place.[61]

3.5 After the Sugar Institute

The half decade that followed the spring of 1930, when the Placé minutes trail off, saw a constantly changing legal environment for the refiners. In the spring of the next year, the Department of Justice filed suit. 1933 saw the passage of the Agricultural Adjustment Act (AAA) and the National Industrial Recovery Act (NIRA), both of which held out the promise not only of government relaxation of antitrust restrictions on industry association activities but, initially, of government enforcement of those actions as well. In 1934 the government passed the Sugar Act, which established quotas on the importation of raw sugar and the production of beet sugar and marked the beginning of continuous government involvement in the industry. Though not directly collusive, this act did protect domestic refiners from entry in the form of offshore refiners and beet producers. But two months later the District Court found against the refiners in the *Sugar Institute* case. Around this time, the refiners became aware that the government would not enforce the AAA or NIRA codes. The beginning of the end of the New Deal experiment in corporatist economics came in the 1935 Schechter decision, which declared the NIRA unconstitutional. The Supreme Court annulled the AAA as unconstitutional in January 1936, shortly before issuing its verdict in the *Sugar Institute* case.

Several times during this period, the Sugar Institute tried to reinvent itself—first as a code of fair competition under the AAA, then as an all-encompassing sugar-producer association, and finally as a revised institute that would be in compliance with the Supreme Court decision, before abandoning any attempt at a trade association in November 1936. Although none of these plans ever came to fruition, they nonetheless reflect what refiners learned from the Sugar Institute experience, and how they responded to the changed legal environment.

The refiners' first response to the New Deal legislation was to move to dismiss their case. The motion was rejected; nonetheless, the district court decision did stipulate that the decrees could be modified if the refiners so requested under the NIRA.[62] In the meantime, the refiners had submitted a code of fair competition under the AAA in August 1933.[63] Like many other such codes,

---

61. At one institute Executive Committee meeting, the representative from the Domestic Sugar Bureau displayed a map he intended to circulate showing a potential division of markets. Nevertheless, the plans for circulating this map were quickly abandoned (Placé Memoranda, Executive Committee meeting, 8 March 1929, 16 May 1929).

62. *United States v. Sugar Institute,* 15 Fed. Sup. 910 (1934).

63. The proposed code is reproduced in *Weekly Statistical Sugar Trade Journal,* 10–31 August 1933, 327–63.

it called upon the secretary of agriculture to restrain new entry and capacity expansion, to allocate production directly if necessary, and to license all members of the industry.[64] It conferred upon the refiners the right "to confer among themselves" to halt ruinous price cutting, and its article 3, "Unfair Competition," condemned the same practices as the Sugar Institute's Code of Ethics.

The organizational structure envisioned in the AAA code differed significantly from that of the Sugar Institute. The "one refiner, one vote" system of the institute was supplemented by an additional requirement that gave larger refiners a greater voice. Changes to the AAA code would require approval of not only a majority of directors, but also the assent of refiners with a combined market share of at least two-thirds.[65]

This strengthening of the voting powers of the larger firms was accomplished in the face of the ability of small refiners to block the agreement itself, for the refiners had been informed that the secretary of agriculture would accept only a unanimous agreement.[66] In contrast, individual refiners had no such veto over the formation of the Sugar Institute; indeed, as we have shown, not all relevant sugar producers were at all times members of that association. Evidently, experience under the Sugar Institute had taught refiners that it was important that the larger firms have greater formal voting rights in industry deliberations.

This outcome stands in sharp contrast to that of many other industries. Brand (1988) has emphasized that the political power of small firms led industries to approve codes that were disadvantageous to the larger firms and so unsustainable without government enforcement. Alexander (1997) illustrates this process for the macaroni industry, whose code was crafted to appeal to the majority of smaller, less efficient firms. When the government then failed to enforce the industry codes, the industry's attempts at collusion were undermined by the aggressive pricing of the larger, lower-cost firms. These important cost asymmetries were not accommodated within the industry code, and this proved fatal to its success.

The steel industry affords a more appropriate comparison. As in the sugar industry, a consolidation near the turn of the century had created a dominant firm with a near monopoly that by the 1930s had remained the market leader notwithstanding a sizeable decline in market share over the intervening decades. In granting firms differential voting power in its NIRA code, the steel industry departed from the "one firm, one vote" system even more sharply than the sugar industry. U.S. Steel and Bethlehem Steel possessed 511 and 160 votes, respectively, in the code authority, while each of the other thirty-eight firms possessed only 1 to 86 votes, depending upon firm size (National Recovery Administration 1934). Evidently, the steel firms had also learned the neces-

---

64. Ibid., 10 August 1933, 330–31.
65. Ibid., 31 August 1933, 361.
66. Placé Correspondence, memo from Ellsworth Bunker, 24 July 1934.

sity of giving greater voting power to the larger firms. As with the sugar industry, a prior collusive experience may have determined the response to the New Deal legislation. Lamoreaux (1985) has argued that U.S. Steel's policy after 1902, shortly after its formation, of cutting prices when demand was slack taught the independents to curtail their output in recessions. That industry's equivalent of the Sugar Institute was the Gary dinners, which served as an avenue to notify the independents of U.S. Steel's intentions. History had thus conditioned members to the benefits of an asymmetric cartel headed by U.S. Steel. Baker (1989) has provided the quantitative evidence that the steel industry was able to reap the collusive gains offered by the NIRA.

The AAA code strengthened not only the large firms but the coordinating body itself. Discretion over statistical reports and auditing authority would be transferred from the member firms to the board of directors. It would have blanket, ex ante authority to conduct audits, rather than having to request audit authority on a case-by-case basis. It was now empowered to employ public accountants to make "periodic checks or audits of refiners' books and records in order to determine whether or not [the] Code is being observed" and "to call on any one or all members of the industry . . . for reports and statistics relating to . . . matters concerning which the Board is entitled to have information under this code."[67]

These stronger powers were backed up with new sanctions for violations of the agreement, including nonreporting of statistics or failure to allow auditing. First, since the proposed AAA code included government licensing of all members of the industry, a violation could result in the revocation of a license. Second, the proposed AAA code was to be considered "a valid and binding contract," with violations of the code constituting a breach of contract and therefore making the violator liable for liquidated damages.[68] These sanctions replaced the, perhaps not credible, expulsion of a member refiner and the often-used blackballing of downstream firms under the Sugar Institute.

The secretary of agriculture rejected the proposed code on the grounds that it did not protect consumer interests sufficiently.[69] Delays in revising the proposed refiners' code later ensued because the secretary considered marketing agreements for raw sugar and beet sugar to be a higher priority. By July 1934 ASRC believed that the government would not enforce AAA codes,[70] and no other sugar refiners code was ever submitted under the AAA. Nevertheless, a code of fair competition for a united sugar association that was to encompass both beet and cane producers was drafted in 1935, and in August 1936, in the wake of the Supreme Court *Sugar Institute* decision, a proposed reorganization of the Sugar Institute was drawn up. The first agreement was silent on voting

67. *Weekly Statistical Sugar Trade Journal,* 31 August 1933, 359.
68. Ibid., 359–60.
69. Placé Correspondence, letter to Manolo Rionda, 27 July 1934, and accompanying memo from Ellsworth Bunker, 24 July 1934.
70. Placé Correspondence, letter to Manolo Rionda, 20 July 1934.

rights; the second maintained the same system as the AAA code. Both draft agreements maintained the enhanced powers of the board of directors to obtain any statistics it required, with the sanction of liquidated damages (in the 1935 draft set at 25 cents per hundred pounds, or about one-half of per-unit variable profits, of the relevant quantity). One hears echoes of Placé's earlier call for "delegating positive power to some central authority" in the 1935 draft's anointing of the executive director as the "judge of violations."[71]

3.6 Conclusion

This chapter has been concerned with how refiners learned to ensure the exchange of information among themselves, and how they faced difficulties in inducing the sharing of certain types of information. Some surviving records of the McCahan Sugar Refining and Molasses Company provide a window into how the information that was exchanged was used at the firm level. In several letters to McCahan's president, Placé, who was responsible for all but production and raw sugar purchases at McCahan,[72] uses institute figures to benchmark McCahan's practices or performance. For example, Placé points out that although McCahan's refined sugar stocks had increased from June 1930 to June 1931, institute figures revealed that its *proportion* of industry stocks had declined.[73] Industry statistics permitted a refiner to distinguish between change in conditions specific to the firm itself, and those common to the industry. In this case, the information helped allay any McCahan fears that it was losing sales to other firms through secret price concessions.

Benchmarking was applied to specific markets as well. Some institute figures were reported by states, and that information had never before been available. Due to the geographic dispersion of refiners, with overlapping market areas, the information broken down by state could be a great help to a firm in assessing its own performance. In another letter Placé argued that McCahan was not holding excessive stocks in Illinois because McCahan was selling 16.5 percent of all sugars there but only holding 8.9 percent of the stocks there.[74]

Although perhaps unsurprising, such benchmarking is noteworthy as it is consistent with the models on the competitive effects of information sharing. In particular, information sharing increases the correlation of firm decisions because firms are acting upon common information. This correlation occurs even absent formal collusion by firms. Moreover, this benchmarking is related to a possible efficiency gain of information exchange, by reducing the chances of erroneous firm decisions based upon poor information. In the previous example, McCahan assessed its level of inventories based upon a comparison with other refiners. Absent the Sugar Institute, McCahan might have been led

71. Both agreements are to be found in Placé, Sugar Institute: Reorganization and Closing.

72. Testimony of Louis Placé, Transcript of Record, 2:827, District Court Record.

73. Placé Correspondence, Costs and Melts, 10 June 1931.

74. Ibid., 22 July 1931.

to reduce its inventories below that of its competitors. If its competitors collectively had better information, then McCahan's independent decision to lower its inventories could hurt McCahan and market performance if stockouts occurred.[75]

The enhanced information exchange achieved by the Sugar Institute did not survive it. Although firms could have shared information through the trade press even after the dissolution of the Sugar Institute, this did not occur. An examination of the *Weekly Statistical Sugar Trade Journal* for the years following the Supreme Court's decision shows that the dissemination of information had returned to the preinstitute state. Estimates of weekly deliveries and meltings are reported. But information on the weekly sales of refined sugar, one of the most elusive statistics, is nowhere to be seen. And there are no state-level data.

One's initial inclination is to classify the Sugar Institute as a failure. It could not avoid prosecution, which threat was one of the constraints of the economic, legal, and political environment in which the institute operated. Thus, in the end, the legal changes overshadowed any learning. The sugar refining industry did learn how to manage incentives within an information-sharing agreement, and more broadly, they learned the advantages such an organizational form offered in advancing industry aims, such as collusion. But the Supreme Court decision denied the industry that organizational form, at least as it was conceived and implemented. It was as if the industry had learned how to use a particular tool, and its value, and then that tool was taken away. Within the longer historical context, the changing legal and political treatment of trade-association activities first gave the sugar industry the opportunity to form and operate the institute, and then took away much of the institute's perceived power by limiting its activities.

Like a constitution, the code did not completely specify all future decisions; rather, it specified how those future decisions were to be made. Thus the Sugar Institute was at least a partial success because its structure enabled future decisions to be made that advanced the institute's original aims. In particular, the institute established a framework in which learning and adaptation could take place. First, the institute's organizational structure was sufficiently flexible to allow the institute and its requirements of members to change as members learned about the strengths and weaknesses of the original institute requirements. Second, the institute enabled firms to learn more about their market and their own performance through the information exchange that was accomplished under the institute's auspices. Third, although some of the lessons about organizing information exchange could not be put into practice due to political and legal constraints, those lessons were nevertheless learned.

---

75. This argument can be advanced without invoking stockouts. Since inventories serve to smooth production and thereby minimize costs, an inventory decision that turns out to be a mistake will result in higher costs of production.

Appendix
Code of Ethics of the Sugar Institute, Inc.

Among the purposes for which this Institute was formed were the following: To promote a high standard of business ethics in the industry; to eliminate trade abuses; to promote uniformity and certainty in business customs and practices; and to promote the service of the industry to the Public.

Accordingly, the organization of this Institute was a frank recognition, in and of itself, that customs and practices had grown up in the industry which were unsound and unbusinesslike, and which were harmful to producers and consumers alike. These customs and practices had resulted in confusion in the trade and discrimination as between purchasers, with a consequent uneven and uneconomic distribution of sugar to the public. The more important result to the industry was a demoralization and restriction of the retail trade in sugar and a retardation of the normal increase of consumption.

Believing that the trade will welcome a rectification of those business methods of the industry which have served to promote discrimination between purchasers; and believing that the public will be better served if the present channels of distribution are preserved and enlarged by maintaining equality of business opportunity among merchants of sugar; and believing that the members of the industry will recognize that it is in the interest of the industry to encourage and promote the wider distribution of its product to the end of increasing its consumption;

The Institute declares its policy to be founded upon, and recommends to its members the adoption of business methods in accordance with, the following principles, to wit:

1. All discriminations between customers should be abolished. To that end, sugar should be sold only upon open prices and terms publicly announced.
2. The business of the sugar refining industry is that of refining a raw product, the price of which to the industry is the controlling factor in the price which the industry receives for its own refined product; and the industry as a purchaser of raw sugar receives no concessions for quantity purchased. Concessions made by the industry for the quantity of refined sugar purchased have resulted in discrimination between customers, which discrimination the Institute believes it to be in the interest of the industry, of the trade and of the public to avoid. The Institute accordingly condemns as discriminatory, and in so far as this industry is concerned, as unbusinesslike, uneconomic and unsound, concessions made to purchasers on the basis of quantity purchased.
3. The following trade practices if not uniformly employed with all customers of a refiner are discriminatory. Furthermore, if not secretly employed they will of necessity be generally demanded, with the result that they must then be uniformly employed or abandoned. If uniformly employed they amount

to a general price concession which should frankly take the form of a price reduction. The Institute condemns them as unethical except when practiced openly; as discriminatory unless uniformly employed; and in any event as wasteful and unbusinesslike.

   a. Variations from the open and publicly announced prices and terms, including (but without limiting the generality of this clause) the following: Special allowances by way of discounts, brokerage, storage or advertising; variations from openly announced grade or package differentials; reduction or substitution of grades or packings; delayed billings; full discounts in cases of delayed payment; and rebates or other allowances by any name or of any nature.

   b. Split billings, except on cars moving on an 80,000 lb. minimum and rate.

   c. The use of differential rates on consignments, or otherwise than on direct shipments over differential routes at customers' request.

   d. Payment of brokerage where any part thereof inures to the benefit of the purchaser.

   e. Storage[76] of sugar in warehouses in which customers or brokers are interested, or with which they are in any way affiliated.

   f. Allotments to brokers running beyond the close of business of the day on which an advance in price is announced by the refiner.

   g. Special services to customers without appropriate charges therefor.

   h. The sale of secondhand sugar by refiners.

   i. Sales for export under contracts which do not provide for shipment out of the country.

4. The factors which enter into and determine the cost of his product for the refiner are so largely outside his control, and the probable margin of his profit so small, as to render highly speculative and unsound the giving by him of options to purchase his sugar. Furthermore, unless equally available to all customers alike, the giving of options is discriminatory. The Institute condemns the giving of options by refiners.

5. In the interest of a more even distribution to the trade, the Institute recommends that sugar shall be consigned only to recognized detention points for reshipment, or to recognized markets and then in care of railroad or steamship lines or to public[77] warehouses, and that the control of the sugar shall remain with the refiner.

6. The Institute recommends the use by members of uniform contracts to be adopted by the Institute for Eastern, Southern and Western markets.[78]

---

76. Subparagraph e originally read "Storage of sugar in customers' warehouses" and was amended to read as printed above by resolution adopted 2 May 1929.

77. The words "or brokers," appearing before the word "warehouses," were striken out by resolution adopted 2 May 1929.

78. The Code of Ethics is reproduced from *United States v. Sugar Institute*, 15 Fed. Sup. 817, 910–11 (1934).

References

Albert, Bill, and Adrian Graves, eds. 1988. *The World Sugar Economy in War and Depression, 1914–1940.* London: Routledge.

Alexander, Barbara. 1997. Failed Cooperation in Heterogeneous Industries under the National Recovery Administration. *Journal of Economic History* 57:322–34.

Baker, Jonathan B. 1989. Identifying Cartel Policing under Uncertainty: The U.S. Steel Industry, 1933–1939. *Journal of Law and Economics* 32:S47–S76.

Brand, Donald. 1988. *Corporatism and the Rule of Law: A Study of the National Recovery Administration.* Ithaca: Cornell University Press.

Chandler, Alfred D. J. 1962. *Strategy and Structure: Chapters in the History of the Industrial Enterprise.* Cambridge: MIT Press.

Creane, Anthony. 1998. Risk and Revelation: Changing the Value of Information. *Economica.*

Eddy, Arthur Jerome. 1912. *The New Competition.* New York: D. Appleton & Co.

Eichner, Alfred S. 1969. *The Emergence of Oligopoly: Sugar Refining as a Case Study.* Baltimore: Johns Hopkins University Press.

Ellison, Sara Fisher, and Wallace P. Mullin. 1995. Economics and Politics: The Case of Sugar Tariff Reform. *Journal of Law and Economics* 38:335–66.

Galambos, Louis. 1966. *Competition and Cooperation: The Emergence of a National Trade Association.* Baltimore: Johns Hopkins University Press.

Genesove, David, and Wallace P. Mullin. 1997a. Narrative Evidence on the Dynamics of Collusion: The Sugar Institute Case. Photocopy.

———. 1997b. Predation and Its Rate of Return: The Sugar Industry, 1887–1914. NBER Working Paper no. 6032. Cambridge, MA: National Bureau of Economic Research.

Green, Edward J., and Robert H. Porter. 1984. Noncooperative Collusion under Imperfect Price Information. *Econometrica* 52:87–100.

Hawley, Ellis W. 1974. Herbert Hoover, the Commerce Secretariat, and the Vision of an "Associative State," 1921–1928. *Journal of American History* 61:116–40.

———. 1981. Three Facets of Hooverian Associationalism: Lumber, Aviation, and Movies, 1921–1930. In *Regulation in Perspective: Historical Essays,* ed. Thomas K. McCraw, 95–123. Cambridge: Harvard University Press.

Kirby, Alison J. 1988. Trade Associations as Information Exchange Mechanisms. *Rand Journal of Economics* 19:138–46.

Lamoreaux, Naomi R. 1985. *The Great Merger Movement in American Business, 1895–1904.* Cambridge: Cambridge University Press.

National Recovery Administration. 1934. *Operation of the Basing-Point System in the Iron and Steel Industry.* Washington, DC: Government Printing Office.

Palmer, Truman. 1927. *Concerning Sugar.* Washington, DC: U.S. Sugar Manufacturing Association.

Placé, Louis V. W. J. McCahan Sugar Refining and Molasses Company, Records of Vice President Louis V. Placé, Jr., 1928–45. University of Florida, George A. Smathers Libraries, Braga Brothers Collection, record group 4, series 151.

Rionda y Polledo, Manuel. Papers and Financial Records. University of Florida, George A. Smathers Libraries, Braga Brothers Collection, record group 2, series 10c.

Robert R. Nathan Associates, Inc., for the U.S. Cane Sugar Refiners' Association. 1971. *Cane Sugar Refining in the United States: Its Economic Importance.* Washington, DC: U.S. Cane Sugar Refiners' Association.

Romer, Christina D. 1990. The Great Crash and the Onset of the Great Depression. *Quarterly Journal of Economics* 105:597–624.

Spencer, Guilford L., and George P. Meade. 1945. *A Handbook for Sugar Cane Manufacturers and Their Chemists.* 8th ed. New York: John Wiley & Sons.

Stigler, George. 1964. A Theory of Oligopoly. *Journal of Political Economy* 72:44–61.

United States Congress. Senate Committee on Finance. 1929. Tariff Act of 1929. Vol. 5, schedule 5: Sugar, Molasses, and Manufactures of, June.

United States Industrial Commission. 1900. *Reports.* Vols. 1, 13, 14. Washington, DC: Government Printing Office.

United States Tariff Commission. 1934. *Report to the President on Sugar with Appendix.* Report 73, 2d series. Washington, DC: Government Printing Office.

United States Temporary National Economic Committee. 1941. *Trade Association Survey.* Monograph 18. Washington, DC: Government Printing Office.

United States v. Sugar Institute. Records of the District Courts of the United States, record group 21, Southern District of New York, Equity File 59–103. National Archives, New York.

Vives, Xavier. 1990. Trade Association Disclosure Rules, Incentives to Share Information, and Welfare. *Rand Journal of Economics* 21:409–30.

Whitney, Simon. 1935. Competition under Secret and Open Prices. *Econometrica* 3:40–65.

Williamson, Oliver. 1975. *Markets and Hierarchies: Analysis and Antitrust Implications.* New York: Free Press.

Yano, Hiroaki. 1982. The Cane Sugar Refining Industry in the United States. Master's thesis, Sloan School of Management, Massachusetts Institute of Technology.

Zerbe, Richard O. 1969. The American Sugar Refinery Company, 1887–1914: The Story of a Monopoly. *Journal of Law and Economics* 12:339–75.

Comment   Margaret Levenstein

David Genesove and Wallace Mullin's essay on the Sugar Institute makes an important contribution to our understanding of firm learning by focusing our attention on an important, but oft ignored, subject, the learning that firms do about organizational design. Most of us implicitly assume that the most important learning that firms undertake is learning about new technologies, with perhaps some passing concern given to learning about using existing technology (such as learning by doing). But the profitable adoption of new technologies often requires organizational innovation as well. Even when we do concern ourselves with organizational innovation, our first inclination is to follow Chandler (1977) and others, and focus on organizational innovation within the firm. But as Lamoreaux (1985) has shown, the profitable adoption of new technologies may also require organizational changes at the industry level as well. Firms actively try to shape industry structure through the design of interfirm organizations and interactions. But to do so successfully requires learning: learning about the other firms in the industry and learning about the sometimes less-than-obvious incentive properties of different interfirm organizations.

Margaret Levenstein is assistant professor of economics at the University of Michigan and a faculty research fellow of the National Bureau of Economic Research.

The simplest and most obvious types of interfirm interaction are those intended to facilitate collusion, and collusion seems to have been the primary purpose of the Sugar Institute. Collusion is undoubtedly difficult to achieve. As Stigler (1964) and others have frequently emphasized, collusion is easily undermined by cheating. Many economists have presumed that the difficulties that firms face in colluding would force them to abandon the attempt. But in many industries firms have had a more imaginative response. They turn their creative capabilities toward experimentation with various collusive schemes, learning about the incentive properties of these schemes, learning about their legality, learning about the other firms in the industry as they observe responses to each new scheme.

The case of the Sugar Institute provides a useful example of the kinds of experimentation and learning firms undertake in an attempt to find a stable collusive arrangement. It also provides insight into the limits to the experimentation undertaken, the limits of the learning that sugar firms did during this period. The Sugar Institute's learning was constrained by its own "mental model" of the sugar industry, by its own implicit model of how to respond to problems of excess capacity and falling prices. Genesove and Mullin suggest that the 1887 consolidation of the industry was a critical learning experience for the industry. Following Havemeyer's creation of the Sugar Trust, sugar firms formed a mental model of their own industry. That model suggested that *the* best way to respond to excess capacity and falling prices was consolidation. When it became clear that that solution was prohibited by antitrust law, sugar firms turned to the next best thing. They looked to close coordination that would, as nearly as possible, allow them to replicate consolidation.

Thus we can see that learning does not take place as a smooth or continuous process. Rather there are critical moments when a mental model is formed, and without a "paradigmatic shift," future learning takes place within that mental model (Kuhn 1970). What is striking about the case of the sugar industry is that, during the period covered in this paper, neither episodes of competition nor episodes of cooperation appear to have provided the basis for a paradigmatic shift that would have allowed sugar firms to develop a new mental model. Such a model might have encouraged them to focus their energy on other cooperative tools or strategies as the basis for an increase in profits.

While a different mental model might have led the Sugar Institute to direct more of its energies toward learning about technological change, advertising, and product development, the learning that the members of the institute did seems to have been strictly incremental modifications of their existing "mental model." Their experience with interfirm organization led to no radical or paradigmatic shift in their understanding of how to protect their profit margins. Within that context, however, they do seem to have learned about one another, and about the incentive properties of various institutional forms with which the institute experimented.

The Sugar Institute experimented with a variety of tools to support collusion. Probably the single most important tool was the public announcement of prices. Like other industries adopting the popular "open-pricing" schemes of the period, the sugar firms hoped that publicly announced prices would prove focal, dulling price competition without explicit price setting. But the institute did not rest with one simple tool.

The institute tried to eliminate mechanisms through which secret price cuts could be given. The institute rules banned rebates and special allowances on transportation charges and limited contract duration to a maximum of thirty days. And it banned vertical integration into certain aspects of sugar distribution. These rules then required that the institute collect information regarding members' compliance with them. So it had to learn which information would be necessary to determine compliance. It began by asking for regular reporting of information about vertical relationships, then turned to special investigations on an ad hoc basis. Initially these special investigations were undertaken by an institute investigator, but when firms resisted providing information to him, the institute began to use third-party auditors, like Haskins and Sells, to collect the necessary information.

The institute's most ambitious, but apparently least successful, scheme called for the reporting of all sales. While the institute was legally prohibited from setting output quotas or market shares, sugar firms seem to have had an idea of the share of industry output to which any firm was entitled. If the Sugar Institute could compute and report total sales in any period, individual firms could calculate their market share and use that as an indicator of cheating (as in Green and Porter 1984). While the institute tried a variety of schemes to induce disclosure of sales, and certainly learned something in the process, in the end it did not succeed in making this particular tool workable.

The institute members learned to make information sharing self-enforcing, at least some of the time, by using an exclusionary disclosure rule in which only those who provided information received reports from the institute. The institute adopted this policy after months of attempting to use "moral suasion" to convince member firms that it was in their individual interest to reveal information to the institute. When the institute learned that it could not, given the necessary weakness of its organizational structure, provide all firms with sufficient incentives to report the requested information, it tried other tactics. Exclusionary disclosure was a more credible threat than expulsion, which the institute threatened but was never willing to implement. Expulsion from the institute would have harmed the remaining members as much as the ostracized firm. Because it was clear that such a threat would never be implemented, it, as we would expect, had no effect on firm decision making.

The institute also experimented with the creation of a more centralized organizational form. Two years after the institute was founded, it created the Enforcement Committee. Even the Enforcement Committee's decisions had to be incentive compatible, as participation in the institute was voluntary. But providing an "explicit institutional structure" for resolving members' refusals to comply with requests for information, Genesove and Mullin tell us, changed incentives sufficiently to induce the reporting of information. Perhaps the public precommitments of members to support the committee changed the incentives of member firms. The precommitment itself created a new punishment, since firms had put up their promise as bond. The use of such a technique reflects learning, or at least experimentation, on the part of member firms with tools to influence the incentives of the institute members.

The decision to create the Enforcement Committee reflects continued experimentation by institute members with the overall design of their industry association. While their choices regarding the design of the association were limited by antitrust law, they did learn from the experience in the institute enough about one another to understand that a different voting mechanism might have been able to achieve more satisfactory results. The institute tried repeatedly to create a decision mechanism in which individual firms ceded their veto power to the institute, but given the legal structure under which the institute operated, simple centralization was destined to fail. We can observe further organizational learning in this area by comparing the operations of the institute to the industry code that it proposed under the Agricultural Adjustment Act. Some of the differences between the two undoubtedly reflect the dramatic changes in both the macroeconomy and the regulatory environment in the intervening years. But the differences in the proposed codes in 1934 and the design of the Sugar Institute in 1926 suggest that member firms had learned, and were using the new opportunity and the new environment to put into effect changes that they had learned would allow them to better achieve their goals. Sugar firms understood that the lack of power to impose sanctions limited the effectiveness of the institute. They hoped to solve the problem with tools made available in the new legal environment, which allowed them to propose a code with strong sanctions.

The new code also changed voting procedures, giving greater weight to large firms. Again, this suggests learning about the internal political dynamics of their own industry. Codes adopted in other industries at the same time tried to protect the interests of small and medium-sized firms with a one-firm, one-vote rule at the same time that the sugar industry, having learned the futility of such a system, appears to have abandoned it in favor of one reflecting the political realities of the industry. The new code also centralized decision making in the board to a greater degree than under the institute rules. Again, this was not something obviously required or induced by changes in external conditions, but rather reflects learning and continued experimentation by industry participants. Whether such a voting rule would have allowed implementation of an incentive scheme that would have induced further information sharing we will never know, but it was another, creative attempt to achieve those long-standing objectives.

What do *we* learn about the feasibility of collusion from Genesove and Mullin's story? They argue that implicit collusion was successful, but also that the institute was not able to achieve information sharing that one might well think crucial to collusive success. So we must ask, did the inability to share sales information have any impact on collusion? Or should we revise our ideas about how much or what kinds of information firms need to have to collude?

There are other, important types of interfirm interaction often pursued by industry associations. These include attempts to increase demand for the industry's product through advertising, standardization, and regulation of product quality. They also include attempts to improve production efficiency by improving the information that firms have about fluctuations in demand and sharing information about, or even jointly engaging in, technological innovation. As becomes clear in Genesove and Mullin's paper, the collusive and efficiency-enhancing functions of interfirm organizations are not mutually exclusive. And in their story we observe experimentation with organizational design to better achieve both types of objectives. Genesove and Mullin suggest that information sharing helped to rationalize production and economize on inventory carrying costs by allowing firms to estimate demand more accurately. They also suggest that firms used shared information as a benchmark to evaluate their own employees' success at marketing sugar and perhaps the company's own market strategy. However, the "mental model" of the industry held by the institute and its member firms seems to have led them to downplay the importance of these other activities—except when questioned by the antitrust authorities. In fact, in the case of advertising, Genesove and Mullin suggest that rather than learn how to achieve cooperative outcomes, firms learned about the limits of the usefulness of sharing information and resources. While Genesove and Mullin's description is brief, the advertising activities of the institute look quite beneficial to the industry. But these benefits were captured almost completely by the largest firms. Smaller firms learned that they were getting taxed to pay for advertising that primarily benefited larger firms, and after eight years they opted out. Advertising was not enough of a priority to the institute to experiment with different structures that might have allowed these activities to continue.

The decision to abandon the institute in 1936, when it became clear that antitrust law would limit its ability to facilitate collusion, suggests that members' mental model of the industry, and the role of an industry association in their model, had changed little over the previous nine years. There seems to have been no appreciation of the potential importance of the association as a repository of shared experience. One of the difficulties of interfirm learning is that there is not necessarily a good "home" for the learning that takes place. The institute itself provided such a home for a short period, but it did not have the longevity necessary to provide a long-term resting place, where knowledge could be stored, accumulated, synthesized over time as the external environment changed.

Institute members also never seem to have explored its potential as an agent or repository of learning about technological change. Genesove and Mullin report that there was no significant technological change between the Sugar Trust and the Sugar Institute. Was this because the possibilities for innovation were not there? Or because the collusive structure of the industry diminished the incentives for, or even impeded, technological change? Is there any evidence that information exchanged through the Sugar Institute increased productivity in sugar, say by smoothing production or cutting inventory costs? Was this a complement or a substitute for other kinds of productivity-enhancing technological change? This particular case cannot answer these questions, but it does remind us that learning is not always Progress.

References

Chandler, Alfred D., Jr. 1977. *The Visible Hand.* Cambridge, MA: Harvard University Press.

Green, Edward J., and Robert H. Porter. 1984. Noncooperative Collusion under Imperfect Price Information. *Econometrica* 52 (January): 87–100.

Kuhn, Thomas. 1970. *The Structure of Scientific Revolutions.* Chicago: University of Chicago Press.

Lamoreaux, Naomi. 1985. *The Great Merger Movement in American Business.* Cambridge: Cambridge University Press.

Stigler, George R. 1964. A Theory of Oligopoly. *Journal of Political Economy* 72: 44–61.

4   Learning by New Experiences: Revisiting the Flying Fortress Learning Curve

Kazuhiro Mishina

4.1 Introduction

It has often been argued in recent years that the firm is a dynamic learning organization. This view holds that the firm not only converts factors of production into a salable product, as modeled in the neoclassical theory of the firm, but also learns over time how better to do so. If learning and production indeed occur jointly, firms preoccupied with the optimization of production alone are shortsighted and must be encouraged by either management or public policies to invest in learning. Is there merit to considering yet another challenge to the traditional theory of the firm? The issue, of course, is not whether the firm learns at all. That is a question of semantics. The real issue is materiality. Do the productive powers of labor increase above and beyond the level predicated on the theory of the firm, and is it sensible to attribute that increase, if any, to learning on the part of the firm? The first of these two questions has been addressed by the literature on the learning curve, albeit incompletely, and the second of the two remains an open question. The gaps that exist in the story of firm-level learning are the focal point of the essay that follows.

This essay, at its core, visits a factory—one of the twenty-two airframe factories studied by Alchian (1963) in his pioneering work of the learning-curve literature—and, aided by the recent advance in the study of operations management, examines what happened behind an authentic learning curve inside the black box of the firm. The factory is Boeing's Plant No. 2 in Seattle, Wash-

Kazuhiro Mishina is associate professor of knowledge science at Japan Advanced Institute of Science and Technology.

The author is indebted to Michael Watkins, who introduced him to some of the data used in this paper, and to Alfred Chandler, Kim Clark, Adam Jaffe, and Therese Flaherty, who made helpful comments on earlier drafts. Daniel Raff, Peter Temin, David Hounshell, and the other conference participants contributed greatly to the final revision of the paper. Financial support from the Harvard Business School, Division of Research, is gratefully acknowledged.

145

ington. This was the primary production site of the famous B-17 heavy bomber, the Flying Fortress, during and prior to the Second World War. This particular production program offers many advantages for a study of this nature. Being a wartime program, it ran for an exceptionally short span of time. The program data therefore escaped external interference such as generic technological progress in the society at large. The B-17 program, moreover, is relatively well documented. The B-17 was virtually Boeing's sole product when it was in production, and its sole customer was the government, which had to justify the cost of heavy bombers vis-à-vis Congress. One would be hard-pressed to find a more attractive case to study when the central theme is firm-level learning.

4.2   The History and the Problems of the Learning Curve

The notion of learning formally entered economics with the discovery of the learning curve. Curiously, however, the learning curve itself was born when the engineering discipline tried to rewrite the theory of the firm in earnest. T. P. Wright, the director of engineering of the Curtiss-Wright Corporation, was apparently inspired by the mass production of automobiles as well as the dream of family airplanes when he began to plot out "the effect of quantity production on cost" (Wright 1936). The resulting graphs, reported in the *Journal of Aeronautical Sciences,* showed a decreasing convex curve with cost—or its components—on the vertical axis and the sequence number of the airplane on the horizontal axis. When converted to logarithmic scale, the graphs looked linear, suggesting not only predictability but also specific mathematical relationship: labor required per unit—or, interpreted more casually, unit cost—is a negatively sloping log-linear function of the cumulative volume of production. It is this mathematical formulation that was later named variously the learning curve, experience curve, and progress function. All three refer to the same phenomenon while emphasizing a slightly different aspect: the process, cause, and outcome of the cost behavior, respectively. In the studies that followed, the formulation fit data quite well in a wide range of industries including, but not limited to, shipbuilding, machine tools, specialty chemicals, and semiconductors.

The learning curve thus established empirically resembles the average-cost function of the traditional theory of the firm in that both strip the firm all the way down to two variables and formalize a widely held belief among industrialists: the unit cost goes down as a firm or a factory makes more of the same product. The learning curve, however, departs from the traditional theory of the firm in two respects. First, it replaces the variable on the horizontal axis. In lieu of the rate of output (output per period), to which economists are accustomed, it inserts cumulative output. Interestingly, though, Wright himself was quite possibly indifferent to the choice between the two variables. He was concerned with the cost estimate of the Nth airplane in production and always labeled the horizontal axis of the graphs N—the sequence number of the airplane—and not as cumulative output. Moreover, he perhaps had no choice but to use the sequence number, as opposed to the rate of output. Given the long time needed to build each unit of an airplane and the small number of units demanded by the market for an airplane, it was not very practical to gauge the rate of output for any natural unit of time, such as week, month, and year, unless a reliable method to measure a fraction of an airplane was devised. In Wright's data, N fell short of 150 in one case and 40 in the other despite years of data gathering. Second, the learning curve departs from the traditional theory of the firm in its adoption of a specific functional form. Although the log-linear formulation was justified only by computational convenience and subsequent good fit, it enabled the learning curve to spell out the cost of every unit in the production sequence and the associated factor requirements once its two parameters—the initial cost and the rate of learning—are estimated.

The two points of departure—the use of cumulative output on the horizontal axis and the specification of the functional form—are thus arbitrary in terms of how they came into being. But it is precisely these two features that led to the widespread appeal of the learning-curve formulation. For one, they together eliminate uncertainty as well as dependence upon decisions, such as setting the rate of output, from the estimation of the unit cost and factor usage, thus opening an avenue to a new possibility of planning operations (Andress 1954) or formulating strategy (Boston Consulting Group 1972) around these deterministic estimates. Those who wish that the pragmatism of engineering ruled management are finally vindicated. For another, cumulative output makes sense as a proxy variable for some sort of production-related experience and, therefore, permits plausible interpretations of the learning curve. In one such interpretation, the learning-by-doing hypothesis, cumulative output is thought to measure the amount of on-the-job practice performed by the direct workers and, consequently, the level of skills they bring to bear on the work they do (Hirschmann 1964). Alternatively, one may think of cumulative output as growing in proportion to the feedback engineers receive from the shop floor regarding the robustness of the process or the manufacturability of the product they developed (Hirsch 1952; Conway and Schultz 1959). Then, the learning curve represents the level of engineering refinement and, in turn, the ease with which direct workers of a given skill level perform their task. Be it direct workers, engineers, or both who actually learn in the firm, those who hold that experience is the mother of improvement are vindicated by these interpretations of the learning curve.[1]

The learning curve is interesting because it seemingly captures a force that

1. If cumulative output merely represents experience, there may well be other proxy variables that are equally good. The one that has been studied most on this line of reasoning is the elapsed time (Fellner 1969). This alternative model makes sense if the stimulus of learning is independent of production and bound by the passage of time. As opposed to learning by doing, one may call it a model of learning by thinking. The same contrast is often framed as induced learning versus autonomous learning (Levy 1965; Yelle 1979; Dutton and Thomas 1984).

is not present in the traditional theory of the firm. However, a question is inevitable. Does it truly mark a departure from economies of scale—a central force shaping the average-cost function in the theory of the firm? Is it not merely the division of labor in disguise? Despite the seriousness of the question, the learning-curve literature offers no clear-cut answers.

The problem is twofold. First, when Wright discovered the learning curve, he was in fact walking familiar territory covered well by Adam Smith. He wrote, "The factors which make possible cost reductions with increase in the quantity produced are as follows: the improvement in proficiency of a workman . . . less changes to disconcert the workman . . . greater spread of machine and fixture set up time . . . ability to use less skilled labor as more and more tooling and standardization of procedure is introduced" (Wright 1936, 124). One may contrast this quote with an earlier well-known observation. Adam Smith, in his inquiry into the causes of the wealth of nations, opened his text with an account of contemporary pin manufacturing practice, in which an ordinary factory employed ten workers to staff approximately eighteen distinct operations and produced upwards of 48,000 pins a day. This amounted to 4,800 pins per worker per day although, he wrote, the workers were not capable of making 20 pins each a day alone. Smith reasoned that the dramatic improvement in the productive powers of labor was due, directly, to a proper division and combination of the different operations and, indirectly, to a large scale of operations—and a large market size—which permitted the division of labor in the first place. He thus established scale—usually measured by the flow rate of output, such as 20 pins a day or 48,000 pins a day—as the most important variable in the cost function or, more broadly, in the theory of the firm. Interestingly, Smith ([1776] 1976, 11) attributed the effect of the division of labor to three factors: "first to the increase of dexterity in every particular workman; secondly, to the saving of the time which is commonly lost in passing from one species of work to another; and lastly, to the invention of a great number of machines which facilitate and abridge labor, and enable one man to do the work of many." These three points correspond almost perfectly to Wright's passage explaining the reasons for the declining cost of airplanes.

Second, the learning curve and the economies of scale are virtually indistinguishable in the majority of econometric studies. The reason is the collinearity between their right-hand-side variables, that is, cumulative output and the rate of output, since the former is nothing but the latter summed over time. Collinearity is especially strong where the rate of output follows an upward trend, as cumulative output always does by definition, and the unit cost or labor hours a downward trend: a pattern predominant in the data used in the learning-curve studies. Thus, it is generally difficult, if not impossible, to properly decompose whatever variations there are in the unit cost data into the part explained by the rate of output, that is, the effect of scale, and the part explained by cumulative output, that is, the effect of learning, so long as the effort to do so relies exclusively on numerical data analysis. Herein lies the promise of detailed case studies.

4.3   The B-17 Program

The Boeing B-17 heavy bomber, known otherwise as the Flying Fortress, was the first four-engined, all-metal, midwing monoplane.[2] It served the U.S. Army Air Forces as a workhorse during World War II. It received much attention, both during and after the war, in part because it was one of the few experimental bomber designs that were deemed combat-worthy when the war broke out in Europe and President Franklin D. Roosevelt suddenly called for 50,000 airplanes a year. The B-17 production program, and in particular its efficiency and ramp-up speed, thus took on a special meaning as a crucial test of the nation's combat readiness. It was in this context that the Air Materiel Command (1946a) later studied this program extensively as an integral part of its postwar planning efforts and issued a comprehensive report on the program performance. This case-study report is the primary source of information for the analysis that follows. The report was compiled on the basis of extensive interviews of Boeing personnel,[3] and the Boeing Aircraft Company concurred that "[a]ll corrections and revisions recommended by us were embodied in this report except those concerning the section on Management"—a section of little interest for the purpose of this essay. The report is generally approving of the choices made by the company during the war, and concludes that the B-17 program's rate of acceleration "compares favorably with that reached by other manufacturers of heavy bombers throughout the country" (ix).

The B-17 began its life in July 1935 as the Model 299—Boeing's answer to an army air corps circular calling for a new multiengined bomber. Boeing developed a semimonocoque all-metal bomber with four engines, by far the largest and boldest entry in the competition.[4] Boeing, however, was disqualified because the only Model 299 it built crashed and burned during the first official test flight. The contract was awarded to a sister model of the Douglas DC-3: a two-engined airplane that was to set the standard for commercial aviation. Boeing's risk-taking was nonetheless rewarded with a small contract for

---

2. A monoplane has only one pair of wings. A biplane has two pairs of wings, one above and one below the fuselage.

3. The report acknowledges the help it received from Boeing's key officers. Their titles are listed as Engineering Historian, Tooling General Superintendent, Liaison Engineer, General Supervisor Training, Assistant to Operations Manager, Assistant to Executive Vice President, Director of Industrial Relations, Assistant to Chief Project Engineer, Assistant to Chief Cost Accountant, Material Manager, Plant Facilities Manager, Personnel Manager, BDV Committee Member, Assistant to the President, Chief Cost Accountant, Operations Manager, Business Office Superintendent, Analyst & Statistician, Quality Manager, Assistant to Production Manager, Superintendent Manpower, Chief Engineer, and Executive Vice President.

4. An airplane with a monocoque structure lets the skin absorb all the stresses to which it is subjected.

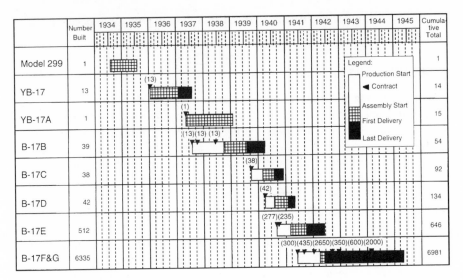

Fig. 4.1   The variations of the B-17

thirteen test units. The YB-17 thus came to life with a new and improved engine, and the B-17 series, despite the criticism in Congress that this heavy bomber was too large and too expensive, eventually evolved through nine official designations (fig. 4.1).[5] Of the nine designations, the last three, E, F, and G, were produced in large numbers and flown over combat theaters. The other designations up to D were more of a prototype, pushing the limit of the basic design. The cruising speed and altitude of the B-17 increased constantly from the Model 299 to the D designation, and thereafter remained unchanged. Between D and E, the rear fuselage was enlarged to accommodate more gunners and heavier defensive armament. Once the basic design was frozen with the B-17E, the subsequent designations differed from E predominantly in terms of added-on armament.[6] Indeed, Boeing internally categorized E, F, and G as "Model 299O" as if they were identical, and so did the Royal Air Force as "Fortress II." In the remainder of the essay, these three designations are collectively identified as the production version of the B-17. Boeing built a grand total of 6,981 units of the B-17, of which 6,847 units were, according to this definition, the production version.

Boeing built almost all B-17s in its main plant (Plant No. 2) in Seattle, which started its life in 1935. Plant No. 2's achievement in both ramp-up speed and productivity is impressive by any standards. Being one of a few proven bombers at the outbreak of the war, the B-17 was called upon as an implement of strategic bombing. The War Department issued a letter of intent ordering 512

5. For the history of the heavy bomber program, see Craven and Cate (1955), Holley (1964), and Rae (1968).
6. Davis (1984), for example, explains the evolution of the airplane in more detail.

B-17Es in July 1940, and thereby made Boeing begin its planning for plant, tooling, and workforce expansion. The delivery of the production version began with five units in September 1941. Monthly production then rose steadily, reaching 100 units in the course of July 1942 and 200 units in the course of May 1943. Plant No. 2 recorded peak production in March 1944 when it delivered a staggering total of 362 units. In the next month, Boeing continued production but also began the conversion of Plant No. 2 from the B-17 to the newer and larger B-29. The effort accelerated in February 1945, but the war ended before the B-29 saw mass production.[7] Plant No. 2 delivered its last 32 B-17Gs in April 1945.

The B-17 was a complex airplane to build, requiring tolerances as tight as 0.005 inches and more than six miles of wiring. The five airplanes delivered in September 1941 consumed on average 142,837 direct labor hours per airframe: the equivalent of approximately 71 worker-years.[8] Thereafter, unit direct labor hours followed a declining trend. They bottomed out in August 1944 at 15,316 hours, almost one-tenth of what had been needed 35 months earlier. Productivity suffered during the cutback phase, and the 100 airplanes delivered in December 1944 embodied 21,357 direct labor hours per airframe. Nevertheless, it is incontrovertible that Plant No. 2 exhibited a dramatic learning effect as measured by the direct labor hours needed for each airframe. The government accordingly reduced the price it paid to Boeing from $242,200 for the first B-17E to $144,824 for the last B-17G despite the vast improvement made to the airplane in between.[9] Figure 4.2 shows a plot of monthly output and unit direct labor hours.

With the information in figures 4.1 and 4.2, it is possible to draw a classical learning curve for the B-17 program. The relevant data here cover the 40-month period between September 1941 and December 1944.[10] The dependent variable of interest is the unit direct labor hours, l_t, which is shown on the vertical axis of figure 4.2. This variable measures the work hours logged by the direct workers of Boeing and its subcontractors, averaged over all airframes that were delivered to the government in month t.[11] One may argue that the unit cost is superior to l_t as dependent variable, but l_t is a major driver of the unit production cost of the airframe.[12] Moreover, where production is labor intensive, l_t makes a cleaner measure of the true unit cost than the accounting cost,

7. See Hershey (1944) and Boeing's 1945 annual report.
8. An airframe here refers to an airplane less such government-furnished items as engines and armament.
9. Note that the total cost of an airplane is dominated by the material cost, and explained only partly by the labor cost.
10. The delivery of the B-17G continued through the first four months of 1945, but data reporting did not.
11. See Asher (1956), Reguero (1957), and Alchian (1963) for a comprehensive account of the original source and the definition of the data.
12. Reguero (1957), for example, estimated that wages represented 60 percent of the unit cost of an airframe.

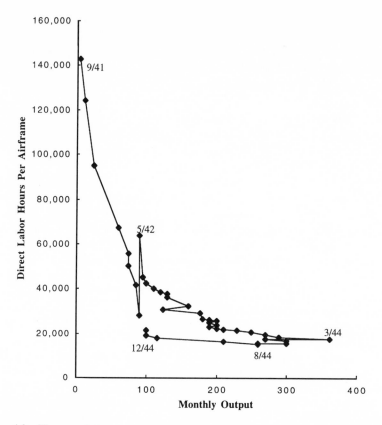

Fig. 4.2   The raw data

which rather arbitrarily allocates overhead expenses and fixed costs (Wright 1936).

The classical learning curve is written as

(1) $\log l_t = a + b \log Y_t,$

or $l_t = aY_t^b$, where Y_t stands for the cumulative output, or $Y_t = \sum_{s=1}^{t} X_s$, where X_s in turn stands for the output in month s. Applying this formulation to the B-17 data, column 1 of table 4.1 reports the result of the popular regression using ordinary least squares (OLS). It indicates that the best estimate of b is $-.472$, that is, every doubling of cumulative output gives rise to 27.9 percent decline in the unit direct labor hours. The coefficient of determination adjusted for the degree of freedom, $\overline{R}^2$, is respectably high and the estimate of parameter b is statistically different from zero. This is where analysis usually ends and specu-lation begins concerning the implications of the learning curve to policymak-ers, business executives, and operations managers.

The problem is that such an estimate of the learning curve is not unbiased

Table 4.1   Linear Regression of $\log l_T$

	(1)	(2)	(3)	(4)	(5)	(6)	(7)
Constant	6.001	6.263	6.534	6.632	4.629	6.741	6.621
$\log k_T$		−.581[a]	−.488[a]	−.567[a]	−.735[a]	−.902[a]	−.547[a]
		(.083)	(.109)	(.089)	(.079)	(.210)	(.093)
$\log X_T$		−.493[a]	−.371[a]	−.285[a]	−.266[a]	−.780[a]	−.292[a]
		(.029)	(.046)	(.043)	(.050)	(.057)	(.044)
T		−.010[a]					
		(.001)					
$\log Y_t$	−.472[a]		−.291[a]				−.052
	(.023)		(.026)				(.065)
$\log Z_T$				−.530[a]	−.524[a]		−.444[a]
				(.039)	(.043)		(.113)
Estimator	OLS	OLS	OLS	OLS	EGLS	OLS	OLS
Degrees of freedom	38	36	36	36	35	37	35
$\bar{R}^2$	.917	.981	.969	.978	.961	.868	.978
Durbin-Watson	1.113[b]	0.908[b]	0.847[b]	1.303[c]	1.485[d]	0.067[b]	1.263[c]

Note: Numbers in parentheses are standard errors.

[a]Coefficients are significantly different from zero at the 1 percent confidence level.

[b]The Durbin-Watson statistic does not exceed the lower bound at the 1 percent confidence level.

[c]The Durbin-Watson statistic exceeds the lower bound but not the upper bound at the 1 percent confidence level.

[d]The Durbin-Watson statistic exceeds the upper bound at the 1 percent confidence level.

despite the strong indications of economic and statistical significance. The result reported in column 1 of table 4.1 reproduces the common problem: the Durbin-Watson statistic is too small to support the null hypothesis of no autocorrelation at the 1 percent confidence level. That is to say, the OLS estimator that led to the fitted learning curve is most likely biased, the meaning of which is that the classical formulation of the learning curve (1) may well be misspecified. Figure 4.3 plots the residuals from the regression of column 1 and makes the issue obvious. The pattern that emerges is clearly far from random. Even if the dip at the beginning is explained away by the changeover from the E designation to the F designation, the systematic deviation occurring throughout 1944 suggests that variables are missing from the regression. This is the problem Alchian (1963) encountered when he found that the learning curve was not able to predict labor hours reliably. The learning curve tells us an interesting story. But as an explanation of quantitative facts it stands on remarkably shaky ground.

4.4   Inside Plant No. 2

It is one thing to find a flaw in the classic learning-curve formulation, but it is quite another to find an alternative explanation for the dramatic decrease in the direct labor hours expended on each B-17. Several hypotheses are conceiv-

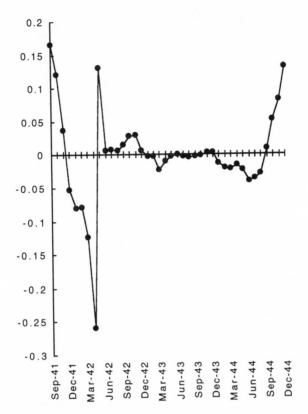

Fig. 4.3 The residuals

able. First, what happened is simply an example of scale economies. On the shop floor, in this interpretation, labor would have been divided more and more as production expanded from 5 airframes a month to 362 airframes a month. A second hypothesis might be that the learning-curve story was not tested properly by the calculations in column 1 of table 4.1 and in figure 4.3. The classic learning curve would be well specified if all the sources of Boeing's production experience were considered. A third possibility is that the quality of the airframes that were produced deteriorated over time or that the B-17 became, because of small design changes, a simpler product to build. This hypothesis amounts not to a claim that efficiency improved but rather to the claim that, as time passed, there was less work involved in building the B-17 airframes. Yet another possibility is that labor input might have improved. On this reading, the learning-by-doing hypothesis is still valid in fact, even though measurement is difficult. One more possibility, of course, is "none of the above." Something other than the division of labor was at work, but it is not quite learning by doing on the shop floor either. The text that follows scrutinizes these hypotheses based on the historical records of the B-17 production program.

4.4.1 Scale Economies

There is no denying that the decrease in the unit direct labor hours in the B-17 program was dramatic. But, then, so was the increase in output. Is it possible that the learning curve is yet another expression of the consequences of the transition from small- to large-scale operations? Answering this question requires a careful examination of the production processes as well as the changes made to them over time.

Boeing built the B-17 in the main building of Plant No. 2.[13] This huge square structure on a 66-acre site covered 37 acres under one roof and boasted a total floor space of 42 acres with balconies. The building was erected with utmost flexibility in mind.[14] Overhead cranes and underground utility tunnels permitted just about any layout configuration. In practice, work in progress moved from the west end of the building, where machine shops were located, toward final assembly on the east end just off the airfield. Between the two production areas was the enormous expanse of the subassembly area.

The subassembly area was divided into many rectangular sections of various sizes. These sections were bordered by a clear boundary because each was filled tightly with only one kind of airframe segment—inboard wing, for example—and adjacent sections were filled with completely different airframe segments. Figure 4.4 shows the inboard wing section (front) as well as the forward fuselage section (back). Between are several completed fuselages heading for final assembly. Figure 4.5 is a close-up view of the forward fuselage section. The production areas, proceeding from parts fabrication to subassembly to final assembly, were sandwiched by the storage areas that occupied the entire north and south sides of the building. The storage areas received shipments from subcontractors and suppliers, and in turn fed the production areas with the parts and materials they needed.

Boeing's production method featured a combination of stationary subassembly and short multiline final assembly. The idea was to minimize the time work in progress spent in the final assembly stage, because once the fuselage and the wings were joined, the airframe wasted space on the shop floor and unnecessarily increased the time workers spent walking back and forth. Thus, Boeing chose to break down the B-17's airframe production into roughly fifty subassemblies upon the arrival of the E designation. These subassemblies were neatly jammed into sections of their own in the subassembly area and completed there as independent units by moving crews while stationary in a holding jig. When a subassembly piece was ready to move on, it was picked up by

---

13. *Aviation* (July 1943) describes this building and the production method adopted therein.
14. When Plant No. 2 was erected, the company faced profound uncertainties with regard to the product mix and production volume both during and after the war.

Fig. 4.4   B-17Es in Plant No. 2: inboard wing subassembly
Source: USAF Museum (Wright-Patterson AF Base).

Fig. 4.5   B-17Es in Plant No. 2: forward fuselage subassembly
Source: Bowers (1976), 81.

an overhead crane and carried all the way to another section that would bolt it together with a few other subassemblies to form a major assembly segment—for example, the inboard wing segment comprising the body of the wing, flaps, engine nacelles, and deicers.[15] Major assemblies likewise joined one another on one of several final assembly lines, where the remaining work, such as attaching propellers, was divided among a few stations. Gigantic airplanes stood immediately one after another in this area, and moved every now and then on their own set of wheels for the first time. Figure 4.6 shows a final assembly line in Plant No. 2 (another is seen starting on the right-hand edge).

The huge plant building as well as the production method described above did not emerge overnight. Understanding the precise timing will prove to be important.[16] When Boeing started building the first B-17 (Model 299), it had only one manufacturing facility (Plant No. 1). In this plant, skilled workers fabricated parts with drop hammers, put together major segments of the airplane on wooden jigs, and installed assorted equipment on the airplane as it sat immobile in the center of the assembly building.[17] In 1935, in expectation of the coming of gigantic metal airplanes such as the B-17, Boeing acquired the land for Plant No. 2 one mile away from its original site. Thereafter, Plant No. 2's main building expanded through four projects. The first two of them, amounting to 9 percent of the floor space of the eventual main building, were carried out in 1936 and 1937. Figure 4.7 shows the very first B-17 (Model 299) being assembled in Plant No. 1 in 1935, and figure 4.8 shows B-17Bs being assembled in the brand-new Plant No. 2 in 1939.

With the coming of the B-17E, both the scale and the method of production changed significantly. The third expansion project commenced in May 1940, immediately following the French order for the DB-7 and President Roosevelt's call for 50,000 airplanes a year. The project added 38 percent of the floor space of the eventual main building, and occupancy began six months after the start of construction. In August 1940 Boeing established the Tooling Department for the first time, because approximately 75 percent of the tools were rendered obsolete by the design changes introduced to the B-17E. This group, staffed fully in one year, added hydraulic presses, steel jigs, and special alterations of general-purpose drilling and milling machines. In October 1940 Boeing obtained government financing and initiated the fourth expansion project. This last phase completed the remaining 53 percent of the main building to increase capacity from ten to sixty B-17s per month. In June 1941 another government-financing contract permitted Boeing to order additional machine

15. Beall (1945) offers an account of the design detail by the vice president of engineering at the time. Bowers (1976) contains the history of the airplane as well as a story told by its original designer.

16. The evolution of Plant No. 2 is reported in great detail in several issues of *Aero Digest,* including February 1937, January 1938, February 1938, November 1940, and October 1941.

17. Laudan (1936) offers an account by a factory superintendent as to how Boeing built the prototype model 299. See also Klemin (1940) and Bowers (1976) for informative photographs of Plant No. 2 when it was building the B-17B.

Fig. 4.6   B-17Es in Plant No. 2: final assembly
Source: USAF Museum (Wright-Patterson AF Base).

Fig. 4.7   Model 299 in Plant No. 1
Source: Bowers (1976), 44.

Fig. 4.8   B-17Bs in Plant No. 2
Source: Bowers (1976), 44.

tools and increase monthly capacity to seventy-five B-17s. Throughout these expansion projects, Boeing chose to extend its production philosophy that valued flexibility rather than reconfiguring the plant layout.

From available evidence, it seems that Boeing's resources for mass production were largely in place by the end of the B-17E run, that is, by May 1942 when the first B-17F was delivered. All told, Boeing added $17.4 million of fixed assets to its balance sheet from 1940 to 1945 for the war effort at Plant No. 2. Of these, 69 percent were in place by the end of 1941 and 96 percent by the following year. The Tooling Department had completed most of the required 70,000 dies and jigs in time for the beginning of the mass production of the B-17E. This included the oft-cited special-purpose equipment that Boeing credited for the productivity improvement. Major additions after May 1942 consisted of the expansion of warehouse space in the summer of 1942, the leasing of six feeder plants that increased plant space by 10 percent in the fall of 1943, and the construction of a cafeteria, an office building, and a wind tunnel in 1943. During the production phase of the B-17F and B-17G, there was no investment in productive capacity.

What does this all mean? The B-17's production version maintained a downward trend of the unit direct labor hours with neither notable capacity expansions nor changes in the production method. In fact, Boeing took the facility, equipment, and method that were designed to turn out 75 airframes a month, and built as many as 362 airframes at the peak of its monthly production. One may well argue, turning the logic of scale economies upside down, that large scale, as measured by the rate of output, is the result, and not the cause, of improved efficiency. Scale, as measured by the size of productive capacity, remained nearly constant, and is likewise unable to explain changes in the unit direct labor hours over a period as long as three years.[18]

What if scale is measured by the batch size? As figure 4.9 shows, the batch size shrank at the beginning with the introduction of the block production system, which was devised to cope with a flock of design changes on the basis of a relatively small standard batch size. The batch size then jumped from 100 airframes to 200 airframes with a period of struggling transition in between. In contrast to this stepwise movement of the batch size, the unit direct labor hours declined smoothly throughout much of these periods. Granted that the changes are by and large in the same direction, the patterns of change are too different to suggest that the batch size is the direct cause of improved efficiency. The reverse causal link—improved efficiency permitted the batch size to expand—seems, if anything, more plausible. To sum, no matter how scale is measured, scale economies cannot provide an adequate explanation for the dramatic efficiency improvement in the B-17 program.[19]

4.4.2 External Experience

The missing variable in the classic learning curve may well be experience external to the B-17 program. That is, the dramatic efficiency improvement is a learning effect after all. It is just that Boeing learned from sources other than its own experience of building B-17s. Does this line of reasoning hold water?

It appears that the answer is no. The Air Materiel Command (1946a, 6) remarks that "Boeing had had very little, if any, production experience prior to the B-17 program. They had produced airplanes, but never in quantity. The B-17 was their first real production program." In its quarter-century history prior to the war, Boeing built only some 2,100 airplanes, most of which had neither the metal construction nor the size of the B-17 (see *Aero Digest* July 1941). In contrast, it built more than three times as many B-17s: a grand total of 6,981 units. Boeing did assemble 240 Douglas-designed DB-7Bs for the French gov-

---

18. To be precise, productive capacity here refers to a concept of scale proposed by Alchian (1959): the contemplated volume of production. In the case of the B-17 at Plant No. 2, it remained basically constant at 75 airframes a month.

19. On the question of different notions of scale, see Alchian (1959) and Gold (1981).

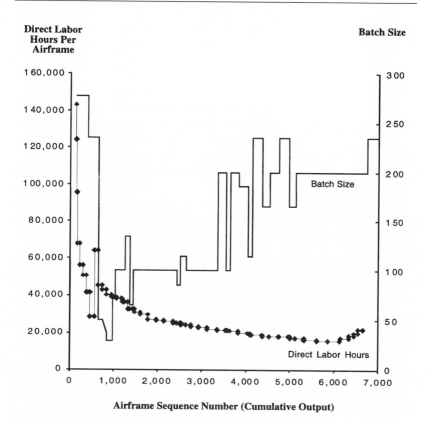

Fig. 4.9   The effect of batch size

ernment in 1940 at Plant No. 2, but even this experience pales in comparison with the B-17 program.

Not only did Boeing produce B-17s without any relevant previous experience, Plant No. 2 also did so without any relevant parallel experience. Boeing did develop another heavy bomber, the B-29, to replace the aging B-17 toward the end of the war, but Plant No. 2 actually built only three prototypes of that airplane. Mass production of the B-29 took place at Renton, Washington, and Wichita, Kansas, in the government-owned facilities, to which Plant No. 2 transferred a nucleus of personnel with a stack of engineering documents. Similarly, when Douglas and Vega joined Boeing in the production of the B-17F and B-17G in response to the solicitation from the government, and under license from Boeing, Plant No. 2 assisted these newcomers, and not vice versa.[20]

20. Chapter 20 of Holley (1964) describes the joint production effort, known as the BDV committee.

Plant No. 2 was always a mother plant rather than a recipient of know-how from external sources. If Boeing did learn from experience, the source of that experience must be found inside Plant No. 2 and with regard to the B-17.

4.4.3 Product Alteration

The B-17 built in 1944 might not have been the same B-17 built in 1941. If newer B-17s required less labor by design, the decrease in the unit direct labor hours observed in the B-17 program is not as dramatic as it first appears. Were there changes in the B-17 in ways that accommodate this line of argument?

The B-17 did undergo numerous engineering changes: 155 of them with the B-17E, 760 with the B-17F, and 634 with the B-17G. Few, however, were introduced to improve manufacturability or otherwise address concerns and suggestions from the shop floor. Boeing's engineering department was in fact overwhelmed by the requests from the battlefield that kept uncovering the B-17's weaknesses in every detail.[21] The most important feature of these changes was that the B-17 acquired more and more armament from batch to batch, and became, if anything, a more complex product to assemble. By the same token, the B-17's quality was always subjected to the toughest of any field tests one can imagine. Nevertheless, quality problems were never cited by any sources I have been able to uncover. On the contrary, the B-17 acquired a reputation of being the most rugged and well built of any heavy bomber as more and more crews returned alive from bombing missions in planes that were severely damaged by fierce enemy counterattacks (see Bowers 1976, chap. 9). To guarantee that this would be the case, the Army Air Forces accepted B-17s only after rigorous inspection by on-site representatives. It is inconceivable that the dramatic decline in the unit direct labor hours was caused by equally dramatic deterioration in the quality of the output, or by improvement in manufacturability.

4.4.4 Learning by Doing

Cumulative output is a proxy variable. It may have failed to represent the rising skill level of direct workers, but it is still possible that the behavior of the unit direct labor hours is explained by improvement in dexterity. Or is it?

Here is what happened with the workforce at Plant No. 2. Boeing initiated all-out hiring efforts in August 1941 as the first B-17Es neared final assembly. In just six months the number of direct workers increased from 9,972 to 21,083. However, this was the peak as far as the head count goes. After February 1942, turnover either outpaced or matched hiring, and the number of direct workers consequently fluctuated around 17,000 for the rest of the B-17 program. In fact, the chronic labor shortage was so severe that Boeing set up

---

21. The working-paper version of this paper (Mishina 1992, 19–21) offers additional data and formal analysis on the subject of engineering's contribution to efficiency improvement. The conclusion drawn is that the pattern of unit direct labor hours has little correlation with the hours logged by design engineers and/or toolmakers.

feeder plants in the summer of 1943 to tap into labor supplies outside the immediate Seattle area. Boeing also tried to make the best use of subcontractors starting with the B-17C, to mitigate the labor shortage. It did not take long to exhaust this source, however: the subcontracting ratio already reached 28 percent with the B-17E and never exceeded 33 percent thereafter. Just like the case of the fixed assets, the size of the workforce already approached its peak figure with the E designation.

Unlike the plant and equipment, the workforce underwent significant qualitative changes during the mass-production phase and its skill deteriorated considerably. The early variants of the B-17 were built by a group of skilled craftsmen who had learned the ins and outs of airframe production through trial and error. With the outbreak of the war, these men either enlisted or were promoted to supervisory positions, and Boeing had to tap into entirely new labor pools to staff Plant No. 2. "During 1941," the Air Materiel Command (1946a, 65) summarizes, "it could fairly be said that hiring specifications were strict, [but] as labor became scarcer the contractor was forced to adopt lower standards and take whatever labor was available." Given this reality, it is difficult to accept an argument that the quality of direct labor may have increased over time.

Moreover, whatever labor Boeing was able to employ did not stay with the company long enough to acquire new craft skills. For example, Boeing started hiring female workers for the first time in its history to cope with the chronic labor shortage.[22] Female employment, which was less than 1,000 in 1941, increased steadily and reached 16,000 by early 1944. In other words, Plant No. 2 attained its peak production as well as peak efficiency predominantly with green hands and *not* with the men who were brought into the plant by the massive hiring program of 1941. The heroic female workers—known generally as Rosie the Riveter—had had a factory job only for a year or two when Plant No. 2 recorded its best performance.[23] Unless labor skill is easily transferable, these facts undermine the learning-by-doing hypothesis that regards direct workers as the principal embodiment of experiential learning.[24]

4.4.5 Production System

It is clear by now that learning, in this case, went far beyond factor inputs. Simply stated, output and productivity did not peak until 1944 whereas the buildup of capital and labor leveled off by early 1942. There is also no apparent

22. See Froelich (1942) for general labor conditions of the industry.
23. The turnover rate was high throughout the B-17 program due partly to wage competition from the shipyards in the immediate vicinity. Absenteeism ranged from 7.2 percent (September) to 10.8 percent (December) in 1943, and from 5.5 percent (January) to 8.6 percent (October) in 1944.
24. The point is not to deny workers' ability to learn. Boeing's 1944 annual report credited workers, for example, by stating that in 1944 the Employee Suggestion System collected 12,493 entries, 2,380 (19 percent of which were awarded and put in use. The point is that Plant No. 2 exhibited a steady learning effect even when the faces of direct workers were constantly changing. Direct workers in this case collectively lacked the ability to accumulate learning.

indication of positive qualitative changes in capital and labor that were employed for the B-17F and B-17G. It is clear instead that learning at Plant No. 2 stretched its effective capacity well beyond the original plan—more than quadrupling, to be precise.

The only way in which this could have happened is through a rising velocity of work in progress that moved through the limited space of the main plant building. This point warrants elaboration, for it highlights the importance of the production system as distinct from factor inputs of production. Space limitation imposes an upper bound on the amount of work in progress (*WIP*) that can be stored on the shop floor. If system cycle time (*SCT*) is defined as the elapsed time between two successive units of output exiting the plant building, and throughput time (*TPT*) as the interval between the entry to and the exit from the plant building of a specific unit of output, the following relationship must hold true for a given unit of time.[25]

$$(2) \qquad \overline{WIP} \geq WIP = \frac{TPT}{SCT} = TPT \times (OUTPUT).$$

When monthly output increases, throughput time as measured in months must decrease accordingly once the plant exhausts all the floor space it can use. This is the precise meaning of the rising velocity. In Plant No. 2 the level of work-in-progress inventory actually declined steeply throughout 1943, and the weighted average throughput time dropped from 1.48 months in the last five months of 1942, down to 0.88 months in 1943, and further to 0.48 months in 1944.

The few accounts put forward in 1943 by the witnesses of wartime production suggest the linkage between the rising velocity and changes in the production system. One of them comes from the superintendent of tooling at Plant No. 2 (Bucey 1943). This manager assigned much of the credit for declining unit direct labor hours to the extensive tooling program, which explicitly focused on speedier production. Interestingly, the point he made was not so much about the time savings in machining: more important was the reduction of rework at assembly thanks to greater interchangeability of parts. Assembly in fact consumed about 80 percent of all direct labor hours, a substantial part of which dealt with rework.[26] Decrease in the amount of rework would certainly help airplanes to leave the plant building more rapidly and free up floor space for more units of work in progress at the same time.

A critical point here is the cause of greater interchangeability. There is no

---

25. *WIP* in equation (2) measures the number of airplanes in various stages of production, counting all of them equally.

26. Boeing's 1939 annual report blamed rework for losses it incurred on the B-17B. According to Bucey (1943, 221), "Incorrectly manufactured parts can result in abnormally high assembly costs which are difficult to segregate. If a part doesn't fit, the amount of rework on the job which must be done by the assembly shops is almost incalculable."

denying that the kind of equipment that arrived with the B-17E made a difference vis-à-vis the old days of low-volume production. Yet much had to do with procedures and simple devices. Bucey (1943) vividly illustrated an example in which a worker used a hand tool on his own discretion to keep production on schedule when regular equipment broke down, and consequently created tolerance problems downstream. Human errors and mistakes like this hurt interchangeability, despite good intentions, where there was, for example, no clear documentation specifying how abnormal situations should be handled under various circumstances. Plant No. 2 reduced these opportunities for human errors with production illustrations, templates, and revisions of tooling development procedures.[27] These initiatives were all an integral part of the production system.

Another account comes from executives of different heavy-bomber producers (Laddon 1943; Perelle 1943). They found that more than 70 percent of their throughput time went into handling and, due to backtracking, some parts traveled more than a mile between two stations that were only fifty feet apart. They concluded that the shop floor's crowded condition caused wastefulness, confusion, and inefficiency with increase in orders. Their solution was to streamline the process so that the right number of fabricated parts could reach the right place at the right time and the entire flow could be in a direct line to the last operation. They abolished the central finished-parts stockroom and made sure that the small stock bins carried only eight to ten days' supplies. This story amounts to a prefiguration of today's just-in-time (JIT) production.

Given Boeing's production method, which relied on overhead cranes for the handling of work in progress, implementation of JIT production must have been inevitable as soon as Plant No. 2 exhausted slack floor space. It was simply impossible to keep a larger number of bulky pieces of work in progress, such as forward fuselage, in transit, that is, hung in the air. Work in progress therefore could not leave one section and move on to the next until the destination section freed up a holding jig. In other words, production had to be pulled strictly from downstream sections. A plant tour report (*Aviation* July 1943, 310) thus stated: "Behind all this fluid activity is a perfect timing. If one division falls behind, it is as instantly apparent as an empty space in a line." It is not difficult to imagine the degree of coordination this plant required for production control.

A primary cause of the rising velocity at Plant No. 2 was the tighter implementation of JIT production. The Air Materiel Command (1946a, 36) pointed to one trend that persisted throughout the growth phase of the B-17 production program: "As the production schedules were increased, the degree of break-

27. Wright (1939) also emphasized similar managerial initiatives and cited Boeing for its use of templates to reduce errors and loss of parts, time, and material.

down [into subassemblies] was of necessity proportionately increased." In essence, Plant No. 2 divided the subassembly area into an ever larger number of smaller sections. As a result, the direct workers could work on a larger number of airframe segments of a given airplane at any given moment in the factory without interfering with one another. The change thus increased the intensity with which an airplane was assembled and, therefore, the velocity of production.

This gain did not come easily. More breakdown into finer subassemblies also meant less slack in each subassembly section and so less leeway for the smooth operations of the entire plant. Behind the rising velocity, the plant was increasingly vulnerable to any deviation from the way in which everything was planned to happen. In order to thrive under this taut environment, the production system must have undergone major changes. The procedures that the purchasing department developed to step up to the challenge of building the B-17E are good examples (*Aviation* June 1941). This group implemented methods to keep track of the status of all outside production parts, check vendors' work on site, and give suggestions to subcontractors. To administer these procedures, the staff expanded from six people at the beginning of the B-17E to a peak of 130. Similarly, production planning and control expanded from 200 people as of January 1939 to a peak of 2,960 in January 1945 (although the second figure contains the personnel for the B-29 and thus overstates the needs of the B-17 program). It is these core managers of the control departments at Plant No. 2 who learned what it took to increase the velocity of production.

4.4.6 Summary

The learning effect manifested itself in terms of declining direct labor hours. Either there was less work to do per airframe, or it must have taken less time to do a given amount of work. For the former to be true, there must have been product design changes that lent themselves to better manufacturability. In the B-17 program, design changes were initiated predominantly for higher product performance rather than improved manufacturability. Therefore, it must be the case that it somehow took less time to do a given amount of work. There are three possibilities corresponding to the different ways in which direct labor hours are typically spent—productive work time, nonproductive work time, and idle time. First, direct workers may have learned to do their real job faster and faster in the spirit of learning by doing or, alternatively, with the aid of capital investment. Second, direct workers may have spent less and less time performing nonproductive work such as material handling and inspection, and more and more time performing productive work. Third, direct workers may have spent less and less time waiting for parts, work pieces, and production instructions. The recent advance in operations management reveals how little of direct labor time went to productive work and how much went to the other two categories.[28] A close examination of the history of the B-17 program, a

---

28. See, for example, Imai (1986).

locus classicus of the learning-by-doing literature, strongly suggests that the measured learning effect stems primarily from the second and third possibilities. It is the system of production that embodies learning, not the direct workers themselves.

4.5   Ford Willow Run versus Boeing Seattle

It should be noted that the conclusion reached in the previous section is not unrelated to how Boeing chose to implement high-volume production. Specifically, Boeing stayed away from mass production pioneered by the Ford Motor Company. The peculiar features of Boeing's approach become crystal clear when Plant No. 2 is compared with a plant Ford operated in Willow Run, Michigan, in order to build the Consolidated B-24 heavy bomber and teach aircraft manufacturers the mass-production methods, equipment, and philosophies of the automobile industry.[29]

Boeing organized for flexibility. The Ford Willow Run plant showcased the hardware-centered approach to high-volume production. The plant covered 67 acres under one roof, and provided two 150-foot-wide areas more than 2,000 feet long. Ford broke down the B-24, which was similar to the B-17 in size, into approximately seventy subassemblies (40 percent more than Boeing did with the B-17), and laid down an assembly line to put them together progressively. The Willow Run plant also differed from Plant No. 2 in the use of permanent steel dies, elaborate fixtures, complex machine tools, and moving chain conveyors. Moreover, all of the jigs, fixtures, and main dies installed by Ford were of heavy, sturdy, long-lasting construction. In other words, Ford tried to achieve high volumes of output by the design of the process—a hallmark approach of mass production. It takes a lot of time and effort to complete tooling up front, but, once it is done, it does not take much thought to produce in high volumes, for the tooling itself embodies a pool of knowledge about how to execute production.

In contrast, Plant No. 2 chose the software-centered approach to high-volume production. Had all the work in progress been removed from the plant, it would have been an enormous empty box devoid of tangible structures suggesting how airplanes were built there. By the same token, Plant No. 2 was scalable in that it could adjust to a wide range of production rates without drastic changes in the operating efficiency. Willow Run, with its fixed production process, needed a certain number of people to run regardless of the production rate because the division of labor there created a predetermined number of positions to be staffed at all times.

Willow Run was highly efficient once it was up and running. However, it refused to run for an unexpectedly long time until minute technical details

---

29. Air Materiel Command (1946b), vii. The Willow Run plant was owned by the government, unlike Boeing's Plant No. 2.

were all sorted out. In fact, the war was over before the plant reached peak capacity. The efficiency of Willow Run was due mainly to scale economies—process design geared rigidly to a large scale of output from the outset. In this respect, it is analogous to Adam Smith's pin manufacturer that set up a process employing ten persons. What appears a learning process here is merely a period of adjustment—much like friction in physics—that is necessary before the process design reaches its potential. As soon as the potential is reached, however, there will be no further progress. Whether a plant is blessed with scale economies or learning economies is largely a question of the process design it chooses to implement at the outset (Zeitlin 1995).

4.6   Indices of Experience

If learning is embodied in the production system, how should the classical learning curve be modified? To answer this question, we must return to the regression. In the context of learning on the shop floor, it has been customary to consider experience somewhat narrowly as representing the history of production activities. To formalize this idea, let X_t stand for the output in month t. Alternative measures of experience as of month T are then expressed by different ways to sum up the raw data, $(X_1, X_2, \cdots, X_T)$. Three summary indices immediately suggest themselves: the elapsed time T, the cumulative output $Y_T = \sum_{t=1}^{T} X_t$, and the maximal proven capacity to date $Z_T = \max_{1 \leq t \leq T} X_t$.

T represents "learning by thinking." Although it is often argued that elapsed time would matter because of the external progress of technology (Fellner 1969), the duration and the surroundings of the B-17 program largely invalidate this interpretation. This variable must therefore stand for the viewpoint that the most scarce input to learning is the time to think. The choice of the time scale was made immaterial in the following analysis by entering this variable in the exponential form of e^T.

Y_T captures "learning by doing" or activity-based experience. This stock variable grows only with stimuli from production activities, but in doing so does not distinguish whether or not activities are simply repetitive. It could thus be associated with either direct labor skill improvement or accumulation of technical know-how.

Z_T in contrast represents "learning by stretching." This boundary variable grows only when the plant stretches its activity level to a new height. It is a good proxy for the production system in place. The plant needs to revamp its production system in order to stretch. Once the production system is revamped, however, it will stay put even when the output level goes back down. Unlike the cumulative output measuring *total* experience, Z_T stands for *new* experience, discriminating whether current production activities push the frontier of experience forward and disregarding any redundant experience.

The bulk of table 4.1 is designed to evaluate these alternative expressions of experience within the following class of model specifications:

(3) $\log l_T = \theta + \alpha \log k_T + \beta \log X_T + \delta \log E_T + \varepsilon_T,$

where k_T is a capital-labor ratio, E_T an index of experience, θ a constant, and ε_T a random disturbance term. This formulation is equivalent, up to the disturbance, to the standard Cobb-Douglas production function:

(4) $X = A K^{\frac{-\alpha}{1+\beta}} L^{\frac{1+\alpha}{1+\beta}} E^{\frac{-\delta}{1+\beta}},$

where A is a constant, $L_T = l_T X_T$ is the total direct labor hours, $K_T = k_T L_T$ is the productive capital stock available in month T, and the last term containing an experience variable works as a shifter of the production function. The appendix discusses the capital data in detail.[30]

Observers of wartime production often attributed the dramatic reduction of unit direct labor hours to the adoption of mass-production techniques.[31] The analysis here controls for this consideration with two variables—the rate of output X_T (Viner 1931) and the capital-labor ratio k_T—while attributing the remainder of the labor-hours reduction to experiential learning.

Rapping (1965) applied model (4) to the Liberty Ship data during World War II. He concluded that the learning effect was related to the cumulative output more than to the elapsed time because the latter's coefficient became insignificant in the presence of the former variable. Argote, Beckman, and Epple (1990) used the same data set and the same formulation with another experience variable of the form $\sum_{t=1}^{T} \lambda^{T-t} X_t$, that is, the cumulative output discounted at a constant rate. They found that this variable, or knowledge after forgetting, explained the learning effect even better than the simple cumulative output. Their result on the depreciation rate λ suggested that only 3.2 percent of the knowledge stock survived one year later and labor turnover had little to do with this high rate of forgetting. These findings are no doubt interesting but demand an explanation as to who knows what in the first place and why a learning agent can forget the content of learning so fast. Answering these questions is difficult within the Liberty Ship data because they contain many independent shipyards.

The analysis of the B-17 data reported in table 4.1 tells a clear-cut story about Plant No. 2, a plant that had only one product. Columns 2 through 4 present the result of employing e^T, Y_T, and Z_T, respectively in place of E_T in equation (3). The coefficients are all statistically significant and the fit is always excellent. They also exhibit scale economies and the effect of capital-labor substitution as expected. In spite of these desired properties, columns 2 and 3 suffer profoundly from serial correlation of the residuals. The character-

---

30. This study actually derived k_T as K_T / L_T. The denominator is not the head count of direct workers because the Air Materiel Command (1946a) stopped reporting this data as soon as the B-29 conversion project made it unclear how many workers were engaged in the B-17 program on a full-time basis.

31. See Middleton (1945) and Simonson (1960) for aircraft production and Searle (1945) for shipbuilding.

istic combination of a high $\bar{R}^2$ and a low Durbin-Watson statistic suggests that these two models capitalize on chance to fit the data. Their residuals indeed show a clear pattern: a model incorporating either e^T or Y_T systematically underestimates the unit direct labor hours whenever they cease to decline. The problem is that both e^T and Y_T consistently grow and, therefore, are unable to explain any reverse movement of the dependent variable. The B-17 data aggravate this problem because the unit direct labor hours reversed the downward trend during the cutback phase of the production program.

In contrast, the Z_T measure in column 4 escapes the problem of serial correlation. First, this model has a high enough Durbin-Watson statistic to exceed the lower bound at the conventional 1 percent confidence level. Test for autocorrelation thus presents no positive sign of missing variables. Second, even if serial correlation does exist, its consequence is minimal for the result in column 4. Column 5 replaces OLS with EGLS (estimated generalized least squares) adopting the two-step Cochrane-Orcutt method.[32] The result of this procedure is parameter estimates extremely close to those of column 4.

The reason only Z_T escapes serial correlation is more than a statistical accident. In other data that consist only of the expansion phase, it would be tricky to separate the effect of the scale variable and alternative experience variables.[33] In the B-17 data the presence of the cutback phase breaks this collinearity. Figure 4.2 shows that the unit direct labor hours at a given rate of output differed between before and after the peak of production. It is this gap that an index of experience ought to explain. The extremely low Durbin-Watson statistic of column 6 in table 4.1 attests to the existence of a missing variable aside from k_T and X_T. Both e^T and Y_T fail to fill the gap because their growth is too regular. From a technical viewpoint, Z_T mitigates this problem because it grows selectively. It too is irreversible, but it at least stays constant during the cutback phase. As a result, column 4 leaves only random residuals and no indication of further missing variables.

The evidence from Boeing's B-17 production program thus offers strong support to the hypothesis of learning by new experiences.[34] The source of learning then is the new experience that is inherent in the challenges of scaling up effective capacity. The alternative hypothesis of learning by doing contradicts the data at least in one respect because they suggest that no learning took place during the cutback phase of the B-17 program.[35] In the last column of

32. The first-step residuals yielded a correlation coefficient of $\hat{\rho} = .307$.

33. In the B-17 data the correlation coefficient with the rate of output X_T for the first thirty-one months of expansion is .608 for e^T, .966 for Y_T, and .996 for Z_T.

34. This empirical finding substantiates widespread intuition and Arrow (1962), in reviewing works of psychologists, alluded to new stimuli as the engine of steadily increasing performance; Dutton and Thomas (1984) similarly referred to the learning opportunities that scale-up brings about.

35. Of course, it is conceivable that confusion associated with the B-29 conversion washed out the effect of learning that did occur even during the cutback phase. Based on the available evidence discussed in the previous section, the present analysis takes a position that at least during 1944

table 4.1, Z_T indeed nullifies the effect of cumulative output Y_T. As in Argote, Beckman, and Epple (1990) a high depreciation rate would technically relax the rigidity of the cumulative output, but would soon run into the difficulties of explaining constant rapid forgetting.

4.7 A Model of Scale-up Economies

This section integrates all the findings from Boeing's B-17 production while attempting generalization beyond a specific historical case. It first converts the empirical formulation of the last section into a schematic model describing the dynamic behavior of manufacturing cost. It then lays out the model's underpinnings by linking the agent, content, and source of learning explicitly to the production system and the operating know-how embodied therein. The section finally discusses the model's implications briefly.

4.7.1 The Model

The quantitative analysis of the B-17 program gave rise to the following formulation in section 4.6 (table 4.1, column 5): $l = \phi k^{\alpha} X^{\beta} Z^{\delta}$. This formulation conceptually translates into a dynamic cost function of the form

$$(5) \qquad\qquad C = C(X, Z) \quad \text{for} \quad {}^{\forall} X \leq Z.$$

The first step is to extend the unit direct labor hours to the total unit cost on the left-hand side and generalize the functional form to accommodate this extension. The rationale is that the unit direct labor hours often signal the efficiency of entire operations. Such was clearly the case in Plant No. 2, where the rising velocity of production was the direct cause of the reduction in the unit direct labor hours.

The second step concerns the right-hand-side variables. Section 4.6 singled out three determinants of the unit direct labor hours: the capital-labor ration k (factor substitution effect), the rate of output X (scale economies), and the proven effective capacity Z (learning effect). Of these, the last two variables explain the bulk of the 89.2 percent labor savings that Plant No. 2 achieved between September 1941 and August 1944.[36] In contrast, the capital-labor ratio is statistically significant but economically unimportant because it did not fluctuate much. Capital and labor tended to grow together rather than one substituting the other. The coefficient of variation is 53.2 for X, 57.6 for Z, and only 33.7 for k. The last figure even drops to 16.1 without the first four months of 1941 when workforce expansion was still catching up with plant expansion.

---

the increase in the unit direct labor hours reflects negative economies of scale due to the cutback itself.

36. During this period, Z increased more than 17 times, which, given the estimated coefficient, would trigger 77.5 percent reduction in the unit direct labor hours all by itself. Likewise, X recorded a 52-fold increase, which alone would cause 65.0 percent reduction. These two effects combined are more than sufficient to explain the actual labor savings.

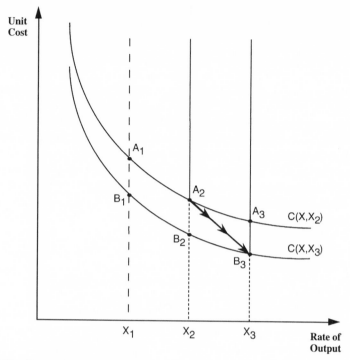

Fig. 4.10   **Dynamic cost function**

The factor substitution effect is therefore omitted from the dynamic cost function.

The cost function (5) is dynamic partly because it departs from the aggregation approach of the past. The classical learning curve aggregates all the determinants of the unit cost in one variable: the cumulative output Y. It was an antithesis to the traditional scale economies where the rate of output X assumed the role of a sole explanatory variable. The dynamic cost function, however, acknowledges the presence of both reversible and irreversible effects on the unit cost. The two variables, X and Z, that it incorporates are measurable in an identical quantitative unit and capture the dynamic behavior of manufacturing cost in a simple diagram.

Figure 4.10 shows the workings of the dynamic cost function. First, let's assume that the plant has experienced the output rate of up to $Z = X_2$. The curve $C(X, X_2)$ depicts the reversible effect, describing the unit cost as a function of the rate of output X. As the plant moves back from X_2 to X_1, so does its cost position from A_2 to A_1. By the same token, the cost declines from A_1 to A_2 as the plant increases output from X_1 to X_2 due to conventional scale economies. The location of X_1 is arbitrary so long as it lies to the left of X_2. The extension of the curve $C(X, X_2)$ to the right of X_2 is illusory since the plant has never operated in this domain. The figure empirically postulates that the curve (5) is downward sloping, that is,

$$(6) \qquad \frac{\partial}{\partial X} C(X,\ Z) = C_X \leq 0 \quad \text{for} \quad {}^\forall X \leq Z,$$

based on the finding that the coefficient of X, or β in model (3), is unambiguously negative.

Now, what happens when this plant scales up from X_2 to X_3? According to the dynamic cost function, the plant's cost position will shift from A_2 to B_3, of which the vertical gap between A_2 and A_3 is due to the reversible effect and that between A_3 and B_3 due to the irreversible shift of the curve $C(X, X_2)$ down to $C(X, X_3)$. The curve connecting B_1 and B_3 corresponds to the new reality that the plant has pushed its frontier from the vertical line $A_2 - B_2$ to $A_3 - B_3$ and irreversibly experienced the rate of output as high as X_3. Once this shift occurs, the cost position reverts to B_1, as opposed to A_1, even when the production is scaled back to X_1. The dynamic cost function thus postulates that

$$(7) \qquad \frac{\partial}{\partial Z} C(X,\ Z) = C_Z \leq 0 \quad \text{for} \quad {}^\forall X \leq Z.$$

The basis for (7) is again the empirical result demonstrating that the coefficient of Z, or δ in model (3), is unambiguously negative. It is this downward shift of the dynamic cost function over the X axis that represents learning, or more specifically scale-up economies.[37]

4.7.2   Discussion

There is no denying that the model of scale-up economies stands on only one study of one plant. More studies are undoubtedly needed to claim the model's applicability elsewhere. It is nonetheless useful to explore the implications of the new model since its merit also depends on the credibility of the story it tells.

One immediate payoff of the new model is its ability to resolve a controversy over the learning curve: whether the learning curve would remain in effect forever or the unit cost would cease to decline at some point. Explanations abound for individual cases where the unit cost did level off (Asher 1956; Baloff 1966; Conway and Schultz 1959). However, there have been no theoretical predictions as to where and when a plateau might appear. With the proposed model, plateauing is a natural consequence for the plants that stop scaling up. If they further cut back production and start operating under longer

---

37. The dynamic cost function suggests a new distinction between short run and long run. In the neoclassical theory of production, this distinction hinges upon whether or not a time period is long enough to permit changes in the plant scale while holding the stock of technical knowledge constant. Instead, it may be more fruitful to consider long run as a time period long enough to permit changes in the effective capacity Z.

system cycle times, the model would predict "toe-up" (Reguero 1957) in which the unit cost begins to climb as it did in Boeing's B-17 data.

The proposed model also offers implications for plant management. If experience is measured by the cumulative output as in the classical learning curve, every bit of production counts equally toward cost reduction and, therefore, there is not much the plant can do except to keep producing. With the new model, there is no learning where there is no challenge. Simply repeating the same production activities would not contribute to cost reduction autonomously because production counts only at the margin of experience. In order to learn, the plant must overextend itself beyond current effective capacity. Even though effective capacity may not be a control variable in the short run, scale-up with minimal investment might focus a plant on a set of activities that propels all functional units toward higher efficiency. It remains to be seen how important the kind of resource constraints that existed in Plant No. 2, especially limited plant space, really is for the learning effect to occur and continue.

The new model raises a subtle question of optimal scaling-up strategy. If $C_{ZZ} \geq 0$ holds as a finer property of the dynamic cost function, it would favor incremental scale-up whereby efforts are devoted to cycle-time reduction whenever possible and however small each gain may be. Otherwise, surpassing a threshold scale becomes a foremost priority. Inference of this property is not straightforward since most functional forms, including the Cobb-Douglas, impose convexity. One way to bring the B-17 data to bear on the question of optimal scale-up strategy is to expand the term $\log Z$ to the second order where the coefficient of Z^2 must be negative if C_{ZZ} is ever to fall below zero. The result shows a small positive coefficient that is not statistically different from zero. Combined with the lack of clear patterns in the residuals of the Cobb-Douglas model, the B-17 data seem to support global superiority of the incremental scale-up strategy.

The model also poses a crucial question about the management of know-how. The best scenario calls for growth that would keep X at rising Z and thereby reap economies of scale and scale-up simultaneously. If the unit of analysis for which this model holds true remains at the plant level, such growth should not scatter over many different plants. Other things being equal, a firm should rather develop a centralized manufacturing complex that would retain all the know-how. A different conclusion will result if it is possible to share know-how effectively within a network of plants. Unfortunately, the present study of one plant is not designed to address this question concerning the organizational boundary of know-how. It only suggests the variables to measure in future research.

Another strategic implication revolves around the role of incumbency. If cumulative output is the adequate measure of experience, the learning effect should give rise to strong first-mover's advantage in terms of manufacturing cost (Spence 1981). The upshot is a high entry barrier and concentrated industry structure, which are strangely missing from certain industries that are believed to exhibit the learning effect. In the proposed model, it is not the incumbency per se that matters. In this regard, the model agrees with the findings of Argote, Beckman, and Epple (1990) in spite of the differences in its specification.

4.8 Conclusion

This essay examines a historical case that resembles a controlled laboratory experiment. Under special circumstances of wartime production, one plant manufactured one product for one customer who kept detailed records of production activities to make sure that weapon manufacturers did not profit from the war. The case further contained a cutback phase where scale shrank clearly but experience did not. This feature allowed the essay to isolate these two critical variables that are highly collinear in most data. From a methodological standpoint, the essay departs from previous studies that used minute differences in the goodness of fit to guide the process of model selection. It instead relies on serial correlation as well as nonquantitative case information. The result is a clear rejection of the learning-by-doing hypothesis that holds direct workers or engineers as the learning agent. The following points summarize the emerging, alternative conception of learning:

1. The source of learning is *new* experiences that scaling-up of effective capacity entails. In Boeing's Plant No. 2, learning did not seem to occur when production was cut back even though production itself continued at a smaller scale. In other words, "quality" of experience mattered. Doing alone, without any regard to the redundancy of experience, did not give rise to learning.

2. Scale-up triggers *system* changes. Changes that took place in Plant No. 2 were subtle, and concentrated in the area of management of operations: how to manage a smooth flow of work in progress from vendors to the plant and inside the plant itself despite space constraints and despite a host of problems that could occur unpredictably. Thus, the content of learning is operating know-how, which makes up the production system.

3. The agent of learning is the core managers of control functions in the plant, that is, those who *coordinate* various aspects of the plant operations to ensure that work in progress flows smoothly without interrupting events so the shop manager can concentrate on his or her job of meeting production schedules while supervising the direct workers. In Plant No. 2, departments such as production control grew most rapidly as the plant exhibited learning effects.

4. During the four years Boeing produced the B-17s in high volumes, the unit direct labor hours declined from roughly seventy-one worker-years to eight worker-years. The magnitude involved here is clearly too large to be explained by skill improvement. In Plant No. 2 the bulk of labor savings appeared to originate from the hours in which direct skill was not being applied in the first place. The key was instead throughput-time reduction and the operating know-how that enabled it.

5. The hardware of production has little to do with learning in airframe fabrication and assembly. In Plant No. 2 the learning effect took place long after capital investment was suspended. The same goes for product and process engineering. These elements may be necessary for production, but not sufficient for the observed cost dynamics. Factor substitution effect was economically unimportant, although scale economies prevailed along with scale-up economies.

Appendix

This study constructed the capital data through three steps: (1) determining the base capital that existed in Plant No. 2 prior to the expansion projects undertaken for the B-17 program, (2) adding to the base the capital expended for the expansion projects on a monthly basis, and (3) adjusting the resulting monthly data for subcontracting as well as the conversion to the B-29. What follows explains each step in some detail.

Base

The base line represents the capital that had accumulated in Plant No. 2 since land was acquired for this new site in 1935, until the beginning of 1940. It excludes Plant No. 1 and a subsidiary facility in Wichita, Kansas. The base was estimated at $1,156,159 from Boeing's annual reports through the following calculation:

$3,230,070	Property and equipment at cost as of 31 December 1939 for Boeing Airplane Company
(1,890,207)	Property and equipment at cost as of 31 December 1934 for Boeing Airplane Company
(371,304)	Property and equipment at cost as of 31 December 1939 for Stearman Aircraft Division
187,600)	Property and equipment at cost as of 31 December 1934 for Stearman Aircraft Company
$1,156,159	

Additions

Four expansion projects involved the main building of Plant No. 2 and increased its productive capacity. The total amount of investment was allocated equally from the month in which occupancy started to the month in which the project was completed. The construction period, typically six months, was ignored because capacity was unavailable for production. Table 4A.1, lists the projects. The Air Materiel Command (1946a) contains more detailed information.

Table 4A.1   **Expansion Projects for Plant No. 2**

Project	Investment ($)	Occupancy	Completion
Private	2,107,218	November 1940	July 1941
EPF W535 ac-16424	7,777,587	March 1941	April 1942
EPF W535 ac-196	3,191,580	November 1941	December 1941
EPF W535 ac-26185	1,238,662	June 1942	September 1942

Table 4A.2   **Feeder Plants**

Plant	Completion of Assembly	Total Square Feet
681	October 1943	38,700
682	November 1943	47,100
683	November 1943	49,630
684	November 1943	37,086
685	December 1943	33,050
686	December 1943	51,000
687	October 1944	33,300

Boeing also added seven feeder plants in 1943 and 1944 as in table 4A.2. These facilities were added to the monthly capital data at $3.50 per square foot, which was typical for Boeing's own investment, in the month when they recorded the first line-off.

Adjustment

To make the capital data comparable to the direct labor hours data, the resulting monthly capital data were divided by one minus the subcontracting ratio to adjust for subcontracting. The subcontracting ratio was 28 percent in 1941 and 1942, 29 percent in 1943, and 32.6 percent in 1944. The data were then scaled down to reflect the conversion to the B-29. The delivery of the B-29 from Renton began in January 1944 and continued throughout the year at a monthly rate between two airplanes and thirty-five airplanes. Hershey (1944) describes the manner in which Plant No. 2 was converted for this purpose from April 1944 to March 1945. Based on this information, the capital data were linearly reduced beginning with April 1944 so that they reach zero in May 1945 when Plant No. 2 was no longer engaged in the B-17 program.

References

Aero Digest. 1937. Specially Planned Modern Building for Final Assembly. (February): 32–34.

———. 1938a. Equipment and Procedure for Constructing Four-Engined Airplanes. (January): 17–19.

———. 1938b. Monorail Crane Equipment at Boeing's New Assembly Plant. (February): 38–39.

———. 1940. Boeing-Stearman. (November): 40–41.

———. 1941a. More Factory Areas Dedicated to Aircraft Production. (October): 60–66, 392.

———. 1941b. The 25th Anniversary of Boeing Aircraft Co. (July): 73–78.

Air Materiel Command. 1946a. B-17 Production and Construction Analysis: Boeing Aircraft Company, Seattle, Washington. May. Typescript.

———. 1946b. B-24 Construction and Production Analysis: Ford Motor Company, Willow Run Bomber Plant, Ypsilanti, Michigan. August. Typescript.

Alchian, A. 1959. Costs and Outputs. In *The Allocation of Economic Resources: Essays in Honor of B. F. Haley,* ed. M. Abramovitz, 23–40. Stanford, CA: Stanford University Press.

———. 1963. Reliability of Progress Curves in Airframe Production. *Econometrica* 31, no. 4:679–93.

Andress, F. 1954. The Learning Curve as a Production Tool. *Harvard Business Review* 32, no. 1:87–97.

Argote, L., S. L. Beckman, and D. Epple. 1990. The Persistence and Transfer of Learning in Industrial Settings. *Management Science* 36, no. 2:140–54.

Arrow, K. J. 1962. The Economic Implications of Learning by Doing. *Review of Economic Studies* 29:155–73.

Asher, H. 1956. *Cost-Quantity Relationships in the Airframe Industry (Project Rand R-291).* Santa Monica, CA: Rand.

Aviation. 1941. 248 Factories Build the Flying Fortress. (June): 74–75, 176, 186.

———. 1943. Fortresses by Boeing. (July): 124–29, 309–13.

Baloff, N. 1966. Startups in Machine-Intensive Production Systems. *Journal of Industrial Engineering* 17, no. 1:25–32.

Beall, W. E. 1945. Design Analysis of the Boeing B-17 Flying Fortress. *Aviation* (January): 121–44.

Boston Consulting Group. 1972. Perspectives on Experience. Boston. Leaflet.

Bowers, P. M. 1976. *Fortress in the Sky.* Granada Hills, CA: Sentry Books.

Bucey, B. K. 1943. Good Tooling Simplifies Production of Flying Fortresses. *Aviation* (January): 107–11, 221.

Conway, R. W., and A. Schultz, Jr. 1959. The Manufacturing Progress Function. *Journal of Industrial Engineering* 10, no. 1:39–54.

Craven, W. F., and J. L. Cate. 1955. *The Army Air Forces in World War II.* Vol. 6, *Men and Planes.* Chicago: University of Chicago Press.

Davis, L. 1984. *B-17 in Action.* Carrollton, TX: Squadron/Signal.

Dutton, J. M., and A. Thomas. 1984. Treating Progress Functions as a Managerial Opportunity. *Academy of Management Review* 9, no. 2:235–47.

Fellner, W. 1969. Specific Interpretations of Learning by Doing. *Journal of Economic Theory* 1:119–40.

Froelich, M. H. 1942. Women in War Work. *Aero Digest* (September): 132–36, 258–64, 298.

Gold, B. 1981. Changing Perspectives on Size, Scale, and Returns: An Interpretive Survey. *Journal of Economic Literature* 19:5–33.

Hershey, S. 1944. Boeing Converts Seattle Plant from B-17 to B-29 Production. *Aviation News* (4 December): 35–37.

Hirsch, W. Z. 1952. Manufacturing Progress Functions. *Review of Economics and Statistics* 34, no. 2:143–55.

Hirschmann, W. 1964. Profit from the Learning Curve. *Harvard Business Review* 42:125–39.

Holley, I. B. 1964. *Buying Aircraft: Material Procurement for the Army Air Forces.* Washington, DC: Department of the Army.

Imai, M. 1986. *Kaizen: The Key to Japan's Competitive Success.* New York: McGraw-Hill.

Klemin, A. 1940. Planning to Assure National Production. *Aero Digest* (May): 42–46, 179.

Laddon, I. M. 1943. Reduction of Man-Hours in Aircraft Production. *Aviation* (May): 170–73, 356–60.

Laudan, F. P. 1936. Factory Procedure in the Fabrication of All-Metal Aircraft. *Aero Digest* (January): 26–29.

Levy, F. K. 1965. Adaptation in the Production Process. *Management Science* 11, no. 6: B136–54.

Middleton, K. A. 1945. Wartime Productivity Changes in the Airframe Industry. *Monthly Labor Review* 61, no. 2: 215–25.

Mishina, K. 1992. Learning by New Experiences. Working Paper 92–084. Harvard Business School.

Perelle, C. W. 1943. Present-Day Manufacturing Problems of the Aircraft Industry. *Aero Digest* (May): 158, 340–47.

Rae, J. B. 1968. *Climb to Greatness: The American Aircraft Industry, 1920–1960.* Cambridge: MIT Press.

Rapping, L. 1965. Learning and World War II Production Functions. *Review of Economics and Statistics* 47:81–86.

Reguero, M. A. 1957. *An Economic Study of the Military Airframe Industry.* Department of the Air Force.

Searle, A. D. 1945. Productivity Changes in Selected Wartime Shipbuilding Programs. *Monthly Labor Review* 61, no. 6:1132–47.

Simonson, G. R. 1960. The Demand for Aircraft and the Aircraft Industry, 1907–1958. *Journal of Economic History* 20, no. 3:361–82.

Smith, A. [1776] 1976. *An Inquiry into the Nature and Causes of the Wealth of Nations.* Ed. Edwin Cannan. Chicago: University of Chicago Press.

Spence, A. M. 1981. The Learning Curve and Competition. *Bell Journal of Economics* 12:49–70.

Viner, J. 1931. Cost Curves and Supply Curves. *Zeitschrift für Nationalökonomie* 3: 23–46.

Wright, T. P. 1936. Factors Affecting the Cost of Airplanes. *Journal of the Aeronautical Sciences* 3, no. 4:122–28.

———. 1939. American Methods of Aircraft Production. *Journal of the Royal Aeronautical Society,* 131–52.

Yelle, L. E. 1979. The Learning Curve: Historical Review and Comprehensive Survey. *Decision Sciences* 10:302–28.

Zeitlin, J. 1995. Flexibility and Mass Production at War: Aircraft Manufacture in Britain, the United States, and Germany, 1939–1945. *Technology and Culture* 36:46–79.

Comment   Ross Thomson

Ongoing productivity growth is not only a critical feature of capitalist development, it also forms a vexing problem for economic analysis, which often con-

Ross Thomson is associate dean of the College of Arts and Sciences and associate professor of economics at the University of Vermont.

ceives technical change as something that happens to firms, not by them. Insightfully taking up this problem, Kazuhiro Mishina forwards both a striking example of productivity growth and a plausible explanation of how learning within the firm led to this growth.

Mishina examines the Boeing plant that manufactured the B-17 bomber, the so-called Flying Fortress, during World War II. Productivity growth was remarkable; labor time per airframe in 1944 had fallen to about one-tenth of that three years earlier. Equally remarkably, after the plant had been tooled up, this output growth occurred without increases in the capital stock, so at its peak the plant produced over four times as many airframes as its rated capacity! The principal argument of the paper is that labor productivity growth resulted from what Mishina calls "learning by stretching," which is learning that occurs when the firm has to scale up production in a given plant. This argument can be read in two steps. First, intrafirm learning, and not other factors, accounted for productivity growth, and second, this learning can best be interpreted as learning by stretching. I will comment on each of these steps and then on the generality of the case.

Boeing's productivity growth is especially intriguing because many of the factors used to explain productivity gains did not apply. Growing labor productivity could not be explained by changes in the quantity or quality of inputs. The plant and its equipment were complete early in the period analyzed and changed little afterward. Workforce skill declined as skilled craftsmen were replaced by workers new to airframe production, by 1944 overwhelmingly women. Nor can growing labor productivity be cast into doubt by product simplification, quality reduction, or the expansion of outsourcing. The product if anything became more complex, and subcontracting increased very little over time. Learning from other firms was unimportant; Boeing was the leader, and others learned from it. Economies of scale cannot explain much of the productivity growth, because plant capacity did not change after May 1942. Having ruled out changing inputs, external knowledge, product deterioration, and scale economies, Mishina concludes that productivity grew through a learning process occurring within the plant.

This is a strong argument, but it makes more sense after the plant had completely introduced mass production than before. As Mishina notes, before mid-1942, the plant was expanding, mass production was inaugurated, and special-purpose equipment was just coming on line. These innovations were associated with embodied technical change and the learning that comes from mastering that technology. It also seems likely that Boeing, untrained in mass production, learned from other firms, which trained workers and managers adept at interchangeable parts manufacturing, sold Boeing machine tools, and perhaps contracted to mass-produce parts. It is true that important elements of the transition to mass production were complete before the first planes were delivered, but there can be no doubt that much of the early productivity growth, which averaged an amazing 14 percent per month through mid-1942, was due to new mass-production equipment and procedures and probably also to economies of scale as rated capacity was approached. For Boeing, like Ford in the beginnings of mass production, superior equipment, learning from other firms, and scale economies all had parts in improving labor productivity. That said, Mishina is likely right that after mid-1942, the still-remarkable 4 percent monthly growth in labor productivity had another explanation.

What is that explanation? Mishina advances narrative and econometric arguments that Boeing "stretched" its capacity and so increased output relative to capital and labor. It multiplied output with a given capital stock (hence increasing the productivity of capital) by reducing the plant's throughput time (the time interval from the first through the last stage of production) by two-thirds. It increased labor productivity by decreasing the time of parts manufacture and more importantly by reducing the time when workers were either waiting for parts or reworking parts not conforming to the required extreme tolerances. Increases in the productivity of capital and labor had similar causes. Growing interchangeability decreased the time of assembly and increased the velocity of throughput (or labor time and production time in Marx's terminology). This growth had its source in both hardware—new machine tools, dies, jigs, and templates—and "software" changes in work standards and procedures and in tool monitoring. A just-in-time production system also reduced idle labor time and throughput time by improving materials flow and inventory control and by coordinating and dividing subassemblies. To implement and monitor these changes required greater managerial coordination, so that increasing efficiencies in the utilization of capital and direct labor came by means of increasing managerial labor, perhaps growing even in relation to output.

This is a fascinating story about which we'd like to know more. Exactly how were these results obtained? Every capitalist would like to increase the productivity of labor and capital simultaneously, but they evidently do not always do so. How did Boeing do it, and do it at such an extraordinary rate? Mishina demonstrates that there was a challenge and a successful response, but not how that success was achieved. In particular, because managers were the key locus of learning, we need to know more about how they were organized, how they learned, and how they used this learning to restructure input coordination, work rules, worker training, and production flows. Furthermore, Mishina's core claim—that it "is the system of production that embodies learning, not the direct workers themselves"—merits further exploration. Many learning theories agree that the learning process is interactive and systemic, such as short-run learning with existing equipment (David 1975; Lazonick and Brush 1985), long-run learning by doing through purchased capital goods (David 1975), learning by using capital equipment (such as Rosenberg [1982] illustrated for commercial aircraft), and learning by selling that transmits product knowledge (Thomson 1989). But such interactive learning can apply just as much to the individual operation as to the relation among operations. We might test the claim that the systemic coordination was more important than improvements in individual operations by inquiring whether machinists making parts increased relative to workers assembling parts. This was likely so, just as it was so in the prolonged period it took firearms and sewing machines to attain interchangeability in the nineteenth century (Hounshell 1984). But then what distinguishes Boeing's systemic learning from that of Singer or Ford?

The econometric analysis counterposes traditional learning approaches, which focus on labor productivity as function of cumulative output or time since invention, to learning by stretching, which focuses on the novelty of overcoming capacity constraints. Econometrically, Mishina favors the last, because while all approaches are statistically significant, learning by stretching overcomes problems of collinearity in the other two. This formulation expects productivity to grow only when output reaches a new maximum, and so—unlike the other two—does not expect productivity growth when output ceases to grow. Mishina's argument is interesting and sensible; learning responding to the challenge of increasing output in a given plant is likely to augment labor productivity. But the argument raises three issues. First, such learning is not universal; there are incentives and opportunities to learn even with constant output and unchanging plant. Second, the argument raises questions of causality. In learning by stretching, managers learn in an effort to increase both output and labor productivity. When successful, learning today results in expanded output and growing labor productivity in current or later periods. The correlation of the two is then the outcome of a third factor, prior learning. If so, why is one the independent and the other the dependent variable? In an important sense, they can be mutually reinforcing. Productivity increases can speed throughput. Output increases might generate new bottlenecks, which in turn lead to learning that increases later output levels or reduces labor costs at existing output levels. This may account for Boeing's continued productivity growth after the maximum capacity had been reached. In this case, learning forms a cumulative process in which productivity growth, output growth, and learning each feeds into the others. Third, when and with what limits does such learning occur? One important factor omitted in the econometrics is management. If managers were the key learners, would expanding numbers of managers be associated with learning and later productivity increases? Moreover, it seems implausible that Boeing could indefinitely increase output within the same plant. Is there then a "long-run" learning by stretching associated with investment to expand the plant or to build others?

The final issue to address is whether this case has general implications. Its 7 percent *monthly* productivity growth rate was far higher than the 2 percent *annual* growth more typical of short-run learning (e.g., David 1975). Was this exceptionally rapid productivity growth rate so unique that the B-17 had no wider lessons? The challenge to increase output with a given plant may be ever-present or at least present when full capacity is approached, and may lead to labor-saving and capital-saving learning. But it rarely has capacity-exceeding and labor-productivity effects as large as those at Boeing.

I conjecture that Boeing's extraordinary productivity growth resulted from the confluence of two trends, each of which also applies to other firms: wartime expansion and radical innovation over the product cycle. The very context in which Boeing's uniqueness appears—the frantic production for a world war—allows us to draw some more general lessons. The rapid, multidimensional growth in B-17 production was mirrored by that in the economy as a whole in the 1938–50 period, when output, labor productivity, and capital productivity annually grew at the then-unprecedented rates of over 5, 3, and 3 percent respectively (Maddison 1991). The peak of this growth was reached in exactly the years of Boeing's B-17 expansion. In some estimates, from 1941 through 1944 aggregate output grew at 15 percent per year, and the 7 percent growth of aggregate labor productivity was exceeded by the expansion of capital productivity (Maddison 1991; Dumenil, Glick, and Levy 1992).

Wartime expansion was constrained not by demand but by supply factors. Producers could sell all they could make. Yet their expansion was constrained by the scarcity of labor, a problem against which Boeing fought constantly. Producers were also constrained by the uncertainty of whether major private capital investments would be warranted after the war, and perhaps additionally by the scarcity of investment funds. For one or both reasons, private investment was modest; the government was key to Boeing's investments. In this demand-abundant, supply-constrained context, firms had incentives to use capacity more fully. In more typical times, excess capacity exists, creating less pressure to produce beyond capacity, especially when this would lead to rising wage costs. At the same time, retained earnings allow investment to occur in anticipation of future demand.

Boeing's experience reflected this wartime productivity boom, but took it to a higher level. In this Boeing shared features with other firms developing new products. Even if demand-constrained growth is normal in capitalist development, firms in the market-expansion phase of product cycles face strong excess demand. Here particularly rapid output growth and labor-productivity growth often occur together, likely accompanied by short-run learning by doing. In periods of rapid product cycle expansion—which distinguished Boeing from most of the wartime economy—labor productivity rises through learning by stretching and doing in the short-run but also through learning by selling that improves products and increases scale, learning by using, and learning by purchasing new capital goods. Productivity growth is especially rapid when the new commodity comes to be produced in a radically different kind of production process, such as in sewing machines in the 1860s and 1870s, automobiles in the 1910s, and airframes in the 1940s.

In my conjecture, Boeing's uniqueness combines the penetration phase of product cycles with the transition to a particular kind of mass production in the context of a supply-constrained, wartime economy. Other war industries expanded output and exceeded capacity, but often without the same labor-productivity increases. Firms introducing assembly-line techniques to produce new commodities dramatically increased labor productivity but not capital productivity. Ford introduced such assembly-line procedures to make B-29s in World War II. Boeing did not; its investments were more flexible, embodied more in management than in hardware. Its output accelerated more quickly as a result. Boeing thus benefited from three circumstances each of which has broader application: wartime, supply-constrained economies; new products facing rapidly growing markets and mass-production requirements; and organizational innovations that reduced fixed capital expenditures and, as Boeing anticipated, eased movement into other new products. These circumstances can occur separately; Boeing grew by combining all three.

References

David, Paul. 1975. *Technical Choice, Innovation, and Economic Growth.* London: Cambridge University Press.
Dumenil, Gerard, Mark Glick, and Dominique Levy. 1992. Stages in the Development of U.S. Capitalism. In *International Perspectives on Profitability and Accumulation,* ed. Fred Moseley and Edward N. Wolff, 42–65. Aldershot, England: Elgar.
Hounshell, David. 1984. *From the American System to Mass Production, 1800–1932.* Baltimore: Johns Hopkins University Press.
Lazonick, William, and Thomas Brush. 1985. The "Horndal Effect" in Early U.S. Manufacturing. *Explorations in Economic History* 22:53–96.
Maddison, Angus. 1991. *Dynamic Forces in Capitalist Development.* Oxford: Oxford University Press.
Rosenberg, Nathan. 1982. Learning by Using. In *Inside the Black Box,* 120–40. Cambridge: Cambridge University Press.
Thomson, Ross. 1989. *The Path to Mechanized Shoe Production in the United States.* Chapel Hill: University of North Carolina Press.

5   Assets, Organizations, Strategies, and Traditions: Organizational Capabilities and Constraints in the Remaking of Ford Motor Company, 1946–1962

David A. Hounshell

During World War II, Detroit became widely known as "the arsenal of democracy."[1] The sheer magnitude of the automobile industry's output of jeeps, trucks, tanks, aircraft engines, machine guns, bombers, and other tools of war was staggering and played a critical role in the Allied victory.[2] After the war, the automobile industry served as an engine of growth for the domestic economy. In the decade after Detroit had fully reconverted to domestic automobile manufacture, factory sales of automobiles increased from 2,148,699 in 1946 to 7,920,186 in 1955. By 1965 that number reached 9,305,561. In that first full decade of domestic production after the war, labor productivity in motor-vehicle factories more than doubled, rising from 4.7 vehicles per worker to 10.2. Total factory sales of vehicles in these two decades were 141,001,445, representing a value of $235.5 billion.[3] Factory sales of motor vehicles in 1955 and 1965 represented, respectively, 3.6 and 3.2 percent of the United States'

David A. Hounshell is the Henry R. Luce Professor of Technology and Social Change at Carnegie Mellon University, where he is a member of three departments: history, social and decision sciences, and engineering and public policy.

1. For evidence of Detroit's role in the war effort, see Thomas D. Wolff, "Safeguarding the Arsenal of Democracy: A History of the Detroit Office of Civilian Defense in World War," M.S. thesis, Wayne State University, 1952; *Freedom's Arsenal: The Story of the Automotive Council for War Production* (Detroit: Automobile Manufacturers Association, 1950); Allan Nevins and Frank Ernest Hill, "Arsenal of Democracy," in *Ford: Decline and Rebirth, 1933–62* (New York: Scribner's Sons, 1962), 197–227.

2. For a succinct statement of Detroit's output of war matériel during World War II, see James J. Flink, *The Automobile Age* (Cambridge: MIT Press, 1988), 275–76.

3. All statistics cited above derive directly from or were calculated from *Automobile Facts and Figures, 1957* (Detroit: Automobile Manufacturers Association, 1957) and *Automobile Facts and Figures, 1967* (Detroit: Automobile Manufacturers Association, 1967). Figures are not adjusted for inflation.

gross national product.[4] The expression "the car culture" well described American's love affair with and dependence upon the automobile.[5]

While the automobile industry grew in size and output in the two decades after the war, it virtually also completed the profound restructuring, commonly known as a shakeout, that had actually begun in the 1910s. By the end of the 1930s, the number of firms in the U.S. automobile industry could be counted on two hands.[6] After the war, the industry became even more highly concentrated. In 1946, the so-called Big Three (General Motors Corporation, Ford Motor Company, and Chrysler Corporation) accounted for 84.7 percent of the passenger cars made in the United States; by 1955, they made 95.6 percent.[7] Most of the "independents" had folded or were near extinction.

When World War II ended, the Ford Motor Company itself, by all accounts, appeared to be heading toward bankruptcy and perhaps even extinction. Ford's market share had declined sharply from its high point in the early 1920s, and the company's once-famous manufacturing assets had eroded greatly during the Great Depression of the 1930s and the war.[8] The company became leaderless during the war when Edsel Ford, the son of the company's founder Henry Ford, died prematurely, when Henry Ford himself became too senile to manage, when the company was bleeding cash at a rate unrealized because its accounting systems were so poorly designed, and when the company's top managers engaged in internecine rivalry for managerial control of the firm. Yet, in spite of these severe problems, the Ford Motor Company endured. For reasons partially explored in this essay, the company actually experienced what the historian Allan Nevins and his coauthors called a "rebirth."[9]

How Ford Motor Company successfully staved off extinction, regained market share, and restored profitability surely constitutes one of the great stories in the history of American business. This transformation is not, however, the central focus of this study, although it certainly motivates it. My goal is to account for the outcome of a single meeting of Ford's Executive Committee—

---

4. These figures are calculated from GNP statistics reported in current dollars in Series F1-5 of U.S. Bureau of the Census, *Historical Statistics of the United States: Colonial Times to 1970* (Washington, DC: Government Printing Office, 1975), 224, and from values of motor-vehicle factory sales reported (in current dollars) in *Automobile Facts and Figures, 1968* (Detroit: Automobile Manufacturers Association, 1968).

5. I borrow this expression from James J. Flink, *The Car Culture* (Cambridge: MIT Press, 1975).

6. Philip Hillyer Smith, *Wheels within Wheels: A Short History of American Motor Manufacturing* (New York: Funk & Wagnalls, 1968). On the shakeout, see Steven Klepper and Kenneth L. Simons, "Innovation and Industry Shakeouts," *Business and Economic History* 25, no. 1 (1996): 81–89.

7. Charles E. Edwards, *Dynamics of the United States Automobile Industry* (Columbia: University of South Carolina Press, 1965), table 1, 13.

8. The Ford Motor Company's Annual Report for 1947 shows that the company's market share had dropped from about 42 percent in 1930 to below 20 percent in 1941 and showed no signs of reversal had the war not intervened. The report also noted that "for five of the past ten years the Company has used up plant, property, and equipment faster than it has replaced it, leaving a substantial capital deficit."

9. Nevins and Hill, *Ford: Decline and Rebirth.*

an outcome that decisively changed the strategic course of the company, a course that had been formulated and implemented with no little care, a course devoted to bringing about a major revitalization of the company in the years after World War II, a course charted to make the Ford Motor Company a formidable competitor of General Motors, which had long since eclipsed it. The meeting itself, however, was not supposed to be about the strategic direction of the company; its nominal purpose was to settle a question about how funds would be allocated to build engine-manufacturing capacity for the company. But, in fact, the meeting transformed an operational question into a strategic one, and in doing so it put on the table the company's history, its in-place physical assets, and its core capabilities alongside its strategic objectives and opportunities.

For our purposes, the archival records surrounding this fateful meeting could not be more ideal. We have detailed reports of the plans that led up to the meeting, and we have reasoned commentaries on those plans. We have documents that executives carried into the meeting. We have a list of all the executives who attended the meeting, and we know a good deal about the backgrounds of these executives and the positions they came into the meeting with. Finally, we have minutes of the meeting itself. Fortunately for us, however, the minutes report only the final decision arrived at in the meeting—a major departure from a unanimous decision reached by the same Executive Committee less than a month earlier. Other than reporting on how the initial positions were laid out, the minutes provide only the barest shreds of evidence of what took place in the meeting, who said what, and who did what. We are left with nothing but our own wits—our theories of firms, organizational behavior, and organizational capabilities—to explain the outcome. This paper is, therefore, an exercise not unlike those relished by Sir Arthur Conan Doyle's fictional character Sherlock Holmes—shifting through seemingly contradictory and often parsimonious evidence, bringing behavioral insights into the analysis, making careful and reasoned inferences, and testing theories against known "facts." Such an exercise can be both entertaining and illuminating.

5.1   The Fateful Meeting

On 2 December 1949, the Executive Committee of the Ford Motor Company, the second largest automobile company in the world, convened a meeting that included not only its own members but also a group of top managers representing the company's manufacturing, marketing, product engineering, and internal control and monitoring organizations. One item stood at the top of the committee's agenda: deciding how the company would produce engines for its future models. But everyone attending the meeting knew that a lot more than engine production lay at stake. All comprehended at some level that Ford's strategic plans and the very organizational design of the company as a whole turned on the meeting's outcome. The issues faced by the group were not new.

Indeed, Ford's top executives had called this meeting specifically to reconsider a decision the Executive Committee had made just a month earlier, after which the full logic of that decision had perhaps become clear.[10]

At its meeting of 4 November, the Executive Committee had adopted the recommendations of its Facilities Committee, a special committee created the previous May by the company's president, Henry Ford II, and his executive vice president, Ernest R. Breech.[11] This new committee essentially functioned as one of the standing committees that reported to the Policy Committee, which had charted all aspects of the company's strategy since its creation three years earlier. The Facilities Committee had been charged with responsibility for resolving production facilities issues. Delmar S. Harder, vice president of Ford's Manufacturing Division, chaired the committee. Other members included Lewis D. Crusoe, the head of the newly created Ford Division, Benson Ford, head of the Lincoln-Mercury Division, Robert S. McNamara, controller, Stanley W. Ostrander, manager of operations for the Lincoln-Mercury Division, and R. T. Hurley, Ostrander's counterpart in the Ford Division.[12] When it was created, the Facilities Committee faced the problem of ensuring the continued manufacture of Ford V-8 engines, which had been in production since 1932, while also providing for the manufacture of completely new overhead-valve engines for new model Fords, Mercuries, Lincolns, and, it was anticipated, a new, small, European-like automobile.

Since Henry Ford II had assumed control of Ford Motor Company in 1945, he and the management team he recruited to rebuild the beleaguered company had been moving toward a decentralized organizational structure modeled explicitly after that of the General Motors Corporation.[13] GM was then widely recognized as the best organized and best managed company in the United States, if not the world, and its diversified, multidivisional management principles and design had been well captured in a now-classic book by Peter Drucker, *The Concept of the Corporation,* published in 1946.[14] Henry Ford II had brought to Ford Motor Company several GM executives, including his executive vice president, Ernest R. Breech; Ford Division head Lewis Crusoe; and vice president for manufacturing Del Harder.[15] Even before Breech joined the company, the young Ford had created the Lincoln-Mercury Division and

10. Minutes of the Executive Committee, 2 December 1949, Ford Industrial Archives, Dearborn, MI, 84-63-1217:1.

11. Minutes of the Executive Committee, 4 November 1949.

12. On the creation of the Facilities Committee, see Ernest R. Breech to D. S. Harder et al., Executive Communication, "Appointment of Special Facilities Committee," 20 May 1949, and Henry Ford II to E. R. Breech, 16 September 1949, Ford Industrial Archives, 65–71:15.

13. Nevins and Hill, *Ford: Decline and Rebirth,* remains the most compelling account of Henry Ford II's accession to the throne of the Ford Motor Company and his efforts to rebuild the company.

14. Peter Drucker, *The Concept of the Corporation* (New York: John Day, 1946).

15. Harder had come from the presidency of E. W. Bliss Company, one of the leading stamping press manufacturers, but he had been in that position only briefly. He spent most of his career as a manager for GM.

given his brother Benson Ford responsibility for its management and performance.[16]

With the arrival of Breech and the numerous executives and managers lured away from GM, commitment to the principle of decentralization grew within the executive ranks of the Ford Motor Company. Throughout 1946, 1947, and 1948, as executives charted the company's strategy for restructuring and renewal in the postwar years, they not only educated employees throughout the company about the principles of decentralization, but they also committed the company to its realization.[17] In early 1949, the company took a giant step in that direction when it created a distinct Ford Division to manage the design, production, and marketing of Ford cars and trucks. Henry Ford II and Ernest Breech tapped the former GM executive Lewis Crusoe to be the first head of the new division, and Crusoe was highly committed to the central tenet of decentralization: achieving the highest performance by a division requires divisional autonomy, thereby providing adequate incentives and demanding full accountability. Throughout this entire period, from mid-1946 through the fall of 1949, all planning in product design and engineering and manufacturing facilities had been predicated on the assumption that the Ford Motor Company was committed to decentralization.

Thus when Del Harder delivered the report and recommendations of the Facilities Committee to the Executive Committee on 4 November 1949, no one could have been surprised by the assumptions and goals that underlay the Facilities Committee's work. Its report laid out four alternative plans for meeting the company's future engine manufacture but endorsed only one plan as being clearly superior to the other three. The preferred plan called for the adaptation of the Parts and Accessories Building at Ford's famous, massive River Rouge plant (the Rouge) to engine production and the destruction of the Rouge's Motor Building. Using machinery and equipment moved from the Motor Building, the renovated facility would produce 4,135 V-8 engines per day to meet the continuing demand for this power plant. To make the new higher-horsepower, higher-performance overhead-valve engine planned for new Ford, Mercury, and Lincoln models, the Facilities Committee recommended the construction of two new engine plants, one to produce the engine for the Ford (a six-cylinder overhead-valve design) at the rate of 2,205 per day, and the other to make engines for the Mercury (1,973 per day) and the Lincoln (376 per day). Both the Mercury and the Lincoln engines were to be overhead-valve V-8 engines manufactured from the same block casting, but they were to be bored differently, contain different crankshafts, have different strokes, and thus be of different horsepower. The Facilities Committee addressed the issue

---

16. For an overview of the organizational aspects of Ford in the postwar period, see David A. Hounshell, "Ford Automates: Technology and Organization in Theory and Practice," *Business and Economic History* 24, no. 1 (1995): 59–71.

17. The company's "master plan" for organizational development and decentralization was adopted by the Policy Committee in July 1946.

of supplying castings to the three engine plants, but the plan specified only that the new engine plant going into the Parts and Accessories Building at the Rouge would continue to rely upon the Rouge's famous foundry for its castings. The other two plants, one to be managed by the new Ford Division and the other to be operated by the older Lincoln-Mercury Division, would either have to contract for their castings or be supplied by new foundries built for those plants. As Harder stressed in his presentation, this plan met two principal criteria—one to supply new engines for new models while maintaining production of the older-model engine, and the other to ensure the principle of divisional autonomy that so much of the revitalization and long-range strategy of the company was predicated upon.[18] Members of the Executive Committee found the Facilities Committee's recommendations compelling and voted unanimously to adopt and implement them. The Facilities Committee estimated the plan would take two years to carry out and cost $187.4 million.

Two weeks later, however, Robert McNamara, Ford's controller and a member of the Facilities Committee, dropped a bombshell on the approved plan. McNamara sent a widely circulated memo to Theodore O. Yntema, vice president for finance, saying that, although as a member he had concurred in the Facilities Committee's recommendation to the Executive Committee, his office had since conducted a "review of the problem [of engine manufacture] on a somewhat broader basis" than had the Facilities Committee. As he noted, his office had gained this "broader" view by relaxing the criteria that had served as the starting point for the Facilities Committee. For example, as already noted, the Facilities Committee had based its analysis on the assumption—flowing out of decentralization principles—that "[e]ngine machining and assembly must be segregated by end product division without regard to engine interchangeability or relative operating costs of different plant sizes." Another criterion, which stemmed from the Executive Committee's earlier decision to lessen the company's dependence on the Rouge (thereby making the company less vulnerable to crippling strikes), called for the Rouge to supply no more than half the engines needed by the company. By relaxing this second criterion while preserving "the rule of organizational separation," McNamara proposed an entirely different strategy for meeting the company's engine needs. He called it "Plan A." The details of Plan A need not detain us here except to note that it also included a provision for the purchase of all castings for the new Ford and Lincoln overhead-valve engines. The bottom line, McNamara promised, was a savings of some $46 million in investment and manufacturing costs.[19]

18. "Forward Engine Program Facilities Study," 4 November 1949, included in the Minutes of the Executive Committee, 4 November 1949.

19. Robert S. McNamara to T. O. Yntema, 18 November 1949, Ford Industrial Archives, 65–71:14. McNamara's Plan A called for the production of the new Ford 6 to be carried out at the Rouge. It thus violated one of the company's explicit criteria, which was to lower the Rouge's

McNamara's Plan A reopened a matter that Harder thought had been settled, and it put Harder very much on the defensive. Above all, it led to the pivotal Executive Committee meeting of 2 December 1949. Several members of the Facilities Committee attended the meeting, plus assorted other managers. Harder began the meeting by presenting the Manufacturing Division's point-by-point assessment of the costs associated with McNamara's Plan A.[20] By the time Harder had finished, Plan A lay in shambles, and the Executive Committee had rejected the principal elements of the McNamara plan.

Harder then distributed—and read—a new memorandum to the Executive Committee in which he reassured the committee members that the plan they had approved a month earlier had been well formulated. The Facilities Committee, Harder stressed, had carefully developed twenty alternative plans of which he had presented only the four most attractive ones. He reiterated that the Executive Committee's decision to build two new engine plants was sound. Presenting locational data for the two new plants, Harder then asked the committee to make a decision about where the plants would be built. The choices included Detroit, Chicago, and Cleveland and combinations thereof. With these choices Harder also presented cost estimates that included site costs, tax burdens, and freight rates but did not include wage rates and "labor efficiency" figures in each of the cities.[21] As the minutes of the meeting note, discussion then "ensued."[22]

When the meeting adjourned, the committee had determined to build only one new engine plant (complete with foundry) and to locate it in Cleveland. But unlike either the previously approved plan or McNamara's Plan A, the Cleveland plant would be built to manufacture 4,000 to 4,500 engines a day— essentially the combined daily output projected for the two previously approved plants. "The actual mix of engines to be manufactured in the new plant," note the minutes, "would be the subject of further study." The Executive Committee also reaffirmed the Facilities Committee's original recommenda-

---

production to 50 percent of the company's parts needs for any major product. (This particular criterion will be discussed below.) McNamara suggested that the company simply purchase castings for the new Ford 6 as well as those for the new Lincoln V-8. With some minor rearranging, he argued, the Rouge's foundry could produce the castings for the new Mercury V-8. He also suggested other alternatives to the approved plan, including using the company's Detroit-Lincoln plant for engine manufacture.

20. The Manufacturing Division's critique of McNamara's Plan A was submitted formally in a memorandum, "Facility Cost Study Comparison," dated 30 November 1949 and distributed to those attending the Executive Committee at its meeting of 2 December 1949. I have not located this actual document but have drawn its conclusions from the Minutes of the Executive Committee Meeting, 2 December 1949.

21. Delmar S. Harder to Henry Ford II et al., "Forward Engine Program—Facilities Study," 2 December 1949, Ford Industrial Archives, 65–71:14. Harder noted in this document that "the location of all three plants in Detroit provides the lowest cost point," but Breech annotated his copy of the locational cost comparisons pointing out that "no effect on costs [is] given to labor efficiency by locations."

22. Minutes of the Executive Committee, 2 December 1949.

tion to raze the Rouge's old Motor Building and to relocate and upgrade the classic Ford V-8 engine production to the site's Parts and Accessories Building. The minutes of the same meeting also show that immediately after making its decisions on engine production, the Executive Committee deferred "consideration of the question of whether or not to make the Buffalo Stamping Plant a part of the Ford Division until such time as the plant was in full production."[23] The Buffalo Stamping Plant was then under construction, the first major components-manufacturing plant built by Ford Motor Company in the postwar period. The Buffalo Stamping Plant accorded with the Executive Committee's clearly delineated strategy of locating manufacturing capacity away from Detroit and the Rouge, thereby lessening the company's vulnerability to the labor militancy that had gripped Detroit and the Rouge since 1937. The committee sought in particular to restrict the company's dependence on the Rouge for any component to no more than 50 percent of total company needs.[24] Although the Buffalo plant had been authorized before the Executive Committee had created the Ford Division, Lewis Crusoe had staked a strong claim on organizational control of the new plant, arguing that its capacity should be devoted to Ford (as distinct from Mercury and Lincoln) products and that such a move would advance significantly the company's commitment to the principles of multidivisional decentralized management. Crusoe had carefully timed submitting his claim to the Executive Committee until it had embraced the recommendations of the Facilities Committee, which, as already suggested, it had done 4 November when it authorized an expenditure of $187.4 million for two organizationally distinct engine-manufacturing plants. To Crusoe, this authorization was the clearest signal yet sent that the Ford Motor Company was truly serious about decentralization.

At this pivotal meeting of 2 December, however, the Executive Committee had undone its original decision to build two separate engine plants of different scales, each to be managed by an autonomous division, and it had decided instead to build a single, large-scale engine plant, the managerial control of which it left in the air. Executives had also equivocated on assigning managerial responsibility for the new Buffalo Stamping Plant. Soon afterward, however, the committee determined to vest responsibility for both the Buffalo Stamping Plant and the Cleveland Engine Plant, as well as their counterparts

23. Ibid. That the organizational responsibility for the Buffalo Stamping Plant was problematic is indicated by a set of documents in Breech's papers in which Harder and Breech struggled to draft a document that laid out the issues surrounding organizational responsibility for the plant. The final draft was issued as an executive communication to all members of the Policy Committee, 15 November 1949, Ford Industrial Archives, 65–71:7.

24. Executives had reaffirmed this decision in May 1949 when Ford Motor Company was hit by a twenty-four-day strike that cost it 1.7 million man-days of labor at a moment when the company was unable to satisfy the market for its cars. For more information and perspective on Ford's postwar labor situation, see David A. Hounshell, "Planning and Executing 'Automation' at Ford Motor Company, 1945–1965: The Cleveland Engine Plant and Its Consequences," in *Fordism Transformed: The Development of Production Methods in the Automobile Industry,* ed. Haruhito Shiomi and Kazuo Wada (Oxford: Oxford University Press, 1995), 56–58.

at the Rouge, in a "group" of the Manufacturing Division named the Engine and Pressed Steel Group.[25]

The decisions made by the Executive Committee were clearly tantamount to the company's abandonment of its strategy to rebuild Ford Motor Company in the image of GM. Without planning on it or considering the issue in a larger strategic context, the Executive Committee had essentially decided to end the three-year drive toward decentralization along product division lines, which Henry Ford II, Ernest Breech, and other executives recruited from GM had seen as the key to the renaissance of the Ford Motor Company. Instead, the Executive Committee set in motion a retreat from reorganizing the company based on products and a return of the Ford Motor Company to its historic, production-centered strategy. The imperatives of production ultimately overrode all other organizational matters. How did this happen?

5.2   What "Ensued" at the Executive Committee Meeting? An Exploration of Decision-Making and Organizational Capabilities

The official minutes of the Executive Committee's meeting of 2 December clearly note that after Del Harder had made his case for the wisdom of the Facilities Committee's original recommendations, "[a] general discussion then ensued." These minutes note further that following this discussion, the Executive Committee made its already-outlined decision "upon motion duly made, seconded, and unanimously carried." The recording secretary included no rationale for the decision, and no discussion is recorded in the minutes.[26]

What went on in the Executive Committee meeting? Why did the committee change its decision about how future engines would be produced and what organizations would manage engine manufacture? What phenomena of organizational behavior or rules for decision making might have governed the final outcome? Did "organizational learning" occur as a result of this meeting or between meetings? What follows is an exploration of several hypotheses that might account for the phenomena observed at this meeting.

One simple possible explanation for the Executive Committee's major reversal in its strategy might go as follows: Henry Ford II and his lieutenants misunderstood or miscomprehended the organizational tenets of GM and the full implications of those tenets for the Ford Motor Company until questions emerged about the Facilities Committee's recommendations for the company's future engine-manufacturing program. Although there is some merit to this argument, it must be weighed against the strong evidence that Ford's executives well understood the organization of GM. Henry Ford II's principal mentor after 1946 was, as has been already noted, Ernest R. Breech, a man who had

25. Henry Ford II to Vice Presidents et al., 27 December 1950, Ford Industrial Archives, 65–71:39.

26. Minutes of the Executive Committee, 2 December 1949.

risen to the top of one of GM's divisions and who succeeded in attracting to Ford Motor Company several highly successful managers who had gained experience in several divisions of GM. After Breech joined Ford as executive vice president, he conducted thorough briefings for Ford's top and middle managers about decentralized management principles through a series of "Management Meetings," which were tape recorded and out of which were published carefully prepared reports that were circulated throughout the company. Delivered 13 May 1947 at a meeting devoted to "Organizational Problems and Plans of the Ford Motor Company," Breech's first, foundational briefing was a tour de force. It presented a clear and persuasively argued case for the decentralization of management at Ford, and it clearly carried the endorsement of Henry Ford II.[27] In subsequent Management Meetings, other top Ford executives laid out how the principles of decentralization were being implemented in their respective domains of expertise and operations.[28] Never before in the history of the Ford Motor Company had such attention been given to matters of organization. In short, the evidence is overwhelming that Ford's executives well understood the principles of decentralized management.

Yet the application of these principles to Ford Motor Company proved to be particularly problematic. Ford was a highly centralized organization that historically had answered to the commands of a single voice—the firm's recently deceased founder, Henry Ford, who had publicly ridiculed the idea of organization and boasted that his company had no organization charts. The Flivver King was now gone, and his grandson commanded the company with a far greater appreciation of organization and organizational principles. But the decentralization of the Ford Motor Company was not straightforward. The company produced only three models of automobiles—the Ford, the Mercury, and the Lincoln. Henry Ford II had created the Lincoln-Mercury Division as one of his first acts of leadership of the beleaguered company, and, as noted, the company had established a Ford Division in early 1949. But deep questions of divisional autonomy existed, and surely much of the discussion on 2 December revolved around this issue. Since 1946, top executives in the company had bandied about the idea of creating an entirely new division of the company to manufacture and market a new European-style "lightweight" automobile. Discussion had grown so serious that the company formally announced the creation of a Light Car Division in August 1946. The new division appeared on organization charts circulated within the company and was always part of strategic discussions at the executive level.

Planning for the design, styling, manufacturing, and marketing of the small

27. Ford Motor Company, Report of Management Meeting, May 1947, Ford Industrial Archives, 65–71:36.
28. See, for example, Del Harder's presentation on the application of decentralization principles to the Manufacturing Division in "The Manufacturing Story," Ford Motor Company, Report of Management Meeting, no. 9, March 1948, Ford Industrial Archives, 65–71:36.

car proved to be problematic, however. The Ford Motor Company had rapidly deteriorated during World War II. Conversion of the company's manufacturing capacity to wartime products, the long, painful death of the company's president Edsel Ford (Henry Ford's son, whose administration had often been undermined by his father), palace intrigue over who would take the reins of the company, and failure to invest in new plant and equipment had crippled the company. During the war, the Roosevelt administration had actually considered taking over the management of the company because it deemed Ford's manufacturing assets and capabilities to be a matter of national security, and when those capabilities began to slip noticeably, alarms in Washington began going off. Reconverting the company's manufacturing capacity to automobile production, getting new models designed and into production, reinvesting in new plant and equipment, and rebuilding the organization proved to be an almost overwhelming task for Henry Ford II and his lieutenants. Thus the launch of an entirely new car division kept getting pushed back as debate grew over whether the American car buyer wanted a light automobile.[29]

From the records I have examined, I have been unable to discern clearly who were the proponents of a European-style car among Ford's top executives. Henry Ford II and Ernest Breech appear to have been among the early advocates, but this assessment is not based on particularly strong evidence. Except for one person, the opponents are even less clear. Lewis Crusoe was clearly opposed to the light vehicle idea. As noted, Breech had recruited Crusoe to Ford where he initially served as vice president for operations (i.e., as Breech's principal assistant). Crusoe and Breech had worked together when Breech headed GM's Bendix Division. After arriving at Ford in 1946, Crusoe moved to various assignments, including head of the Division of Planning and Control, controller, vice president of finance, and then, as noted, as the first head (vice president) of the Ford Division.[30] Crusoe was an ardent champion of decentralized managerial organization and espoused the central tenet of divisional autonomy. Although championing decentralization, Crusoe nonetheless opposed the idea of the Ford Motor Company's manufacturing a light vehicle and thus by definition opposed the idea of a Light Car Division.[31] By 1949 when Crusoe took charge of the new Ford Division, the consumer preferences of Americans

---

29. The 1946–49 debate about the creation of a small "Euro-style" car was not entirely new. Officials at Ford had waged the same debate in the late 1920s and 1930s, as is masterfully recounted in Allan Nevins and Frank Ernest Hill, *Ford: Expansion and Challenge, 1915–1933* (New York: Scribner's, 1957).

30. The best account of Crusoe's background at GM and work at Ford appears in Nevins and Hill, *Ford: Decline and Rebirth*.

31. Crusoe's opposition to the light vehicle emerges in his role as head of the committee examining the company's "forward engine program," the records of which are quite extensive and are contained in the Ford Industrial Archives, largely in the papers of Ernest R. Breech, 65–71. In addition, in an interview with me in Washington, DC, on 7 September 1994, Robert McNamara told me that Crusoe was adamantly opposed to the idea of a small car.

had become increasingly clear. The move was toward bigger and more power-ful cars. Ford's top managers quietly killed the light-vehicle project.[32]

Ironically the abandonment of the Light Car Division may have undermined Crusoe's designs on the Ford Division's gaining control over its own manufac-turing operations, a critical element of divisional autonomy in Crusoe's opin-ion. With the Light Car Division no longer in the strategic plan or on the organ-ization chart, that left only the new Ford Division and the Lincoln-Mercury Division. Some managers had argued for dividing the latter division in two, but the arguments against this easily carried the day, principally because of the small sales of the Lincoln automobile.[33] More important was the overwhelming incongruity between the size of the Ford Division and that of the Lincoln-Mercury Division. The Ford Division was essentially the Ford Motor Com-pany. This asymmetry could well have been a crucial factor in the discussion that ensued at the Executive Committee meeting of 2 December 1949. With the company's having only one significant product division, there may have seemed little point in giving the head of this division authority over new and upgraded components-manufacturing capacity such as the projected Cleveland Engine Plant, the nearly completed Buffalo Stamping Plant, and the refur-bished engine plant that was to be moved into the Rouge's Parts and Accessor-ies Building.[34]

Since the company had first headed down the road toward decentralization, Ford's River Rouge complex had loomed as a huge obstacle to decentraliza-tion, both physically and psychologically. The Rouge was the physical mani-festation of Henry Ford's and his lieutenant Charles Sorensen's obsession with large-scale, high-throughput, integrated manufacturing. Built in the late 1910s and the early 1920s, the Rouge was designed to take iron ore and coal in at one end of the complex and to ship finished automobiles out the other.[35] Henry Ford's goal was to make the Rouge an autarkical empire, and certainly that was

32. The Light Car Division continued its existence until the third quarter of 1947 when the Policy Committee reversed itself within a thirty-day period, going from a decision of "full speed ahead" in mid-August 1947 to total abandonment of the Light Car Division in September after the results of a Ford-commissioned survey showed that Americans wanted bigger, roomier, faster, more powerful cars. Nevertheless, the idea of a light car remained fixed in some executives' minds and thus intruded into much of the company's long-term planning process (Nevins and Hill, *Ford: Decline and Rebirth,* 333). Even as late as 8 February 1949, the idea of a small car was still a major agenda and discussion item at the meetings of the Forward Product Planning Committee. See the minutes of the committee for that date, Ford Industrial Archives, 65–71:14.

33. Even as late as October 1949, the idea of splitting the Lincoln-Mercury Division in two was still being bandied about but not very seriously. See C. E. Bosworth to Ernest R. Breech, 19 Octo-ber 1949, Ford Industrial Archives, 65–71:39.

34. Breech's thinking about the problems of organizationally situating a plant that produced parts for two or more product divisions is interesting and is laid out nicely in Ernest R. Breech to All Members of the Policy Committee, "Question of Organization Responsibility—Buffalo Stamping Plant," 15 November 1949, Ford Industrial Archives, 65–71:7.

35. On the development of the Rouge, see Nevins and Hill, *Ford: Expansion and Challenge,* which remains the best treatment of this subject. See also Lindy Biggs, *The Rational Factory: Architecture, Technology, and Work in America's Age of Mass Production* (Baltimore: Johns Hop-kins University Press, 1996), 137–60.

the image that he liked to promote and that the complex itself conveyed. But by no means was that the reality, at least not in the period under discussion. After Ford Motor Company changed over from the Model T to the Model A in 1927/28 and then was forced soon after to introduce the V-8, the company had increasingly relied upon outside suppliers for its components to save on capital costs associated with model changes and to decrease changeover times.[36] Indeed, when Ernest Breech and his associates defected from GM to Ford, they were shocked to learn that the degree of integration at Ford was significantly lower than that of GM. They immediately set about to reintegrate the Ford Motor Company.[37]

The Rouge figured only negatively in Ford's decentralization and reintegration plans, however. Soon after GM was humiliated with the Flint sit-down strike and was forced to recognize the United Auto Workers as the collective bargaining agent of its workers, GM's executives had initiated a strategy of dispersing its factories—locating them away from Detroit in areas where labor was believed to be less well organized and less militant.[38] Ford's GM expatriates quickly brought this policy into force at Ford, and the Buffalo Stamping Plant was the first of many, many plants that Ford built away from Detroit in the two decades after World War II. Ford pursued this policy in spite of its economic studies showing that unit costs for components such as steel stampings and engines would be lower if capacity were added in Detroit (including at the Rouge).[39]

This policy of dispersing Ford's manufacturing capacity caused enormous confusion among the company's workforce (including middle managers), especially because it was implemented after the company had begun to espouse and then execute its program of decentralizing its organizational structure. Confusion about what "decentralization" really meant reached such a level soon after the company announced its plans for the Cleveland Engine Plant that Ernest Breech, Theodore Yntema (vice president for finance), Del Harder (vice president for manufacturing), and John S. Bugas (vice president for in-

36. On Ford's increasing reliance on outside suppliers, see David A. Hounshell, *From the American System to Mass Production, 1800–1932: The Development of Manufacturing Technology in the United States* (Baltimore: Johns Hopkins University Press, 1984), 300. A good indicator of Ford's reliance on outside suppliers is the company's purchase of bodies at the time the Buffalo Stamping Plant was undertaken. Ford purchased 40 percent of its bodies from outside suppliers. See Project Appropriation Request, 23 June 1949, bound in "Proposed New Pressed Steel Plant," Ford Industrial Archives, 65–71:41.

37. Oral History Interview with John Dykstra, Ford Archives, accession 975, box 1, Dearborn. For quantitative estimates of Ford's and GM's relative degrees of integration, see Harold Katz, *The Decline of Competition in the Automobile Industry, 1920–1940* (New York: Arno Press, 1977), especially chapter 6.

38. On GM's dispersal policy, see Douglas Reynolds, "Engines of Struggle: Technology, Skill, and Unionization at General Motors, 1930–1940," *Michigan Historical Review* 15, no. 1 (1989): 69–82; James M. Rubenstein, *The Changing U.S. Automobile Industry: A Geographical Analysis* (London: Routledge, 1992).

39. Studies for what became the Buffalo Stamping Plant and the Cleveland Engine Plant showed Detroit, especially the Rouge, to have the lowest costs.

dustrial relations) felt compelled to give a company-wide briefing to tell managers and workers that the geographic dispersion of Ford's manufacturing capacity was not what the company meant by decentralization of management.[40] Geographic dispersion and organizational decentralization might have confused the bulk of Ford's workforce, but certainly the company's top managers understood these two strategies were not to be confused with each other even though they could be complementary. As Lewis Crusoe well recognized, the Facilities Committee's recommendation to the Executive Committee to build two separate engine plants away from Detroit, each managed by a different division, would simultaneously meet each condition.

The configuration of the huge Rouge plant's operations, which reflected the obsession of the post-1918 Model T Ford Motor Company with technically "efficient" production to the exclusion of other cost considerations, stood as a huge impediment to decentralization of management. In many respects, the Rouge *was* the Ford Motor Company, and to parse the company into autonomous divisions meant parsing the Rouge. And it simply would not parse along product lines. Despite considerable efforts by managers and executives who truly wanted to see the decentralization of Ford management *and* who truly understood the company's manufacturing operations, the Rouge would parse only along functional lines (steel production, foundry, engine plant, parts and accessories, etc.). The Ford Motor Company's assembly operations appear to have been the only easily product-parsed manufacturing facilities of the company, but this situation must have been so self-evident to executives that they never spent any time discussing it.

So, to return to the original hypothesis, does possible confusion over organizational principles on executives' parts stand up to the test? The evidence suggests that Ford's top executives well understood the principles of decentralization but that Ford's in-place physical assets—especially the Rouge plant—made the literal decentralization of the company along product lines problematic at best and impossible at worst. The simultaneous dispersal of manufacturing capacity away from the Rouge and the vesting of managerial responsibility for these new manufacturing assets in the hands of autonomous product divisions would certainly have moved the company toward its publicly articulated strategy of decentralization. Even committing the company to the long-term reorganization of the Rouge along product lines without dispersal away from the Rouge would, in theory at least, have been possible but was apparently ruled out. This discussion has centered only on the company's physical assets, and surely the Rouge's physical structures were paralleled by human, organizational assets that might also have seemed difficult to parse along product as opposed to functional lines.

But what explanation will hold up? In his Fels Lectures on Public Policy

40. Ernest R. Breech, "Decentralization—What It Is and How It Works"; T. O. Yntema, "The Profit Center System"; Delmar S. Harder, "Decentralization in Practice"; John S. Bugas, "Decentralization and Ford Men and Women"; all in Ford Industrial Archives, 71–20:5.

Analysis, published in 1974 under the title *The Limits of Organization,* economist Kenneth Arrow suggests that individuals and organizations develop "codes" that govern their operation over time. He uses the term "code," as he notes, "both literally and metaphysically. It refers to all the known ways, whether or not inscribed in formal rules, for conveying information." As Arrow argues,

> [O]rganizations, once created, have distinct identities, because the costs of changing the code are those of unanticipated obsolescence.
> Becker and others have stressed that a significant part of accumulation of human capital consists of training specific to the needs of a firm, an input of information to the worker which increases his value to the firm but not to other firms. . . .
> One might ask, as one does frequently in the theory of the firm, why all firms do not have the same codes, so that training in the code is transferable? In the first place, in this combinatorial situation, there may easily be many optimal codes, all equally good, but to be useful in a firm it is important to know the right code. . . .
> In the second place, history matters. The code is determined in accordance with the best expectations at the time of a firm's creation. Since the code is part of the firm's or more generally the organization's capital, as already argued, the code of a given organization will be modified only slowly over time.[41]

Arrow's notion of "code" has not been developed directly by many scholars, but it bears some semblance to ideas developed in the late 1980s and early 1990s by a wide range of scholars, all writing in one way or another about organizational capabilities.[42]

In their highly influential, now-classic article, "The Core Competence of the Corporation," C. K. Prahalad and Gary Hamel identify "core competencies" as those things that provide a firm competitive advantage over another firm, all else being equal.[43] David Teece, Gary Pisano, and Amy Shuen define core

41. Kenneth J. Arrow, *The Limits of Organization* (New York: Norton, 1974), 55–56.

42. This paper cannot purport to offer a comprehensive review of the literature on the organizational capabilities view of the firm. The following pieces do offer such a review: Alfred D. Chandler, Jr., "Organizational Capabilities and the Economic History of the Industrial Enterprise," *Journal of Economic Perspectives* 6, no. 3 (1992): 79–100; Richard N. Langlois, "The Capabilities of Industrial Capitalism," *Critical Review* 5 (1992): 513–30; Dorothy Leonard-Barton, "Core Capabilities and Core Rigidities: A Paradox in Managing New Product Development," *Strategic Management Journal* 13 (1992): 111–25; Ross Thomson, ed., *Learning and Technological Change* (New York: St. Martin's, 1993) (see especially the chapters by Chandler and William Lazonick); Richard S. Rosenbloom and Clayton M. Christensen, "Technological Discontinuities, Organizational Capabilities, and Strategic Commitments," *Industrial and Corporate Change* 3 (1994): 655–85; William Lazonick and William Mass, eds., *Organizational Capability and Competitive Advantage: Debates, Dynamics, and Policy* (Brookfield, VT: E. Elgar, 1995). Of course, the work of Edith Tilton Penrose, *The Theory of the Growth of the Firm* (New York: Wiley, 1959), is fundamental.

43. "The Core Competence of the Corporation," *Harvard Business Review* 68 (May 1990): 79–93.

capabilities as "a set of differentiated skills, complementary assets, and routines that provide the basis for a firm's competitive capacities and sustainable advantage in a particular business."[44] Historians such as Alfred Chandler and William Lazonick have for a long time been using the concept of organizational capabilities to account for some firms' superior performance relative to their competitors, all else being equal.[45]

Dorothy Leonard-Barton, however, has argued that core capabilities carry with them a Janus-faced twin, "core rigidities." As she explains, "Core rigidities are the flip side of core capabilities. They are not neutral; these deeply embedded knowledge sets actively create problems." Leonard-Barton maintains, moreover, that "core rigidities are more problematic for projects that are deliberately designed to create new, nontraditional capabilities."[46]

Within the evolutionary economics framework constructed by Richard Nelson and Sidney Winter, we find concepts that bear some similarity to Arrow's notion of codes and the core capabilities ideas described above.[47] Nelson and Winter speak of informal decision rules and routines that economic actors, including firms, develop over time, which in large measure govern their behavior and performance. Some firms' decision rules and routines bring favorable (i.e., asymmetrical) returns in an environment. These firms flourish. A change in the environment (e.g., a change in the underlying technology of an industry) can eliminate these firms unless either these decision rules and routines work well in the new environment or a firm changes its decision rules and routines.[48]

Was the Executive Committee meeting of 2 December 1949 an occasion in which the "code" of the Ford Motor Company, which the organization acquired early in its history when Henry Ford and his lieutenants were committing the company to mass-production principles, overtly expressed itself in the decision to build a single, large-scale plant that would yield engines of the lowest unit cost? Was the "GM code" brought to Ford by Breech and the other high executives too meager to produce any radical shift in the company's behavior? Were the costs of changing the Ford code too high? Had the former GM executives, such as Vice President for Manufacturing Del Harder, fallen into the Fordist decision rules and routines of old, opting for the principle of lowest unit cost at whatever the cost of organizational design, product flexibility, and other benefits attributed to decentralized divisional autonomy? Did the decision to build

44. "Firm Capabilities, Resources, and the Concept of Strategy," Consortium on Competitiveness and Cooperation Working Paper 90–9, Center for Research in Management, University of California, Berkeley, 1990, as quoted in Leonard-Barton, "Core Capabilities and Core Rigidities," 112.

45. See note 43 above. See also Alfred D. Chandler, Jr., *Scale and Scope: The Dynamics of Industrial Capitalism* (Cambridge: Harvard University Press, 1990).

46. Leonard-Barton, "Core Capabilities and Core Rigidities," 118.

47. Richard R. Nelson and Sidney G. Winter, *An Evolutionary Theory of Economic Change* (Cambridge: Harvard University Press, 1982).

48. See also the now-classic paper by M. L. Tushman and P. Anderson, "Technological Discontinuities and Organizational Environments," *Administrative Science Quarterly* 31 (1986): 439–65.

a single plant revolve around Ford executives' realization that rather than emulate GM the company had to rely upon and indeed renew Ford's fundamental core capabilities—efficient production engineering—to gain competitive advantage? Or was the decision a manifestation of core rigidities in which the logic of "but we've always done it this way" gained the upper hand?

The work of the Facilities Committee had been carried out in parallel with that of another committee created by the Executive Committee, the Forward Product Planning Committee, the group charged with developing medium- and long-range strategies for putting new Ford products on the market. Membership on the two committees overlapped to a certain degree, and clearly the most important overlapping member was Del Harder. Harder was joined on the Forward Product Planning Committee by, among others, the vice president for engineering (Harold Youngren, another defector from GM) and the vice president for finance (Theodore O. Yntema, who came to Ford from the business school at the University of Chicago). When the committee took up its work in the autumn of 1948, it had to deal with the question of exactly what engines would be going into the company's projected models. Indeed, the company's entire "forward product planning" revolved around decisions about engines. This fact is made clear by the review of the forward engine program carried out by the Finance Division when it was headed by Lewis Crusoe, just before he became the head of the Ford Division. This review fed into the work of the Forward Product Planning Committee.

For its review, the Finance Division, with the concurrence of both the Engineering Division (product design) and the Manufacturing Division, established at the outset five first principles or basic assumptions to guide the formulation and execution of its strategy vis-à-vis engines. One principle simply stipulated which new engine would be built first, while the second stated that the daily capacity figures were to be derived from estimations of anticipated sales of the new models. These two principles were highly pragmatic and had virtually no radical implications for the company's organization and operational routines. The third and fourth principles had rather profound implications that may well have conditioned the discussion that ensued on 2 December. Engines put in future products, the third principle specified, "would be processed without limitation by present practice." That is, the company would not be bound by present manufacturing technology in the manufacture of new engines. This principle in effect declared that the company would pioneer new manufacturing technologies. The fourth principle stated that the new engines "would be made without regard to the present facilities" (i.e., the Motor Building at the Rouge and perhaps even the entire Rouge plant). This principle was certainly consistent with the company's emerging policy of dispersing capacity outside of Detroit. For the purposes of establishing high and low investment information, the cost of the "ideal" production process for engines would be estimated if installed in an entirely new plant (high) and if "fitted into existing buildings with a minimum of outside plant" investment (low). The committee's fifth principle was that the Ford Motor Company should manufacture all its engines rather than relying upon any suppliers.[49]

The Executive Committee, therefore, carried out its discussion on 2 December in the context of several of its members' having earlier committed themselves to the principles of self-sufficiency and of not being bound by present manufacturing technology and present manufacturing facilities. Did these commitments conflict with the organizational design principle of building two separate engine plants, each different in scale, each with different unit costs, and each managed by autonomous product divisions? In other words, did the organizational design principle so conflict with the self-sufficiency and technology principles as to be undermined by the latter?

Or did the plan that was adopted by the Executive Committee represent a compromise among those who attended the meeting? Here, too, history matters. When Henry Ford II took charge of the Ford Motor Company and set out to rebuild the failing enterprise, one of his first high-impact decisions was to hire as a package a group of ten young, intelligent, ambitious men who had been part of the enterprising and highly successful Office of Statistical Control within the Army Air Forces during World War II. Headed by their commanding officer, Charles B. "Tex" Thornton, who had created and managed the Office of Statistical Control, the group quickly became known as the Whiz Kids. Although none had ever set foot in an automobile plant, the group (both individually and collectively) maintained that they had the analytical skills necessary to manage any complex undertaking, including automobile manufacturing. Henry Ford II bought into this argument, and even after Ernest Breech and the other GM managers joined the Ford Motor Company, the Whiz Kids continued to impress their mark on the company. Two of the Whiz Kids would go on to become presidents of the company, and four would become vice presidents. Only the commander of the Whiz Kids, Tex Thornton, encountered rough waters at Ford. Thornton aspired to great things; Breech did too. Soon after joining Ford and seeing Thornton's mode of operation, Breech informed Henry Ford II that the company was not big enough for both Thornton and himself and that the president had to choose who was going to stay. Henry Ford II chose Breech. The remaining Whiz Kids, however, played critical roles in the rebuilding of the Ford Motor Company, and their talents and drive were quickly appreciated by Breech and his lieutenants from GM.[50]

49. L. D. Crusoe to Henry Ford II, "Preliminary Review of Proposed Engine Program," 13 December 1948, Ford Industrial Archives, 65–71:14. As already noted, the GM personnel who came to Ford in the immediate postwar period were surprised at the extent to which Ford relied upon external suppliers for its major components. They believed that a high priority for the new Ford company should be to reintegrate manufacturing. The construction of the Buffalo Stamping Plant was predicated in large part in reducing Ford's dependence on outside suppliers for 40 percent of its bodies and body parts.

50. The history of the Whiz Kids is treated in Nevins and Hill, *Ford: Decline and Rebirth;* David Halberstam, *The Reckoning* (New York: Morrow, 1986); John A. Byrne, *The Whiz Kids: Ten Founding Fathers of American Business and the Legacy They Left Us* (New York: Currency Doubleday, 1993).

Since none of the Whiz Kids possessed experience in manufacturing operations, their principal work at Ford centered on organization, information, and analysis. Their fundamental premise was that, if the company could develop an effective system of information flow and control, they could maximize its performance using decision methods that some had learned at Harvard Business School before the war and that the group had developed further in the Office of Statistical Control during the war. Fundamental to this process was the reduction of information into quantitative units. Quantification of information allowed its manipulation while also ostensibly eliminating the bias that typically attended assessment of qualitative information. In the postwar years leading up to the 2 December meeting, the Whiz Kids had worked valiantly to develop an information-generating and -control system that Ford's top management could use to know truly what was going on within and at all levels of the corporation. This system went well beyond a traditional financial accounting system that kept tabs on monetary transactions. The Whiz Kids developed a control system that measured a wide spectrum of corporate performance—all based on quantitative indices.

The epitome of the Whiz Kids' fundamental belief structure was Robert McNamara, who by the time of the 2 December meeting was the Ford Motor Company's controller. He had studied and taught business management at Harvard Business School, where he had become a disciple of Robert Anthony, a professor of accounting whose philosophy was that accounting should provide the principal means of control and decision making in the corporation. Under Anthony, McNamara had mastered the case on return-on-investment calculations and decision criteria that Donaldson Brown had developed at the Du Pont Company and had then transferred to GM after Du Pont gained control of GM in 1919.[51] Under Tex Thornton, McNamara had carried out statistically rich analyses of the Army Air Forces' operations that he believed could both account for and optimize that service's performance in the conduct of the war. At Ford, McNamara fell under Lewis Crusoe's wing, essentially following Crusoe's movement up the command structure while mastering the lessons the former assistant treasurer at GM taught him. McNamara had backed up Crusoe's work on the Forward Product Planning Committee, and after Crusoe became the first head of the Ford Division, McNamara, now controller, had served on the Facilities Committee with Crusoe, where he clearly supported Crusoe's pursuit of a GM structure and strategy at the Ford Motor Company.

Yet McNamara went beyond Crusoe in his work as controller. Under McNamara, the Controller's Office extended its reach throughout the corporation, gathering increasing amounts of information and using that information to assess—and challenge—the operations and decision making of units throughout the company. McNamara's 18 November memorandum questioning the Executive Committee's 4 November decision to build two engine plants in accor-

---

51. In an interview with me in Washington, DC, 7 September 1994, Robert McNamara was still able to recite chapter and verse of the principal aspects of Donaldson Brown's ROI formulation.

dance with the recommendations of the Facilities Committee (of which he was a member) typified his mode of operation, forcing managers like Del Harder to develop arguments that could withstand McNamara's quantitative challenges to operational and strategic decisions.

McNamara's memo was unquestionably the catalyst that forced the Executive Committee's reassessment of its earlier decision to build two separate engine plants. But what role did McNamara actually play in the 2 December meeting? Certainly the minutes of the meeting make clear that Del Harder succeeded, point by point, in showing how McNamara's plan to supply engines—developed only from numerical analysis rather than operational experience that took account of reality—simply would not work. But if McNamara's plan was rejected, does this mean that McNamara's credibility was effectively undermined at the meeting and in subsequent events at Ford? Certainly the postmeeting evidence suggests that McNamara's star continued its meteoric rise at Ford. (McNamara succeeded Crusoe as head of the Ford Division and then became president of the entire Ford Motor Company not long before he departed to become secretary of defense under President John F. Kennedy.)[52] McNamara's challenge to the Facilities Committee's recommendations, as he went out of his way to point out, in no way questioned the organizational design criterion of preserving divisional autonomy over engine manufacture that had been fundamental to all product planning and corporate-wide organizational changes during the previous three years. Yet when the Executive Committee ended its meeting on 2 December, it had taken actions that, (1) essentially realized the spirit of McNamara's 18 November memo, which was fundamentally intended to save the company money, and (2) essentially abandoned the principle of divisional autonomy over manufacturing operations.

Was this outcome a compromise offered by Controller McNamara? Did it provide the proponents of Fordist lower unit costs with what they wanted (presumably a bigger, more specialized plant) while promising the proponents of divisional autonomy an attractive alternative? What was the alternative, and what role would McNamara have had in offering it? Although evidence is lacking from the meeting itself, postmeeting evidence suggests that McNamara could well have forged the compromise, a compromise in which his own office stood to gain as well. The compromise was simple: maintain the historic strength ("code," "core capability," "routine") of the Ford Motor Company by building the largest-scale, most technologically advanced, lowest-unit-cost facility to be managed by the Manufacturing Division; at the same time, employ the emerging information and control system being developed by the Controller's Office to allow the heads of product divisions to monitor costs and quality of components being made by the Manufacturing Division and "sold" to the

---

52. Byrne, *Whiz Kids,* provides a biographical sketch of McNamara and his subsequent career beyond Ford, but the best biography of McNamara published to date is Deborah Shapley, *Promise and Power: The Life and Times of Robert McNamara* (Boston: Little, Brown, 1993).

product division. The development of what became known as "transfer pricing systems" would allow the Ford Motor Company to develop itself into a hybrid organization—a firm showing many of the dominant characteristics of the highly centralized, efficient-manufacturing company that Henry Ford had first built while providing an ersatz or virtual expression of the information flows, accounting mechanisms, and control structures that characterized a multidivisional, decentrally managed organization like GM. Massive flows of quantitative data and sophisticated methods of analyzing these data—things that the Controller's Office was specializing in—provided the key to this step. The controller would provide the heads of divisions with the means to gain all the benefits of decentralization without its higher unit manufacturing costs.

5.3 The Outcome

Whether Robert McNamara actually invoked transfer pricing as a kind of deus ex machina at the Executive Committee meeting of 2 December can only be a matter of pure speculation.[53] The same is true with our own offering of "codes," "core capabilities," "core rigidities," and "organizational routines," as mechanisms that account for the Executive Committee's about-face of 2 December 1949. Readers may well have their own framework for explaining what ensued at the meeting. But the actual *outcome* of the Executive Committee's decision at this fateful meeting is definitely not subject matter for speculation. The decision led directly to the design, construction, and opening of the Cleveland Engine Plant, complete with its own automated foundry. Less than six weeks after the Executive Committee's meeting, the Ford Motor Company purchased a 200-acre tract of land in Brookpark, Ohio, a community adjacent to the Cleveland Airport. Five months later, construction began at the site, and in December 1951—two years after the fateful meeting—production of six-cylinder overhead-valve engines began at the Cleveland Engine Plant.[54] The plant itself was hailed as the most advanced factory in the world, and its opening will forever be tied to the advent of "automation," a word that Ford's Del Harder coined to describe the automatic loading and unloading of workpieces in machinery such as stamping presses and machine tools and the automatic movement of these workpieces between such machines.[55] The Cleveland Engine Plant was a piece of pure Fordism. It consisted of highly specialized ma-

53. This statement is only partially true. In my 7 September 1994 interview, McNamara asserted that his control system and especially the development of transfer pricing allowed Ford to reap the benefits of centralized management of production while maintaining a semblance of decentralization. McNamara went on to say that many of the Ford executives from GM remained so wedded to the GM way of doing things that they could not function well in the new Ford organization.
54. The development and early operation of the Cleveland Engine Plant are treated in Hounshell, "Planning and Executing 'Automation.'"
55. James R. Bright, *Automation and Management* (Boston: Harvard Business School, 1958); Joseph Geschelin, "Engine Plant Operation by Automation," *Automotive Industries* 106 (1 May 1952): 36.

chinery tied together with materials-handling equipment and fed by a continuous stream of raw materials. The pace of work at the factory was determined not by those who worked there but by the machines that dominated the factory. The Cleveland Engine Plant was the progenitor of several other automated engine plants built by Ford in the decade after 1952. Cleveland Engine Plant II was planned soon after Cleveland Engine Plant I opened; its product was geared to providing Ford's first major entrant into the rapidly developing "horsepower race" of the 1950s and early 1960s. Engine plants at Lima, Ohio; Dearborn, Michigan; and Windsor, Ontario, followed, each advancing the automation technology of the previous plant.

Although Del Harder's Manufacturing Division presided over the planning, construction, and operation of these engine plants and a host of other components manufacturing plants such as transmission factories, brake plants, and the like, the Controller's Office vigorously pursued control over the performance of these plants. The Cleveland Engine Plant itself became a battleground over cost accounting in a struggle between the Manufacturing Division and the Controller's Office. McNamara and his minions developed a costing system that projected theoretical costs and held them up against actually observed costs. This system provided algorithms by which observed costs could be adjusted to account for less-than-capacity output, but then these adjusted costs were held up against the theoretical costs to expose less-than-satisfactory operational performance. A long, heated dispute between the Manufacturing Division and the Controller's Office over Cleveland Engine Plant costs probably occasioned an actual tour of the plant by Ford's board of directors in 1954, at which time the Manufacturing Division gave an extended—and pointed—briefing about the manufacturing economics of the Cleveland plant in which data at variance with the Controller's Office was presented.[56]

The battle between "the bean counters" and "the operations people" continued at Ford during the 1950s. The company's accounting and control systems became the stuff of legends during this period, and the Ford Motor Company became an important training ground for an entire generation of managers committed to quantitative analysis and management by numbers. At the same time, Ford's operations people continued to pioneer in the development of automation, and in the late 1950s the company took a vital leadership role in the standardization of transfer machines, the heart of "Detroit automation."[57] The

56. "Review of Cleveland Operations," October 1954, Ford Industrial Archives, 65–71:8. An example of McNamara's department's reviews of Cleveland Engine Plant costs is "Comparison of Monthly Costs with Planned Costs, 1952 Ford 6 Overhead Valve Engine," 24 November 1952, Ford Industrial Archives, 65–17:10. As one member of the Controller's Office wrote in 1954, "[T]he whole subject of the cost differential on engines has been such a touchy one for several years" (W. H. Guinn to L. P. Hourihan, 3 February 1954, Ford Industrial Archives, 71–2:4).

57. Ford's work on standardization of automation equipment, particularly transfer machinery, is reviewed in David A. Hounshell, "Automation, Transfer Machinery, and Mass Production in the U.S. Automobile Industry in the Post–World War II Era," paper delivered at the annual meeting of the Society for the History of Technology, London, 2 August 1996.

Executive Committee meeting of 2 December 1949 clearly offered a portent of this future.

During the 1980s, with the apparent growing weakness of the U.S. automobile industry vis-à-vis that of Japan, ironically both "bean counting" and "Detroit automation" came under attack as the root causes of U.S. decline, and of the Ford Motor Company.[58] Assessing whether this facile diagnosis was accurate will, I suppose, occupy historians and business analysts for a long time. Those who take up this subject should unquestionably ponder the events that led up to the Ford Motor Company's Executive Committee meeting of 2 December 1949 and ask what decision rules, organizational principles, and interpersonal dynamics were in operation that day that changed the course that the company had charted a mere three years earlier.

Was the outcome of this fateful meeting preordained or inevitable? When examined through the lens of Arrow's "codes" or Nelson and Winter's "routines," then perhaps the reversal taken at the meeting seems virtually inevitable. When viewed through the lens of history, Ford's long-time and deep commitments to mass production, as embodied at the River Rouge plant, seem to have run over the attempts by some to reorient the company and to do things in a different way; the sheer mass of these commitments—both physical and psychological—moving through time gave them an inertia that was simply too great to redirect.[59] The demands of the post–World War II automobile market also surely played a role in the Executive Committee's decision to reverse its course. Increasingly, Ford's executives realized that, if they could just make enough cars to satisfy the enormous demand, they could return the company to profitability. The imperatives of production were enormous, and as as those who have studied the postwar automobile industry have recognized, manufacturers (including the independents) pursued the same strategies of committing more deeply to Fordist production regimes. As Womack, Jones, and Roos write in *The Machine That Changed the World* (63), in 1955 "six models accounted for 80 percent of all cars sold" in the United States.

Yet even within Ford's top ranks, sentiment remained for building a broader product line through the creation of an entirely new division that would have autonomy in both production and sales. Although most histories of the Ford Motor Company's attempts to introduce the Edsel in 1957 focus on the car's terrible design as contributing to the Edsel's becoming one of the greatest disasters in marketing history, they often overlook the original idea for the Edsel. The Edsel was "created" in 1955 both to broaden the company's product line

58. See, e.g., Michael L. Dertouzos, Richard K. Lester, and Robert M. Solow, eds., *Made in America: Regaining the Productive Edge* (Cambridge: MIT Press, 1989); James P. Womack, Daniel T. Jones, and Daniel Roos, *The Machine That Changed the World* (New York: Rawson, 1990).

59. Although my (more scientifically precise) language here varies from that used by the historian of technology Thomas P. Hughes, we are essentially discussing the same phenomenon. See Hughes, "Technological Momentum in History: Hydrogenation in Germany, 1898–1933," *Past and Present* 44 (August 1969): 106–32.

and to serve as the vehicle by which the company created a new division. It led to Ford's splitting the Lincoln-Mercury Division into two separate divisions (recall that this was the same goal pursued in the immediate postwar period), an independent Lincoln Division and an independent Mercury Division (headed by the Edsel's chief promoter). The Edsel was supposed to give the Mercury Division enough product to warrant its autonomy in both sales and manufacture.[60] Ultimately, the strategy did not work, and the Lincoln and Mercury divisions were reunited. Robert McNamara, by then head of the Ford Division, opposed the plan for the Edsel. While the debacle unfolded, he pursued a different strategy of broadening his own division's product offerings, introducing the Falcon compact at the lower end and moving toward what became the Galaxie at the top end, with the traditional Fairlane in the middle. McNamara, whose promulgation of Plan A had led directly to the fateful meeting in 1948 that had reversed the strategy of decentralization of production, had triumphed again in the centralization of the Ford Motor Company. Soon, he would do the same for the U.S. Department of Defense under Presidents Kennedy and Johnson.[61]

Comment   Sidney G. Winter

David Hounshell's paper sets forth a historical question about what happened at a single meeting that occurred at the Ford Motor Company in December 1949—but he doesn't answer the question. He just frames it very nicely, explores some possible interpretations, and then leaves it up for grabs. "Fortunately," he remarks, we do not know what actually happened during the meeting itself. We can only operate in the Sherlock Holmes mode, making inferences based on the specific historical facts that Hounshell carefully describes, and guided by our general theoretical understanding of organizations.

It is an understatement to say that I welcome the opportunity to address this challenge. In his sharply focused study, Hounshell not only invokes broad theoretical issues that have fascinated me for many years, but also raises more specific questions with historical connections to ones that I have previously encountered and thought about.[1]

---

60. On Edsel, see Nevins and Hill, *Ford: Decline and Rebirth,* 380, 384–87.

61. On McNamara's centralization of the Pentagon, see David R. Jardini, "Out of the Blue Yonder: The RAND Corporation's Diversification into Social Welfare Research, 1946–1968," Ph.D. diss., Carnegie Mellon University, 1996.

Sidney G. Winter is the Deloitte and Touche Professor of Management at the Wharton School of the University of Pennsylvania.

1. In particular, I have had the occasion to reflect on the managerial style and skills of one of the key protagonists in Hounshell's story, Robert S. McNamara. I had the opportunity for a relatively close-in view when I did a brief stint in the systems analysis office of McNamara's Pentagon in 1962.

In his quest for an explanation of the outcome of the December 1949 meeting, Hounshell considers a range of potentially helpful concepts and theoretical schemes. The key words here include several that happen to be current favorites in the strategic management literature, such as organizational capabilities, codes, routines, core competencies, and so forth.

Although there are distinctions among the ideas evoked by these terms, there is a sense in which they all come from the same family. In his classic book *Essence of Decision* (1971), Allison laid out three broad "models" (or paradigms) for understanding organizational decisions: unitary rational actor, organizational process, and bureaucratic politics. In the Allison typology, all of Hounshell's candidates for an explanatory role fall under the organizational-process heading. In different ways, they all assert the tendency of an organization to adhere to its own established, and often idiosyncratic, behavioral patterns. To understand what an organization did or might do in a particular situation, one must look at how it responded to similar situations in the past. In this paradigm, the very idea of a *choice* of actions is subject to skeptical scrutiny. At most, top decision makers choose from menus defined and limited by organizational processes rooted in the past. Attempts to choose things that are not on those menus produce no result, or at least no coherent result.

The puzzle that Hounshell presents relates to the *outcome* of a *meeting*. It matters which word is conceived to hold the heart of the puzzle. I am going to proceed, tentatively, on the assumption that the mystery is in the meeting. A short period of unobserved behavior of a few individuals appears to hold the key to a mysteriously sharp discontinuity between the lines of strategic thinking favored by top management prior to the meeting and the actual course of action the Ford organization subsequently followed. We have, thanks to Hounshell, a large amount of background information about the meeting, but know nothing of its details. What could possibly have happened at the meeting?

If this is the puzzle, then the organizational process model is not the right tool kit, for it is not about meetings. Allison's bureaucratic politics model,[2] on the other hand, *is* about meetings—in fact, about precisely the sort of meeting that is at issue here. In Allison's terms, this is a meeting of "Chiefs"—of top managers who have distinct and generally dissimilar realms of authority and responsibility in the organization. The Chiefs in this case are gathered in the presence of a Senior Chief (Henry Ford II), and their legitimate role in such a setting is to advise their superior on questions relating to the overall direction of the organization.

Before applying the model to the case, let me review its key features. Organizational actions are viewed as the outcomes of internal political processes or "games."[3] The participants are "players in positions"—the players are differ-

---

2. Also known as the *governmental* politics model.

3. Allison notes (1971, 163) that his use of the "games" terminology owes something to game theory (particularly of the Thomas Schelling variety), but at least as much to Wittgenstein's discussion of "language games."

entiated by their managerial responsibilities. These responsibilities are not merely different but, in general, asymmetrical—the players have different *sorts* of responsibilities. In particular, they may have different ranks in the formal hierarchy of the organization, and different status in its informal hierarchies as well.

The situation of a player in a bureaucratic politics game is complex, both motivationally and cognitively. It is axiomatic that players have personal goals, especially career goals; they would not have attained the positions that admit them to the game if they were not both smart and ambitious. Typically, both the present position of a player and the organization as a whole can be viewed, from the player's perspective, as means to the end of greater personal success in the future. It is true, of course, that some basic goal alignment between the players and the organization is provided by the fact that few players are likely to gain if the organizational ship sinks under them. Similarly, the success of the organization *tends* to advance the interests of its top managers. In general, however, a given manager has strong grounds to prefer some directions of organizational success to others; indeed, there may be successful directions that are even more disadvantageous to an individual manager than a major organizational failure would be. "A successful career in a successful organization" is the common goal of managers—common in form but sharply different in substance from one manager to the next.

These considerations underlie the bureaucratic politics principle "Where you stand depends on where you sit." It is not to be expected, for example, that a player will be the leading advocate of the view that his or her own unit should play a diminished role in the organization's future.

Cognitive biases associated with organizational positions tend to amplify the effects of imperfect goal alignment. Indeed, it is simplistic to interpret the divergent views of different managers merely in terms of their individual proclivities to pursue personal goals at the expense of the organization. In myriad ways, the player's position shapes not only the information the player receives about what is going on in the organization and the environment, but also the mental models used to interpret that information and to project the consequences of action.

For example, much of the information the manager receives is filtered through subordinates; these subordinates typically have at least as much stake in the future standing of their organizational unit as the boss does and are consequently predisposed toward an "us against them" interpretive framework for many situations ("them" being the rest of the organization). To promote morale and loyal followership, an effective leader will repeatedly emphasize the importance of the unit's work—and even if these pep talks are largely role-playing when the leader is new in the post, mechanisms of cognitive dissonance and other considerations tend in the course of time to align the leader's beliefs with the talk. Also, the leader's intraunit credibility and influence depend on his or her success in conflicts with other units; this tends to make the leader a more ardent advocate for the unit's cause (and for subordinates' views) than might otherwise be the case.

The list continues. An important section of the list is under the heading "top managers are presumptively subject to the same cognitive biases that psychologists have repeatedly verified in experimental subjects." These biases include tendencies to overoptimism, overconfidence (an exaggerated sense of the precision of judgments made under uncertainty), a preference for dealing with confirming rather than disconfirming information (even in the absence of a motivating stake in the relevant proposition), and the "hindsight bias" of believing retrospectively that what happened was largely foreseen. Considering the nature of the processes by which people arrive in top managerial positions, it would be logical to expect that these common biases are, if anything, *more* prevalent in the selected group than in the population in general. These general biases tend to reinforce the effects of the more situational biases noted above, making them highly resistant to challenge.[4]

These cognitive effects are aspects of the principle "What you see depends on where you stand." The evidence considered, its evaluation, and the stakes identified in the situation differ from player to player because of their different stands on the issues. More precisely, what you see depends on where you stand because, for example, of the preference for confirming information. It thus depends indirectly, and partially, or where you sit. But what you see also depends *directly* on where you sit, because, for example, of information filtering by subordinates.[5]

In the context of a meeting among managers from different units—and especially a meeting of Chiefs—the above considerations establish the following structure of stakes for an individual player: (1) Enhance your long-term prospects for promotion, expansion of authority, and other rewards. (2) Increase your power, or at least don't lose power. "Power" is reflected concretely in the allocation of control of action channels, that is, the buttons and levers that actually make things happen in the organization, in the specific action channels chosen for the problem at hand (you generally want your unit to "have the action on this problem"), and in influence derived from access to superiors. (3) Be on the winning side at the end of meeting; considerations of future influence and credibility are relevant here along with the specific issues of the meeting, so there are advantages to "winning" that extend beyond those of winning on the issues, and may even outweigh the costs of an unacknowledged loss on the issues.

Turning to the case at hand, the first thing that the bureaucratic politics model does for us is to deepen the mystery considerably. To see this, consider

---

4. See Gilovich (1991) for a lively discussion of some of the cognitive biases explored by psychologists. These biases are highly relevant to theories of decision making, and in many ways the psychologists' findings lend support to Allison's (unacknowledged) favorite among his three models, bureaucratic politics.

5. See Allison 1971, 178.

the winners and losers from the Executive Committee meeting, invoking the above conceptualization of the players' stakes and extending the evaluation beyond the end of the meeting proper to the few weeks that followed.

The Winners: (1) Vice President (Manufacturing) Delmar Harder. Harder ultimately emerged with control of important new action channels—the Cleveland Engine Plant and the Buffalo Stamping Plant, retained his authority over the Rouge, and seemingly scored a victory at the start of the meeting over Robert McNamara's challenge to the work of the Facilities Committee that he chaired.[6] (2) Controller Robert McNamara. In spite of Harder's demolition of his "Plan A," the meeting outcome reflected greatly increased sensitivity to the cost issues raised in his 18 November memo, and a corresponding subordination of the goal of decentralization along product lines. Further, his own office could, and did, offer a path to partial reconciliation of the competing demands of divisional autonomy and cost control.

The Losers: (1) Lewis Crusoe, vice president and head of the Ford Division. Crusoe had sought organizational control of the new Buffalo Stamping Plant, which ultimately wound up under Harder. Further, as head of the dominant (by far) product division, he had the most to gain in power terms from the company's embrace of GM-style decentralization—an embrace that ended abruptly with the meeting, leaving him with a much-diminished brand of autonomy. (2) Ernest Breech, executive vice president. From the time of his move from GM to Ford in 1946, Breech had taken the lead in promoting and explaining decentralization as the key to the revitalization of the company. Had the company stayed on track in that direction, Breech would surely have played a key role in more substantive implementation decisions—but by the end of the meeting, the company had jumped that track. (3) Henry Ford II, president and CEO. Even before the arrival of Breech, Crusoe, and Harder, Ford had taken a small step in the direction of divisionalization by creating the separate Lincoln-Mercury Division. The movement toward decentralization that Breech spearheaded obviously had Ford's support, according to Hounshell. Hence, the setback suffered at the meeting by the general cause of decentralization necessarily reflected adversely on the credibility of the company's leader. Only by embracing a compromise that differed sharply from his orientation of the preceding years did Ford manage to emerge, formally, "on the winning side."[7]

What is striking about this list of winners and losers is that the winners are junior in status to the losers. Hounshell does not concern himself explicitly with the status ranking of the participants, but, based on the evidence put forward, a reasonable estimate would be Ford, Breech, Crusoe (?—head of dominant product division), Harder (?—head of preeminent functional division),

6. "Plan A lay in shambles" (Hounshell's paper).
7. Hounshell does not tell us of any change in Ford's leadership role in the aftermath of the meeting. One might speculate that it would evolve toward something more analogous to a constitutional monarch and less to a prime minister—but whether that would happen depended substantially on Ford's own choices.

McNamara (subordinate to VP finance, functional division). Hence, the basic mystery acquires the added dimension: how did the little guys prevail over the big guys? Curiouser still: how did Harder and McNamara emerge as winners in the immediate aftermath of a period of intense conflict between them? Fratricidal warfare is not generally recommended as a tactic for coalitions. These features of the meeting's outcome would be *extremely* unexpected and puzzling in almost any organization at any time; I confine myself to the italics rather than spelling out that case at length.

To unravel this deepened mystery, I first note the possible relevance of the bureaucratic politics maxim "Beware of Option B."[8] This maxim is a warning to the holder of formal decision-making authority, in this case Henry Ford II. It warns against a particular threat to his or her de facto control: if the task of defining decision options is delegated to staff and subordinates, there is a possibility that the real discretion will be exercised in the design of the options, reducing the leader's "decision" to an act of pro forma ratification. The appearances of decision can be preserved as this goes on, if only one of the options presented can really withstand scrutiny. More specifically, it often happens that options A, B, and C can be arrayed along a continuum, and A and C can be deliberately designed to be too extreme, each in its own direction. The problem left for the leader is one that Goldilocks would get right. The important issues were those addressed in the design of a particular candidate for the role of Option B; some of those issues may have nothing to do with the A-B-C continuum. The staff work on the problem leaves those issues hidden below the surface when the leader finally sees the options.[9]

There are some parallels between this general "Beware of Option B" scenario and what happened in the Executive Committee. There are three options, McNamara's Plan A (which comes to us as the prelabeled candidate for the role of Option A), Harder's plan (which we label Option C), and the course of action that actually emerges from the meeting, Option B. The three options can be located on a continuum of degree of conformity to the company's decentralization principles, as those were interpreted prior to the meeting. Harder's Facilities Committee accepted those decentralization principles as axiomatic and reported accordingly. McNamara's 18 November memo rejected the axioms, particularly the idea that "[e]ngine machining and assembly must be segregated by end product division without regard to engine interchangeability or relative operating costs of different plant sizes." Conciliatory words about the "rule of organizational separation" notwithstanding, McNamara's plan was

---

8. Option B is discussed briefly in Halperin 1974, 210. I cannot provide a specific cite for the maxim, but it (the maxim) is definitely out there.

9. This can all transpire regardless of whether those involved in the staffing actually conspire to withhold some issues from the leader's decision, or are simply and sincerely trying to help out. The process generally is helpful to the leader in at least the following senses: (1) the task of designing Option B forces resolution of conflictual issues among subordinate Chiefs, and (2) time and attention demands on the leader are reduced. The latter benefit is less valuable when a key strategic problem is faced, as in this instance.

essentially defiant of the company's decentralization thrust. The actual outcome, Option B, is intermediate on the decentralization dimension, and intermediate in a particular way—a way that turns out to be quite favorable to the bureaucratic interests of Harder and McNamara. Finally, it seems reasonable to doubt that Option B would have been well received by Ford if it had been advanced without the context provided by A and C. Thus, there are some hints here that boss Ford was "taken"—though perhaps to his long-term benefit— by his subordinates Harder and McNamara, by means of mechanisms suggested by "Beware of Option B." But, of course, the standard analysis does not literally apply, because Harder and McNamara did not act as a team in framing the options.

Or did they? Here, my quest for an answer to Hounshell's challenge comes to a fork in the road. Down one branch lies the suggestion that the essential dynamics of "Beware of Option B" might have arisen accidentally in the meeting, and the thought that this might have happened makes a very puzzling course of events marginally less puzzling. It is "as if" the Option B device had been employed. This interpretation has some appeal, but it requires that the "winner" status of Harder and McNamara be regarded as coincidental, and it still leaves the basic outcome quite puzzling. In particular, virtually everything that is known about the episode up through Harder's demolition of McNamara's Plan A seems to point toward a reaffirmation of the committee's decision of 4 November, supporting Option C. How could McNamara's deviant and demolished plan have carried the weight required of it in this story?

I will take the other fork, which addresses these objections but is considerably more adventuresome. On this alternative interpretation, the hints of "Beware of Option B" mechanisms are valid clues to what happened, and the dramatic conflict between Harder and McNamara was, well, drama. I postulate that Harder and McNamara reached a meeting of minds on three points: (1) that the decentralization rhetoric of Breech and Ford was fundamentally out of touch with the economic and technical realities of the Ford Motor Company, (2) that the fact that President Ford himself was firmly identified with the decentralization cause, together with the bureaucratic power and stakes of Breech and Crusoe, made it very unlikely that any straightforward challenge to the policy would succeed, and (3) that a feigned conflict between the two of them could create an opening that would get key facts on the table for discussion. Implicitly at least, they also agreed that their individual interests in "a successful career in a successful organization" could be better served by this risky maneuver than by keeping their heads down while the boss made a big mistake. In "A Docudrama" (see below) I offer my speculation as to how the Harder-McNamara interactions might have been initiated.

Even the bold assumption of a Harder-McNamara conspiracy still seems inadequate to account for the outcome. The question of how McNamara's "demolished" plan could play the role required of it still rankles. There can be only one answer: regardless of what happened to his *plan,* not all of McNamara's *analysis* was demolished. The point to the feigned conflict, I suggest, was this: when the dust settled, the Executive Committee was left staring at an important area of agreement between the combatants. From Hounshell's discussion, it is plausible that this area of agreement might have embraced (1) the existence of significant economies of scale in engine manufacture, (2) the fact that the River Rouge plant remained a valuable asset when its costs were correctly assessed on a forward-looking basis, and (3) the fact that the Rouge "simply would not parse along product lines." Taken seriously, these considerations are enough to open the door for Option B. Of course, these points could have been raised without the feigned conflict setting—but the question "what is your main point here" would probably have arisen early, and giving the answer "to challenge decentralization" would not have promoted constructive discussion. There had to be some cover.

A Docudrama

Conversation in a hallway at the headquarters of the Ford Motor Company, circa third quarter, 1949.

Controller Robert McNamara and Vice President (Manufacturing) Del Harder are in a group leaving a meeting led by Executive Vice President Ernest Breech. Breech has spoken, once again, about the virtues of GM-style decentralization. As Harder departs, McNamara strides alongside him—this is not the way to the controller's office.

McNAMARA: I think decentralization will bring great things to the Company in the future . . .

HARDER [*noncommittally*]: Yeah.

McNAMARA: . . . assuming of course that you don't mind losing money.

HARDER [*startled*]: How's that?

McNAMARA: Well, we're finally coming to crunch time between the GM model and Ford realities. We're going to see whether the model fits. Frankly, I don't see how it can—except in some very costly and unprofitable way.

HARDER: Why shouldn't it fit? It worked pretty well at GM, even if Breech does exaggerate that point a bit.

McNAMARA: For openers, Ford is a smaller company than GM and has fewer makes of cars—and the Ford models dwarf the other two makes in sales. Are we really going to have vertically integrated divisions where each division has its own manufacturing? That would mean big cost sacrifices because of the small scale of those operations. But that seems to be the picture that's developing.

HARDER: Yeah, a multidivision company with one division that counts. You can see why Lewis Crusoe cheers for "divisional autonomy."

McNamara: Then there is the Rouge, which is part of your responsibility. My figures show that, with reasonable utilization, costs there could be quite low compared to anything we could do in a new facility—partly because so much of the capital cost at the Rouge is sunk. But how can you divide up the Rouge among different divisions? It just doesn't divide that way—attempting to do so flies in the face of the idea that motivated the Rouge in the first place.

Harder: I think you're right.

McNamara: —and there's the question of the organizational future of the Rouge facility. I've heard people say "The Ford Division is the Ford Motor Company," and I've also heard "The Rouge is the Ford Motor Company." Now, what does that tell you?

Harder: Crusoe expresses nothing but contempt for the Rouge—white elephant, antiquated, insuperable union problems, and so forth. But I'm not sure that he fully expresses his views.

McNamara: Neither am I.

[*Long pause: McNamara looks at Harder; Harder stares blankly into space.*]

Harder: You know, I've been puzzled myself about how this would all work out in the end. Maybe the two of us should have lunch somewhere and talk it through.

McNamara: Fine by me. I'll have my secretary set it up. [*He turns and walks back in the direction from which they came.*]

A final question about the meeting is who proposed Option B, the idea of pursuing a shallower type of decentralization using transfer pricing and other control schemes to reconcile a degree of product-division autonomy with the traditional Ford pursuit of economies of scale in production. Hounshell suggests that it might have been McNamara. While it is very plausible, almost inescapable, that McNamara was a principal architect of the compromise, it would not be tactically sound for him to offer it in the meeting (certainly not in the context of my interpretation of the events, but also more generally). My candidate for this role is Theodore Yntema, McNamara's immediate superior, an economist who would attend carefully to an argument revolving about costs, present values, and transfer pricing schemes, and a comparatively disinterested party in the battle over control of production facilities. Yntema need not have been aware of the postulated Harder-McNamara conspiracy. For example, one could imagine McNamara approaching Yntema with concerns about possible conflict at the 2 December meeting, and making a request for his assistance in keeping the strongest and most important points of his analysis from being lost from view in the scuffle. With Yntema's cooperation in that regard, both Harder and McNamara could play a subdued role in the latter part of the meeting and avoid looking like the winners they were.

So much for my speculative solution to the mystery of the meeting. I now reopen the question of whether the meeting, the outcome, or something else entirely deserves to be at the focus of attention. In many ways, my account of the meeting simply adds color to the interplay of considerations that Hounshell set forth and interpreted from an organizational-process viewpoint. Indeed, so far as the *outcome* is concerned, the episode must be scored as a triumph for the organizational process/organizational inertia family of theories. Here is the question: in its first major postwar expansion of engine capacity, the Ford Motor Company will build X new engine plants; what is X? Three years of top management talk suggest $X = 2$ or more; a historical look at capabilities and practices suggests $X = 1$, and the latter is correct. So who needs to understand meetings?

Allison's unitary rational-actor model also deserves a credit line here. Bureaucratic stratagems and skills aside, Harder and McNamara had, in my view, something very important going for them: they were basically right. They were right at least in the sense that their analyses started from the given situation in the company—its actual "idiosyncratic resource endowment," as the proponents of the resource-based view of the firm would describe it.[10] By contrast, the decentralization efforts seem to have started from a vision of a desired end state, "be organized more like General Motors." The difficulties encountered in explicating this goal to the Ford community may reflect the persistence of organizational "codes," as Hounshell suggests—but it could also reflect the failure of the proponents to think the problem all the way through. Thus, in spite of dramatic contrasts between the decision process and the conventional image of rational decision, one could argue that the outcome of the meeting was largely a consequence of reality constraints surfacing. (I am more tempted by this interpretation than Hounshell appears to be.) It is a virtue of the rational-actor model that it leads one to expect reality constraints to surface sooner or later—but it can be quite misleading about when.

A final lesson about the comparative merits of the organizational process and bureaucratic politics approaches can be drawn from this discussion. The trouble with the bureaucratic politics approach is that it has an unbounded appetite for data. Hounshell's experience of discovering a great deal of information about the meeting, but not what actually "ensued," is illustrative of a general problem. Even if he had a videotape of the meeting, he still would not know whether my conspiracy theory is correct; there is no record of the conversation in my docudrama. While I have taken unusual liberties in filling the gaps in my story with my own speculations, no one can write a bureaucratic-politics account of a decision episode without some gap-filling—particularly the passive kind that accepts "absence of evidence as evidence of absence" when ignoring the possibility of hidden manipulations, stratagems, and other factors. This is a critical weakness in the bureaucratic-politics paradigm as a scientific program, and even more critical for real-time prediction pur-

10. See, e.g., the papers in the volume edited by Cynthia Montgomery (1995).

poses—though the paradigm remains a valuable area of study for aspiring players.

The models in the organizational-process family do not suffer this weakness. Relative to bureaucratic politics, the proponents of organizational-process models take a more positivistic view: give us enough opportunity for thoughtful study of how observable events up to T have apparently shaped those at $T + 1$ in various contexts in the past, and we will come up with insights that are helpful even though T's events are imperfectly known and even when $T + 1$ is next year. I remain committed to my own "evolutionary" version of that general approach, and must accordingly concede that Hounshell's interpretive efforts were on the right track after all.

References

Allison, Graham T. 1971. *Essence of Decision: Explaining the Cuban Missile Crisis.* Boston: Little, Brown & Co.

Gilovich, Thomas. 1991. *How We Know What Isn't So.* New York: Free Press.

Halperin, Morton H. 1974. *Bureaucratic Politics and Foreign Policy.* Washington, DC: Brookings Institution.

Montgomery, Cynthia A., ed. 1995. *Resource-Based and Evolutionary Theories of the Firm: Towards a Synthesis.* Hingham, MA: Kluwer Academic.

6   Sears, Roebuck in the Twentieth Century: Competition, Complementarities, and the Problem of Wasting Assets

Daniel M. G. Raff and Peter Temin

6.1 Introduction

The American frontier closed around 1890. This assertion in its obvious meaning—that there was no unsettled land—is not true: much land waited to be settled in 1890. But after 1890 there was no place where settlers were beyond easy contact with the rest of society. By 1890 the railroad reached throughout the country. Mail, newspapers, periodicals, and publications of all sorts could travel by post and reach everyone quickly.

These conditions created an opportunity for the successors to the peddlers who in earlier years had carried or carted their wares to the otherwise isolated. Previously, relatively large retailers—however small their volumes may have been in absolute terms—sold only in cities and towns. But in 1890 the country's population was still two-thirds rural. Now mass retailers could use the mails to sell goods where people lived (Chandler 1977). They advertised goods in newspapers and magazines that reached farmers. They even published their own catalogues as the extent of their offerings and the value of direct control over the presentation grew.

One of the most successful of these retailers was Richard W. Sears, the founder and for several decades the guiding light of Sears, Roebuck and Company. This paper follows the career of the company after Richard Sears's retirement and death.

Daniel M. G. Raff is associate professor of management at the Wharton School of the University of Pennsylvania, an associate professor of history at the university, and a faculty research fellow of the National Bureau of Economic Research. Peter Temin is the Elisha Gray II Professor of Economics at the Massachusetts Institute of Technology and a research associate of the National Bureau of Economic Research.

The authors thank Naomi Lamoreaux, Walter Loeb, Thomas Misa, Walter Salmon, participants in the preconference, and seminar attendees at Cal Tech and the Wharton School for helpful comments and discussions. The usual disclaimer applies.

The company's history is well-plowed ground in business history. Why another pass? We regard previous treatments as being in important respects incomplete: large and interesting questions deriving from the interaction of economics and history seem to us to have been almost completely ignored. The two most salient settings for analyzing these interactions in the history of Sears are clusters of decisions made by the company in the 1920s and 1980s. It is on these that this essay focuses.

In both these periods, Sears, Roebuck faced challenges. In the first period the company acted brilliantly, in the second not nearly so well. On the strength of the early period's strategic investment decisions, a company that had been merely large and profitable grew into the nation's single largest retail firm and a pervasive factor in the economy as well as in the purchase behavior of a remarkably large number of households. In the second, however, challenges unanswered nearly destroyed the company. This paper analyzes the elements behind the success in the twenties and the near disaster in the eighties and places them in a broader and more systematic context.

We argue that a company succeeds as Sears did when it combines two types of advantages to make itself ineffaceably different from the mass of actual and potential competitors. The first of these types bears on demand. The company identifies and offers goods or services for which many customers are willing to pay a price in excess of production and distribution costs. Indeed, it makes its offering on terms such that customers turn to it rather than other possible suppliers of the same or similar product. The second type concerns supply. The company utilizes assets that have scarcity value the company can itself appropriate. For the company's supply to have these features, the assets must be difficult to do without. (Another way of putting this is to say that it must be difficult for potential competitors to provide the offering without the assets in question.) The assets also must be difficult for potential competitors simply to reproduce. And the company must not be at a disadvantage bargaining with its suppliers. For the success to be long-lasting, and not just a momentarily advantageous transaction, the assets (and indeed all these attributes of them) must be durable.

Achieving each of these two types of advantages in isolation may be a relatively straightforward matter. The harder task, the one that makes for a sustainable competitive advantage that is truly valuable, is to develop them both together. Effecting the combination, and so frustrating the familiar forces of competition and free entry, represents developing the competitively valuable asymmetries possession of which distinguishes successful firms from mediocre ones, firms that earn supranormal profits from those either losing money or earning merely ordinary returns.

There is more. Because environments change, the task is never complete. Successful firms adapt in ways that sustain and enhance the value of the two sets of characteristics we have identified. New activities are undertaken aimed at entrenching the firm in emerging markets, activities that exploit and extend the companies' defensible strengths. Less successful firms may blunt the force of competition in one market. But they do not adapt, and the value of their asymmetries wastes. Preventing such wastage (at a cost, of course, less than the value to be gained) is the trick of enduring success.

This process is ongoing. (It is dangerous to rest on your laurels.) But it does not move evenly through time. There are opportunities for bold decisions, and there are times when action must be taken even without clear objectives. Decisions taken at such times are good if they move the firm toward growing markets and if, at the same time, they exploit the distinctive capabilities of the firm. It is the interaction of these two characteristics that distinguish brilliant from mundane decisions. And it is a characteristic of good business leadership to recognize and anticipate this interaction because it is often hard to discern and predict in a rapidly changing world.

Two episodes in the history of Sears, Roebuck and Company illustrate this argument. In each time frame, Sears moved into a new activity. In each case the new activities were profitable at least at an ordinary level from the start. But only in the first case did the new activities also build on the distinctive and durable strengths of the existing organization. As a result, the innovations of the 1920s left Sears stronger at the end of the decade than at the beginning. The innovations of the 1980s did exactly the opposite. Sears's retailing resources were not maintained and supported relative to competitive standards. Naturally their value depreciated.

How could the managers of Sears have made such a mistake? They understood the point made above that Sears needed to use its existing capital to provide leverage for its next ventures. But they appear to have been prisoners of the way this capital had been used in the boom following the Second World War. They could not free themselves from modes of doing business that were tried and true but rapidly becoming outmoded. The case is vivid but the point is general.

The remainder of this paper is organized into four sections. The first sets the stage by describing the company's initial mission and growth under Richard Sears and his colleagues, most notably Julius Rosenwald. The two following sections describe the decision-making process and the decisions in the two periods of interest. A final section concludes.

6.2   The Early Years

Department stores, predominantly creatures of the post–Civil War urban boom, established the basis on which mail-order houses did business. The department stores initiated uniform prices, departing from the individual bargained price of the bazaar. The uniform price had several advantages over individual prices. It allowed stores to hire a large staff that could be given simple instructions and evaluated far more easily on the quantity sold than if the employees could influence both price and quantity. The uniform price also allowed stores to offer a money-back guarantee, as there was an easily ascertained price to give back (Hower 1946).

Department stores carried a wide and growing range of products. They benefited from economies of scope in selling goods that specialized stores could not realize. They did a volume business and often bypassed wholesalers to cut costs, a move made possible by their large volume in each good. They even circulated small catalogues to sell by mail the stock they had in stores.

Montgomery Ward began its mail-order business in the 1870s, soon after the advent of the urban department stores. It followed the model of the department stores in terms of its wide offerings and fixed prices, but it brought the goods to the consumer—not the other way around. Business was good in the late-nineteenth-century economic expansion, and Montgomery Ward prospered.

Richard Sears aspired to get into this growing market. He began by selling watches, a lot of which he had been able to acquire at an unusually good price, with a money-back guarantee. He did well and expanded. But he was not able to build on his success and was close to bankruptcy in the depression of the 1890s. His partner, Alvah Roebuck, sold his third of the business for $25,000; but Sears convinced a potential supplier, Aaron Nussbaum, to buy half the firm for $75,000 (Worthy 1984, 25). The difference between the implicit value of the firm when Roebuck was the salesman and the implicit value when Sears was suggests some of the skills that propelled the company forward in its early years under Sears's direction.

Sears possessed both manic energy and real writing ability, and he made the Sears catalogue a potent selling tool. The Sears product line broadened in the 1890s. From watches and jewelry, it expanded to virtually all goods used by rural farming families, from clothing to buggies, kitchenware to farm equipment, hunting supplies to patent medicines. The Sears catalogue, advertising all of them, became one of the wonders of the modern world, a monument to Sears's ability to portray a remarkably wide range of merchandise in an appealing manner.

The catalogue presented such a cornucopia of goods that it created what we might now call a virtual reality in the minds of Sears's rural customers. It seized their imagination at the same time that it offered countless items that would make their lives more convenient and productive. No other retailer—fixed or mail—offered the range and verve of Sears.

Yet considered as a business, Sears's company was a helter-skelter operation. As the catalogue expanded and farm incomes grew after the depression of the 1890s, the difficulty of assembling and sending orders threatened to swamp the company. Goods were shipped only with long delays. Many reached farmers in damaged condition, and returns under Sears's money-back guarantee were increasing. As tension within the firm rose, labor turnover increased as well.

Sears, Roebuck was saved from this morass by Julius Rosenwald, a businessman brother-in-law of Nussbaum. Rosenwald had purchased half of Nussbaum's interest and came increasingly to run the company. Rosenwald sought to increase the efficiency of the operation and the quality of the goods at the same time. That is, he wanted to reduce effective costs without selling poor or damaged goods. There were two ways to go about this: first, buying, distributing, and generally administering more cheaply; and second, pricing to take less profit on each item. Buying more cheaply required being an attractive customer to vendors. As a large and growing national outlet in an age of localized retailing, Sears could do this; and it did so ruthlessly. The second, which was also implemented, built on the same foundations of large outreach—potential as well as actual—as the first. Because the average cost curve sloped downward, overall profits were in fact enhanced by the increase in volume. Rosenwald actively pursued the first way. This is less straightforward but more interesting for our story, so it merits more detailed discussion.

Sears, Roebuck initially shipped goods directly from the factories in which they were made. There often were delays in shipping. The factories that received the orders from Sears were supposed to report back to Sears what they had shipped, but the advices were often slow in coming. When a customer complained to Sears, the factory was sent a new order to ship. In that age of handwritten ledger books, there was no easy way to check the new order against the records of the outstanding old ones. The result was that orders frequently were sent out over and over again. The cost to Sears of all this duplication was large since Sears paid the freight for returns, and the effect on consumer perceptions of the company was very bad. One customer in the 1890s is quoted: "For heaven's sake, quit sending me sewing machines. Every time I go to the station I find another one there. You have shipped me five already" (Emmet and Jeuck 1950, 116).

Rosenwald undertook a massive investment for a new mail-order facility in Chicago, which opened in 1906. It was a large structure—large even by today's standards—with all sorts of mechanical equipment for moving goods. But the concept underlying the building was more important than the machinery.

Otto Doering, the operations superintendent, assigned each goods order as it arrived a time and place. That is, he introduced a system where each order was assigned a particular shipping room for a particular fifteen-minute period. Each department supplying an item in the order was notified of this time and place and directed to deliver the item then and there. Items not arriving in time were shipped separately. The supplying department was billed for the extra cost.

Why did this system work so well? At a formal level, it worked because it subdivided the process of mailing goods into its component parts and provided the opportunity and the incentives for each part to be done well. The component parts were finding the goods, assembling the order, and packaging it.

Working backward, packaging the goods was made straightforward because all the goods to be sent were assembled by the end of the fifteen-minute period. They could be packed well and sent off.[1]

Assembly was done well because Doering's system placed the incentives where the work was to be done. The product departments had the responsibility to supply the ordered goods to the shipping location. By fixing a time and providing a penalty for late delivery, Doering enlisted the departments in the effort to get completed orders out quickly. The penalty was tied to the cost of late delivery; it therefore was "just" rather than arbitrary or punitive. The cost of late delivery appeared as a carrot for on-time delivery instead of a stick used for late delivery.

Finding the goods in the component departments was left to the departments. As in the earlier chaotic system, they were the best placed to organize their products to be easily found and dispatched. But unlike in the previous system, the departments did not send goods to consumers: the goods were dispatched to Sears's mail-order facility instead. Given the incentives for delivering goods to the shipping rooms in fifteen-minute segments, the departments had derivative incentives to organize their goods in an efficient manner.

The discipline was not as strict as in the modern Japanese just-in-time delivery system. Given the technology of the time, there was no way it could be. So the Sears plant in Chicago had places for goods from the manufacturers to be stored, identified by their Sears catalogue identification number. Orders could be assembled from these holding bins. The supplying departments were responsible for keeping them filled.

All this was done without computers or telephones. Pneumatic tubes were a popular mode of communication in department stores, and they were mentioned in the 1905 catalogue description of the new plant. Since Nussbaum had first approached Sears in an effort to supply pneumatic tubes to the company, their use may have been one of his contributions to more efficient operations. Doering undoubtedly used pneumatic tubes to let product departments know of delivery times and places and to get information on the assembled goods to departments dealing with finance.

The new procedures also solved the information problem that had resulted in multiple shipments for the same order. The supplying firms no longer communicated directly with consumers. All communications went through Sears. The need for feedback on which orders had been fulfilled between Sears and its suppliers had vanished, and the problem of duplicate shipping information at Sears and its suppliers evaporated.

The difficulty of implementing this new vision is reflected in the length of the period required to make it operational. Forms used within the company show that it was being used widely two years after the new facility was opened.

---

1. The prevalence of goods reaching the consumers damaged under the old system reveals the need for care in this step.

But Lessing Rosenwald, who joined the shipping department in 1912, six years after the building was opened, reported that the new system was only then becoming fully effective (Emmet and Jeuck 1950, 134).

While the new facility improved Sears's operations, it should not be thought that the earlier chaos had put Sears behind other companies of the time. For the other resources of Sears were valuable. In the four years preceding the new plant, Sears's operating expenses averaged 3 percent lower as a percentage of sales than Macy's (Emmet and Jeuck 1950, 175). Sears's gross margin was larger than Macy's—a tribute to Sears's ability to exploit the scale of its business by buying low or even integrating backward to make its own merchandise. Profits as a percentage of sales were higher than Macy's even before the new plant was opened.

Nonetheless, the new plant represented a tremendously valuable asset. The real competition Sears faced at this stage of its history came from other mail-order firms. The new plant helped address customer needs. Considered as a complex asset in itself—facility, systems, people, and know-how all together—the plant possessed all the subsidiary features supporting scarcity value. It enabled the company to trade in volumes that freed Sears from upstream appropriation threats and supported low prices to customers. And the company complemented this by monitoring its downstream activities—the pricing and presentation of its offerings relative to that of its competitors—to make sure it stayed up to the mark where not actually defining it.[2]

In the early years of the century, then, Sears had a large market, attractive goods, a well-deserved national reputation for reasonable prices and general reliability, and distribution assets unusually well suited to getting and keeping this all before the public. These are complementary with one another, and success fed success. The company was in an unambiguously advantageous position.

6.3 Operations and Choices in the 1920s

Sears faced a double challenge after the First World War. The postwar recession had nearly bankrupted the company. Farm income was down after the war as European farms came back into production. The agricultural depression reduced the income that farmers had to spend on mail-order products. The long-term population trend was off the farm and into cities, and during the 1920s the trend accelerated. The result of these long-run and short-run forces was that Sears's traditional market was anything but buoyant during the 1920s.

Sears also faced new and vigorous competition for this diminished market. Chain stores had grown rapidly before the war and had become widespread by

2. The Sears household actually subscribed to the Wards catalogue—presumably under Mrs. Sears's maiden name! Offerings, prices, and even the quality of the stock on which the catalogue was printed were all carefully monitored. See Rosenwald to Sears, 26 February 1902, Julius Rosenwald Papers.

the 1920s. J. C. Penney, F. W. Woolworth, W. T. Grant, United Cigar, A&P stores, and many such others were spreading all over the country. Growing automobile ownership made these stores increasingly accessible. The rural customer in particular was no longer dependent on the Post Office to bring merchandise to her. None of these stores by itself offered the range of products that Sears did. But the position of Sears in each market was nevertheless diminished.

Richard Sears, for all his gifts, was never the steadiest of influences; and by this point he was out of the picture. Rosenwald was a man of much more appropriate abilities for managing a complex organization, and, unambiguously in control, he successfully steered the company through the shoals of the postwar depression. He then had to chart a course for the open water ahead. The requirement for success was to find a more attractive market to replace Sears's stagnating rural one. To preserve, much less enhance, profitability, the new market needed to be one that could be exploited from Sears's great operating and merchandising strengths. Exploiting the accumulated organizational capital of the existing business would, if the match were good, provide protection from competitors already trying to exploit the opportunity or contemplating entry.

Rosenwald hired a retired World War I general named Robert Wood after Wood was fired from a senior position at Montgomery Ward in 1924 in a dispute over strategy.[3] Wood had been a devotee of the *Census of Population* and the *Statistical Abstract of the United States* for many years.[4] He read and reread the statistics. He projected the population trends he discerned and saw that the mail-order firms' market was moving away from it into the territory of urban department stores. As he had at Montgomery Ward, Wood championed the development of urban retail stores as a way to hang on to customers (Wood 1961, 42).[5] To the opposing argument that the stores would simply divert the mail-order business to the stores, Wood responded briskly that it was "[b]etter to lose that business to one's self than to someone else" (Emmet and Jeuck 1950, 341). Wood was concerned with maximizing the overall profits of Sears; his opponents, the profits of one part of the company (albeit then the largest part).

Despite the force of this argument, Wood did not convince much of the Sears management. Perhaps many of the skeptics were defending specific vested interests. Perhaps they were simply fearful of change. Wood did convince the

---

3. For a glimpse at this and at the competitive environment for mail-order firms, see Wood 1924.
4. This habit dated back to his time as a logistics officer in the army helping build the Panama Canal. Library facilities had been limited.
5. Wood may have meant that if one part of the Sears operation was declining, it would be nice to have another expanding. He may also have anticipated (correctly) that there were economies of scope and that store business would help support Sears's fixed costs—its administration, buyers, transport, etc.

head of the company, however; and that was all he needed. Indeed, Wood's ideas had persuaded Rosenwald even before Rosenwald decided to hire Wood. "You need us and we need you" were the words with which Rosenwald began their relationship (Wood 1961, 43).

The first store was opened in 1925 on the site of the Chicago mail-order plant. It was followed in that same year by seven more stores. Sears had over three hundred by 1929, and 40 percent of its sales that year were made in them.

The first stores were located in mail-order facilities, in part to minimize the cost of the real estate and maximize the ease of supervision. But soon Wood had to decide where else to place stores. He set out to differentiate his stores from the plethora of others already existing. His stores would not compete for central-city locations with department stores: they would instead be located on the outskirts of cities, where rent and parking were cheap. They would not emphasize "soft goods" (clothing, food, etc.) like chain stores, though they would make a point of carrying some. They stocked most prominently "hard goods"—hardware, furnishings, farm implements, plumbing—Sears's traditional lines. They were men's stores far more than women's.[6]

Each of these characteristics of the new stores was the result of a decision. Wood, in his perusals of the *Statistical Abstract,* had noted that, in addition to becoming more urban, people were becoming more mobile. In a talk given in 1937, much after the fact, Wood explained that the center-city location of department stores was determined by the means of transportation (Worthy 1984, 83). Railways, first horse-drawn and then electric, converged at the center of cities. Stores in outlying districts could draw only customers who could walk there. But the advent of the automobile meant that the center city was losing its advantage. People could drive to stores that were outside the city center. In fact, they would prefer to drive there because the traffic was less and the parking easier.

It is no accident that this reasoning sounds like the argument for the shopping centers that grew after World War II and the shopping malls that have grown since. Wood was the first to recognize this opportunity, and Sears was well-placed to exploit it.

An alternative strategy can be seen in stores opened by Sears, Roebuck's main competitor, Montgomery Ward. Faithful to their rural customers, Montgomery Ward opened stores in small rural towns. (The facilities were initially intended simply to showcase merchandise. They were converted into stores in the face of customers' desires to take the demonstration items home.) The distinctive feature of this strategy is shown in the comparison of store locations in table 6.1. Sears stores were located in cities almost an order of magnitude larger than cities where Montgomery Ward opened stores.

Montgomery Ward had been faithful to its rural clientele in its retail loca-

6. For an interesting retrospect, see Wood 1950.

Table 6.1   Population of Sears's and Ward's Store Cities, 1925–29 (number of cities)

Population	Sears Only	Sears and Ward	Ward Only
Under 25,000	18	20	320
25,000–99,999	52	84	47
100,000–499,999	47	10	6
500,000 and over	11	1	0
Total	128	115	382
Median population	82,682	43,573	11,647

Source: Worthy 1984, 87.

tions. It therefore shared in the agricultural depression of the 1920s. Sears had been faithful to its merchandising tradition—bringing a wide range of goods to working families. But it also had recognized that the occupations and locations of these families were changing. It operated at a higher level of abstraction than its principal competitor. It found a way to exploit the growth of the urban market with the experience it had accumulated serving the rural one. In this it was unlike A&P, Woolworth, and so forth, which only exploited a new market, and Montgomery Ward, which only relied on its experience. It succeeded because the features of its assets that were valuable in the one setting were, properly mobilized, valuable in the other as well.

Sears also targeted regions of the country. Wood, ever on the hunt for trends in the statistics, observed that the population of the United States was shifting westward and southward. He therefore located Sears's retail stores disproportionately in the South, Southwest, and West (Worthy 1984, 90).

The decision to carry a wider range of goods than other retail stores was a continuation of Sears's policy. The Sears catalogue of course included everything from underclothes to farm machinery. The new stores would do the same. There would be goods for the home craftsman and remodeler just as there had been goods for the farmer. There also would be the opportunity to buy a wide variety of products in a single store. Sears even would supply parts and service for the cars that customers used to get to the store.

The new stores initially were designed to look like the warehouses to which they often were attached. Wood thought the young people setting up households would like to buy their goods in a no-frills atmosphere, reminiscent of the farms they had left or the bare houses they were beginning to furnish. General Wood thought of his stores as military commissaries, a term he used frequently. But this decision was at best ahead of its time. Only now are warehouse clubs thought to indicate good values. Customers in the 1920s were not so fond of the warehouse atmosphere. The times were expansive, and Sears discovered that merchandise both looked and sold better when it was displayed well. Unlike the decision where to place the stores, the decision how to design the stores had to be reversed. Fortunately for Sears, refixturing stores is relatively inexpensive. And business bounced back: people did trust the Sears name.

There were many reversals of policy like this: the redirection of company efforts was not accomplished without false starts and great effort. The postwar inside history of the company argues that there was no clear conception of how retail operations fit into Sears's overall strategy. Its summary sentence reads, "It appears in retrospect that almost the only thing that Sears, Roebuck knew about retailing in the first years after 1925 was that it had entered the field" (Emmet and Jeuck 1950, 341–47). But this is an overstatement. It is true that retailing from a store was a new activity for Sears, Roebuck. The staff at Sears was used to the procedures of a mail-order business. The company's mail-order policies and procedures were by the 1920s well developed and smoothly operating. Retail stores were different, however, and the company had to learn how to manage them. There naturally were confusion and false starts along the way. But the learning process should not be confused with lack of insight into the overall logic. It is apparent that Wood had a clear vision for his company. The problems were all in its implementation.

And the difficulties should not be overdrawn. Sears, Roebuck had been profitable even before the 1906 Chicago mail-order plant was opened. The retail stores were profitable from the start as well. Improvements were made that enhanced the prosperity of the stores, but there was never a time when the problems of retailing threatened to overturn the decision to sell from stores.

As before, the profitability came partly from the company's low costs. The stores were located in outlying sections of cities not only to attract motorized customers. They also took advantage of lower rents outside the city center. Despite later claims that the locations were chosen solely for the customers, the low rents may have been at least part of the initial motivation for outlying locations.

Store rents were only a small part of Sears, Roebuck's expenses. Sears kept costs low and its competitive position strong relative to a whole class of potential competitors by buying cheaply (Raff 1991). The traditional way to accomplish this was to use the large size of Sears as a bargaining tool and force the price of goods down. Sears buyers traditionally had no loyalty to supplying companies. They would switch in an instant if a newcomer offered a lower price.

Wood had a different philosophy. He wanted continuity in his suppliers. While he wanted low prices as much as any of his predecessors, he wanted to use stable relations with the producers of his merchandise to ensure high quality. He replaced the adversary relationship that had characterized Sears before the First World War with a cooperative one. "The tremendous volume in which Sears bought was not to be used as a club to beat down the source's prices but as a foundation on which the source as well as Sears could build a prosperous business" (Worthy 1984, 68). The need to beat down source prices was not even great. The production runs for Sears were typically vastly in excess of those for competitors, even those in the new urban setting. The scale-economy advantages were often large. Even sharing some of these advantages with the vendors, Sears product costs were unusually low.

Sears even integrated backward to a limited extent, extending its operations further into the manufacturing stage than it had before. The story is told that Wood, reading a newspaper this time, saw that steam locomotives were no longer being made in the United States. He called an acquaintance who was the head of a firm making locomotive parts and asked him what he was going to do. The hapless friend responded that he was at his wits' end. Wood suggested that the manufacturing firm could make refrigerators for Sears. Sears would finance the new machinery needed to change products and guarantee the firm a secure market. The deal was consummated, and the manufacturer grew to be a principal in what is now Whirlpool, Inc. (Worthy 1984, 71).[7]

The attractiveness of this locomotive parts firm did not lie in its machinery. The machinery was all junked in favor of new tools for making new products. Instead the assets of the manufacturing firm lay in its human capital, both the manual skill of its workers and the management skill that held the company together. These human assets were fungible, an attractive feature to Wood, and they were employed by him in a process that resembles the European recovery after World War II and the Japanese response to changing relative prices in the 1970s.[8]

Sears participated actively in the design of many of the products it sold. The buyers worked with the manufacturer to create a product that the buyer could sell and that would fit in with other products the buyer was handling. Sears created a testing laboratory to help this process by evaluating new products and providing a mechanism to introduce new ideas and further modifications.

Sears also designed its orders to keep manufacturing costs as low as possible. Goods were ordered in large quantities to capture economies of scale. And Sears kept its orders steady over time in order to smooth the impact of demand fluctuations on its suppliers. Sears absorbed the inventory costs, of course, but it calculated that they would be less than the start-up and waiting costs involved in irregular orders. The cooperative relationship between Sears and its suppliers that itself verged on vertical integration allowed Sears to effect this kind of optimization (Worthy 1984, 73).

Finally, Sears took on much of the distribution function of getting products from manufacturers to the merchant. Sears by the 1920s had ten regional mail-order plants. The Sears buyer took an active part in the transport of goods to these centers. The manufacturer was relieved of the need to plan, and Sears could reap the advantages of centralized distribution.

---

7. On Sears and refrigerators more broadly, see Tedlow 1990, 305–28.

8. Changes were made in response to new conditions in those places and times within existing business organizations. It was easier in those settings to use the existing hierarchies to redirect labor than it was to create new organizations to pursue new objectives. (See Toniolo 1995; Dore 1986.)

Sears was not, however, fully vertically integrated. It took only minority positions in its supplier companies. Wood wanted to influence the manufacturers, but he wanted them to be working for themselves. Sears also tried not to buy the entire output of a manufacturer, so that the manufacturer would have to keep up with the general market. Sears kept clear that its primary role was selling, not manufacturing.

Retailing was challenging, particularly in a time of transition in which the time-hallowed stereotypes of the lives and wants of the potential customer base became more problematic. The inherited organizational structure actually magnified this problem. Mail-order operations were national and high volume. Demand variations in any one region—whether for reasons of style or local income—would be small relative to the whole. The law of large numbers stabilized demand at the company level. Retail stores by contrast were far smaller and by their nature local. Fashion tastes and income could vary greatly across the nation, with potentially massive impact on the profitability of individual stores. Buyers had to be far more nimble to stock stores than mail orders.

Indeed, the buyers in Chicago did not stock the stores themselves. Store managers, and a territorial organization that grew up over them, purchased from the buyers the goods that were sold in the local stores. General Wood came to believe that selling from stores on the Sears scale was "too vast and complicated" for centralized control. He made the organization, in a much-repeated phrase, into a federation of independent merchants, each local store manager to a considerable extent autonomous within the four walls of his own store. The buyers therefore had to do far more than simply procure goods on favorable terms. They had to persuade the store managers to stock them.

The store managers were the appropriate people to make these decisions under the circumstances. They oversaw the sales, often in the most literal fashion; they lived in the communities; and their jobs involved understanding on the one hand the desires and needs of the local customers and on the other the local competitive situation. They were, so to speak, close to the consumer purchase decision; and the information they gleaned from this perspective, otherwise difficult to capture with the technologies of the day, undoubtedly helped in merchandising, pricing, and ultimately, revenues (Raff 1991). Unlike the managers and the individuals called buyers in the local department stores, these Sears employees did not have a free hand as to which vendors they used. But equally unlike their counterparts, they benefited on the cost side from the advantages Sears scale and reliability offered to suppliers. These advantages were all complementary, of course; and all helped sustain the advantageous position from which Sears started.

Within the Sears procurement operation, conflicts developed between the older buyers used to the strictly mail-order ways and the younger ones who recognized the new complexities of the job. Wood and the Sears management flirted with the idea of developing two different sets of buyers, that is, of essentially splitting the company in two. Growing antagonism between the two downstream parts of business certainly encouraged a split. But the decision was made to keep a unitary buying organization and preserve the advantages of large scale and clear lines of authority. It took many years to work out the problems of unifying procedures for both branches of the business (Emmet and Jeuck 1950, 355–57), and, as we shall see, the problems of coordinating buying and sales never entirely went away.

The automobile provides a dramatic example of how actually observing the customer can help exploit and extend competitive strengths. Farm machinery was not of course a big seller in the new stores, many of them being in suburban sites. But the customers owned, and cared for, the cars they parked. Thus automotive equipment replaced farm equipment in the merchandise selection as Sears became a major auto parts seller. The buyers figured out that tires wore out quickly, and Sears brought automobile tires within the four walls of the Sears stores. Tires, indeed, for many years provided the highest sales dollars per square foot of any product category in Sears. Sears became a major channel.

It was only a small managerial step from there into automobile insurance. The idea of Allstate was to take advantage of the one-stop buying experience of the stores. If customers trusted and were buying parts, even those on which safety depended so directly as tires, why not try to sell them insurance while they were in the store as well? As Wood recalled,

> I called a meeting of my outside directors in 1931. Business wasn't good at that time . . . and I proposed we found this insurance company. . . . [T]hey asked me two very pertinent questions. They said: "In the first place, why should we start anything now, when times are bad? In the second place, what the hell do you know about insurance?" Which was also true.
>
> "Well," I said, "I don't know much about insurance, but I do know this— that Sears has the largest tire and battery and auto accessory business in the country, and every car owner goes to Sears or knows Sears. In the second place, we've got this system of stores and instead of the agent pounding the pavement for a prospect, they'll come to our agent in the stores, and our cost of acquisition will be far less than with ordinary insurance companies." (Wood 1961, 74–75)

The shift into selling a service was made almost without strain. Healthy profits flowed freely almost from the first.

The 1920s represented a critical time for Sears. Its traditional market was eroding, and action was needed to revive the company. General Wood seized the new opportunities created by urbanization and the automobile and gave his company a new lease on life. There were of course problems and difficulties in shifting direction, but two qualities of the innovations made them ultimately beneficial. First, they were responsive to the market. As every history of Sears notes, the new stores and focus on the automobile were prescient innovations. Second, the innovations were conservative in terms of Sears's operations and mission. Sears's buying operations, internal procedures, and customer base evolved relatively smoothly into servicing the new operations. These assets were valuable in the new setting, too. Problems were noted prominently at the time and in company histories, but the change was effected without reducing company profitability or threatening the integrity of the organization. Sympathy with the market coupled to a keen sense of what Sears could do unusually well was the hallmark of Wood's innovations.

There was nothing inevitable about the decision to open retail stores and the associated decisions about where to site them and what products to carry. Wood is noted so prominently in histories of Sears because he seems to have made the decision largely on his own. He had no support among Sears's senior management. As we have discussed, he had active opposition among the rank and file. His ex ante arguments convinced only one person: Julius Rosenwald. But that was the only person who had to be convinced to initiate Sears, Roebuck's transformation. The ex post success of Wood's innovations made everyone into a believer and Wood himself into a cult hero. Wood became Sears's CEO in 1928 when the previous president died. He was chosen over Doering, the able organizer of the mail-order facility in Chicago. He was elevated because he was thought by Rosenwald to have the vision to carry Sears in the interwar years and because, being younger, he would have more years in which to do this.

General Wood turned out to be very long-lived. He did not retire early, and he did not depart when he retired. Nor did the sense of his presence fade. His apotheosis proved, as the years passed and times decisively changed, quite unfortunate for the company. It was the reasons for his success in the 1920s, and not the details of how it came about, that ought to have been honored. Wood's logic was his valuable legacy. The specific content of his vision wore much less well with time.

6.4   Operations and Choices in the Late 1970s and 1980s

Sears, Roebuck faced a crisis in the late 1970s that was similar to its problems in the early 1920s. It found its customers' business slipping away. It needed to do something new to replace the old. But unhappily the leadership of Sears at this time was not as insightful as General Wood. His inheritors suffered from a profound misperception of what their fundamental assets were and what made these assets valuable.

Over the half century following the events described above, Sears had pursued both catalogue operations and retail sales. It also pursued the Allstate initiative, which not only sold insurance but branched out into a number of financial products and even came to operate a large savings and loan in California. Overall, this was a very successful period in terms of the company's financial results. And Sears became a dominant presence in general merchandise retailing: there were years in which the firm's annual revenue approached 1 percent of GNP. Sears, it seemed, developed a franchise with urban America in the middle half of the twentieth century just as it had had with rural America at the end of the nineteenth.

By the late 1970s, however, the franchise's customers were changing. Deindustrialization and demography were at the root of the changes. Employment in manufacturing grew slowly in the 1970s and reached a peak in 1980. Employment in services meanwhile was booming. More important still, the population under five years of age peaked in 1960 and fell for the next twenty years. The young blue-collar families Sears was accustomed to fitting out were a fading force in the marketplace. There were fewer and fewer new households eager simply to equip their houses with Sears furnishings and appliances and to clothe their young children in utilitarian Sears pants and dresses. In retrospect, it seems clear that by the late 1970s Sears's earnings growth had essentially flattened out. There had been decades of boom since the move into retailing, but now they seemed to be over. The company's earnings from retailing were even unambiguously lagging behind those of its principal competitors.

As in the 1920s, other firms already existed to serve newer markets. Discount department stores, focused specialty stores, and other chain stores were growing rapidly. Even local department stores were doing relatively well. The company's own research indicated that the customer base was still intact and that the Sears name was just as trusted as before. The customers even came in just as often. But now they also shopped elsewhere; and far more frequently than previously, they stayed to purchase elsewhere too. The issue was only partly price. Sears was losing some sales to discounters, but it was also losing sales to these other competitors (Brennan 1980, unnumbered p. 5). The notion that the nation had excess capacity in retail space—that it had become "overstored"—became as much discussed within the company as in the trade press.

This overstoring was ironic. It seems very likely that many of the specialty store, chain, and outlet stores in question were located near or even in suburban and regional shopping malls anchored by the Sears stores in question. The casual accessibility of other stores within a mall or in adjacent ones made price comparisons more convenient. Any contrast between Sears's offerings and those of the other retailers—or even a contrast between the attractiveness of the two presentations—could be easily noticed and acted upon. The proximity made things much harder for Sears. Wood's move to sites with cheap land and plentiful parking was far less attractive when other retailers made the move right along with Sears.

Less attractive as it might be, cash flow was still strong. Borrowing capacity remained ample. So Sears could lay its hands on money to change how it did business. As the sense of crisis in retailing operations grew, the question arose of what to do. As in the 1920s, Sears faced a stagnating market. It needed to find a way to use its existing tangible and intangible capital to effect a movement into more attractive markets or positions. In the 1920s, Sears seems to have come to its new role in a relatively autocratic fashion. This time the future of the company was subject to extensive debate.

One group of managers, within the retailing group and up from the Field, that is, up from working in and supervising Sears's many stores, believed radical means were required to execute the Wood's traditional strategy. There were too many private deals between the buyers and the store managers. There were excessively broad selections of goods on display and in inventory. Store managers faced excessive temptations to advertise and have sales to keep revenues up and to get goods they had purchased out the door. This party wanted to revitalize Sears retailing by shaking up the organization: they wanted to change who made decisions. This was a retailing alternative, though a disturbing one to the traditional culture of the Field.

Indeed, this party discovered, as it explored its intuitions, that it was hard to tell from the Sears control system just how well or badly the Field and the catalogue were doing. For it emerged that Wood and his successors had not even adequately differentiated the stores and the catalogue operations. Goods ordered and purchased by Sears's buyers went into a common pool from which they were sold through both outlets. How could Sears corporate decision makers know which outlets were profitable? How could they tell about the catalogue? And how could demand in an outlet or in a location be communicated back to a buyer? And if it were communicated, how could the buyer's actions be evaluated? The cost of information processing may have necessitated this aggregative view in the 1920s. But a lot had changed in the ensuing fifty years. New modes of knowing were now possible, and they revealed, this group felt, a need for dramatic changes both in what was done and in how the decisions of what to do should be made.

The overall thrust of this group's proposals was back-to-basics. "[The] overall strategies . . . we recommend for these next five years are embarrassingly fundamental . . . no revolutionary insights, no earthshaking revelations," wrote the head of the buyers in a key internal document (Sears, Roebuck and Co. 1978). "They are as basic as blocking and tackling." The strategies included superficially novel departures from past practice such as limited selling of nationally branded products, but the focus was on centralized control of the breadth of product lines (variety within categories was to shrink radically to five or even three) and of other aspects of operations—to a substantial extent even advertising and pricing—that had since the 1920s been left to the Field organization and store managers. This seems to have been a conscious rejection of Wood's emphasis on democracy in the organization. This group hearkened instead back to an earlier phase in Sears's history where centralization achieved economies of scale in selling to a national market and everything else adapted to the centrally made decisions. The executive appointed to head the retailing group shortly thereafter told reporters in 1981 that he felt very strongly that Sears needed to approach its business as though it were a single store. If there were a right way to do something, then that right way should be used in New York, Los Angeles, and Miami.

Another group, this one in the corporate office, saw the solution to the problem of Sears's earnings differently. This group's adherents appear to have taken the overstoring notion very seriously indeed. But they do not seem to have seriously envisioned any fundamental change in the autonomy of the store managers within their four walls and in their local market. They proposed to drop nothing. Instead, they wanted to fit new services into Wood's stores.

This was an essentially conservative group, identified with the Field rather than with headquarters. It wanted to preserve the Field's independence through decentralized responsibility. That was, the view ran, the heart of what it was to be a Sears store manager. They also had no desire to abandon the four-walls approach that gave that decentralized responsibility effective influence: the mosaic of stores all across the country, carefully sited to be in optimum locations in individual neighborhoods and carefully spaced so as not to intrude upon one another's market areas was not the problem either. Nor did this group feel that the problem lay in the time-hallowed selection of product categories Sears presented to the public. The problem was just that the presentation was tired. Sears needed to jazz things up. New fixturing was in order. Popular culture figures like Cheryl Teigs should be recruited to lend their names to private-label product lines. The catalogue covers should evoke a slightly hipper life.

The concept of Sears stores and their operations would be essentially unchanged. Demand would be stimulated with advertising and brand names. And people would be attracted to Sears by the addition of new businesses. These executives sought to find new businesses that would appeal to the customer they understood, the customer who valued the Sears that had been. They thought in terms of buying existing companies rather than, in the spirit of General Wood, developing their own new lines of business. Since the executives wanted to improve nationwide performance, they needed companies whose operations were also large and so, almost by construction, national in scope. They looked at companies in whose businesses trust was an important component, to complement the powerful positive reputation all polls showed Sears itself had with the American consuming public.[9]

They conducted market research. They had been in the credit-card business for two decades, principally to support their own sales, and were surprised to discover that their customers were undersupplied with financial services. Nearly 70 percent of Sears card holders with income greater than $36,000 a year (over $60,000 in 1996 terms) had no brokerage account. Fifty-seven percent of American households held Sears cards, more than any other. For households all across the income distribution, financial services were purchased from a wide variety of vendors. Surveys turned up evidence of some desire to consolidate these relationships.

9. One can trace the contours of this search in the files of Philip Purcell in the Sears Archive.

Developments in the external environment around this time made financial services operations attractive. Demand was visibly increasing. While the rate of family formation was down, existing families were aging. Having furnished their houses, they were beginning to save for their children's education and their own retirement. Sears could follow them through this life cycle. The customers could stay with Sears.

Inflation in the late 1970s had been in double digits, and investors were becoming both more sensitive to yields and more sophisticated. Entry was becoming easier. Because of technical legal details, Sears could enter this business unburdened by many of the regulations that would constrain competitors. If it could turn long-term (or even long-past and trusting) Sears appliance and insurance customers into financial-services customers, there was hope of avoiding the intense direct competition then going on between the Wall Street firms. Perhaps economies could also be reaped in distribution and selling costs through using the Sears national network of stores. Finally, the huge and relatively stable Sears cash flow provided a substantial resource in facing the investment risk. And parts of the business were even familiar. The Sears organization itself had immense cash flows to manage, and it did so successfully. By the early 1980s, when all this came to a head, Sears had run credit cards for thirty years. It had sold insurance for fifty. Allstate had dabbled in other financial products. All these ventures had basically been successful.

What would expanding into the financial services sector in a serious way do for the historic Sears operations (as opposed to the Sears income statement)? A significant amount of the investment in store sites and in advertising and public relations designed to generate store traffic was sunk. The Sears management hoped to build on this base. Sears customers were in the stores and in a buying mood. They could be induced, the managers thought, to buy financial services as well as durable goods. The consumer, in short, would benefit from one-stop shopping across an even wider range of goods and services than anyone previously had offered. The value of the fixed costs of running the store and of the real estate would rise.

The corporate managers at Sears clearly thought there was synergy between such new activities and the old activities of the firm. Philip Purcell, head of Sears's strategic planning group, said at the time that "[t]here is no reason why someone shouldn't go into a Sears store and buy a shirt and coat, and then maybe some stock. I don't consider that any more outrageous than the first idea like that that came up, that someone might buy a coat and tie, then buy auto insurance" (Weiner 1980).

The reasoning behind such a view is curious. The idea that people in the 1930s came in to Sears to buy clothes and then happened to buy insurance is far from Wood's conceptualization of his stores. Wood thought that people would come to buy tires and get their car repaired—and then also buy auto insurance. The intimate connection between specific products and services had become unclear in the following fifty years.

The parallel between auto insurance and, for example, stock purchases also misses important aspects of the services in question. Auto insurance is like a warranty on a product. It protects the purchaser of a car and of car parts against problems that may come in the future from the car. It is like a guarantee against defects in an appliance. But most financial-services products have none of these qualities. Instead of protecting purchasers, the products expose them to risk. There is no sense in which the consumer was to be protected or insured from a poor choice of stocks. The law of large numbers was not on the customers' side in financial services.

The imprecision of this parallel suggests strongly that the anticipated synergies between Sears and a financial-services firm would not come about. However profitable such an acquisition might be as a portfolio investment, it would not have a revitalizing effect on Sears retailing operations.

The conservative option, championed by the corporate leadership and the Field, carried the day. Resources were invested in store renovation. Images of Cheryl Teigs went into the stores and the catalogue. Merchandising was also simplified and decision making became somewhat more centralized. To this extent, the first group got its way. But these were small things. There was no large-scale reconfiguration of organization and infrastructure. In the traditional lines of business, the locus of control shifted a little. But in terms of infrastructure, it was more business as usual than not. On the other hand, the company began an extended process of considering financial-services acquisition targets. Two leads were pursued to fruition. First, Sears bought the real-estate brokerage Coldwell Banker. Shortly thereafter, it bought the securities brokerage house of Dean Witter.[10]

This managerial decision was not inevitable. The first group described above could have been given its head. There were other, even more radical alternatives for Sears. Before discussing the actual subsequent history of Sears in the 1980s, we want to flesh out a counterfactual Sears. It is hard to know how a large organization like Sears would have looked in this alternate world; we know from the history of the 1920s that change did not come easily to its far-flung operations. Nevertheless, two models of merchandising were emerging at the time of this decision about the future of Sears. Each connects with the reasons the move into retailing earlier in the century had been successful. Either or both of them could have been the result of the first alternative, if that path had been chosen.

The avatar of the first model is Wal-Mart. This company generated tremendous profits in the 1980s through a commercial strategy that focused on keeping in touch with its workaday customers and keeping costs low. The most obvious foundation of its success was locational, but the means through which location was exploited is the theme we want to pursue. The parallels with Sears's strategy in the 1920s are striking.

10. The search and negotiation processes are described in detail in Katz 1987.

Wal-Mart set up stores in towns its competitors reckoned to be too small to support a general-merchandise store. This was Montgomery Ward's policy of the 1920s in a new and more appropriate context. Wal-Mart was able to make a success of operating in these locations because its costs were significantly lower than those of its competitors. Some of the reasons this was so were site-specific. Ground rents were lower. Staff compensation expenses tended to be relatively low because the stores were in places in which the opportunity cost of labor was relatively low. Advertising expenses were relatively low in part because rates in county papers tend to be lower than in big-city dailies and in part because the largest retailer in a district, particularly if it follows an every-day low pricing strategy, does not need to inform its potential customers about its existence and price levels as much as it would if it had real competitors and price competition through sales.

These savings are all in the cost category of selling, general, and administrative expenses, an important category but one much smaller than the cost of goods sold. Wal-Mart acquired goods cheaply. It got them to the stores cheaply. It used the shelf space extremely productively. These practices were the real foundation of its overall low costs. The low costs supported stores in smaller markets, and the markets were to a substantial extent expanded beyond what potential competitors might have thought possible by passing on some of the lower costs in lower prices.

Wal-Mart acquired goods cheaply the way Sears had traditionally operated: it offered economies of scale to suppliers while making sure whenever it could that the suppliers were more dependent on Wal-Mart than Wal-Mart was on them. The scale economies derived from the fact that Wal-Mart placed orders centrally, that is, on behalf of the entire company rather than on a store-by-store basis. Since Wal-Mart ran a high turnover business, these orders were large. Wal-Mart took care to use multiple sources whenever the good was not branded. This limited the bargaining power of suppliers. Wherever possible, Wal-Mart arranged that its orders were very important to each of its partial suppliers. Sometimes it accomplished this end simply by being a very large (if not the dominant) customer. Sometimes it did this by encouraging the supplier to make sunk investments in the relationship, thus creating barriers to exit from it. Wal-Mart's policy echoed Sears's policy in its incomplete but still powerful vertical integration with its suppliers.

Wal-Mart also had several strategies that were novel to the industry for getting goods to the stores cheaply. The first of these concerned its use of distribution centers. Rather than have vendors ship goods directly to store doors, Wal-Mart had 80 percent of the goods channeled through a small number of Wal-Mart distribution centers. In these, the truckloads of shipments from individual vendors were broken down and combined into full-truck shipments for particular (clusters of) Wal-Mart stores. (Since Wal-Mart stores were commonly relatively close to one another, it was often efficient to supply several at once.) Since the quantities of an individual item destined for a particular store in such a truckload were often small, resupply had to be frequent. But since the trucks were running full and the stores were clustered, this did not represent a serious inefficiency.

The second supply strategy supported the first. Wal-Mart encouraged national vendors and vendors from other regions of the country to set up production facilities in the regions in which the Wal-Mart stores were. That way, the trucks could fill up with goods bound for the distribution centers once they had disgorged their cargo. This strategy was obviously limited by the extent to which the vendors' production processes had economies of scale beyond Wal-Mart's needs. But Wal-Mart trucks typically ran back 60 percent full, so the limitations cannot have been extreme.

The third important aspect of how Wal-Mart was able to operate profitably in these previously infeasibly small markets strikes our theme of keeping in touch with customers: it kept revenues high and unit costs low by using its shelf space efficiently. Very early on, Wal-Mart began investing in data-capture and transmission technology that enabled it to track the precise details of what was selling where. Its product line was focused, generally speaking, on unflashy categories for which there was steady demand. Nonetheless, tastes did vary across space and time. Getting the maximal value out of the available shelf space, both in terms of the speed with which products put out would be sold and in terms of the prices they would command, turned on monitoring what was in demand at each location and making sure some was available when customers sought it out. Instead of relying on high-variable-cost and low-reliability staff inventories (that is, physical counts, inevitably taken only at intervals), Wal-Mart monitored the incoming shipments and the outgoing sales through scanners at the registers and could for practical purposes do this continuously. The company kept detailed statistics on which products and brands (even in which aisle locations) generated maximum profits per square foot of shelf space. It exploited the frequency of shipments to avoid stockouts without having to keep large in-store stocks. And it minimized in-store storage facilities in order to maximize productive selling space. The warehouses, after all, were in even lower-rent districts.

Wal-Mart pursued lines familiar to Sears. But it pursued them in a streamlined way based on investment in new information technology. Sears was operating with an older version of this technology in which only highly aggregated information reached management. Sears's practices kept its costs high, its ordering cycle long, and its stores operating separately rather than as a unit. For Sears to have competed directly with Wal-Mart, it would have had to rethink from the ground up how goods passed from manufacturers to consumers. Sears managers told themselves that Wal-Mart and other low-price firms succeeded because they sold cheap goods, representing a move down-market that Sears would not follow. The focus on the goods sold obscured the innovations in the way Wal-Mart and other firms organized like it handled the products. The goods were cheap partly because Wal-Mart's costs were low.

Wal-Mart pursued this approach selling goods for which there was a reasonably steady and predictable overall demand. A different approach to keeping costs low and keeping in touch with the customers suggests itself for goods with a more substantial fashion content, that is, goods for which demand is not reasonably steady and predictable but is, rather, quite volatile over time.

This second approach may be identified with the practices of companies such as The Gap and The Limited, both enterprises that for practical purposes started after scanner technology was developed and computing power became cheap. The approach they used also relies importantly on rapid and inexpensive capture of sales data.

In traditionally organized department-store retailing, merchandising decisions were made by buyers who supervised both the selling and the procurement function. The advantage of this bundling was that these individuals could oversee the customers making up their minds and could therefore gather information not only on what actually was selling but also about what would have sold if only it were in stock. The disadvantage of this arrangement was the limited nature of the scale economies it afforded. No matter how good the taste of individual buyers or how thorough their knowledge might have been of one store's clientele, they could under this traditional system only buy for the department and the clientele they could see. For many scores of years, there was one buyer for each department for each store, even after the growth of chains of department stores. Even until quite recently, aggregation was confined to narrowly defined regions.

A further consequence of this system was that the orders booked with individual vendors tended to be small even when the aggregate orders coming from the company that owned the store were large. Individual buyers therefore did not have much bargaining power with the vendors. It was difficult for the vendors to minimize setup costs of machinery, dyeing equipment, and even cloth procurement under such circumstances. Needless to say, the vendors would have preferred to have these economies (if for no other reason than for the reduction in complexity of their own operations). To some extent they insisted on being paid for the inefficiencies, in effect ignoring the fact that orders from Macy's New Haven and Macy's 34th Street were both orders from R. H. Macy and Company. To some extent they maneuvered around the inefficiencies by insisting on long delivery lags. Under this system, Macy's had to commit to cuts and colors five to nine months before the goods reached the shelves. This was obviously a disadvantage in selling fashionable goods. Mistakes were inevitable and expensive—either heavy discounts or expensive staff time and resources were required to get the unwanted goods out of the way and replaced by goods with better prospects.

A system in which orders were placed on the basis of much more current information and then delivered promptly would have been better. There would have been fewer fashion mistakes and less expense in rectifying them. Such a system could be made attractive to the vendors if setup costs were lower because production runs were longer. Regional and even national orders from chains, that is, from integrated buying, would call for these longer runs. Companies like The Gap and The Limited delivered precisely such orders. There were some savings from requiring fewer buyers. (These were offset only a little by needing to pay these individuals more. The old system had required very many buyers.) There were some savings from tying up working capital for shorter periods and some—though less than one might have expected—from economies of scale in production. But the buying companies using this system did not want to claw back all the cost reductions their larger orders were yielding the vendors. Time, in the twin guises of savings on reduced markdowns and increases in sustainable initial markups, was far more valuable. These improvements were made possible during the 1980s by the growth of information technology, in which computers were used to record sales as they occurred, integrate and analyze the resulting data, and communicate the results directly to producers (Abernathy et al. 1995).

Raff and Salmon (1992) contains provisional estimates of how much of an advantage this system offered circa 1988 (around the time of a famous leveraged buyout that correctly identified the consequences of the inefficiencies of traditional department store practice but wildly overestimated how substantial the improvements might be). The estimates prove to be quite substantial. The final yardstick concerns the difference between the two types of stores in operating income as a percentage of sales in a key apparel category. The system's advantages come to 55–60 percent of the difference. The individuals behind the two companies in question became billionaires during the decade in which their companies introduced this system and the traditional department stores did not adapt. These billions were, like those of the founder of Wal-Mart, the fruit of keeping in touch with what consumers wanted to buy and of keeping costs low in ways competitors found difficult to replicate.

These savings depended on having accurate and current information. The means by which the most accurate and most current information could be obtained were changing rapidly in the 1980s, and the standards of accuracy and currency were rising fast. Sears would have had to be on top of the new information technology to transform itself into a chain like Wal-Mart or The Gap. To do so would have been harder than it was for these new competitors because Sears had disadvantages growing out of its prior success. Its very size was in some respects an impediment. It needed an information system that would be able to handle national-scale transactions and inventory tracking for the very large product line that Sears offered. It even needed, on a more mundane level, some way to track its catalogue and retail operations separately. They were all in the same rich soup around 1980, and it was impossible for Sears's management to tell which orders had done well and where the purchase variances were relative to plan. Although Sears's great size made the problem hard, it also bestowed one advantage for solving it: Sears was big enough and rich enough to have been able to hire the best people and to stay at the forefront of the new possibilities.

The profits of Sears's competitors were partly the result of opening free-standing specialty stores. Customers knew exactly what was contained in these stores, and they entered them to buy specific goods. The Sears concept of four walls, by contrast, was a vision of one-stop shopping. People in this view thought hard about a shopping trip and then bundled the whole family into the car for a trip to Sears. It was far from The Gap's and The Limited's notion that a shopper would make a trip just for a sweater or a bra. For Sears to follow the lead of these specialty stores, it would have had to do more than update its computers. It also would have had to breach the four walls of the Sears store and establish independent specialty outlets between the large stores.

What is the relationship between these two examples? The Gap and The Limited sold goods where fresh information was absolutely critical to success because goods that did not sell soon would never sell at first price. The cost of fashion mistakes was high. Wal-Mart sold goods that would always sell eventually, but it too wanted to stay in stock with goods that were selling now. In apparently very different categories, the efficient use of shelf space was a prime cause of the competitive success of both. Sears, diverse as it was, might have had something to learn.

These firms provide models of radical innovations available to Sears. We do not mean to argue that Sears should have blindly imitated all details of operations of Wal-Mart or The Gap. Instead we maintain that innovations like those of the firms we have just discussed were becoming the competitive standard in all categories in which any firm adopted them. We therefore believe that such innovations represented a more appropriate program for Sears than the acquisitions being contemplated unless Sears intended to abandon the categories in question entirely. If Sears had been able to adopt some of the new technology that enabled more rapid capture and exploitation of information, it might have kept up with the rapidly changing market. If Sears had rethought its internal operations and taken advantage of some of the progress of technology since Rosenwald's distribution plant was built, it might have been able to maintain its traditional economies of operation into new decades.

This is not a wildly speculative alternative. It was rumored in this period that Sears was contemplating opening chains of free-standing auto equipment stores, chains of hardware stores, chains of children's clothing stores. These are all categories in which Sears products had good reputations and substantial market share. They are all categories in which other entrepreneurs set up in the course of the 1980s in the style we have described and operated extremely profitably. The most famous such success took place in retail terrain as apparently unattractive as the usually highly seasonal category of toys. But even there, entrepreneurs with the new information technology in hand succeeded in making the narrow-and-deep approach (Raff and Salmon 1992) with its tremendous selections within the narrow categories profitable. If it could happen there, where might it not? Sears had a business it valued in each of the categories listed above. But it proceeded in the new aggressive ways in none of them. The very idea seems to have been thought too organizationally disruptive.

Why were the stores so sacrosanct? Perhaps these people feared cannibalization of the vast network of stores already in place. Perhaps they feared that it would be impossible to evaluate the success of any of the parts in a mixed system. Perhaps it was all cultural: perhaps they felt that too much of the company's working management had come up through the old decentralized system, could not imagine life at Sears without it, and would simply quit, leaving Sears in the lurch, if too much changed.

The resistance to free-standing single-category stores was an even more profound constraint than it appeared. It was clearly feasible to implement the information technology required to run such category-killer-like operations on a free-standing basis: this was the foundation—"the stick that stirred the drink," to borrow a phrase from the sports pages—of the blossoming of the category killers themselves. But modifying the vast corporate software that coordinated and controlled all the multifarious lines of Sears was a task of immensely greater proportions and impediment, and was clearly not feasible at the time.[11] The four walls were not just ramparts. They were tremendous barriers to progress.

Sears held onto Coldwell Banker and Dean Witter for a decade. The financial results were basically strong. (Indeed, in some years, they were the bulwark supporting a generally anemic performance of the merchandising and sales operation.) The operations of these two divisions even compared well to the results of comparable firms in their own industries. But these operations' successes did not show the synergies that had been foreseen. The financial companies found that locating offices in Sears stores offered no advantages to them. In fact, outlets at Sears fared worse than independent locations, and Dean Witter's agents resisted assignment to Sears with all their might (Hoge 1988, 250). Sears's customers were not attracted to a single source for consumption and savings vehicles. They seem to have trusted Sears to make washing machines—which could be returned if they did not operate properly—but not to make investments—which couldn't.

The outcome was actually much worse than a simple lack of development of the hoped-for synergies. Merchandizing group sales at Sears did not grow nearly as rapidly in the 1980s as those of Kmart and Wal-Mart. As shown in table 6.2 Kmart surpassed Sears in in the early 1980s. So did Wal-Mart by the end of the decade, despite the fact that Wal-Mart had started from a much smaller base. Despite some relatively good years in the mid-1980s, the profile of Sears results by the end of the decade was such that the retail operations actually appeared to be a drag on overall performance. The requirements of

11. Gretchen Kalsow, personal communication, 21 February 1997.

Table 6.2   Total Revenues of Sears Merchandizing Group and Some
Competitors (millions of dollars)

Chain	1982	1985	1988	1991
Sears	18,779	22,092	24,252	24,757
Kmart	16,772	22,420	27,301	34,580
J. C. Penney	11,414	13,747	14,833	16,201
Wal-Mart	3,376	8,452	20,649	43,886

Source: Annual reports.

competitiveness were evolving. Large volume was not sufficient in itself for a firm to keep up. Sears was not making the complementary investments. The asset value of the Sears name was wasting.

Shareholder activists, and others, noticed this. They thought they could make their portfolio investment decisions for themselves, and that the job of Sears management was to nurture and exploit the Sears retailing franchise. They were therefore opposed to improving the stock returns by divesting retail. The Sears retailing operations, they thought, were still a potentially valuable asset. Instead, they demanded improvement in the retailing performance. Market share had been eroding. Entry-driven increased competition was clearly a part of this, but it was suspected that intractable bureaucracy and an out-of-line cost structure driven in part by a failure to keep up with the infrastructure investments being made by firms competing for the Sears customers' business played significant roles as well.

By the early 1990s this process had gone far enough to put Sears onto the list of potential takeover targets. Senior management took defensive actions. They also began more structural changes. Among the changes offered was selling the financial acquisitions and, equally, a stake in Allstate. Now retailing would have to be fixed or there would be nothing.

By 1996 in-store boutiques were the leading market concept. Sears could still get good procurement prices: it was the largest single customer of Levi Strauss. The head of Sears logistics had come to the job straight from the analogous army staff position in Operation Desert Storm.[12] The changes he oversaw were dramatic. The number of channels store managers had to order through shrank by up to two-thirds. Suppliers began to make output more promptly after receiving orders and shipped more frequently. The goods were therefore fresher. Sears could also cut its own inventory holdings and thus inventory carrying costs. The capacity utilization of delivery trucks that ran from Sears's distribution centers to the stores rose from 60 percent to 90. The more frequent deliveries freed up in-store storage space for sales use. Altogether, selling, general, and administrative expenses (SG&A) had fallen by midsummer of 1996 to 21.6 percent of sales, more than two points better than the close

---

12. For these details and more, see Berner 1996.

competitor J. C. Penney and only two points worse than the superbly organized May Company. And it was not clear that forward progress had stopped.

6.5 Conclusion

We have argued in this paper that Sears, Roebuck and Company faced similar challenges in the 1920s and 1980s. In both periods, the retail operation was working well and generating respectable returns. But both times Sears also faced a stagnating market. In neither decade did the prospect of carrying on in the traditional fashion offer much promise.

In each period, the company set off on something new. In the earlier period, Sears added retail stores to its mail-order operations. In the later period, Sears added financial services to its retail stores. Retail stores proved to be wildly successful; financial services ultimately a distraction. Why?

We opened this discussion by asserting that successful responses to situations like these focus on an attractive market that can be supplied exploiting a firm's existing competitive strengths. Retail stores in the 1920s embodied this combination. The attractiveness of the market was the result of demographic changes and a new technology. The automobile and its related activities created new jobs for Sears's customers and new opportunities for them to spend their earnings. Retail stores enabled these customers to continue to patronize Sears with the aid of the new technology.

Information technology was to the 1980s as the automobile was to the 1920s. It provided a new way for consumers to interact with retailers. But while the change in the 1920s was due to the consumers' use of the auto, the change in the 1980s was due to the stores' use of information technology. Cars brought consumers to the stores that had a wide range of products; computers enabled stores to bring to consumers the selection of products that consumers demanded. We have described in each case how the new technology was used by some merchants to attract a profitable and defendable base to their stores.

But it was not used to this effect in Sears's stores in the 1980s. Where Wood had really shaken up the organization, the new changes shook up people in the organization without really shaking up the organization at all. Sears in effect opted to ignore investment possibilities in retailing that would have had a powerful positive effect on its future viability and instead concentrated its entrepreneurial energies on expanding into financial services instead. Why did they think this was a good choice, and why was it not?

Financial services were presented as a way to utilize the presence of the customer in a Sears store. Instead of tailoring the merchandise to the customers' demands—as the new information technology allowed—Sears placed its bets on deciding what the consumers wanted. Instead of altering the merchandising of goods, merchandising was carried on roughly as it had been and financial services were simply added in on top. But the hoped-for synergy between financial and retail services did not materialize. The presumption that people would make yet another major purchase on their trips to Sears was erroneous.

Sears was able to disentangle itself from its new operations as easily as it began them. While there is no doubt that financial services were a profitable market, Sears had no special advantage in that market.

While this seems obvious in hindsight, it must not have been so obvious at the time. Sears debated its strategy in 1980 as it faced the dilemma of a stagnating market. If individuals reasoned exactly along the lines of this paper, their thoughts seem to have gotten no farther than the rumor stage. The group that reasoned most closely to the analysis of this paper lost out to the group that led Sears into finance. Management very nearly lost control of the company in consequence. Facing vigorous new entrants once the company refocused on retailing, the task of regaining place and momentum was only harder. That it proved possible to regain some place and momentum is a credit to management. But it is no measure of the forgone profits.

References

Abernathy, Frederick H., John T. Dunlop, Janice H. Hammond, and David Weil. 1995. The Information-Integrated Channel: A Study of the U.S. Apparel Industry in Transition. *Brookings Papers on Economic Activity: Microeconomics,* 175–246.

Berner, Robert. 1996. Retired General Speeds Deliveries, Cuts Costs, Helps Sears Rebound. *Wall Street Journal* (16 July): A1, 7.

Brennan, Edward. 1980. Challenge 81. Speech delivered 6 August. Sears Archive, Hoffman Estates, IL.

Chandler, Alfred D., Jr. 1977. *The Visible Hand: The Managerial Revolution in American Business.* Cambridge: Harvard University Press.

Dore, Ronald. 1986. *Flexible Rigidities: Industrial Policy and Structural Adjustment in the Japanese Economy, 1970–1980.* London: Athlone.

Emmet, Boris, and John Jeuck. 1950. *Catalogues and Counters: A History of Sears, Roebuck and Company.* Chicago: University of Chicago Press.

Hoge, Cecil C. 1988. *The First Hundred Years Are the Hardest: What We Can Learn from the Century of Competition between Sears and Wards.* Berkeley: Ten-Speed Press.

Hower, Ralph. 1946. *History of Macy's of New York, 1858–1919: Chapters in the Evolution of the Department Store.* Cambridge: Harvard University Press.

Katz, Donald R. 1987. *The Big Store: Inside the Crisis and Revolution at Sears.* New York: Viking.

Purcell, Philip. Diversification Files. Sears Archive, Hoffman Estates, IL.

Raff, Daniel. 1991. Robert Campeau and Innovation in the Internal and Industrial Organization of Department Store Retailing. *Business and Economic History* 2d series, 20:52–61.

Raff, Daniel, and Walter Salmon. 1992. Allied, Federated, and Campeau: Causes, Outcomes, Consequences. Harvard Business School Working Paper.

Rosenwald, Julius. Papers. Regenstein Library. University of Chicago. Chicago.

Sears, Roebuck and Co. 1978. The Yellow Book. Typescript. Sears Archive, Hoffman Estates, IL.

Tedlow, Richard. 1990. *New and Improved: The Story of Mass Marketing in America.* New York: Basic Books.

Toniolo, Gianni. 1995. *Economic Growth in Europe since 1945.* New York: Cambridge University Press.

Weiner, Steve. 1980. Sears Finds Broadening Its Image Takes Time, Presses Staff to Adjust. *Wall Street Journal* (31 October): A1, 20.

Wood, Robert. 1924. Past, Present, and Future of the Mail-Order Business. Robert E. Wood Papers, Herbert Hoover Presidential Library, West Branch, Iowa.

———. 1950. On to Chicago. Speech delivered 4 May. Sears Archive, Hoffman Estates, IL.

———. 1961. Oral History. Butler Library, Columbia University, New York.

Worthy, James. 1984. *Shaping an American Institution: Robert E. Wood and Sears, Roebuck.* Urbana: University of Illinois Press.

Comment   Thomas J. Misa

Daniel Raff and Peter Temin revisit the story of Sears, Roebuck in the twentieth century to advance an analytical agenda of exploring certain neglected aspects of the interaction of economics and history. Their paper analyzes decision making at Sears during two critical periods in the company's history: in the 1920s and in the 1980s. Their analysis focuses on changes in technology, markets, entrepreneurship, and information flows. They repeat the well-known finding that Sears successfully met the challenge in the 1920s of expanding urban markets and increasingly mobile consumers by opening retail stores advantageously placed in the outlying districts of urban areas. Sears customers not only drove their automobiles to the stores but also bought automobile parts, automobile tires, and automobile insurance there. In company with other writers, they are impressed with Robert Wood's prescient vision for the company as well as the way that his decentralized policies optimized information flows—for instance by decentralizing decision making about stocking individual stores while aggregating the resulting orders to gain economies of scale from suppliers.

Given hindsight, Raff and Temin are deeply critical of the decisions made in the 1980s. While Sears in the 1920s captured competitive advantages by understanding the opportunities presented by the interaction of changing markets and new technology, in the form of urban consumers driving automobiles, the company in the 1980s apparently did not appreciate that the emerging in-

Thomas J. Misa is associate professor of history at the Illinois Institute of Technology. His book, *A Nation of Steel: The Making of Modern America, 1865–1925* (Baltimore: Johns Hopkins University Press, 1995), received the 1997 Dexter Prize given by the Society for the History of Technology.

formation technology presented opportunities for retailers to coordinate production, distribution, and consumption and that demographic and economic changes were undermining the purchasing power of its customer base of young, blue-collar families. These market- and technology-driven opportunities were captured more fully by Wal-Mart and specialized retailers like The Gap. After lengthy debate, and absent a strong entrepreneurial vision like Wood's, Sears diversified into financial services. While earlier writers, including Worthy (1986, 260–69), extolled the logic of these purchases and confidently predicted that the company would go from success to success, Raff and Temin have the benefit of more-recent hindsight. It turns out that not enough Sears customers, however underprovided they were with financial services, wanted to go to Sears and—at one stop—choose a washing machine, buy a house (from Coldwell Banker) to put it in, and invest in securities (from Dean Witter) with the leftover money. There are a number of puzzling questions that follow from the statement of Philip Purcell, head of Sears's planning group, "there is no reason why someone shouldn't go into a Sears store and buy a shirt and coat, and then maybe some stock." Would customers choose the securities of their shirt company? Does one choose government bonds and a white refrigerator to accompany a Federal-style house? Apparently Sears top management thought that family decisions about consumption are taken at the same moment as family decisions about investment. Raff and Temin hint that the centralizing tendencies of the executives backing diversification made the company even less nimble, less consumer-sensitive, and hence less competitive in present-day fluid, segmented markets. After reviewing the alternative technology and business strategies of The Gap, The Limited, and Wal-Mart, the authors conclude that these firms' innovations in capturing sales data and using them to guide shelf stocking and coordinate purchasing "were becoming the competitive standard in all categories in which any firm adopted them."

At least three dimensions of the Sears story merit greater attention for the themes of this paper: advertising, scale, and gender. Advertising appears prominently only in the prehistory to the 1920s, in the form of the famous Sears catalogue; it appears obliquely in the brief comments that Wal-Mart found advertising rates to be lower in small-town papers compared with big-city dailies and that Sears placed images of Cheryl Teigs in the stores and catalogue. Otherwise, it appears that Sears in the 1920s and 1980s engaged in little or no advertising to speak of. A company's advertising is one easily located historical source, which often speaks volumes about who the prospective consumers are, or who the company hopes them to be. After all, it was just in the 1920s that advertising itself becomes an industry. Indeed, Sears's history seems to be one long "fable of abundance" (Lears 1994). Greater attention to Sears advertising would not only flesh out the company's views of its customers, but would also link this present paper to other historians' efforts to examine the cultural productions of American business.

Second, there is the question of scale and the dynamics of decision making.

While I appreciate the point that decision making by committee is not inherently superior to decision making by executive fiat, there is some unfairness in assuming that Sears in the 1980s could have been reformed if only an entrepreneurial figure like Wood in his prime had been at the helm.[1] In the 1980s Sears, as the authors recount, was a vast enterprise. Unlike the 1920s its employees through stock ownership held the largest single share of the company. On the notion that stakeholders (not only stockholders) in a company ought to have some say in how the enterprise is managed, I am not persuaded that autocratic decision making is desirable. Another intriguing point briefly touched upon in the paper is the outstanding quality of General Wood's lieutenants. In the steel industry such "heroic" entrepreneurs as Andrew Carnegie and Charles Schwab were remarkably well served by loyal lieutenants.[2] Not only are such lieutenants the proximate source of information, ideas, and alternatives; they also may constructively dissent from the top executive's initial judgment. The necessity of going Inside the Business Enterprise (Temin 1991) to uncover the dynamics of such decision making remains an important insight. In this regard, I wanted more information on the "extensive debate" within Sears during the early 1980s and more analysis of it. Both groups of managers offering rival strategic plans for the company (should they be labeled the retail-reformers and the corporate-diversifiers?) had a strong identification with "the Field," that is, the store-level managers. There were a great many managers with field experience, and any retailing strategy required their active assistance and enthusiasm. Indeed, reconceptualizing business "strategy" as an emergent and negotiated phenomenon—relaxing the rigid notion of strategy being solely a top-down creation—helps comprehend the puzzle of why "the store" was so sacrosanct (at Ward in the 1920s and at Sears in the 1980s).

Third, the analytical category of gender is hinted at in this paper and, to understand the success of the retailing concept in the 1920s, it seems a useful category to pursue. In contrast to the full line of "hard" and "soft" goods presented in the Sears catalogue, from underwear to farm machinery, Raff and Temin indicate that the early retail stores focused on so-called hard goods (hardware, furnishings, farm implements, plumbing). "They were men's stores far more than women's," they write. Yet fieldwork at our local Sears store, located in an once-outlying area of urban Chicago, as well as inspection of my family's credit-card statements, confirms that consumption today is largely in the hands of women. I imagine that behind such a gender reversal—something

1. Wood continued past his prime, resigning the board chairmanship of Sears in 1954 at the age of seventy-five; meanwhile, in the mid-1950s, Ward was crippled by the incoherent leadership of Sewell Avery. See the unflattering anecdotes recounted about both men in Tedlow (1990, 330–37).

2. It can be fairly argued that Andrew Carnegie, absent the loyal opposition of Charles Schwab and persistent advocacy of outsider Henry Oliver in 1897, would not have bought the Minnesota ore lands that made Carnegie Steel into a vertically integrated company. Similarly, Schwab as owner of Bethlehem Steel, absent a crucial intervention by Archibald Johnston in 1907, would have stopped the firm's entry into manufacturing special heavy-duty structural steel beams, a market that Bethlehem dominated to great profit for decades. See Misa (1995).

like the transformation of the Marlboro brand from a woman's product to a man's—must be an intriguing story of markets, advertising, and the gendered construction of consumption patterns.

Finally, I would like to take a step back and reflect on the style and focus of this essay, and on the presumed audience for business and economic history. I would label Raff and Temin's present essay as lessons learned from a manager's perspective. The managers of Sears, they state, "could not free themselves from modes of doing business that were tried and true but rapidly becoming outmoded." The worst prospect in view was that "management very nearly lost control of the company." I think there must be larger questions at play, relating to the "interaction of economics and history" that the authors hint at in their introduction. Given the present diversity of approaches in business and economic history (a short list must include Chandlerian, institutional, evolutionary, and cultural approaches),[3] this essay needs more explicitly to justify its approach and to relate its approach to these others. I would also welcome a further elaboration on the large and interesting questions relating to the interaction of economics and history. By positing that long-range profitability results when firms develop competitively valuable asymmetries that frustrate the familiar forces of competition and free entry, and showing how a large firm can survive while making below-average returns on investment, they appear to wipe out one classic rationale for capitalism. From a public-policy perspective, the phenomenon of "wasting assets" seems to be a justification for regulatory intervention.

References

Lears, T. J. Jackson. 1994. *Fables of Abundance: A Cultural History of Advertising in America.* New York: Basic Books.

Lipartito, Kenneth. 1993. Innovation, the Firm, and Society. *Business and Economic History* 22, no. 1:92–104.

———. 1995. Culture and the Practice of Business History. *Business and Economic History* 24, no. 2:1–41.

Misa, Thomas J. 1995. *A Nation of Steel: The Making of Modern America, 1865–1925.* Baltimore: Johns Hopkins University Press.

———. 1996. Toward an Historical Sociology of Business Culture. *Business and Economic History* 25, no. 1:55–64.

Sicilia, David B. 1995. Cochran's Legacy: A Cultural Path Not Taken. *Business and Economic History* 24, no. 1:27–39.

Tedlow, Richard S. 1990. *New and Improved: The Story of Mass Marketing in America.* New York: Basic Books.

Temin, Peter. 1991. *Inside the Business Enterprise: Historical Perspectives on the Use of Information.* Chicago: University of Chicago Press.

Worthy, James C. 1986. *Shaping an American Institution: Robert E. Wood and Sears, Roebuck.* Updated edition. New York: New American Library.

3. See Lipartito (1993, 1995), Misa (1996), and Sicilia (1995) as well as the publications issuing from the Hagley conferences.

7 Marshall's "Trees" and the Global "Forest": Were "Giant Redwoods" Different?

Leslie Hannah

7.1 The Problem

How can we generalize from the case studies in this volume? How representative are they? Are alternative post hoc rationalizations equally plausible? In altered circumstances (inherently unpredictable at the time), would different outcomes have been observed? Many of these questions are unanswerable: the lessons of the cases are often sui generis, the counterfactuals are unknowable, the data for comparable firms are unobtainable or no such firms exist. This does not mean that cases cannot enrich our understanding, but it has sometimes led frustrated business historians to claim rather more for their craft than is justifiable. This essay reviews some of their problems and suggests how we might focus their research on areas where significant progress is more likely. It addresses, particularly, the experience of large firms, in the context of differences in national industrial systems and performance outcomes.

Writing at the time that large corporations were being built on an unprecedented scale, Alfred Marshall felt the need to modify his favored analogy of firms in the economy as trees in the forest. In his first (1890) edition of the *Principles of Economics,* he had suggested that, like trees in the forest, there would be large and small firms, but "sooner or later age tells on them all." However, by the sixth edition of 1910 he was cautioning that his earlier sentence could appropriately be put in the past tense, for "vast joint stock companies . . . often stagnate, but do not readily die" (Marshall 1961, 316). Marshall was an acute observer of the contemporary real economy in Britain, Germany,

Leslie Hannah is dean of the City University Business School, London, and a nonexecutive director of London Economics, Europe's largest independent economic consultancy.

The author is grateful to the Centre for Economic Performance, London School of Economics, for funding and to Alfred D. Chandler, Nick Crafts, John Kay, Danny Quah, John Sutton, members of LSE seminars, and the editors and commentator for helpful criticisms of earlier drafts.

and America: he would not have modified his view without substantial evidence that the Giant Redwoods he observed in these economies were qualitatively different from the nineteenth-century firms on which he had based his generalizations of two decades earlier.

The work of business historians—even those who profoundly disagree with Marshallian perspectives on industrial economics—has generally concurred with his view that something new was happening in the twentieth-century corporate world. Chandler (1990) and Lazonick (1991), for example, have suggested that large corporations, by the beginning of this century, built significant technical, organizational, and marketing capabilities, thus acquiring often unassailable first-mover advantages, so that they generally still dominate the global oligopolies they first created. The purpose of this essay is not to question whether they (and Marshall) are right, for they clearly are, but rather to establish the degree to which the traditional analogy of rising and declining trees, or the implied new one of Giant Redwoods with a charmed life, perhaps of centuries rather than decades, best describes the reality of the modern corporate economy. I will suggest that—on the evidence of the century so far— there is some life in the old view and that understanding *where* and *why* helps us diagnose the nature, strengths, and limits of dynamic organizational capabilities.

Skepticism about corporate capabilities is not universal among business historians. The tendency to overemphasize successes (and to rationalize them ex post)—what has been criticized as the "Whig" misinterpretation in the context of political history—is chronically endemic among them, as it is also among businessmen and management consultants (see, e.g., Hamel and Prahalad 1994). It commonly coexists with the conviction that they have found the unique recipe for rectifying the failure of firms or countries (a trait particularly well-developed in the Anglo-Saxon world of one-time leaders that have allegedly failed). I believe that some of the insights this process has generated have been valuable: it has, for example, helped us to understand the role of corporate learning and organizational capabilities in generating asymmetries between firms that provide a key to understanding competitive performance. Like Molière's Monsieur Jourdain and his prose, "new" industrial economists and business historians are now beginning to formulate explicitly what thoughtful businessmen have long implicitly understood about the limits of the simpler, neoclassical models of "old" industrial economists. The following comments are not intended to undermine that endeavor, but to reinforce it by disciplining some of its more adventurous generalizations.

7.2 A Proposed Test

The overuse of the survivor technique, distorting our understanding of the process that has led to the present state of things, has affected several disciplines besides business history. If we merely observe that many of the firms that now dominate the economy are of ancient lineage,[1] or that some of today's top firms were also at the top a century earlier, we might conclude that giant firms are *generally* long-lasting; yet the stated observation is equally compatible with the hypothesis that some initially small firms grow rapidly to become large, while corporate giants have, over reasonably long periods, a poor survival rate. Our current knowledge of survivors dominates our impression of the typical experience, and their triumphs are lionized, while the history of the failures is forgotten or considered untypical.

The first step in rectifying resulting misinterpretations has usually been to examine a population of firms defined ex ante. For this essay I have extended Schmitz's work (1995) to generalize about the global industrial giants of 1912. While there are no doubt still some omissions, I believe the amended list in appendix A includes almost all the industrial (i.e., mining and manufacturing)[2] firms in the world with an equity market capitalization[3] of $26 million or more in 1912. These were large firms even by today's standards: the largest (U.S. Steel) employed 221,025 workers in 1912; other firms on the list typically employed more than 10,000.[4] They were also, generally, firms that had already stood the test of time, being on average thirty-two years old in the corporate sense, and often much longer established as partnerships or earlier private firms. They were not the outcome of temporary stock market bubbles: these were the survivors of a brutal shakeout process after the global turn-of-the-century stock market booms and merger waves, in which many giants with watered stock but few capabilities had drastically declined (Livermore 1935; Lamoreaux 1984; Hannah 1974; Tilly 1982; Samber 1996). They were, on the whole, firms that contemporary stock market analysts considered attractive and safe because of their consistently reliable record of generous but sustainable

1. Harris Corporation (1996) shows that 39 percent of the Fortune U.S. top 500 are more than 100 years old and a further 50 percent were founded between the 1880s and 1920s. The oldest American firm in the 1912 list, Lorillard and Company, can be traced back to 1760. European firms are, of course, generally older: some (relatively small) modern firms had medieval origins and the large French firm St. Gobain can plausibly be traced back to the mid-seventeenth century, though it did not take modern corporate form until the nineteenth century.

2. The study is confined to these sectors because they most clearly approximate to being globally competitive in the twentieth century and I wish to test how corporate evolution in such markets works.

3. A few giant companies (mainly American and German and often family-owned) had no quoted equity capital in 1912; I have taken total balance-sheet assets, net of any bonded debt, or similar proxies for equity market capitalization in such cases. I have also treated Western Electric (which had recently become a subsidiary of AT&T) in this way. All nationalized or substantially state-owned firms of 1912 have been excluded.

4. These employment figures are provided only for illustrative purposes. Because the population is defined by a capital measure (equity market capitalization), some firms in capital-intensive industries will be included but employ under 10,000. Employment data is more readily available for British and German firms than for other countries: see, e.g., Shaw (1983), Kocka and Siegrist (1979).

dividends (Meyer 1910, 196). A population of the largest firms of ten years earlier would almost certainly show earlier exits and faster rates of decline than this population of maturing Giant Redwoods.

In order to assess their propensity to decline or develop, it was necessary to devise a comparable measure of the size of the 1912 firms in 1995. Equity market capitalization is again available for survivors, but the comparison needs to take account of inflation. The deflator I have used is U.S. stock market prices, more specifically Standard and Poor's industrial 500 index. The rise in U.S. stock prices (measured thus between 1912 and 1995 and averaging about 6 percent compounded per year) clearly partly reflects the declining value of the dollar (averaging 4 percent per year in 1912–95) but also some real growth. It seems appropriate to use a deflator that also captures the fact that even firms merely sustaining their market position would have participated in this growth, which in the OECD countries has, over the century as a whole, attained levels just above 2 percent per annum, per capita, with some extensive growth in the number of industrial workers also (Maddison 1989, 15).

One intuitive interpretation of the 1995 equity market capitalization, thus revalued "at 1912 stock market prices," is that it reflects the difference between how the long-run strategy of the 1912 managers actually turned out and what they would have left posterity if they had instead decided they had no distinctive capabilities, retired, and handed their assets to a hypothetical index-matching fund manager. If the 1912 and 1995 values were found to be equal, it would imply they would have lost nothing (except their managerial incomes) if they had followed that path, while a ratio of 1995 to 1912 "size" below one would suggest that giving up in 1912 would have been a better bet. A ratio above one would suggest that, in the long-term, the firm's capabilities were broadened (e.g., by extensive growth into wider geographic or product space) or deepened (by adding new competitive advantages, perhaps from R&D, or branding).

This appealing intuition should not be pressed too far, however. A sellout in 1912 of firms of this size, even where possible, would not necessarily have been at the market price: breakup values were less than the going-concern values reflected in the market price; but takeover values could be higher. Equally the ratio of 1995 to 1912 size should not be taken as a measure of investor returns: that would require an analysis of the intervening dividends (and other flows to and from shareholders), which could have been higher or lower than Standard and Poor's average. In principle, investor returns could be better even if no firm existed at the end: a monopoly well-milked is better for investors than a residue of unprofitable corporate assets. By the same token, a firm may have been under bankruptcy protection, severely compromising its equity investors' assets, but still remain large-scale, reflecting its other capabilities rather than temporary financial mismanagement or ill luck. A recent example is Texaco, which was under bankruptcy protection in 1987, but still retains significant capabilities and, by our measure, is the fifth-best performer of the hundred 1912 giants. Several German firms have also had parallel experiences in their frequently disrupted and dismembered national past. Our concern is not the outcome for investors, but rather the survival, development, or decline of capabilities embodied in the firm. In that spirit we are primarily interested in the "size" of the 1995 firm relative to that of 1912: the 1912 firm's adjusted 1995 stock market value reflects in some sense whether the "lump of corporate capability," defined by the boundaries of the firm, has grown or declined.

Of course that size will have been affected by many factors other than its assets in 1912 and the skill with which its 1912 managers then deployed them.[5] Market position and scale often conferred first-mover advantages, but the competitive process was one of continuous movement, not just initial position: the capabilities needed (and their potential usefulness in the marketplace) naturally were transformed over time. New corporate resources were also added, not just in ways indirectly captured in our stock exchange price deflator (e.g., reinvested profits), but by new capital issues or new stock issued for firms acquired (and acquisition activity was one to which many of these firms were strongly prone). By implication, we assume all of Unilever's "organizational capability" came from the British half (Lever Brothers) not the Dutch half (Margarine Unie) with which it merged in 1929, while Du Pont's stock of skills implicitly came entirely from its chemical rather than oil-company (Conoco) heritage. Because of shares issued to finance such mergers and acquisitions or to finance internal expansion, shareholders probably did worse than our measure of changes in the "lump of managerial capability" suggests.[6] In that sense, adopting a ratio of one between the 1995 and 1912 values as the threshold defining corporate capability enhancement (rather than decline) should be considered a *very* weak test, biased in favor of diagnosing corporate growth. I will be making simple, comparative, long-run judgments, and my choice of deflators and benchmarks is usually biased against the hypothesis being tested.

A major problem remains for firms that disappeared by liquidation, acquisition, or nationalization. The treatment of these firms is more fully discussed in appendix A, but for the most common case—acquisition—the best estimate of its capability enhancement seemed to be the price paid at the time of acquisition, converted (as with 1995 survivor values) to 1912 stock exchange prices. Since acquired firms were generally declining, but taken over at a premium, this probably gives an upward bias to the results.[7]

---

5. For that reason, I would expect correlations between 1912 size and 1995 outcomes to be very low; but since much has been made in the literature of first-mover advantages, dynamic increasing returns, and the sustainability of core corporate capabilities, it is worth defining the extent of the phenomenon more precisely.

6. E.g., four of these firms appear on a list of the top ten firms that destroyed shareholder value by overinvesting in the 1980s (Jensen 1993).

7. The average terminal ratio of surviving firms was three times that of acquired ones, and firms acquired prior to 1950 had twice the ratio of firms acquired after 1950. See table 7.1 and appendix A.

7.3   Did Giant Firms Grow or Decline (1912–1995)?

Four-fifths of the giant companies in the 1912 list were based in the major industrial countries of their day: Germany, Britain, and, above all, America, which alone accounted for over half. They had amassed substantial assets— physical, human, and/or reputational—to become the largest corporations globally. Most had distinctive accumulations of skills, architectures of internal or external relationships, first-mover advantages, economies of scale, scope, or experience, or technological leads, of a kind that asymmetrically endowed them with competitive advantages over other firms. That these were in many cases the outcome of a path-dependent (and difficult to replicate) process of organizational learning is also clear. The parables of learning that we have told[8] are prominently represented among the 1912 giants, and they could be replicated many times over. They include Westinghouse Air Brake, whose market power over its railroad customers—then the dominant transportation providers—derived from network standard setting in which exclusive private ownership (at least in the days before Microsoft) was not common. Some— including Shell, Jersey Standard (Exxon), and Rio Tinto (RTZ)—derived market power from control of raw material resources or distribution networks, or—like Eastman Kodak or Siemens—from popularizing new technologies. Others—like Guinness, Procter and Gamble, and Lever Brothers—had pioneered branded products in mass urban markets.

The business-history literature understandably focuses on companies such as these which, because they have been sustained successes, remain familiar to us today. There is, however, a danger in this perspective of developing a somewhat Panglossian view of giant corporations as repositories of capabilities that are self-sustaining. Indeed, their long-run success easily reinforces the stronger view that such corporations were able to entrench their existing market position and developed organizational routines that reinforced what they had already learned, creating dynamic, learning organizations that would, through geographic (often multinational) expansion, through diversification into new product markets, or through the institutionalization of innovation by R&D, constantly expand the ambit of their capabilities. That some firms—Procter and Gamble, Du Pont, Shell, Siemens, and others—did so is undoubtedly true, but how typical were they? That question is rarely answered in relation to a population defined at the start of the process, rather than by the remembered survivors.

Yet who now remembers German giants of 1912 like Hohenlohe Iron and Steel, British ones like Metropolitan Carriage, or U.S. ones like Central Leather, the Utah Copper and Nevada Consolidated group, or Cudahy Packing? And when firms that have drastically declined, like U.S. Steel and Ohio

---

8. E.g., Usselman (chap. 2 in this volume) for Westinghouse Air Brake, Samber (1996) for Pittsburgh firms, Genesove and Mullin (chap. 3 in this volume) for American Sugar, Lamoreaux and Sokoloff (chap. 1 in this volume) for Pullman.

Table 7.1   **Summary Measures of Long-Run Performance of the Hundred Largest Firms of 1912 by 1995**

Outcomes	Probability of Outcome (%)
Survives in top hundred	19
Survives and larger in 1995 than in 1912	28
Experiences bankruptcy or similar[a]	29
Larger in 1995 or on earlier exit than in 1912	35
Survives in any independent form	52
Disappears	48

Capability Expansion (below 1 = decline; above 1 = growth)	
Mode[b]	0
Median[b]	0.4
Mean[c]	1.0–1.4

Source: Author's calculations from data in appendix A.

[a]Including liquidation, bankruptcy protection, extensive corporate breakup, or nationalization.

[b]Including all exiting firms at their disappearance ratio.

[c]Including all exit values and terminal values, the unweighted mean value is 1.4 and the mean weighted by 1912 values is 1.2; if all exits are valued at 0, the unweighted mean value falls to 1.1 and the weighted mean to 1.0. The average terminal ratio of the fifty-two survivors in 1995 is 2.0; that of the forty-eight disappearances is 0.6.

Oil (now combined as USX Marathon), are remembered, it is usually as exemplars of their failure to expand their capabilities, as elephants that did not learn to dance in a world in which corporations (if they are wise or well-advised) normally do.

Our 1912 population—and our tracking of the outcomes by 1995—enable us to judge how typical the firms we remember are, relative to those we have largely forgotten. Is it easy to expand corporate capability (whether at the terminal date of 1995 or by earlier exit at a respectable size) or are cumulative corporate learning and capability expansion difficult tricks for giant firms to pull off? Table 7.1 indicates that the typical firm declined: nearly a half of them disappeared and more than a quarter experienced bankruptcy or a similar close shave with it. The modal value of the capability expansion ratios is zero, while the median company registers 0.4, that is, it was only 40 percent of its 1912 size at the terminal date. Yet the distribution is highly skew, with the firms that we remember, particularly the three spectacular performers—Burmah/BP, Procter and Gamble, and Du Pont, with capability expansion ratios above 7— rescuing the mean performance, which, depending on the assumptions made, was between 1.0 and 1.4. Just over half the firms survived and just over half these survivors grew; indeed a number of them did sufficiently well to remain in a similar list of the hundred largest firms today.[9]

9. To outrank the hundredth-ranked firm in the 1995 giant industrials, the lowest-ranked firm of 1912 would have had to achieve a ratio of 4.0. The average giant firm of 1912 would have had to

Yet for the 1912 top hundred overall, the record was not impressive. Not only was decline twice as common as growth, but mean capability expansion ratios slightly above 1 imply that, if these giants issued new capital to shareholders or to pay for firms acquired in 1912–95, as many of them did abundantly, they did notably worse than the average company in Standard and Poor's index. The minority of growth-oriented firms that dominate the literature are by no means typical. The low median value of the ratio suggests that most giant firms are incapable over a long period of sustaining their initial endowment of capabilities. However, a significant group of firms achieves ratios between 1.0 and 9.1, implying that some giants could create new capabilities, in addition to those they manifestly inherited, an arguably more challenging task.

To extend Marshall's analogy of the population of firms as the "trees of the forest," the Giant Redwoods among them were in the long run prone to death and decline. Economists are notoriously shy about defining what they mean by the long run, but it is certainly a shorter time in economics than in silviculture: we are talking about corporate "redwoods" with a distinct propensity to die over decades, not the centuries of their natural cousins. The "quarter-life" of the 1912 giants (i.e., the time taken for a quarter of them to disappear in bankruptcy, nationalization, or merger) was thirty-three years, and they are, as we approach the millennium, now hovering around their half-life.[10] The time elapsed since 1912—eight decades or so—is not much longer than the business "half-life" of a single human being,[11] though, of course, personally managed businesses *generally* had much shorter average life spans than this. Small firms certainly have shorter average lives than giant firms[12]—it usually takes longer to walk down a mountain than to roll off a hillock—but both large and

grow to 2.7 times its 1912 size to achieve the average size of the 1995 top hundred, from $81 million to $218 million in 1912 stock exchange prices. The nineteen 1912 giant firms that were still in the 1995 global top one hundred achieved an average ratio of 3.8, though one of them (RTZ) managed to stay in with a ratio as low as 0.8 (falling from thirteenth place to eighty-eighth).

10. Fifty-two of the 1912 top hundred firms still formally exist independently, though arguably some—e.g., Singer (Bicoastal) and U.S. Rubber (Uniroyal)—are so small that they are as good as disappeared. The problem of reincarnation also complicates the calculation: paradoxically rather more 1912 giant firms still existed in 1950 than earlier, in 1945 (largely because of the breakup of IG Farben and Vereinigte Stahlwerke, which in the 1920s had absorbed half the German giants of 1912); similarly at least two firms (Nabisco and Imperial Tobacco) are about to be demerged from their recently acquired parents at the time of writing. Because of such reincarnations, it is wrong to conclude from the longer interval between the quarter-life (1912–45) and the half-life (–1999?) that the rate of disappearance declines over time, though, in the limit, that will become true. Moreover, if economic evolution is Lamarckian rather than Darwinian (and the process of corporate learning clearly implies that), we might expect organizational death rates to decline with age; see, e.g., Hannan and Freeman (1984). In calculating half-lives of giant firms I have assumed they were born giants in 1912, rather than when founded as small firms.

11. Demographers do not conventionally use the concept of half-life to describe life expectancy, but in advanced industrial economies the half-life of an eighteen-year old male would be about fifty years; see Registrar General (1914), table 3.

12. Most studies of new, small firms show a half-life in very low single digits. At the time Marshall began writing, English joint stock companies had a half-life of about seven years (Shannon 1933).

small firms commonly die. They differ only in the length of time they take and, even in that respect, by surprisingly little: to raise a joint-stock company's half-life by one year, it is necessary to increase its size by twenty-three times.[13] The proposition that it would be possible to fritter away $3 billion (much less $90 billion) in a human lifetime is one I personally find daunting, but business leaders are evidently made of sterner stuff. $3 billion is the value (in 1995 stock exchange prices) that the market placed on the smallest of these firms' "lump of capabilities" in 1912 (and $90 billion that of the largest); yet overall these firms barely increased their value; many had decimated it or dissipated it completely. The supposedly exceptional turbulence in corporate rankings (now modishly asserted by businessmen to have followed the liberalization of world trade, oil crises, unprecedentedly rapid technical change, and the spread of industrialization) is in fact also observed in the earlier periods of increasing national autarky and relative economic stagnation. Corporate dinosaurs are ubiquitous in an ever-changing world. As the old English music hall joke had it: Q. How do I build a successful small firm? A. Easily! Buy a large one and wait!

One interpretation of the strong tendency to stagnation or decline would be that it was the rational strategy of dominant firms pursuing shareholder profit maximization, a point argued for U.S. Steel's early decline by Stigler (1968). Rather than set an entry-preventing price, it may be sensible for dominant firms to milk their monopoly position while yielding market share to competitors. This was particularly likely where it helped firms appear respectable to anti-trust authorities, especially when rivals thus indulged respected price levels. Casual inspection of the business histories of the declining firms in this population suggests that planned decline was rarely their explicit objective, though it may have been implicit in their muddled reactions. We have not investigated overall stockholder returns, but the general impression in these companies' histories is of depressed profits desperately used by managements to paper over the cracks of declining capabilities, not of generosity to stockholders during a preplanned yielding to competitors of market share they could not have expected to keep. Stigler's hypothesis could clearly be investigated further, but it appears unlikely to account for more than a small proportion of the 1912 giants' propensity to reduce their size.[14]

The implications of these observations for industrial economists are clear. While we naturally focus on success—on corporations that did learn to expand

---

13. In the range between the average English joint stock company and the average global 1912 giant firm. Around 1885, joint stock companies, whose half-lives are referred to in note 12, averaged paid-up capital of about £60,000 (Jeffreys 1938, 130), compared with equity market values averaging £16.6 million in the 1912 global top hundred, a ratio of about 1:275. Their half-lives were in the ratio 1:12.

14. Even in Stigler's study (1968) of U.S. Steel, the returns to its stockholders peaked in real terms ten years after the merger, that is, in 1911, and U.S. Steel stockholders did worse on average than other steel companies for the remainder of his analysis (1912–25), which covers the period of this study. The impression of U.S. Steel post-1925 is also not very favorable to an extension forward in time of the Stigler hypothesis.

or sustain their capabilities—this is not something that giant managerial hierarchies have normally been very good at. In fact the alleged twentieth-century tendency to increased industrial concentration is by no means universal or sustained in all national markets (Hannah 1995a), and probably is quite mild on a global basis also.

The implications for the parables that business historians tell and for understanding individual corporate evolution are that we should be as sensitive to the sources of eroding capabilities as of their building. Corporations can forget as well as learn; their inherited learning can become redundant (or even dysfunctional) in a changed environment; "first-mover" advantages appear fleeting; supposedly distinctive capabilities can be replicated or improved upon by competitor firms.[15] Such outcomes appear to be twice as common as successful expansion of capabilities for giant corporations.

Clearly if we could distinguish ex ante what determines how firms can beat the normal form and do well, we could change the balance of economic evolution and (presumably) become very rich men. The reader will not, then, be surprised that it is in fact very difficult to do so, and that those who have so far been brave enough to attempt it are quite unconvincing. While this population of firms is not large enough—given the variability of outcomes—to generate many statistically significant results,[16] it does enable us at least to call in question some generic recipes for corporate success, even those generated with hindsight. If ex post "prediction" is difficult, we can be reasonably certain that ex ante prediction will pose a few problems; the strategic management consultants we should most respect are the modest ones.

7.4   National Differences in Corporate Performance

Perhaps the most widely used systematic model of corporate failure is Chandler's invocation of Britain's failure to develop professionally managed corporate hierarchies as a reason for Britain's twentieth-century economic decline, relative to Germany and the United States (Chandler 1990). This thesis is appealingly grounded in a compelling argument about corporate capability, but its vigorously stated comparative perspectives are vulnerable from a number of angles (Kleinschmidt and Welskopp 1993; Alford 1994; Hannah 1995a). Our population of Giant Redwoods certainly provides no support for the hy-

15. See, e.g., Raff and Temin (chap. 6 in this volume), Hounshell (chap. 5 in this volume), and, more generally, Lieberman and Montgomery (1988) and Henderson and Clark (1990).

16. Why not, then, increase the size of the sample? Because this is not a sample; it is (or is very close to being) the whole population of giant firms in 1912. Though inclusion of very large firms in the $15–$25 million range would be possible, that suffers from the same problem as the econometrics of national growth rates and convergence (do we really want Iceland to have the same weight as the United States?). The truth is that, for assessing corporate or national performance, the world has not generated enough human experience for us to generalize econometrically. Disciplined parables are a more realistic scholarly objective. For some indication of the likely results of adding firms in a lower size range to the study, note 21 below.

Table 7.2   **National Performance Differentials of 1912 Giants**

	U.S.	Germany	Britain	Other
No. of firms headquartered there in 1912	54	14	15[a]	17[a]
Average equity capitalization in 1912 (millions of dollars)	90	59	95	56
Outcomes (%)				
Survival in top hundred 1995	17	29	47	0
Any independent survival	48	57	60	53
Proportion showing positive growth (i.e., ratios above 1.0)	26	43	40	18
"Capability enhancement"[b]				
Unweighted average[c]	1.5	1.2	1.9	0.5
Coefficient of variation	(135)	(104)	(123)	(164)
Median[c]	0.4	0.6	1.3	0

Source: Author's calculations, from appendix A data.
[a]Counting Royal Dutch Shell as wholly British.
[b]Defined as terminal equity capitalization ÷ 1912 equity capitalization.
[c]Including exits.

pothesis that large British firms were less likely to sustain their capabilities than German and American ones; indeed, the reverse is true. As table 7.2 shows, British firms were most likely to survive, most likely to remain in the top hundred, and generated higher performance ratios than American or German ones, however measured.[17]

Nearly half the British giants of 1912 survived, but less than a fifth in other countries overall. Germany came nearest to Britain, with a 29 percent survival ratio for its 1912 giants; however, Germany seriously lagged in building new giant firms in the twentieth century, an activity in which the United States excelled.[18] Of the new giant firms entering the top hundred after 1912 and still there by 1995, the United States built 50 percent more even than Japan, which had no giant firms in the 1912 top hundred list but twenty-one by 1995. Europe generally built fewer new giants than the United States or Japan, but within Europe, it was Britain, not Germany, that stood out, both as a builder of new giant firms and a sustainer of existing ones.

17. The use of the U.S. rather than the British stock exchange index (which rose by less) as the deflator biases the results against British-based firms.

18. Between 1912 and 1995 the German representation in the top hundred halved from 14 to 7 because it created only 3 "new" giant firms to replace its declining firms. The United States' share fell proportionately less, from 54 to 40, because, despite its standing as the worst performer of the three leaders in table 7.2, it created 31 "new" giant firms. Between 1912 and 1995 Britain's share of the world's giant firms declined least of the three, from 15 to 14 (if the 1 Anglo-Dutch firm of 1912 and the 3 of 1995 are counted as entirely British), not only because it had more survivors than Germany but also because it created more new giant firms than Germany in the course of the century (though proportionately fewer than the United States). The 1995 data is from an unpublished study by the author, based on the industrial firms in *Business Week*'s listing of the world's giant firms on 31 May 1995 by equity market capitalization.

These results invite speculation on whether entrenched oligopolists weaken rather than strengthen the national economies in which they are headquartered. Some postwar international comparisons (Geroski and Jacquemin 1988; Geroski and Mueller 1996) suggest that the stability of dominant firm positions exhibited in the British case is associated with poor national economic performance, and this reinforces the traditional economist's emphasis on market assortment rather than persisting corporate capabilities as a source of efficiency gains.

However, a more benign interpretation is possible for the British Giant Redwoods in the 1912 population, consisting as they did of giants that had established their global status in competitive conditions before World War I, rather than in Britain's more sclerotic phase of post-1932 protectionism and cartelization (Broadberry and Crafts 1992). The British giant corporations arguably had more staying power because in 1912 they were domiciled in a free-trade country, while American giant corporations were already then substantially overprotected by high tariffs and German ones moderately so (Capie 1994, 59). British 1912 capabilities were thus already disciplined by more stringent (because more global) *market* tests. British giant corporations also tended already to spread an unusually high proportion of their corporate *resources* globally. Since perhaps a third of the British giant corporations' activities were located overseas in 1912, probably twice as much as the average American or German giant corporation at that time (Hannah 1996), they were less constrained by their home market performance and already more fitted to compete globally.

Another explanation of the poor U.S. performance could be that U.S. firms were inhibited by antitrust laws from expanding, earlier and more seriously than their German and British counterparts. Antitrust laws clearly did restrain the smaller U.S. giants from some acquisitions, yet some of the best U.S. performers were vigorous independent companies deriving from antitrust action, notably the 1911 breakup of Standard Oil and Du Pont, while the 1912 giant that was "lucky" *not* to be broken up, U.S. Steel, then performed abysmally both in absolute terms and relative to the industry average.[19] Antitrust enforcement thus had positive as well as negative effects on U.S. corporate giants. Moreover, European firms were subject to parallel constraints from nationalization or expropriation: the British firm Vickers, for example, saw its assets in cars, computers, aircraft, and shipbuilding eventually nationalized, and RTZ lost its core assets (in Spain) to Franco's postwar nationalization program. German firms suffered from extensive nationalizations in the 1930s,[20] and German giants sustained massive expropriations, in both 1914–19 and 1939–45, of sub-

19. The later demerger of Northern Telecom from Western Electric also performed well, as did the 1914 British company split of Burmah (later Burmah Castrol) and Anglo-Persian (later BP). Even the four companies demerged from American Tobacco in 1911 achieved an average performance of 0.7, compared with the only independent tobacco company's performance of 0.5.

20. Nationalization was the greatest risk in the "other" countries, which performed worst; see table 7.2.

sidiaries in enemy countries and beyond their shrinking western and eastern national borders. Giant corporations faced large and diverse political risks *wherever* they were based in a turbulent century; but the best firms were the ones that turned this to their advantage; no nation had a monopoly of severe challenges to big business.

My results thus decisively reject the notion that there were exceptionally few large British corporations or that they were especially notable for failing to sustain or develop their capabilities; and a case can be made that the opposite is true. Certainly matched pairs of roughly equal British and American firms appear to confirm this: in oil Shell did more than twice as well as Exxon and by 1995 was the largest industrial firm in the world; in tobacco, BAT did three times as well as American Tobacco; in textiles, J&P Coats did three times as well as American Woolen; in copper, RTZ did three times as well as Phelps Dodge. Even when one American firm did markedly better than its British twin (e.g., Du Pont did three times as well as Brunner Mond [Zeneca]), the superior U.S. performance was cancelled out by U.S. firms in the same industry that declined markedly (e.g., American Agricultural Chemical and Virginia-Carolina Chemical).

Of course, the British success could simply be the outcome of random variations in the performance of a relatively small number of firms. What is clear is that the leading industrial countries all had some significant capabilities in managing leading corporations. There are strong indications that Britain's firms slightly lower down in the size range of moderately large corporations also show a clear tendency to outperform Germany and the United States, though the data on these are less standardized and relate to changing populations of firms.[21]

It is abundantly clear, then, that Chandler was wrong in identifying the failure to entrench oligopolies in manufacturing corporations as the key to Britain's fundamental twentieth-century weaknesses. Paradoxically, the country that best exemplifies the Chandlerian thesis about dynamic and sustained corporate capabilities is Britain, the country where he least expected to find it. Yet this conclusion leaves an unresolved puzzle. British GDP by 1995 was only four times in real terms its 1912 level, while the United States and Germany achieved twice this rate of growth.[22] The well-known statistics that first focused Chandler's attention on manufacturing as the root cause of Britain's slow

21. Teece (1993, 214) noted that in *Chandler's own data* on the top 200 firms in each country, leading German firms had a low probability of maintaining their position, though he was inclined to excuse it as the effect of war at the 1953 benchmark date for Germany. But Cassis (1997) observes that the poor German performance persists in longer-run comparisons with the longevity of large British and French firms. See also Hannah (1995a). Table 7.4 also suggests that large British firms were faster than continental European ones in adopting what Chandler defined as appropriate structures, despite the contrary impression in *Scale and Scope*.

22. The United States' GDP increased eight times, and Germany's nine times, both in real terms. All countries grew both by increasing labor productivity and by increasing the population, but the latter kind of growth was most noticeable in the United States and least in Britain.

growth are still eloquent: Britain's share of world trade in manufactures declined more rapidly than that of Germany, while America's share actually rose.[23] The proportion of Britain's labor force in manufacturing fell markedly relative to Germany.[24] If large British industrial firms were *not* generally performing badly, it seems reasonable to examine whether *smaller and medium-sized* manufacturing firms in Britain were in some sense underperforming relative to those in the United States and Germany. If this alternative hypothesis were nearer the mark, we would expect the decline in British manufacturing to be reflected *especially among smaller firms;* while, if the Chandler view were correct, it would be the larger firms that had suffered most. The industrial concentration data supports the former hypothesis: Britain has become significantly more reliant on its large firms than either the United States or Germany (though in the first decades of this century the United States was probably the leader); Britain now has the highest levels of industrial concentration of any major modern economy.[25] The statistical record of industrial structure and performance is consistent with the view that the capabilities embodied in Germany's midsized *Mittelstand* or in the vigorous competitive fringe of small and medium-sized firms in Germany and America are what have given them their competitive edge in manufacturing; the data simply are not compatible with the Chandler view of changing national competitive advantage of these countries' large firms and those of Britain. Far from neglecting to develop the core capabilities of its large corporations, Britain seems to have done so proportionately more than its two main industrial rivals over the century as a whole.

There are, moreover, strong indications that it is a mistake to focus the debate on changing national competitive advantage solely on the manufacturing sector. Indeed, on Broadberry's estimates, between 1909–11 and 1990 Britain *improved* its manufacturing *productivity* performance relative to both the United States and Germany.[26] Some of this is arguably due to the reversal since 1979 of the British government's former promanufacturing, pro-large-

23. Britain's share of world manufactured exports declined from 30 percent in 1912 to 9 percent in 1991, while Germany's fell only from 26 percent to 20 percent; the United States' rose from 13 percent to 17 percent over the same period (Tyszynski 1951, 286; Central Statistical Office 1992, 142).

24. The share of manufacturing in total employment fell slightly faster between 1910–13 and 1990 in Britain (from 32 percent to 20 percent) than in the United States (from 22 percent to 15 percent), while in Germany the manufacturing share was stable at around 30 percent of employment (Broadberry 1996).

25. By 1970/71 the largest one hundred manufacturing firms controlled 40 percent of net output in the United Kingdom, 33 percent in the United States, and perhaps only 30 percent in Germany; around the First World War, concentration had been lower in Britain than in the United States and about the same as in Germany (Hannah 1995b, 58).

26. U.S. manufacturing productivity in manufacturing was 103 percent higher than the United Kingdom's in 1909–11 but only 75 percent higher by 1990; German manufacturing productivity was 19 percent higher than the United Kingdom's in 1911 and only 8 percent higher (in West Germany alone) by 1990 (Broadberry 1996). Of course, productivity in East Germany is now markedly lower than in either Britain or West Germany.

corporation stance; the encouragement of small-firm growth by small-business programs, similar to those adopted earlier in the United States and Germany; and the espousal of a more free-market and free-trade policy stance that Britain had championed in 1912 but soon, along with other countries, abandoned for interventionist policies.

In that changing environment, the long-run decline of British manufacturing employment and exports is less worrying than might at first appear. As Britain latterly became self-sufficient in oil, it had less need of manufacturing exports to pay for oil imports than Germany or the United States (i.e., it moved nearer to the United States' position in 1912, as a net oil exporter achieving only *low* manufacturing exports). This is not to say Britain had no economic troubles: its living standards have fallen relative to Germany and the United States in the twentieth century. Yet careful sectoral analysis of the components of growth suggests that some of this was inevitable (Britain had already industrialized more than the United States and Germany in 1912, so had far less scope for overall productivity improvement by shifting resources out of agriculture), while insofar as any British sector fell behind its rivals, it appears to have been, not manufacturing, but services, particularly the utilities and communications sectors, in which America has done markedly better than Britain.[27]

7.5   Are There "Sunset" and "Sunrise" Industries or "Sunset" and "Sunrise" Firms?

The various industries in which the giant firms of 1912 were concentrated appear at first sight to have exhibited more consistent patterns of performance than their nationality.[28] As table 7.3 shows, about half the firms are in five industries—coal mining, textiles and leather, nonferrous metals (including other mining), iron and steel (including related heavy industries), and mechanical engineering—in which the average firm had substantially declined in size at the terminal date; very few giant firms increased in size, and only one (RTZ) remained in the 1995 top hundred. The "successes" in these "old" industries[29]

27. The U.S. productivity lead over Britain in utilities was only 50 percent in 1909–11 but 290 percent by 1990; Germany's lead was 4 percent in 1909–11 and 30 percent in 1990. Britain's transportation and communications sector has, however, had a better productivity record relative to Germany (Broadberry 1996).

28. Though the poor performance of Germany and "other" in table 7.2, relative to Britain, is partly due to their having a higher proportion of their giant firms in the "old" industries. Germany was strong in two "new" industries (electrical engineering and chemicals) but had *no* giant firms in either petroleum or branded products. (Britain had old industries but they were generally organized on the basis of Marshallian industrial districts, with external economies substituting for economies of scale internal to large firms.) However, America's poor performance cannot be explained by industrial composition: it had the same proportion of giant firms in "new" industries as Britain.

29. Of course they were often considered important and significant industries at the time: railroad manufacturers were then bigger than car manufacturers; gold, diamond, and copper mines were felt to have excellent prospects, as were high-tech armaments and ship manufacturers. They are "old" only in retrospect.

Table 7.3   Industrial Performance Differentials among 1912 Giant Corporations

Industry	No. of 1912 Giant Firms in the Industry	Aggregate 1912 Market Capitalization of the Industry's Giant Firms (billions of US$)	Median Industry Performance	Average Industry Performance	Coefficient of Variation
Textiles and leather	4	0.4	0.1	0.1	79
Coal mining	7	0.4	0	0.2	185
Mechanical engineering	10	0.9	0.1	0.4	164
Nonferrous metals, etc.	14	1.2	0.2	0.4	116
Iron/steel/heavy industry	18	1.5	0.3	0.6	125
Branded products	18	1.6	0.9	1.3	142
Chemicals	10	0.4	2.2	2.4	79
Electrical engineering	5	0.4	3.4	2.7	70
Petroleum	14	1.2	3.6	3.7	62
All 1912 giant firms	100	8.1	0.4	1.4	140

Source: Author's calculations from data in appendix A.

often achieved it by selling out early (e.g., the railroad-equipment manufacturer, Metropolitan Carriage, in 1919 with a ratio of 1.9); others succeeded in their core old activities as well as new ones (e.g., Mannesmann, with the best ratio for this group of industries of 2.7 in 1995). A few well-performing survivors shifted industry completely: for example, American Can into financial services (with a ratio of 1.9) and the French steel giant Schneider into electrical engineering (achieving the stability ratio of 1.0). Such "new" industries undoubtedly offered better growth opportunities but, of course, many of the "old" 1912 industries did not have any relevant capabilities to transfer to such new industries in order to escape constraints in individual markets. Judging from giant firms in coal, textiles, and railroad-equipment manufacture, the collapse of their markets and the limitations on interindustry transfer of their capabilities posed particularly tough obstacles. The most promising solution for such firms may have been the absorption into other firms that many of them suffered, presumably to maximize the value of what few transferable skills they still embodied.[30] By the same token, firms that were in 1912 already in the rapidly growing industries of petroleum, chemicals, and electrical engineering (industries whose giant firms more than doubled in real size on average) perhaps had a somewhat easier task in converting their initial stock of skills and building dynamic capabilities. Branded products firms—the most numerous of the "new" industries in the 1912 list—also tended to grow on average.

However, it would be wrong to suggest that giant firms had clearly predestined outcomes depending on their initial "sunrise" or "sunset" industry base. In fact, there was more diversity of performance *within* industries than *between* them.[31] Even in an industry as promising as electrical manufacturing—where three out of five firms scored above 3.3—Westinghouse (0.7) and AEG (0.3) performed weakly. Oil companies overall did well, but relative laggards, when nationalized or taken over, could be below their 1912 size. The branded-product firms include some of the great twentieth-century successes like Procter and Gamble (8.1) and Lever Brothers (Unilever) (3.4) but also some of the more remarkable failures like American Tobacco/Brands (0.4) and Cudahy Packing (0.1). In industries where decline was the typical outcome—like the steel and related engineering industries—not all had to go the way of U.S. Steel (0.1), International Harvester (0.1), and Krupp (0.2); Gewerkschaft deutscher Kaiser (Thyssen) (0.9) and John Deere and Company (0.9) did distinctly better. As the last column of table 7.3 shows, both old and new indus-

30. U.S. coal firms were absorbed into firms like Du Pont; in Europe the post-1945 solution was nationalization (Britain's National Coal Board and Charbonnages de France) or publicly subsidized private corporations (Ruhrkohle in Germany): a solution that seems more often to have expensively delayed decline than facilitated diversification or skill transfer.
31. The coefficient of variation of the average ratios for the nine industries is 95; thus there is more variation *within* the majority of the industry groups (coal, mechanical engineering, nonferrous metals, etc., iron and steel, and branded products) than *between* industry groups and, within the four less variable groups (textiles, chemicals, electrical engineering, and petroleum), there is still almost as much variability as there is *between* industry groups.

tries showed considerable variability of growth outcomes: the coefficient of variation exceeded 60 in all industries and exceeded 100 in half of them. This pattern of diversity of experience within industries is consistent with the pattern revealed by wider samples of firms over shorter periods (e.g., Schmalensee 1985; Rumelt 1991). Dynamic economies—of which the global economy in which most of these firms in varying degrees operated is the largest case—indeed consist of rising and declining industries, but businesses can develop and sustain competitive advantages in *either* kind of industry. Simplistic recipes for industry portfolio management may have earned consultants fortunes, but a surer key to sustained success is learning to operate distinctively and profitably anywhere, rather than paying expensively for fashionable diversifying acquisitions in industries in which no distinctive new proprietor value can be added (Kay 1993).

How, then, can large corporations retain their positions, continue to add value, and expand their capabilities? The only reasonable answer is: with great difficulty. Samuel Johnson's view, that "business could not be managed by those who manage it if it had much difficulty," has often appealed to academic analysts and is probably true of the generality of businesses; but the generality of businesses—in the short or long term depending on their initial size—are dead. It is a pleasant conceit of us all—from business-school professors, through academic analysts to management consultants—that the world would be a better place if systematic analysis could change that. Given the high incidence and costs of corporate decline and failure—and the distance of the specter of global domination by a few exceptionally competent firms—it is doubtless in the social (as well as the private) interest that all possible steps should be taken to encourage such systematic analysis. To date, however, we have made great strides in storytelling, but a clearer, surer recipe for sustained success for large corporations has remained elusive.

This outcome is not accidental: it is inherent in the competitive market process that underpins the success of twentieth-century capitalism. Most of the companies I have described were remarkable successes in 1912; their high stock market valuation reflected their ability to earn supernormal profits. These profits were often a reward for large-scale investments in production, management, and marketing, along the lines described by Chandler (1990). There was often something more—a technological advantage, exclusive possession of raw materials or of valuable distribution networks, a strong brand image—to entrench the position of the first movers in the Chandlerian sense. Yet, as Lieberman and Montgomery (1988) have emphasized, such advantages are often fleeting and contingent. Patents were of limited effectiveness, advertising built up rival brands, new mines and oil wells were discovered, techniques of management, production, and marketing were copied. Even where this could not easily happen, exogenous changes in the technology of production or in the nature of markets could make the initial advantage insecure; entrenched positions could also be challenged by antitrust or by expropriations (both nationalizations and those following defeat in war).

Where such challenges were ineffective, or where they were neutralized by the firms' own strategic initiatives, the giants survived, but, given the power of competitive forces, it is arguably no surprise that disappearance or decline was nearly three times more likely among the giants than growth. The process of copying was one that often competed the profits of the onetime leaders down to normal levels, spreading the benefits of their initial advantage more widely. Firms that limited this process and maintained some competitive advantage once could, in principle, have had a run of further luck that enabled them constantly to entrench new capabilities. A more plausible explanation of capability enhancers is that they had some distinctive architecture that enabled them— but not others—constantly to replicate their early success (Kay 1993). Such corporate architectures must be complex and difficult to identify, describe, and copy, for, if that were not the case, their value would be competed down by emulators. *By definition,* we do not know what those architectures are, though it is plausible that their corporate operators have acquired that knowledge through a process of collective, tacit learning, transmissible between managerial generations.

This points up starkly the catch-22 of their craft for all business historians and management gurus. They naturally view that bleak scientific point skeptically, as the fund manager views the financial economist's "efficient markets hypothesis," with which it has close affinities.[32] It is perfectly possible, in both cases, to discover a generically effective strategy but, when we do, its profitability will be competed down by the emulation our discovery prompts. The gold we have unearthed will very soon turn into the dross of normal profits, as its benefits are widely spread, but the private dross represents the broad social benefit of expanding average capabilities.

Both the incentive to develop competitive advantages and the incentive to emulate them were strong in the societies in which the giant firms of 1912 operated.[33] Large firms themselves became very efficient surveyors of the possibilities, increasingly competing with and emulating each other. In that sense, the averagely weak ability of large firms to develop the distinctive capabilities that had once generated their size is a sign, not of their individual weaknesses, but of their collective strengths within the capitalist market system. Marx understood the "contradictions" in this dialectical system well. Paradoxically, capitalist firms are induced by the search for surplus value (supernormal profits) to grow; but competition between them also tends to destroy the dis-

---

32. And, as with stock picking, it is easier to give business-strategy advice retrospectively than prospectively!

33. At least in the United States, the United Kingdom, and Germany. The "other" countries— many what we would now call "emerging markets"—actually show the worst performance in table 7.2, perhaps reflecting that they did not have these social capabilities in such large measure.

tinctive sources of supernormal profits. Marx's mistake was to consider this a weakness in the stage of economic evolution he then saw unfolding. In fact, the mix of incentives and checks it created has been capitalism's fundamental strength as the (now globally favored) system of social organization.

7.6   Which National Differences Were Most Sustainable?

If that view of the world is accepted, we might expect international differences among giant firms to diminish in all except a few cases of well-entrenched or undiscoverable competitive advantages. We can see some of this process in the chemical industry, which accounted for ten of the world's largest hundred industrial firms in 1912 and for twenty in the 1995 top hundred. In 1912 the chemical giants of Britain, Germany, and America were substantially differentiated. The Germans, with excellent universities and moderately paid scientists, were strongest in the research-intensive sector, where these cheap human resources were a particular advantage, that is, in fine chemicals (then mainly dyestuffs). The British, with plentiful and cheap supplies of capital, excelled in the capital-intensive sector. The major technological innovation in this sector, the Solvay process, had been licensed by its Belgian owners to separate British, U.S., and German companies: of these, only the British firm, Brunner Mond, was large enough to enter the top one hundred (the other licensees, Deutsche Solvay and the U.S.-based Solvay Process Company, though operating in bigger national markets, were less profitable). The largest U.S. chemical firm was Du Pont, an explosives specialist, with its national market among mines and gun owners larger than European equivalents (the London-based Nobel Dynamite Trust had a near monopoly in both the British and German explosives markets, but was still just too small to qualify for entry to the 1912 list).

However, these superficially strong national differences among giant chemical corporations were short-lived. Du Pont had already in 1912 begun to focus its R&D strategy, so that it was poised to become an engine of growth and diversification for the company *nach deutscher Art* (Hounshell and Smith 1988). In the next quarter-century, the somewhat diverse chemical giants of Britain, Germany, and America all became very much more like each other: as research-intensive as the Germans, as capital-intensive as the British, and as market-oriented as the Americans. This occurred partly by expropriation (notably by the British and Americans of German patents and other assets) but also by processes of competition and emulation of advantages seen in domestic and overseas competitors. Chemical engineering and financing techniques, research laboratories, patent pools, and multinational investment all played their part in the process. The competitive advantages that had once seemed nationally distinctive rarely remained so. Indeed, with the widespread post–World War II entry of the oil companies into downstream chemical operations, it became obvious that not only rival chemical companies but also vertically related

Table 7.4   Adoption of the Multidivisional Structure (% of the top 100 corporations with M-form structure)

	1913	1932	1950	1960	1970	1980–83	1993
U.S.	0	8	17	43	71	81	—
Japan	1	0	8	29	55	58	—
Germany	1	—	5	15	50	60	70
France	1	3	6	21	54	66	76
Italy	—	—	7	17	48	—	—
U.K.	0	5	13	30	72	89	88

Sources: See appendix B.

producers could copy and acquire the chemical companies' various research, production, and marketing skills. The process was not all one-way, for there were still some good reasons for pursuing distinctive strategies in a changing and complex world,[34] but, except in the pharmaceutical sector (where patent protection is unusually effective), it was difficult for companies to entrench any distinctiveness (and the supernormal profits that brought) for long.

The process of competitive emulation of distinctive advantages nationally and internationally can be traced more precisely for what has been seen by many business historians as the distinctive generic capability facilitating the management of the giant diversified corporations that allegedly prospered in the twentieth-century world. Chandler (1962) showed the postwar spread of the multidivisional organization through U.S. industry, after its pioneering in the 1920s by firms like General Motors.[35] Table 7.4 shows that its postwar spread throughout the five other major industrial countries was less rapid, but, with only a slight lag, the M-form was widely adopted in Britain and, soon after, in Germany, France, Japan, and even Italy, which was notorious for having relatively few giant U.S.-style corporations.

Yet, in many respects, these countries' business cultures are undoubtedly profoundly different; the spread of the M-form simply demonstrates that these national differences are minimized by large-scale business institutions. Techniques of managing large corporations, of harnessing central research laboratories to diversification, or of advertising national brands may easily be copied by the large corporations of one nation from another, or a multinational may

---

34. A recent example is the rise of the British pharmaceutical industry in the last quarter of a century. In 1970 the largest British pharmaceutical company rated only sixteenth in the world; now Glaxo Wellcome is the largest in the world, and several others are ranked in the top twenty; even a foreign company like the merger of U.S. Upjohn with Swedish Pharmacia chose to base its new headquarters in London. This change in the British position in research-based fine chemicals is probably due to the advantages of London as a commercial and financial center and the availability of cheaper scientists from good universities than the United States and Germany now offer (i.e., a similar advantage to pre-1914 Germany, though not one that any sensible country would like to base its competitive advantage on for long, since it implies sustaining low living standards).

35. Though Hounshell (chap. 5 in this volume) suggests the problem of applying it to different corporations, e.g., Ford.

enter the market to spread them. Competition and emulation thus do a great deal to homogenize the giant-firm sector in reasonably competent advanced industrial countries.[36] In that sense, we should not be surprised at our earlier conclusion that some popular characterizations of national differences in large corporations appear to be baseless caricatures.

Where, then, is national differentiation in business cultures and business institutions likely to reside, if it is not in industrial giants? There are, I suggest, two main locations. First, the culturally embedded characteristics of business are often reinforced by local institutions underpinning small and medium-sized businesses: such essentially localized businesses are inherently less subject to (though, of course, not entirely immune from) many of the pressures for international emulation and homogenization (Piore and Sabel 1984; Kogut 1993; Knight 1995). Well-known examples in the literature are the German apprenticeship training system (which underpins the powerful world-market position of German *Mittelstand* firms in the engineering industry) and Italian small-firm networks (typified by Porter's well-known example [1990] of Sassuolo's ceramic tiles). Firms may find it difficult to capture the resulting rents—so they do not generally appear in lists of large firms like mine—but the positive impact on national living standards (and the sustainability of the differences underpinning that) are likely to be considerable.

The second likely area of substantial and sustained national differentiation is in the utilities and communications sectors. Public ownership or state regulation of competitive processes dominate here and frequently prevent international convergence of institutions and standards. It seems quite likely, for example, that the United States' ability to increase its lead over Britain in living standards in the first half of the twentieth century was more due to its relative performance in these services (in some of which Britain had an initial lead which was reversed) than in manufacturing (in which the British productivity gap remained remarkably stable) (Hannah 1995a; Field 1996; Broadberry 1996).

Research on contrasts in national economic performance and their relationship to business institutions is difficult and not yet systematically developed. There may be some mileage in further international comparisons of giant industrial corporations, but, if my findings are a pointer, business historians may more productively focus their research on national institutional differences in other directions. The prize of focusing our efforts accurately is an attractive

36. Even here, however, note that the adoption of the M-form stabilized in continental Europe and Japan at lower levels than in the "Anglo-Saxon" countries. One plausible explanation is contrasts in their capital markets: the monitoring processes of M-form head offices may, for example, be undertaken by universal banks or other agents in less fluid capital markets. Significantly, while in the United States and United Kingdom a positive correlation is found between profitability and M-form adoption (Armour and Teece 1978; Steer and Cable 1978), no such correlations appear in Germany and Japan (Cable and Dirrheimer 1983; cf. Ingham 1992).

one: the understanding of the microeconomic foundations of the macroeconomic convergence processes that economists have identified in the modern economic development of advanced industrial nations, and also of the limits on such convergence processes.

Appendix A
The World's 100 Largest Capitalist Industrial Enterprises of 1912

All industrial enterprises[37] with equity market capitalization of $26 million or more in 1912 are listed in rank order within industry groups. For a fuller account of the construction of this population see Hannah (1998) and Schmitz (1995). I am grateful to Alison Sharp for research assistance and to many national specialists for advice, which is more fully acknowledged in Hannah (1998). For industry averages see table 7.3; for national averages see table 7.2; for overall totals see table 7.1.

There are two major problems of the capability survival test for our 1912 giant firms: identifying the precise "heir" of the 1912 firm, and dealing with giant firms that were themselves taken over or otherwise "disappeared" between 1912 and 1995. Some arbitrary judgments are inevitable—the genetic descent of corporations is less unambiguously defined by economic than by human reproductive processes—but I have tried to apply standard rules to resolve difficult cases. Corporate descent is defined in organizational (rather than legal or technological or marketing) terms. The successor firm of American Tobacco is American Brands, even though it no longer sells tobacco in America and recently disposed of the subsidiary bearing its original name in that business.[38] Considered strategic decisions to change business lines are accepted as the corporate destiny: American Can is now Travelers Group (not part of the Triangle Group that bought the can-making subsidiary), Singer is now Bicoastal (not the Hong Kong–Bermudan sewing machine and computer company that laboriously reassembled a world-class sewing-machine business that Singer's managers had believed had no future and had broken up).[39] Where mergers have been reversed, the intervening life is ignored: Bayer is the successor of

37. Defined as all nongovernment enterprises with more than 50 percent of their activity in mining and manufacturing.
38. Such decisions can notably affect the results: the American Tobacco subsidiary was sold in 1994 for $1 billion, whereas at the 1995 benchmark the rest of American Brands was worth $8 billion.
39. While in individual cases choosing these successor companies affects the calculated outcome, overall the swings may well cancel out the roundabouts: the alternative option would show American Can performing much worse and Singer performing rather better.

Elberfelder Farbenfabriken (the intervening IG Farben notwithstanding), Zeneca is the successor of Brunner Mond (the intervening ICI notwithstanding). Where voluntary demergers have occurred, the larger core is taken as the continuing firm. However, when demerger derived from government action, large resulting entities are credited as joint successors: Du Pont became Du Pont plus Hercules and Atlas, Lothringer Hüttenverein became Knutange and Klöckner, Burmah is now Burmah Castrol plus BP, Western Electric is now Lucent Technologies plus Northern Telecom.[40] Firms may leave archeological remains—as in the survival of the Armour and Swift brand names as a small part of a subsidiary of Conagra—but both firms are (reasonably) judged no longer to exist.

Yet some firms that have "disappeared" into a larger entity retain substantial, separately identifiable capabilities in "quasifirms," clearly deriving from the 1912 entity. The National Biscuit Company is traceable in 1995, but had "disappeared" into RJR Nabisco; similarly Imperial Tobacco is now a division of Hanson Industries. In both cases the larger entity built on the surviving capability of the acquired company and sometimes recognized its independent viability. Indeed, in these two special cases, both parents were discussing demerger of their subsidiary, so that it would again become an independent firm. Clearly such cases on the verge of corporate "reincarnation" are different from a 1912 firm that had truly "disappeared" in the sense of being liquidated (e.g., Central Leather), sold at a price reflecting long-run decline (e.g., Pullman), or acquired from bankruptcy protection by an optimistic corporation that proved unable to turn it around (e.g., AEG). Valuing surviving subsidiaries or divisions in 1995 as separate entities is problematic: AEG, for example, if valued on the basis of capitalizing divisional profits, would actually have a negative value (which would probably be too pessimistic an assessment of its surviving capabilities). I have therefore valued acquired firms at the estimated price paid for acquiring their equity[41] *at the time of their substantive disappearance,*[42] converting this to "1912 stock exchange prices" by the appropriate Standard and Poor's 500 index point, as with 1995 survivors. Acquisition prices are usually at a substantial premium to market values, and as acquired firms were generally declining,[43] the earlier date of the acquisition imparts an upward bias, relative

40. However, most problems of this kind have been avoided by our choice of dates: 1912 is after the major 1911 divestitures imposed on Standard Oil and American Tobacco and before the major German mergers (Vereinigte Stahlwerke and IG Farben) which were later reversed by allied antitrust action.

41. Where this was not published in the press at the time, I have estimated it from market price data at the time of the merger.

42. Some judgments verge on the arbitrary; e.g., where firms were temporarily absorbed into a larger firm, then demerged, then later merged more completely, I have generally taken their later disappearance, to preserve some symmetry with the treatment of surviving (but once merged) firms.

43. As my data imply, see note 7.

to surviving firms valued in 1995. This measure is, therefore, presented separately in parentheses in table 7A.1. Recognizing its upward bias, it will be used when a full sample of outcomes is required or where it is clear that it is biased against the hypothesis being tested.

A final problem is nationalization. This was, for reasons not unconnected with their size,[44] a serious risk for the giant firms of 1912. All the Russian, Mexican, and French firms in the 1912 list, many of the German ones, and parts of some British ones[45] were at some stage nationalized, and some remain in state hands. Nationalized firms like BP and St. Gobain continued to be managed like private firms and by 1995 were privatized, so can be treated in the normal way. Giant Russian companies (of which there were three in 1912) pose difficulties. Nobel Brothers (the only Asian firm in the 1912 list, with St. Petersburg headquarters but mainly Azerbaijani operations) was expropriated after the Russian Revolution; the company's rump of Western operations (e.g., in Poland) was worth little when finally liquidated in the 1950s. Two other Russian firms in industries with no large quoted 1995 successors (one iron and steel firm, the other in railroad engineering) are also pessimistically treated as declining to zero value. However, where Western firms remain nationalized, I have taken the 1995 balance-sheet assets less any traceable dedicated debts as a proxy for market value.

Since this work was undertaken, one further omitted firm has been identified: Alpine-Montangesellschaft, an iron and steel firm with equity capital of $72.4 million in 1912, based in the Hapsburg Empire (Austria). This firm became majority-owned by Vereinigte Stahlwerke in 1926, then, after the *Anschluss,* part of the Hermann Göring Werke, and was nationalized in postwar Austria as Vöst-Alpine. Its inclusion (ranked thirty-fourth in 1912) would displace the Belgian-based Lothringer Hüttenverein from the hundredth position, but would not materially affect any of the major reported results.

---

44. On the Caligulan principle ("I wish the Roman people had but a single neck"), governments were more likely to nationalize large firms than small.

45. BP was majority-owned by the state for most of its twentieth-century existence, but not in 1912 or 1995; parts of several other 1912 companies were nationalized in Britain, but they were left with a range of capabilities that have been considered the surviving firms. In some cases (e.g., Vickers) the effects of nationalization of large parts exaggerate their measured decline.

Table 7A.1   **The World's Hundred Largest Industrial Firms of 1912**

Rank in Global Top 100 in 1912 (and in parentheses, 1995, where still in top 100)	1912 HQ Location	Name of Company in 1912 (in parentheses, 1995 changed name or alternative outcome)[a]	Market Capitalization of Equity (in millions of US$ at 1912 stock market prices)[b] 1912 Initial	1995 Multiple[c]
		Textiles and Leather		
3	UK	J&P Coats (Viyella acq. 1986)	287	(0.3)
68	US	Central Leather (liquidated 1952)	40	(0)
69	US	American Woolen (Textron acq. 1955)	40	(0.1)
82	UK	Fine Cotton Spinners (Courtaulds acq. 1964)	34	(0.1)
		Coal Mining		
23	F	Mines de Lens (Charbonnages de France)	94	0*
28	F	Mines de Bruay (nat. 1945)	87	(0)
29	G	Gelsenkirchener (Ruhrkohle/RWE acq. 1968/69)	86	(0.2)
47	F	Mines de Courrières (nat. 1945)	55	(0)
61	F	Mines d'Anzin (nat. 1945)	47	(0)
72	G	Harpener Bergbau (VEW acq. 1992)	38	(0.1)
91	US	Pittsburgh Coal (Continental acq. 1966)	31	(1.0)
		Mechanical Engineering		
4	US	Pullman (Wheelabrator-Frye Acq. 1980)	200	(0.1)
8	US	Singer (Bicoastal)	173	0*
10	US	International Harvester (Navistar)	160	0.1
21	US	Westinghouse Air Brake (American Standard acq. 1968)	102	(0.1)
36	US	John Deere	70*	0.9
50	US	American Car and Foundry (Icahn acq. 1984)	52	(0.3)
64	R	Briansk Rail and Engineering (nat. 1917)	45	(0)
79	US	American Locomotive (Worthington acq. 1964)	37	(0)
88	US	Baldwin Locomotive (Armour acq. 1965)	32	(0.1)
95	UK	Metropolitan Carriage (Vickers acq. 1919)	27	(1.9)
		Nonferrous Metals and Other Mining (including related refining and smelting)		
6	US	Anaconda (ARCO acq. 1977)	178	(0.2)
12	SA	De Beers	158	0.3
13 (88)	UK	Rio Tinto (RTZ)	148	0.8

Table 7A.1   (continued)

Rank in Global Top 100 in 1912 (and in parentheses, 1995, where still in top 100)	1912 HQ Location	Name of Company in 1912 (in parentheses, 1995 changed name or alternative outcome)[a]	Market Capitalization of Equity (in millions of US$ at 1912 stock market prices)[b]	
			1912 Initial	1995 Multiple[c]
18	US	Utah Copper and Nevada Consolidated (Kennecott acq. 1923–33)	116	(1.1)
22	US	Phelps Dodge	95	0.3
25	US	American Smelting (ASARCO)	92	0.1
42	SA	Rand Mines	65	0
43	SA	Crown Mines (Rand Mines acq. 1968)	63	(0)
45	US	International Nickel (Inco)	57	0.4
54	US	Calumet & Hecla (Universal Oil acq. 1968)	51	(0.1)
60	UK	Consolidated Goldfields (Hanson acq. 1989)	47	(1.6)
70	US	National Lead (NL Industries)	39	0.2
83	US	U.S. Smelting Refining & Mining (Sharon acq. 1979)	34	(0.2)
86	SA	E. Rand Proprietary	33	0
		Iron, Steel, and Heavy Industrial[d]		
1	US	U.S. Steel (USX Marathon)	741	0.1
14	G	Krupp	130*	0.2
38	G	Phoenix (Thyssen acq. 1963)	67	(0.1)
46	US	American Can (Travelers Group)	57	1.9
48	G	Deutsch-Luxemburg (Vereinigte Stahlwerke acq. 1926)	55	(0)
49	G	Gewerkschaft Deutscher Kaiser (Thyssen)	54	0.9
51	UK	Vickers	52	0.2
65	US	Pennsylvania Steel (Bethlehem acq. 1916)	43*	(0.5)
67	UK	Armstrong, Whitworth (bankrupt 1926)	41	(0)
71	F	Schneider	39	1.0
77	R	Russo-Belge (nat. 1917)	37	(0)
80	G	Hohenlohe Iron & Steel (dismembered and liquidated 1921–39)	36	(0)
81	Lux.	ARBED	35	0.2
89	G	Mannesmann	32	2.7
90	G	Gutehoffnungshütte (Maschinenfabrik Augsburg-Nürnberg)	32*	1.0
93	US	Crucible Steel (Colt acq. 1968)	30	(0.3)
96	US	Republic Iron & Steel (LTV acq. 1984)	27	(0.5)
100	Belg.	Lothringer Hüttenverein (Schneider et. al. acq. Knutange 1919, Klöckner insolvent 1992)	26	(0.6)

(continued)

Table 7A.1 (continued)

Rank in Global Top 100 in 1912 (and in parentheses, 1995, where still in top 100)	1912 HQ Location	Name of Company in 1912 (in parentheses, 1995 changed name or alternative outcome)[a]	Market Capitalization of Equity (in millions of US$ at 1912 stock market prices)[b]	
			1912 Initial	1995 Multiple[c]
		Branded Products[e]		
9	US	American Tobacco (American Brands)	169	0.4
11 (38)	UK	British-American Tobacco (BAT Industries)	159	1.3
15 (44)	US	Eastman Kodak	128	1.3
16	US	Armour (Greyhound acq. 1970)	126*	(0.1)
17	UK	Imperial Tobacco (Hanson acq. 1986)	120	(0.5)
19	US	American Sugar (Tate & Lyle acq. 1988)	110	(0.1)
20 (75)	UK	Guinness	109	1.2
27 (19)	UK	Lever Brothers (Unilever)	87	3.4
30	US	U.S. Rubber (Uniroyal)	80	0*
31	US	B.F. Goodrich	75	0.2
32	US	Swift (Beatrice acq. 1984)	75	(1.0)
34	US	National Biscuit (RJR acq. 1985)	72	(1.8)
44	US	Liggett & Myers (Grandmet acq. 1980)	58	(0.4)
52 (10)	US	Procter & Gamble	51	8.1
66	US	P. Lorillard (Loews acq. 1968)	42	(0.7)
75	UK	Reckitt & Sons (Reckitt & Colman)	38	1.0
87	US	Corn Products (CPC International)	33	2.3
97	US	Cudahy Packing (General Host acq. 1968)	26*	(0.1)
		Chemical[f]		
37 (20)	US	Du Pont (+ Hercules + ICI acq. Atlas 1971)	69*	7.2
53 (94)	G	Farbwerke vormals Lucius & Bruning (Hoechst)	51	2.0
57 (85)	UK	Brunner Mond (Zeneca)	49	2.4
62 (67)	G	Elberfelder Farbenfabriken (Bayer)	45	3.0
63 (95)	G	BASF	45	2.3
73	US	American Agricultural Chemical (Continental acq. 1963)	38	(0.2)
76	US	Virginia-Carolina Chemical (Mobil acq. 1963)	38	(0.2)
84	F	St. Gobain	33	2.5
85	Belg.	Solvay	33*	1.1
92	US	General Chemical (Allied-Signal)	30	3.1
		Electrical Engineering		
7 (2)	US	General Electric	174	4.7
24	G	AEG (Daimler-Benz acq. 1985)	93	(0.3)

Table 7A.1 (continued)

Rank in Global Top 100 in 1912 (and in parentheses, 1995, where still in top 100)	1912 HQ Location	Name of Company in 1912 (in parentheses, 1995 changed name or alternative outcome)[a]	Market Capitalization of Equity (in millions of US$ at 1912 stock market prices)[b]	
			1912 Initial	1995 Multiple[c]
39	US	Westinghouse Electric	67	0.7
41 (32)	G	Siemens	65	3.4
59	US	Western Electric (Lucent Technologies + Northern Telecom)	47*	4.7
		Petroleum		
2 (3)	US	Jersey Standard (Exxon)	390	1.9
5 (1)	N/ UK	Royal Dutch Shell	187	4.8
26 (22)	US	Indiana Standard (Amoco)	88	3.2
33 (14)	US	New York Standard (Mobil)	73	4.4
35	US	California Standard (Chevron)	71	3.7
40	US	Ohio Oil (U.S. Steel acq. 1982)	66*	(3.5)
55	US	Prairie Oil & Gas (Sinclair acq. 1932)	50	(0.3)
56	Mex.	El Aguila (Shell acq. 1919)	50	(2.4)
58	R	Nobel Bros. (nat. 1917, rump dissolved 1959)	48	(0)
74 (16)	UK	Burmah Oil (Burmah Castrol + BP)	38	9.1
78	US	Mexican Petroleum (PNP acq. 1919)	37	(2.3)
94 (58)	US	Texas Co. (Texaco)	29	5.2
98 (52)	US	Atlantic Refining (ARCO)	26	5.9
99	US	Vacuum Oil (New York Standard acq. 1931)	26	(5.1)

[a]*Acq.* = acquired; *nat.* = nationalized.

[b]An asterisk indicates that market valuation was not available. An approximation (usually based on balance-sheets assets net of quoted debt) was used.

[c]I.e., 31 May 1995 equity capitalization, revalued at 1912 stock exchange prices by the Standard and Poor's industrial 500 index, divided by 1912 equity market value, that is, what in the text is described as the "capability enhancement ratio."

[d]Many firms in this category included vertically integrated coal mines and shipbuilding yards in 1912.

[e]In addition to the core food, drink, and tobacco industry, this category includes branded household chemicals, rubber tires, and photographic goods.

[f]This category includes St. Gobain, which in 1912 (as now) was mainly a glass producer, though in 1912 it also had a major interest in chemicals.

Appendix B
Sources for Table 7.4

United States

1913 inferred from Chandler (1962).

1932 from Chandler (1962) and based on fifty companies, but with no multi-divisionals in the next fifty assumed.

1950–80 percentages estimated from the chart in Kogut and Parkinson (1993, 190), based on 150 firms—this may underestimate multidivisionals in the top one hundred.

However, Rumelt (1974), basing his study on samples of 183–207 of the top 500 firms, suggests figures of 20 percent for 1949, 50 percent for 1959, and 77 percent for 1969, which rather surprisingly implies no greater propensity to adopt multidivisional organization among very large than among more moderate-sized corporations, at least after the war.

Japan

1913–32 inferred from Morikawa (1992, 113–14).

1950–80 from Suzuki (1991), based on 114 companies. He has a category "mixed functional and divisional," half of which I have allocated to the multidivisional category.

Kono (1980, 80) gives very similar results, though cf. Fruin (1992) for the view that multidivisionals were not so common in Japan as these figures imply.

Germany

1913 "at least one," that is, Siemens, in Kocka (1978, 577).

1950–70 from Pooley-Dyas and Thanheiser (1976).

1983–93 from Whittington, Mayer, and Curto (forthcoming).

France

1912 from Levy-Leboyer (1980) (but cf. Daviet 1988).

1932 from Fridenson (1997).

1950–70 from Pooley-Dyas and Thanheiser (1976, 186–87).

1983–93 from Whittington, Mayer, and Curto (forthcoming).

Italy

1950–70 from Pavan (1970, 67), percentages based on 6/84 firms in 1950, 16/94 in 1960, and 48/100 in 1970.

United Kingdom

1913 inferred from Hannah (1976).

1932 from Hannah (1976), based on approximately fifty companies, with the assumption that lower-ranked companies did not adopt the multidivisional structure, as for the United States at that date.

1950–70 from Channon (1972, 67), percentages based on 12/92 in 1950, 29/96 in 1960, 72/100 in 1970.
1983–93 from Whittington, Mayer, and Curto (forthcoming).

References

Alford, B. W. E. 1994. Chandlerism, the new orthodoxy of U.S. and European corporate development. *Journal of European Economic History* 23, no. 3:631–43.

Armour, H. O., and D. J. Teece. 1978. Organizational structure and economic performance: A test of the multidivisional hypothesis. *Bell Journal of Economics* 9 (spring): 106–22.

Broadberry, S. N. 1996. How did the United States and Germany become richer than Britain? A sectoral analysis and comparative productivity levels, 1870–1990. Paper for Leuven preconference, November 1996, to Seville International Economic History Congress, August 1998.

Broadberry, S. N., and N. F. R. Crafts. 1992. Britain's productivity gap in the 1930s: Some neglected factors. *Journal of Economic History* 52:531–58.

Cable, John, and Manfred F. Dirrheimer. 1983. Hierarchies and markets: An empirical test of the multi-division hypothesis—in West Germany. *International Journal of Industrial Organisation* 1, no. 1:3–62.

Capie, Forrest. 1994. *Tariffs and growth: Some insights from the world economy, 1850–1940.* Manchester: Manchester University Press.

Cassis, Youssef. 1997. *Big business: The European experience in the twentieth century.* Oxford: Oxford University Press.

Central Statistical Office. 1992. *Monthly review of external trade statistics: Annual supplement.* No. 13. London: Government Statistical Service.

Chandler, Alfred D., Jr. 1962. *Strategy and structure: Chapters in the history of the American industrial enterprise.* Cambridge: MIT Press.

———. 1990. *Scale and scope: The dynamics of industrial capitalism.* Cambridge, MA: Belknap Press.

Channon, Derek F. 1972. *Strategy and structure of British enterprise.* London: Macmillan.

Daviet, Jean-Pierre. 1988. Some features of concentration in France. In *The concentration process in the entrepreneurial economy since the late 19th century,* ed. Hans Pohl. Stuttgart: Zeitschrift für Unternehmengeschichte.

Field, Alexander J. 1996. The relative productivity of American distribution, 1869–1992. *Research in Economic History* 16:1–37.

Fridenson, Patrick. 1997. France: The relatively slow development of big business in the twentieth century. In *Big business and the wealth of nations,* ed. A. D. Chandler, Jr., F. Amatori, and T. Hikino. Cambridge: Cambridge University Press.

Fruin, W. Mark. 1992. *The Japanese enterprise system: Competitive strategies and cooperative structures.* Oxford: Clarendon Press.

Geroski, Paul A., and Alexis Jacquemin. 1988. The persistence of profits: A European comparison. *Economic Journal* 98 (June): 375–89.

Geroski, Paul A., and Dennis C. Mueller. 1996. *The dynamics of company profits: An international perspective.* Cambridge: Cambridge University Press.

Hamel, G., and C. K. Prahalad. 1994. Competing for the future. *Harvard Business Review* 72, no. 4:122–30.

Hannah, Leslie. 1974. Mergers in British manufacturing industry, 1880–1918. *Oxford Economic Papers* 26.

———. 1976. Strategy and structure in the manufacturing sector. In *Management strategy and business development,* ed. Leslie Hannah. London: Macmillan.

———. 1995a. The American miracle, 1875–1950, and after: A view in the European mirror. *Business and Economic History* 24, no. 2:197–263.

———. 1995b. The joint stock company, concentration, and the state, 1894–1994. In *Proceedings of the Annual Conference 1994,* ed. Adrian Allan. London: Business Archives Council.

———. 1996. Multinationality: Size of firm, size of country, and history dependence. *Business and Economic History* 25:144–54.

———. 1998. The world's largest industrial firms, 1912, 1937, 1962, and 1987. Unpublished paper.

Hannan, M. T., and J. Freeman. 1984. Structural interaction and organisational change. *American Sociological Review* 49:149–64.

Harris Corporation. 1996. Founding dates of the 1994 Fortune 500 U.S. companies. *Business History Review* 70 (spring): 69–90.

Henderson, Rebecca M., and Kim B. Clark. 1990. Architectural innovation: The configuration of existing product technologies and the failure of established firms. *Administrative Science Quarterly* 35, no. 201:9–30.

Hounshell, David A., and John Kenly Smith, Jr. 1988. *Science and corporate strategy: Du Pont R&D, 1902–1980.* New York: Cambridge University Press.

Ingham, Hilary. 1992. Organisational structure and firm performance: An intertemporal perspective. *Journal of Economic Studies* 19, no. 5:19–35.

Jeffreys, J. B. 1938. *Business organisation in Great Britain, 1850–1914.* Reprint, New York: Arno Press, 1977.

Jensen, Michael. 1993. The modern industrial revolution, exit, and the failure of international control systems. Harvard Business School Working Paper, May. Quoted in *Economist,* Another Victory for Myopia, 2 December 1995, 111.

Kay, John. 1993. *Foundations of corporate sources: How business strategies add value.* Oxford: Oxford University Press.

Kleinschmidt, Christian, and Thomas Welskopp. 1993. Zu viel "Scale" zu wenig "Scope": Ein Auseinandersetzung mit Alfred D. Chandlers Analyse der deutschen Eisen und Stahlindustrie in der Zwischenkriegzeit. *Jahrbuch für Wirtschaftsgeschichte* 2:251–97.

Knight, Michael J. 1995. Organization and coordination in geographically concentrated industries. In *Coordination and information: Historical perspectives on the organization of enterprise,* ed. Naomi R. Lamoreaux and Daniel M. G. Raff. Chicago: University of Chicago Press.

Kocka, Jürgen. 1978. Entrepreneurs and managers in German industrialisation. In *The Cambridge economic history of Europe,* vol. 7, *The industrial economies: Capital, labour, and enterprise,* part 1, *Britain, France, Germany, and Scandinavia,* ed. Peter Mathias and M. M. Postan. Cambridge: Cambridge University Press.

Kocka, Jürgen, and Hannes Siegrist. 1979. The hundred largest German industrial corporations, late 19th and early 20th centuries: Expansion, diversification, and integration in comparative perspective. In *Law and the formation of big enterprises in the 19th and early 20th centuries,* ed. Norbert Horn and Jürgen Kocka, 55–122. Göttingen: Vandenhoeck and Ruprecht.

Kogut, Bruce, ed. 1993. *Country competitiveness: Technology and the organizing of work.* New York: Oxford University Press.

Kogut, Bruce, and David Parkinson. 1993. The diffusion of American organizing principles to Europe. In *Country Competitiveness,* ed. Bruce Kogut. New York: Oxford University Press.

Kono, T. 1980. *Strategy and structure of Japanese enterprise*. London: Macmillan.

Lamoreaux, Naomi R. 1985. *The great merger movement in American business, 1895–1904*. New York: Cambridge University Press.

Lazonick, William. 1991. *Business organisation and the myth of the market economy*. New York: Cambridge University Press.

Levy-Leboyer, Maurice. 1980. The large corporation in modern France. In *Managerial hierarchies: Comparative perspectives on the rise of modern industrial enterprise*, ed. A. D. Chandler and H. Daems, 117–60. Cambridge: Harvard University Press.

Lieberman, Marvin B., and David B. Montgomery. 1988. First-mover advantages. *Strategic Management Journal* 9:41–58.

Livermore, Shaw. 1935. The success of industrial mergers. *Quarterly Journal of Economics* 50:68–96.

Maddison, Angus. 1989. *The world economy in the twentieth century*. Paris: OECD.

Marshall, Alfred. 1961. *Principles of economics*. Variorum edition. Ed. C. W. Guillebaud. London: Macmillan.

Meyer, Edgar J. 1910. Industrial stocks as investments. *Annals of the American Academy of Political and Social Science* 35 (May).

Morikawa, Hidemasa. 1992. *Zaibatsu: The rise and fall of family enterprise groups in Japan*. Tokyo: University of Tokyo Press.

Pavan, R. J. 1970. Strategy and structure in Italian enterprise. Ph.D. diss., Harvard Business School.

Piore, M. J., and C. F. Sabel. 1984. *The second industrial divide*. New York: Basic Books.

Pooley-Dyas, Gareth, and Heinz T. Thanheiser. 1976. *The emerging European enterprise: Strategy and structure in French and German industry*. London: Macmillan.

Porter, Michael E. 1990. *The competitive advantage of nations*. London: Macmillan.

Registrar-General. 1914. *English life tables*. Cd. 7512.

Rumelt, Richard P. 1974. *Strategy, structure, and economic performance*. Cambridge: Graduate School of Business Administration, Harvard University.

———. 1991. How much does industry matter? *Strategic Management Journal* 12: 167–85.

Samber, Mark. 1996. Firm Behaviour and Financial Panic in an Industrial District. Paper presented at conference, Business History, 18–19 October, National Bureau of Economic Research, Cambridge, MA.

Schmalensee, R. 1985. Do markets differ much? *American Economic Review* 75, no. 2:341–51.

Schmitz, Christopher. 1995. The world's largest industrial companies of 1912. *Business History* (October): 85–96.

Shannon, H. A. 1933. The limited liability companies of 1866–1883. *Economic History Review* 4:290–316.

Shaw, Christine. 1983. The large manufacturing employers of 1907. *Business History* 25:42–60.

Steer, Peter, and John Cable. 1978. Internal organisation and profit: An empirical analysis of large UK companies. *Journal of Industrial Economics* 27 (September): 13–29.

Stigler, George J. 1968. The dominant firm and the inverted umbrella. In *The Organization of Industry*. Homewood, IL: Richard D. Irwin.

Suzuki, Yoshitaka. 1991. *Japanese management structures, 1920–1980*. London: Macmillan.

Teece, David J. 1993. The dynamics of industrial capitalism: Perspectives on Alfred Chandler's *Scale and scope*. *Journal of Economic Literature* 31 (March): 199–225.

Tilly, Richard. 1982. Mergers, external growth, and finance in the development of the large-scale enterprise in Germany, 1880–1913. *Journal of Economic History* 42: 629–58.

Tyszynski, H. 1951. World trade in manufactured commodities, 1899–1950. *Manchester School of Economic and Social Studies* 19, no. 3:272–304.
Whittington, Richard, Michael Mayer, and Francesco Curto. Forthcoming. Back to Harvard: Strategy, structure, and performance in contemporary Europe. In *Proceedings of the British Academy of Management Conference.*

Comment   Bruce Kogut

Leslie Hannah's paper is one of a few solitary gulls flying in the midst of the storm of protest against the fascination of the large firm in business history over the past few decades. Since a good deal of the storm is also no other than Hannah, the paper provides an excellent venue to take a perspective of the issues.[1] The target of the attack is not simply the interpretation placed by Alfred Chandler on the British "failure" due to personal capitalism, but the facile reasoning by which careful academics and less than careful pliers of the trade in the auctioning of ideas have come to associate size with success, a success dressed up with the honey glaze of "organizational capabilities."

There is not madness in the idea that big means good. Countries such as the United States, France, Japan, Germany, and the United Kingdom are rich, and they have what Prais has called "giant" enterprises. This generation of big firms, moreover, has appeared to lead to ever larger shares of their national economies. Table 7C.1 gives a summary of the data, and the data are simply very impressive. Since these countries differ in their per capita incomes and since these big firms play such a large role in their economies, it is entirely reasonable to conclude that a good part of the explanation for country differences must lie in the capabilities of their large enterprises.

Hannah wants rightfully to rethink this conclusion. Business historians may wince at the implications. For if governments would rather nationalize big companies than many small ones, academics prefer to study them for the same reason. "I wish the Roman people had but a single neck," Hannah writes, citing Caligula. The population of small and medium-size business firms is large; Marshall (1921) estimated the U.K. manufacturing population to be 45.8 percent in 1901. We applaud the accomplishment, even if not to the satisfaction of all, of Chandler tracking the records of 200 companies for each of his three countries. Nevertheless, he left out hundreds of thousands of other firms, including innovative small firms, breweries, and pubs. It is not surprising that researchers have preferred the histories of large firms, but a principal message of Hannah's story is that small and medium-size firms are essential parts of the comparison among countries. I return to this point below.

Bruce Kogut is the Felix Zandman Professor of Management and codirector of the Reginald H. Jones Center at the Wharton School of the University of Pennsylvania.

1. See, for example, Hannah (1995).

Table 7C.1   Share of Industrial Output by Hundred Largest Firms (percentage)

Country	~1915	~1950	~1970
France	16	25	40
	(1912)	(1955)	(1970)
Germany		22	46
		(1949)	(1966)
Japan		39	34
		(1950)	(1980)
United Kingdom	16	21	41
	(1909)	(1949)	(1968)
United States	22	30	33
	(1909)	(1954)	(1970)

Sources: For France, Daviet (1988); for Germany and Japan, Suzuki (1991); for the United Kingdom and the United States, Prais (1976).

Let's put aside for now the implications and consider the critical thesis. Hannah suggests that the virtuous association of size and capabilities should be subjected to analysis. In this regard, he has hit upon a fundamental point of confusion in the studies of large firms, namely, that the cross-section of the largest firms tends to obscure a survivor bias. Take a cross-section at any point of time and large firms are revealed. The important issue is why some large firms grow and prosper and others dwindle and, sometimes, die.

To initiate this analysis, Hannah creates a list of the hundred largest firms in several advanced industrialized countries for 1912, and then compares their capitalization against survivors for 1995. In this exercise, he makes some assumptions, such as the use of the U.S. Standard and Poor's deflator for all countries, a crude pass that one suspects nevertheless goes a long way to make the data for the years 1912 and 1995 comparable. The findings indicate the following: (1) Only one-half of the large firms avoided merger, liquidation, or nationalization.[2] (2) Big firms in the United Kingdom survive more often than those in the United States.

The first result casts doubt on the value of first-mover advantages over a long period of time. Of course, the period is eighty-three years. Wars have occurred, boundaries have changed, and dividends have been paid. Still, it is fair to ask, given the assumption that size matters, what is the story of survival and growth? The answer is that 21 percent of the firms listed in 1912 were still in the top hundred in 1995, and over half were still alive. Two-thirds of the large firms failed to keep up with the movement in the overall market.

These conclusions are not unlike those of other studies on sustainable advantage. Pankaj Ghemawat (1991) took 692 businesses from the Profit Impact of Market Share database, split into two samples for 1971 ROI. Sample 1 was

2. We can quibble over the significance of ignoring the distinction between debt and equity in market capitalization and the difference in liquidation versus nationalization.

39 percent, sample 2 was 3 percent. In 1980, it was 21.5 percent and 18.0 percent. What is true at the business level applies also at the corporate level. Not only are corporate effects on business profits hard to identify (Rumelt 1991), past innovative success is a poor predictor of future success (Mansfield 1963).

Given these sorts of baselines, it is not surprising that there is considerable reversion to the mean, if not outright reversal. Without information on the annual average changes and their variance, it is hard to calculate the expected distribution. Moreover, since there is considerable industry variation, one would expect that firms in older industries would face less attractive growth opportunities than those found in newer industries. In fact, Hannah finds evidence for this. Yet Burmah Oil, Procter and Gamble, ARCO, and Du Pont accounted for about a fourth of the total relative growth in the population. These outliers might represent spontaneous drift, or superior "organizational capabilities." The presence of three in the petroleum and petrochemical industries suggests also a simple market-opportunity story.

The second result, as listed above, argues against the statement that the United Kingdom lost relative ground due to the failures inherent in personal capitalism. Contrary to Hannah's finding that nationality is not a significant variable in the performance of large corporations, his data show that U.K. membership was a decidedly significant asset. Table 7.2 indicates that only 17 percent of the U.S. firms survived in the top one hundred of 1995; German and British firms evinced survival rates of 29 percent and 47 percent, respectively. The rate of survival in any independent form, however, was more tightly grouped, with British firms showing the *best* rate (60 percent), and the U.S., the *worst* (48 percent).

Hannah offers the speculation that British firms were hardened by a more open economy in 1912, while German and American firms were overprotected. Of course, British productivity growth ranked behind its major competitors prior to 1913 and was second to last from 1913 to 1929; Weimar Germany did worse. From a position of 25 percent of world trade in 1925, it fell to 12 percent by 1929.

There is a more conventional complaint to be made against the use of size. To what extent can we say that growth in size is an indication of success? What happened to the Hannah (and Kay) of 1977 who, taking on the dragon of spontaneous drift (the argument that the tendency toward large-firm concentration is an outcome of a random log-normal process), found that four-fifths of the growth of British large business was due to mergers and acquisition? Surely, Chandler's wild goose chase (one suspects he would have preferred ducks as the hunting target) did not entail the rounding up of bulimic giants who grew by their appetites rather than by their wits.

Size is interesting in a few ways directly, but it is mostly interesting as part of a larger drama. There is little evidence that size is clearly associated with scale economies. In the famous study by Rostas (1948) comparing U.S. and

U.K. productivity, no evidence was found for scale economies leading to productivity; even though the United States led absolutely in productivity for all industries, the United Kingdom frequently had larger plants when measured by unit output. Similarly, Prais (1976) found essentially no evidence for scale.

However, we do know that the industry distribution of firm sizes is correlated among countries, as are concentration rates. I normalized the data taken from Chandler's appendices, creating Z-scores for each firm in a given country (Kogut 1992). Regressing these scores on industry dummies generated coefficients that indicate the effect of membership in a given industry on a member firm's size. These industry coefficients are highly correlated across countries, and their correlations increased over the three panels (approximately 1912, 1936, 1950). Extending this analysis to Japan and France generates similar results. In short, Chandler's claim that variations in technical conditions lead to large firms in some industries and not others is consistent with these results. And it is not a terribly bad story, given its simplicity and the magnitude of the problem, to claim that the United States and Germany often led the exploration of these technical possibilities in the new industries of chemical, electrical equipment, and transportation.

It is a story, however, that is frequently puzzling. For example, contemporary observers in Europe often claimed that their national markets did not support the scale economies found in the United States, hence the causes of their weakness. Yet American firms were increasingly important investors in Europe; many of these firms were not large, and even when large, their plants were often not unusually large (Kogut 1992). What American firms embodied was a kind of knowledge, call it national organizing principles, that had developed steadily and cumulatively over the course of a century of experience (Hounshell 1984). To read the reports of the productivity missions from France and England to the United States is a test of will to endure long accounts of what appears to be common sense; the pages are filled with minute description of the routinization of work that was, strikingly, often absent in the European factories.

The ambiguity of size is, of course, that big size is as likely to be the outcome of firms who know how to do it better as to represent a source of advantage itself. Now, if size was the first-mover advantage, then Hannah should be finding more powerful evidence for sustainable advantage. But if size is the outcome of an unobserved advantage (be it organizational capabilities, patented technology, or government contracts), then a firm's duration is contingent on the evolution of its broader competitive and institutional landscape.

This broader landscape consists of firms, workers (sometimes organized in unions), governments, political interests, research centers, suppliers and buyers, idea merchants, and, of course, mechanisms of financial intermediation and corporate governance. To think of big firms as the engines of growth is not silly. The economic development of Korea, Malaysia, India, Mexico, and many other countries suggests that big firms are an integral part of the process. Some, such as Amsden and Hikino (1994), point to this recapitulation as evidence of technical efficiency.

Large firms arise in industrializing markets because the diffusion of managerial knowledge is unevenly distributed across the space of firms, regions, and nations. Smith was right, and Stigler echoed this theme. The encapsulation of economic knowledge in the organizing principle of the division of labor was a source of British industrial strength. Where it was absent in other countries, it would have to be created. Stigler noted the same, adding that this division of labor would be recreated through the greater vertical integration of firms in countries where development was lagging.

In the 1800s, institutions of labor, finance, and suppliers were weak, as if the industrial landscape was unpopulated. The explosion of powerful new technologies opened up these vistas for exploration. Large firms represented peninsulas of competence jutting into the unorganized space of economic relations in rapid transition; they also represented powerful political counterweights to governments, often intervening, often corrupt. This was the Cambrian explosion in the exploration of organizational form in the absence of organizing templates.

The boundaries of nations, like the boundaries of firms, are meaningful. The simple reason is that governments make laws and levy revenues. But nations are also characterized by the systemic interdependence of labor markets, managerial hierarchies, governance and financial intermediation, and product market competition. (See, for example, Soskice 1990.)

Consider, for example, France, for which Houssiaux (1957) has made an especially exhaustive study of the emergence of large firms. He compiled a list of the largest stock firms for 1912, based on their total assets. He followed their evolution through successive panels conducted for 1936 and 1952.

There are a few minor, but still informative, points to observe. First, because Houssiaux did not restrict his attention to manufacturing firms, his list for 1912 shows a surprising dominance of mining firms (as notes Hannah in his list) but also of maritime transportation companies, department stores (e.g., Printemps), and water companies; to this day, the Compagnie Générale des Eaux remains a remarkable company, large, multinational, and never nationalized. Also, France, like the United Kingdom, was unusually strong in food and beverage sectors, though its success in these areas is less provoking of bewilderment.

Second, the French firms evidenced a reasonably strong stability, despite a very difficult period from 1929 to 1945. Table 7C.2 reproduces Houssiaux's findings (1957, 295). Houssiaux concludes that "this rate of mortality confirms the hypothesis of the stability of the large enterprises."

The riposte is to concentrate on the list for 1952, for which it is noticed that seventy-two firms are older than thirty years. (Houssiaux dates age from the time of incorporation, which can underestimate age considerably, especially for firms founded in the previous century.) Eight firms are dated to be less than

Table 7C.2   **Mortality of the Hundred Largest Firms in 1912**

	1912–36	1936–52	1912–52
Unchanged	77	92	69
Merger, restructured	12	7	16
Dissolved	11	1	15

ten years old. But these, Houssiaux notes, were descendants or were founded by the largest firms.

It is in this small observation of the entrepreneurial ties among the firms that the contrast between focusing on firm size or focusing on systemic relations is clearly drawn. In 1952, Houssiaux (1957, 794) notes, the portfolio investments (poste) of the hundred largest French companies rose to more than 200 billion francs, while their gross assets had a value of 237 billion francs. These enterprises had 900 known financial ties, averaging 9 ties per firm. One hundred twenty-seven of these ties tied these hundred to each other. Their administrators, numbering 975, disposed of a total of 3,120 board seats. "In spite of a production structure that was too little concentrated," concluded Houssiaux, "the most essential businesses in France is under the control more or less directly by the largest companies." Nor has the importance of industrial groups in France declined, as witnessed in the persistence of current studies.

The significance of understanding the firm in relation to its environment does not only imply the importance of interfirm ties. One of the most troubling periods in German economic history was the collapse of the traditional craft institutions during the Weimar Republic. The inflation had led to a compression in wages, and the introduction of techniques of mass production threatened to diminish the attractiveness of attaining craft skills. The number of apprentices fell compared to the prewar years, and the system was not repaired until the 1930s. The impact of these strains is starkly evident in the data on productivity, and is reflected in Hannah's observations on the low stability of German enterprises during the interwar period (see his footnote 28). The weakness of German firms was partly the consequence of the breakdown of Weimar labor institutions. Large firms provided critical support to these institutions; their hesitations, especially given the experiences of the revolutionary period just after World War I, were a major source for the breakdown in the education and advancement of skilled workers in the 1920s.

In other countries, the dominance of large firms hides a dynamic small-firm sector. (See footnote 18 in Hannah's chapter.) To leave aside the familiar example of Italy, Sweden of the interwar period revealed an unusual dynamism despite the depression. Dahmen (1950, 420) reports that between one-third and one-half of the workers employed in 1939 belonged to firms started after 1918. Behind the success of a Volvo or Asea were the foundings of many small firms that served as suppliers and sources of funding. Again, large firms rise to prominence because of their instrumental role in national innovatory networks.

In all, the most important implication of Hannah's analysis, as he notes in his conclusions, is that the comparison among countries must look at the entrepreneurial conditions for the emergence of new firms. In this regard, the higher mortality rate of American firms is an indication of a healthy entrepreneurial climate. Should it be cause of celebration that almost half of British firms in 1912 still make the top one hundred list some eighty-three years later?[3] If there is weakness in the British performance of this closing century, it is odd to fault the large corporation for its survival rather than look for causes on the shop floor, or at the small and medium-size portion of the distribution. No doubt the appeal of Caligula's maxim for academic research explains the hesitation of business and economic historians to take the plunge into a historical analysis of small-firm birth and growth.

If Hannah is right that Chandler rode off, like the uncle in *Tristram Shandy*, on his hobbyhorse, only to have the horse return riderless, then attention paid to the large firms in this paper has nevertheless paid handsome dividends. The substance of Hannah's investigation into firm size fits a bit the irony Isaiah Berlin noted about Marx, that the success of his ideas in the world offered his own contradiction. The study of big firms remains a good horse to ride, even if the interpretative landscape has radically changed.

References

Amsden, Alice H., and Takashi Hikino. 1994. Project Execution Capability, Organizational Know-How, and Conglomerate Corporate Growth in Late Industrialization. *Industrial and Corporate Change* 3:111–47.

Dahmen, Erik. 1950. *Svensk Industriell foretagarversamhet.* Stockholm: Industrins Utredningsinstitut.

Daviet, Jean Pierre. 1988. Some Features of Concentration in France, End of the 19th/20th Centuries. In *The Concentration Process in the Entrepreneurial Economy since the Late 19th Century,* ed. Hans Pohl and Wilhelm Treue. Stuttgart: Franz Steiner Verlag Wiesboden.

Ghemawat, Pankaj. 1991. *Commitment: The Dynamic of Strategy.* New York: Free Press.

Hannah, Leslie. 1995. Afterthoughts. *Business and Economic History* 24 (winter): 246–62.

Hannah, Leslie, and John Kay. 1977. *Concentration in Modern Industry: Theory, Measurement, and the U.K. Experience.* London: Macmillan.

Hounshell, David. 1984. *From the American System to Mass Production, 1800–1932.* Baltimore: Johns Hopkins University Press.

Houssiaux, Jacques. 1957. *Le Pouvoir de Monopole.* Paris: Sirey.

Kogut, Bruce. 1992. National Organizing Principles of Work and the Erstwhile Dominance of the American Multinational Corporation. *Industrial and Corporate Change* 1:285–325.

Mansfield, Edwin. 1963. The Speed and Response of Firms to New Techniques. *Quarterly Journal of Economics* 77:290–310.

---

3. One can, in this respect, empathize with Hannah's lack of restraint in noting that respect should be reserved for modest strategic management consultants.

Marshall, Alfred. 1921. *Industry and Trade: A Study of Industrial Technique and Business Organization, and of Their Influences on the Conditions of Various Classes and Nations.* London: Macmillan.

Prais, S. J. 1976. *The Evolution of Giant Firms in Britain.* Cambridge: Cambridge University Press.

Rostas, L. 1948. *Comparative Productivity in British and American Industry.* Cambridge: Cambridge University Press.

Rumelt, Richard. 1991. How Much Does Industry Matter? *Strategic Management Journal* 12:167–85.

Soskice, David. 1990. Wage Determination: The Changing Role of Institutions in Advanced Industrialized Countries. *Oxford Review of Economic Policy* 6:36–61.

Suzuki, Yoshitaka. 1991. *Japanese Management Structures, 1920–1980.* New York: St. Martin's.

8 Can a Nation Learn?
American Technology as
a Network Phenomenon

Gavin Wright

What is the relationship between the performance of business firms and the growth of the national economy? Economists who study economic growth commonly treat nations themselves as the performing units that save, invest, and experience technological change. But business historians following the lead of Alfred Chandler often imply that the record of the national economy is not much more than the aggregation of the successes and failures of its major corporations. To quote Chandler (1994, 57): "First, and most important, the United States is not going the way of the United Kingdom in terms of long-term competitive strength. . . . Today American companies remain powerful competitors in the most dynamic and transforming industries of the late twentieth century."

To resolve this dichotomy, we have to ask who does the learning that constitutes technological progress for the economy, and how that knowledge is accumulated and implemented over time. With specific reference to the American surge into world economic leadership in the decades bracketing the turn of the twentieth century, this paper advances two propositions: First, that technological progress was a network phenomenon, growing out of the actions of large numbers of interacting people—not necessarily in formally structured institutions of coordination. Second, that these networks were strongly national in character. An implication is that American industrial firms were able to institutionalize research and development systems after 1900, in large part because

Gavin Wright is the William Robertson Coe Professor of American Economic History at Stanford University.

The author would like to thank the organizers (Naomi Lamoreaux, Daniel M. G. Raff, and Peter Temin) for inviting and encouraging this paper. Critical readings by Alexander Field and the other conference participants are greatly appreciated. Useful suggestions were also received from Nate Rosenberg and the members of the Economic Growth Program of the Canadian Institute for Advanced Research, and from the anonymous reader for the University of Chicago Press.

they could draw upon, extend, and channel the energies of previously existing technological networks. In a real sense the learning was national.

The term "network" has many valid meanings in economics. It may refer to a physically connected infrastructural system, such as railroads or pipelines, or by extension to an established pattern of interfirm supply relationships. As used by sociologists, "networks" are extrafirm linkages among business leaders, based on common social backgrounds and political interests over extended periods (Granovetter 1995). The usage here is broader and perhaps less precise, a technological learning network composed of people who are not necessarily acquainted with each other personally, but who share a common technical language and problem-solving environment—an "invisible college" in the language of the history of science (Price 1963, 85). The premise is that technology is not simply a body of abstract information, but is inherently social, embedded in terminology, in procedures, in physical equipment, and in products.

The point of this conceptualization is to try to draw insights from the analogy to interdependent physical systems, in which technological choices are affected by "network externalities." Most technological progress entails network externalities in that it builds upon an installed base of existing technology and improves some aspect of that base incrementally. Processes of this sort are subject to increasing returns to scale, multiple equilibria, and path dependence, in that historical events may have lasting effects on future developments.[1] Technological spillovers at the local or regional level have been conceptually familiar since Marshall (1920), and confirmed empirically with modern data (Jaffe, Trajtenberg, and Henderson 1993). This paper goes further, and argues that major historical spillovers were national. Although it would hardly be appropriate to say that the American economy became "locked in" at an early point to particular techniques of production, the paper contends that certain features of the process of technological change were distinctively national, and persisted across the vast organizational and scientific space dividing the nineteenth and twentieth centuries.

The paper begins by establishing that American economic growth in the nineteenth century did entail learning, and that this learning was substantially a national network phenomenon. The first of these assertions may seem trivially obvious, but it requires special attention here because of the practice now entrenched among economists of equating "learning" with changes in "total factor productivity," also known as the "residual." As will be argued, collective national learning may reside just as much in the discovery, expansion, and accumulation of the factors of production as in their productivity. Following the lead of Abramovitz and David (1973, 432), "Our point is that there may be *more* to technological change than the residual can capture, rather than less" (italics added).

---

1. The recent economic history literature on these topics begins with David (1985) and Arthur (1989). A theoretical review may be found in Katz and Shapiro (1994).

Pursuing this theme, subsequent sections focus, not on the rationality of technological choices (a preoccupation of much of the New Economic History), but on its network character. The venerable example of ring versus mule spinning in cotton textile technology is used as an example. The argument is then applied to minerals, building on evidence that the United States was far ahead of the rest of the world in resource development, and that these sectors drew increasingly upon advanced forms of knowledge and expertise. The following section identifies elements of continuity between these nineteenth-century patterns and the organized science-based industrial research technologies that arose after 1900. A salient feature of both regimes was the persistence of collective learning beyond the boundaries of sponsoring firms. A concluding section speculates on the implications of modern research institutions for national learning networks.

8.1   Dimensions of American Economic Performance

On one reading of American economic history, there is nothing to be explained. According to Angus Maddison's figures, the United States overtook the United Kingdom in gross domestic product per capita or per work hour around 1890, and moved into a position of world leadership for the subsequent century. But perhaps these events were only a reflection of favorable natural conditions and the rapid growth of factors of production, as opposed to technological progress. The historian Paul Kennedy (1987, 242–43) has written:

> With the Civil War over, the United States was able to exploit [its] many advantages—rich agricultural land, vast raw materials, and the marvelously convenient evolution of modern technology (railways, the steam engine, mining equipment) to develop such resources; the lack of social and geographic constraints; the absence of significant foreign dangers; the flow of foreign and, increasingly, domestic capital—to transform itself at a stunning pace. . . . Indeed, given the advantages listed above, there was a virtual inevitability to the whole process. That is to say, only persistent human ineptitude, or near-constant civil war, or a climatic disaster could have checked this expansion—or deterred the millions of immigrants who flowed across the Atlantic to get their share of the pot of gold and to swell the productive labor force.

Economists might find confirmation of this account in standard macroeconomic data, at least if they have become habituated to dividing growth into parts attributable to "expansion of inputs" on the one hand, and "technological progress" on the other. Not only did the United States enjoy a rapid increase in the size of its territory and population, but between 1890 and 1910 its rate of gross nonresidential capital formation was the highest in the world, culminating a century-long increase (Maddison 1991, 41). In this view, only in the twentieth century did the country experience knowledge-based economic growth—perhaps generated by the newly organized research efforts of modern

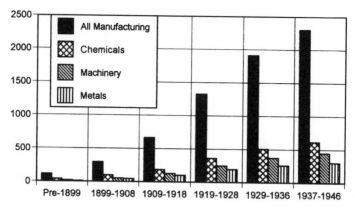

Fig. 8.1   Cumulative laboratory foundations in U.S. manufacturing
Source: Mowery and Rosenberg (1989, table 4.1).

business enterprises (fig. 8.1). By international standards, however, American leadership in science was long delayed. As late as 1940, the United States ranked a poor fourth to the United Kingdom, Germany, and France as a cumulative winner of Nobel Prizes in physics and chemistry (fig. 8.2).

To press this view further, Steven Broadberry's new estimates of productivity in manufacturing show that the United States maintained roughly a 2:1 lead over Britain and Germany in this sector as early as 1869, perhaps as far back as 1840 or even earlier (Broadberry 1993, 1994a, 1994b). The rise of the United States in world rankings could not therefore have come from an acceleration of relative productivity growth in manufacturing, despite the emphasis on that sector in much of the literature. Broadberry concludes that U.S. leadership must have originated elsewhere in the economy, and that high relative labor productivity in manufacturing was simply a feature of the environment. The difference between the United States and other leading countries, he suggests, "must surely be due to natural resources" (1994a, 536). Indeed, the United States was the world's largest producer of nearly every one of the major industrial minerals of that era, and Wright (1990) shows that the coefficient of relative resource intensity in American manufacturing exports was actually *increasing* across the period of ascendancy to economic leadership, from 1879 to 1928.

To accept these facts as indications that nineteenth-century American growth involved "no technological progress" or "no learning" would be unwarranted, a triumph of conventional methodology over history and common sense. The rapid expansion of the factors of production was not exogenous to the flow of American history, no more so than the "marvelously convenient evolution of technology." After showing that crude total factor productivity accounts for only about 10 percent of U.S. economic growth in the nineteenth

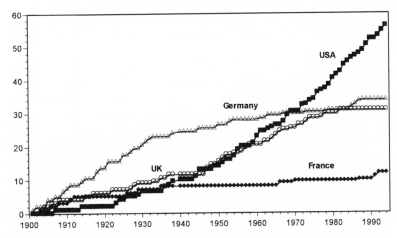

Fig. 8.2   Cumulative Nobel Prizes in physics and chemistry, 1901–94
Source: Nobel Foundation Directory (1995–96).

century, Abramovitz and David (1973) go on to argue that the stimulus to new investments was continually renewed by biased, capital-using, and scale-dependent technological change. Similarly, Olmstead and Rhode (1993) emphasize that the territorial expansion of American agriculture was not simply a replication of existing techniques on additional acreage, but was a vast learning experience in biological adaptation. And as will be argued below, world leadership in mineral production was not primarily the result of a fortunate geological endowment, but represented a return to advances in exploration, training, and the technologies of extraction, refining, and utilization. Only in retrospect was the national ascendancy a "virtual inevitability": clearly many people were gaining new and useful knowledge in nineteenth-century America.

In a sense this view is implicit in the literature on the "American system of manufactures," arising from the interpretive treatments of Habakkuk (1962) and Temin (1966). British engineers visiting the United States in the 1850s were struck by certain novel American technologies in small-arms manufacture and other industries, and economic historians have subsequently struggled to translate these observations into recognizable economic categories. Without attempting to summarize this entire discussion, we may say that one of its results has been a list of identifiable traits that differentiated American from British manufacturing practice. Some examples include

1. Greater use of natural resources relative to both capital and labor (David 1974). Particularly in the early years, American machines and products tended to be made of wood, which was relatively cheap, and the United States became a leader in woodworking (Rosenberg [1981] 1995).

2. The use of special-purpose machinery, allowing long production runs of

standardized commodities (Ames and Rosenberg 1968; Hounshell 1984, chap. 1). These products were adapted to American tastes and to the relatively equal distribution of income.

3. American manufacturing firms operated *faster* than their European counterparts, from machine speeds to the intensity of the work pace (Field 1983; Clark 1987). The intense use of the capital stock was a forerunner of the "high-throughput" systems perfected by large corporate enterprises around the turn of the twentieth century (Chandler 1977).

4. American technology did not necessarily substitute capital for "labor" generally, but deployed machinery to substitute unskilled labor for skilled craft labor (Harley 1974). Early American factories relied heavily on women and child labor, and subsequently on immigrants (Goldin and Sokoloff 1982; Sokoloff 1984). High labor mobility and frequent turnover were the norm, to which mechanization was an adaptation.

Putting these attributes together, and eschewing the fruitless effort to select one of them as the "single bullet" driving all of the others, what mattered most was the emergence in the nineteenth century of an indigenous American technical community, pursuing a learning trajectory to adapt European technologies to the American setting (cf. David 1974, chap. 1; Broadberry 1994b).

Hounshell (1984) throws much cold water on the notion of a continuous American technological thread joining Eli Whitney to Henry Ford, but his book presents numerous examples of individual mechanics who moved repeatedly from one industry to another during their careers, applying a common set of skills and principles to a diverse set of challenges. A notable case is Henry Leland, founder of the Cadillac Motor Car Company, who began in 1863 as an apprentice to a loom builder in Worcester, Massachusetts, moving on to Samuel Colt's armory in Hartford, and then to the sewing-machine section at Browne and Sharpe (p. 81). Through these years of employment, Leland gained a generalized mastery of the cutting-edge machine technologies of that day, to which he in turn contributed. As Rosenberg (1963) has argued, the high mobility of individuals among firms as well as regions, and the flexibility of machinery firms in adapting their skills to new industrial users, constituted a powerful mechanism for diffusing new paradigms throughout the economy. Even for a newer and more science-based technology like the telegraph, Israel (1992) shows that improvements grew largely out of a "shop culture" of practical experience, and many practitioners moved from the operating room into the manufacture of equipment. Other telegraph operators moved on to inventive careers in still newer industries like the telephone and electrical machinery, of whom Thomas Edison was only the most famous.

In a similar spirit, Thomson (1989) recounts the path from the sewing machine to mechanized shoe production at the end of the nineteenth century, tracing the lines of personal and technological linkage in minute detail. Thomson places particular emphasis on the spread of knowledge through networks of trade, or "learning by selling." During the early period of craft production, many improvements originated for the simple motive of self-usage. But the inventions that spread and were refined into an advanced state were those that entered into commodity exchange, greatly widening the circle of diffusion and feedback. Thomson shows that the impetus for technological change in shoe manufactures often came from outside the industry, through the efforts of "cross-over" inventors who saw an opportunity to apply their expertise in a new setting (pp. 185, 203). He concludes: "Established and potential inventors were integrated in a communications network that tied the diffusion and improvement of some machines to the birth and introduction of others. . . . New machines came to sustain their own learning processes, pulled inventors in to improve them, but at the same time generated inventors oriented to other new operations. . . . By the time Goodyear developed its system of machines, it could call on well-established solutions and professional inventors" (pp. 211–12).

8.2   Technological Independence in Cotton Textiles

These generalizations may be illustrated by the case of cotton textiles, the largest early manufacturing industry in both the United States and Britain. Aided by a protective tariff, the New England industry grew rapidly during the 1820s and 1830s on the basis of some famous innovations: the power loom (originally a British invention, but perfected in the United States); integration of spinning and weaving; and the dormitory or Lowell-Waltham system, under which young unmarried women were recruited to work for a few years prior to marriage—an institutional adaptation to labor scarcity. Although the dormitory system disappeared with the advent of mass immigration in the 1840s, in major respects the industry was set on its course of development for the next century.

American and British textiles technologies evolved very differently.[2] In cotton spinning, the two major technological alternatives were the ring and the mule. The mule was a British specialty dating from the eighteenth century, embodying the principle of intermittent spinning: the spindle travels on its carriage while drawing out and spinning the yarn, and then returns to its original position while the yarn is wound. The ring, descended from Arkwright's water frame, was a continuous spinning machine, effecting both spinning and weaving simultaneously. Continuous spinning simplified the machine-tending job, but put extra strain on the cotton fibers and produced a coarser yarn. Over more than one hundred years, the pace of development of these two competing strategies was uneven. The mule was in the ascendancy from the 1830s, following the introduction of the more highly mechanized self-actor. But the self-acting mule never became dominant in the United States, because of ongoing improvements in ring spinning, which increased the operating speed to 5,500

---

2. This section draws upon Saxonhouse and Wright (1984). The best technical account of the evolution of spinning technology is Catling (1970).

Table 8.1   **Ring and Mule Spindles in Place, 1907–8**

	Total Spindles in Place	% Mule	% Ring
United Kingdom	43,154,713	83.6	16.4
United States	23,200,000	17.7	82.3
Germany	9,191,540	55.8	44.2
Russia	7,562,478	50.2	49.8
France	6,609,105	60.0	40.0

Sources: Copeland 1909–10; International Federation of Master Cotton Spinners' and Manufacturers' Associations 1908.

rpm in the 1850s, to 7,500 rpm by the 1870s (the Sawyer spindle), and to 10,000 rpm by 1880 (the Rabbeth spindle). By the 1870s, American mule spinning was on a path to extinction, and by 1907–8 the United States and United Kingdom were at opposite ends of the international spectrum in their commitments to their favored spinning technology (table 8.1).

How can we explain this divergence? Although critics of the British have portrayed their love for the mule as an example of technological backwardness, scholars such as Sandberg (1974) and Lazonick (1981) suggest that the choices of technology were well-suited to initial conditions in the respective countries. Mule spinning was a skilled male occupation, while ring spinning was a machine-tending job that could be performed by girls and young women. Continuous spinning was less flexible, placing more stress on the cotton fibers; hence it was better suited for longer-staple cottons used in long production runs of standardized yarns and cloth. The mule was better adapted to variations in cottons and yarn counts, and thus allowed Lancashire to take advantage of its proximity to the world's largest cotton market in Liverpool, and to produce for diverse markets all over the world. Thus, the original divergence had a reasonably clear economic logic.[3]

For present purposes, the important point is that this logic of divergence became more compelling over time, because of positive feedback from the initial choice of technique to patterns of factor expansion and learning. The British began with a skilled labor force, and extended this "factor endowment" by training new mule spinners, through an informally organized program comprising "migration" (moving from machine to machine, or factory to factory), "following-up" (attaching a young worker to an experienced worker), and "picking up" (an even less formalized mode of learning by observing).[4] The

3. Sandberg's analysis is complementary to that of Harley (1974), stressing the relative scarcity of skilled labor in the United States. Lazonick's interpretation is more institutional, emphasizing both craft unions and vertical specialization between spinning and weaving as factors favoring the mule. Temin (1988) notes the role of the early U.S. tariff structure in channeling production toward the low-quality end of the product spectrum, and hence toward vertical integration and ring spinning.

4. See the account in More (1980, 107–30) and the estimated wage structure in Boot (1995).

American industry began with an unskilled labor force and replaced it many times over with new generations of immigrants. The dexterity and stamina of the factory workforce undoubtedly improved over time, but the primary locus of improvement was in the machinery, which soon came to be produced by specialized firms. These textile-machinery producers continued to improve the performance of ring-spinning machinery through cumulative incremental advance, moving on to the perfection of automatic weaving by the 1880s. Technology coevolved with the structure and labor force of the U.S. industry, including its southward migration as of the late nineteenth century.

Thus the two leading national textile industries came into the twentieth century with sharply contrasting systems. In each country, industry experts believed that theirs was the superior choice. Yet both industries were successful, the two largest in the world before World War I.[5] The "national" character of these choices pertained not just to the identity of the technicians, but to their coevolutionary interaction with domestic textile firms, the primary users.

American textile-machinery manufacturing had important technological linkages to many other branches of the machine-tools industry. As early as the 1830s, machine shops that were initially attached to textile factories began to diversify their product lines into steam engines, turbines, locomotives, and other machine tools. Through a process that Rosenberg (1963) calls "technological convergence," a common body of metalworking and mechanical knowledge came to be applied to a diverse range of industries. In contrast to the bifurcation across national boundaries, a tendency toward standardization within the country was observed very early, promoted both by long-distance sales of specialty firms and by the high geographic mobility of nineteenth-century mechanics. Leading machine-tool firms like the Matteawan Manufacturing Company of Beacon, New York, trained several generations of expert machinists only to find that these "alumni" left to take management positions or to found their own firms in new locations. A study of the careers of ten leading machinists found that they had worked for an average of 5.5 employers in 4.2 industrial centers (Lozier 1986, 33, 202).

8.3 Conceptual Issues

The existence of an American technological network in the nineteenth century seems well established. But what forces or institutions held it together? Why and in what sense was it national? For many years economics has grappled with the question, why does any private operator invest in the generation of new knowledge? To be sure, these investments are productive. But as

---

5. The ironic implication of recent research is that, despite its technological sophistication and leadership in productivity, the U.S. textile industry itself may never have achieved true international competitiveness. For evidence that most of the antebellum industry required tariff protection for survival, see Harley (1992). Yet this industry generated innovations that ultimately set the standard for the world!

formulated most clearly by Arrow (1962), investments in knowledge differ in two fundamental ways from conventional investments: they are subject to severe uncertainty, and even if successful, the discoverer may not be able to appropriate the resulting returns. The textbook conclusion is that market economies will tend to underinvest in knowledge generation.

In grappling with these issues, one must distinguish between "basic" technology on the one hand—pure ideas or information about scientific principles—and applied, or practical technologies on the other, which typically combine abstract ideas with a large component of "know-how," or experience-based knowledge. Uncertainty and appropriability are problems in both cases, but the institutions identified as mitigators of these problems tend to operate most effectively at the applied end of the spectrum: patents or other forms of intellectual property rights; cooperative or nonprofit research institutions; government procurement policy; private market power, existing or potential, which offers the promise of sufficient "first-mover advantages" to reward the investments; large, diversified research portfolios that protect against concentrated risk. Industries with long track records of successful research and development programs are those that have "solved" the uncertainty and appropriability problems through some combination of institutional arrangements like these. For example, Teece (1992) argues that firms investing in new technologies seek to embed their new knowledge deeply in product design, marketing, specific assets, personnel systems, and so forth, to make them as firm-specific as possible.

Yet this list of possibilities seems inadequate to account for nineteenth-century America's enthusiasm for new technologies. The search for patents was sometimes crucial, but many innovations were not patentable, and many patents were difficult to enforce or were subject to protracted and costly litigation. Government demand was important in a few areas like firearms. But neither the size of government nor the size and national market power of the largest private companies were anywhere near what they became in the twentieth century. Where else can we turn?

An article by Robert Allen (1983) considered this question and proposed a mechanism that he called "collective invention." Allen noted the steady incremental progress in the iron and steel industries of England and the United States, along such dimensions as the height of furnaces, the level of blast temperature, and the spread of fast driving. These improvements were not generally patentable, yet the firms involved disseminated all the relevant facts about their latest operating results, and this information in turn became the basis for further improvements elsewhere. The question is why. Allen suggests four possible mechanisms.

1. Owners and managers may have had professional ambitions that would be advanced by publishing information about their firm's operation and performance.

2. Where construction entailed participation by suppliers, contractors, and

consulting engineers, it may have been more difficult to maintain secrecy than to release the information.

3. Releasing information may actually have been profitable, if the firm had a stake in asset values that would be enhanced by dissemination (such as the value of regional mines).

4. Firms may have been party to norms of reciprocity, explicit or implicit, whereby divulging information gave them access to similar information from the other firms in the group.

These mechanisms have many plausible applications to nineteenth-century America. The role of professional ambitions became increasingly important as the century progressed, with the formation of engineering societies and growing interactions between business and universities. But long before "professionalization," skilled mechanics and machinists openly published detailed specifications of their machinery as a form of self-advertising.[6] Hoke (1990, 252) notes the pattern of hiring experienced watchmaking mechanics from established firms, as a mode of spreading a technology lodged in a "subculture of watch factory mechanics." These effects were intensified by the rise of specialized firms and individuals committed to "invention" as their primary occupation (Thomson 1993, 88–93). Whereas a chef with a recipe has reason to keep it secret, a machinery maker with command of a "general purpose technology" has every reason to spread the news and expand the range of its potential customers. Misa (1995) identifies producer-user interaction as the core element in the evolution of a distinctive American steel technology, taking up such examples as railroads, skyscrapers, factories, and automobiles.

A collective interest in property values could also serve as the basis for public or quasi-public support for investments in knowledge. Land-rich Stephen Van Rensselaer sponsored one of the first geological surveys in America in the New York county that bears his name, for obvious economic reasons (Hendrickson 1961, 358). By 1860, twenty-nine of thirty-three state governments had followed his example. The funding of state geological surveys was the leading form of direct aid that state governments provided for science in the antebellum era. In their dual role as landowners and suppliers of transportation services, American railroads also sponsored geological surveys and metallurgical research (Mowery and Rosenberg 1989, 38).

But behind these mechanisms and others that one might cite was an overarching factor serving to enhance their efficacy, namely the *scale* of the national economy. The importance of scale in the incentive structure for innovation is a major implication of models from the new or endogenous growth theory, pioneered by Paul Romer (1986, 1990). We may not be able to identify with precision the microlevel basis for positive returns to new knowledge, but

---

6. For specific examples, see Calvert (1967, 7). Calvert also notes the popularity of the sections in early mechanical-engineering periodicals called "shop kinks" or "shop hints," in which ideas and techniques developed in one shop were broadcast for all interested parties to share.

as Romer (1996, 204) argues, "a nonrival idea can be copied and communicated, so its value increases in proportion to the size of the market in which it can be used. . . . If people can sometimes establish property rights over a nonrival good like an operating system or a recipe . . . differences in scale will change the rewards for producing new ideas." Many of the mechanisms discussed above are scale economies at the industry or national level. Only an economy of sufficient size could support specialized machine-tools firms, inventors, and professional associations. The size of the national economy clearly differentiated the United States from other resource-abundant countries of recent settlement, such as Argentina, Australia, and Canada; and by the mid-nineteenth century, extensive growth was rapidly pushing the United States into a unique total-national-income size bracket.

But scale is a tricky economic concept. Mere bigness counts for little if the regions of the country are not integrated economically; other things equal, longer distances actually reduce the size of the relevant market. Sokoloff (1988) finds that inventive activity as measured by patents tended to concentrate in locations where cheap transportation offered access to larger markets. But even if the costs of distance are reduced by investment in transportation and communication, national "market size" would not be effective as an incentive to innovators unless the country were reasonably homogeneous in its patterns of consumer demand, and in the geographic characteristics to which technological change is adapting. Thus, the question of scale is intimately linked to what might seem to be cultural questions: why and in what sense were the learning networks national in scope? Fundamentally, they were national because the "problem-solving environment" was increasingly national, and this unity of focus reflected the growing integration of national product markets and the high level of internal population mobility across state lines.

Of course this national differentiation had a cultural dimension. A Scottish visitor of 1849–50 complained that American mineralogists disdained to label geological formations with the names of European localities, but insisted on using an independent national terminology (Bruce 1987, 26). But whereas such chauvinism in a small country might have generated isolation and backwardness, for the United States national technological particularity was positively reinforced by the ongoing expansion of the economy and of the relevant technological community along national lines. Scale economies may ultimately reside as much in the way knowledge is organized—the terminology, the conceptual categories, the standardized routines for testing and measurement—as in the incentives facing profit-seeking producers and innovators. But the realm of "ideas" and the realm of "things" were continually interacting. Historians of technology stress that knowledge often diffuses through the spread of producers' goods that physically embody esoteric scientific information and procedures, as in the example of the Prony dynamometer, which was of great importance in the indigenous American development of hydraulic turbines. According to Constant (1983, 186), in contrast to the European practice of custom turbine design, American producers "concentrated on development of cheap but highly efficient, empirically designed 'stock' wheels which could be merchandised like agricultural implements or hardware." By the 1880s, although the technology of turbine design was patentable and proprietary, knowledge about turbine testing was communal and consensual, "the common property of a well-defined community of practitioners" (p. 194).[7] National engineering associations and technical curricula were institutionalizations of the national focus of nineteenth-century technological networks.

An illustration of the advanced state of the American technological community as of the 1880s may be found in the contrasting experience of the South. Although the term "national" has been used to this point as a convenient shorthand, in many ways the South was not a part of the larger national accumulation of knowledge. Regional production problems were different in essential ways, from wage rates, education, and race to the resource base and the climate. But the South did not develop an early indigenous regional technological community, and found that the startup costs of a late beginning were high. When a group of Georgians set out in the 1880s to establish a state school of technology as a spearhead for regional industrial development, they chose the "shop culture" approach of the Worcester Free Institute over the "school culture" approach associated with Boston Tech (later MIT). The result was highly practical "trade school" training, producing "graduates who could work as machinists or as shop foremen, but who were not well prepared for engineering analysis or original research" (McMath 1985, 9). This may have been the only feasible choice at that time.

Even a quarter-century later, when U.S. Steel acquired the largest southern steel producer and embarked on an ambitious project of upgrading and modernization, it encountered a series of unexpected problems in labor costs and discipline, idiosyncrasies in resource quality and conditions of extraction, and problems with product quality control and marketing. After their initial burst of enthusiasm, the company largely neglected its Birmingham interests. Southern nationalists have seen this as part of a conspiracy to keep them down, but a more plausible interpretation is that the company's technological expertise—representative of the emerging "national" technology—was not well suited to conditions in the South (Wright 1986, 156–77).

8.4 American Mineral Development as a Knowledge Industry

One of the earliest and largest American technological networks was focused on exploitation of the nation's mineral potential. Contrary to learned intuition, resource-based development was not "low-tech," and world leadership in mineral production was not primarily based on geological endowment. David and Wright (1997) show that U.S. mineral production as of 1913 was

---

7. See also Layton (1979).

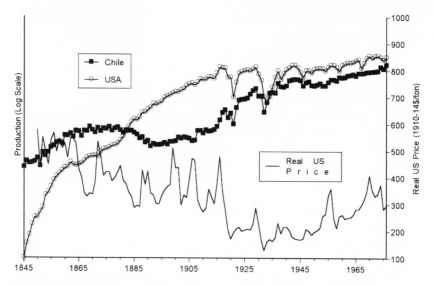

Fig. 8.3   Copper mine production, United States and Chile, and real U.S. price of copper, 1845–1976
Source: Schmitz (1979, 63–78, 270–72).

substantially disproportionate to what we now know to be the country's 1913 share of world mineral reserves. Within a thirty-year period, the United States achieved leadership or near leadership in coal, iron ore, copper, lead, zinc, silver, tungsten, molybdenum, petroleum, arsenic, phosphate, antimony, magnesite, mercury, salt, gold, and bauxite, a degree of simultaneity too extreme to have been coincidental. The example of copper is illustrative (fig. 8.3). Until the 1880s, Chile was the world's leading copper producer, and by the 1930s had nearly recovered its number-one ranking. During the fifty years in between, the action was in the United States.

Developing America's mineral potential was fundamentally a collective learning phenomenon, a return to decades of investment in exploration, transportation, and the knowledge infrastructure of mineral deposits; in training mining engineers and geologists; and in metallurgical revolutions that expanded the range of minerals that could be profitably extracted. Provision of geological information was the initial step. Geologists were among the most conspicuous of those antebellum scientists listed in the *Dictionary of American Biography* (about 14 percent of the total) who drew livelihoods chiefly from private industry rather than government or educational institutions (Bruce 1987, 139). As noted, state geological surveys were the leading form of direct aid for science in the antebellum era. The states supported not only the fieldwork of geologists, but also the publication of their sometimes voluminous reports (pp. 166–67).

Discoveries in the Michigan copper region in the 1840s provide a striking early instance of the role of these surveys and geologists' involvement in exploration and mineral-resource exploitation. A federal survey under the direction of Charles T. Jackson, a leading geologist and chemist in Boston, was completed in 1850, providing the first geological maps adequate to support rational exploration and development work. This venture launched not only the development of these copper fields, but a number of scientific careers. Josiah Whitney, a young protégé of Jackson's who had been sent off to Europe to pursue interests in chemistry, returned in the summer of 1845 to work as a geologist for a mining company. Forsaking chemistry, Whitney soon joined the staff of Jackson's survey in 1847, and within a few years had established himself as a leading industrial consultant. "Making five hundred dollars a month, he could not afford to be a Yale professor" (Bruce 1987, 139–40). His reputation was further enhanced by his publication the following year of *The Metallic Wealth of the United States,* the first comprehensive work on American ore deposits, a book that became widely known and helped him gain a position as director of a state survey for California in 1860.

Despite Whitney's remark about relative salaries, university professors of that era could sometimes be highly entrepreneurial while on the job. An early example was J. P. Lesley, who graduated from the University of Pennsylvania in 1838, and then worked on the first state geological survey.[8] After a decade in the ministry, he published *A Manual of Coal and Its Topography* in 1856, and in the same year became secretary of the American Iron Association. He also worked as a private consultant, and in 1857 his office stationery carried the following letterhead: "Geology and Topography. Geological and other Maps constructed; Surveys of Coal Lands made; Mineral Deposits examined; Geological Opinions given to guide purchasers, and Reports made to Owners and Agents. Orders for elaborate Topographical Surveys from Rail-road and other companies, will be executed in scientific principles, and in the highest style of the art." Two years later he joined the faculty of his alma mater, was made dean of the science department in 1872, and dean of the new Towne Scientific School in 1875. He was librarian, secretary, and vice president of the American Philosophical Society, and a charter member of the National Academy of Sciences. During all this time he continued his consulting activities, traveling in 1863 to Europe for the Pennsylvania Railroad to study the Bessemer steel process. He also served as state geologist, directed the second Pennsylvania geological survey, and for four years edited a weekly newspaper, *United States Railroad and Mining Register.* The overlapping sectoral engagements in Lesley's career vividly illustrate the learning spillovers among mineral exploration, transportation, and industrial development.[9]

With the opening of the trans-Mississippi west after the Civil War, there was

8. This account is adapted from Pursell (1972, 241–45).

9. The chemical labs set up by railroads and steel companies during the 1860s for testing materials were the first scientific laboratories in American industry. See Rosenberg (1985).

a commensurate expansion in the scale of resources committed to geological surveys. A number of ad hoc projects culminated in the establishment of the U.S. Geological Survey in 1879. Under directors Clarence King and J. W. Powell, the Survey emerged as the leading governmental research agency of the nineteenth century. The payoff to its early topographical and metallurgical work had a lasting impact on popular appreciation of the practical benefits of scientific research (Manning 1967, 4–14; Paul 1960; Owen 1975, 225). Although private professional work while on the Survey staff was not permitted, the organization acquired a reputation as an ideal stepping-stone toward career success in the mining sector (Spence 1970, 60). The Survey was particularly effective in changing attitudes toward petroleum geology in the industry, by publishing reliable field data and popularizing the anticlinal theory of the oil-bearing strata—a distinctively American doctrine (Owen 1975, 56, 95). While the major elements of the theory had been worked out before 1900, the discovery in 1911 of the rich Cushing pool in Oklahoma offered tangible evidence of its practical value. For the next fifteen years, most new crude discoveries were based on the surface mapping of anticlines (Williamson et al. 1963, 45–46).

Over roughly this same period, the United States also became the foremost location for education in mining engineering and metallurgy. Until the 1860s, advanced American mining students often attended the Bergakademie in Freiberg, Saxony; but with the founding of the Columbia School of Mines in 1864, enrollments abroad largely ceased. As early as 1871, mining expert John A. Church declared Columbia to be "one of the best schools in the world—more scientific than Freiberg, more practical than Paris" (quoted in Spence 1970, 38). The fact that an institution in New York City was training engineers for work in remote western localities is strong evidence that learning was nationally structured. But by 1893, more than twenty American schools offered degrees in mining (Christy 1893). Enrollment continued to grow over the next ten years or more, especially in the western states. With over 300 students enrolled in its mining college in 1903, the University of California claimed to be "without doubt the largest mining college in the world" (Read 1941, 84). The continuing flow of trained American mining specialists was reflected in a distinctly national professional identity. When the British Institution of Mining and Metallurgy held its first meeting in London in 1892, the organizers "found it more than a little irksome to have to acknowledge that in the United States some such organization had been operating successfully for nearly twenty years" (Wilson 1992, 8–9).

The national identity of mining engineers derived not just from their training within the United States, but from the interaction between mining schools and industry. Columbia organized the Summer School of Practical Mining, which helped students become familiar with working conditions they would meet after graduation. Professor Robert H. Richards perfected the Mining Laboratory, where practical problems in ore dressing and metallurgy could be worked out by students (Christy 1893, 461). Mining engineers increasingly assumed managerial and executive roles within large firms, and this expectation came to be reflected in the curricula of mining schools (Ochs 1992). Herbert Hoover, surely the most famous mining engineer of this era, favored this trend toward combining executive and technical functions, viewing it as an American strength (Hoover 1909, 185–91). The contrast was with the European tradition of training mining engineers to serve as inspectors, and in regulatory positions directing the activities of state mining monopolies. Large mining corporations became increasingly prominent after 1900.[10] Surveys of mining school graduates, however, indicate that most maintained professional independence throughout their careers, taking on a wide range of job assignments and consulting positions, often founding independent companies (Ochs 1992; Spence 1970, 79, 136–39, 275).

Perhaps the best evidence of the distinctive national character of American mining engineers is their role in overseas development. A 1917 manpower census for military purposes counted 7,500 mining engineers, 2,112 of them with working experience in foreign countries. Although Canada and Mexico were the two largest of these, the experience was in fact widely dispersed among the continents of the world (table 8.2). A survey of graduates of the Colorado School of Mines between 1900 and 1940 found that 64 percent had worked abroad at some time, 39 percent for several years (Ochs 1992). The American impact was notable in Australia, where into the 1880s most of the largest mines were managed by Cornishmen, who had much practical experience but were untrained in metallurgy and resistant to the use of new technology. A turning point came with the move in 1886 to recruit highly paid engineers and metallurgists from the Rocky Mountain states, a decision that "linked Australia to a new powerhouse of skills and attitudes" (Blainey 1969, 154, 252). In South Africa, because hard quartz-rock mining required techniques "unknown to most British mining engineers," Americans were offered princely salaries to come and direct mining operations in the 1880s and 1890s. An American served as the state mining engineer in the Transvaal in 1888, another was the first president of the South African Association of Engineers and Architects, and a third was one of the first presidents of the Chemical and Metallurgical Society formed in 1894 (De Waal 1985).

Many of these themes are well illustrated by the case of copper. The early developments in Michigan have been touched upon already; beginning in the 1870s, the national totals were augmented by production from newly discovered deposits in Arizona and Montana, though Michigan production continued to grow absolutely until the 1920s. What truly propelled the industry into the twentieth century, however, was a revolution in metallurgy, overwhelmingly an American technological achievement. In the 1880s and 1890s, the major

---

10. Of the fifty-eight U.S. companies represented in the world's largest hundred as of 1912, nearly one-third were in minerals, including petroleum (Schmitz 1995).

Table 8.2   **Experience in Foreign Countries of U.S. Mining Engineers and Chemists, 1917**

	Mining Engineers	Chemists
Africa	74	13
Australia	46	19
Canada	384	203
Central America	74	15
Cuba	68	60
Europe		
Austria-Hungary	7	24
Belgium	6	6
Denmark	1	19
France	23	38
Great Britain	116	117
Germany	61	231
Holland	2	10
Italy	5	11
Norway-Sweden	19	21
Russia	25	30
Spain	7	5
Switzerland	8	18
Others	22	10
Not specified	101	171
Far East	3	
Greenland	3	
India	11	
Mexico	679	117
Newfoundland	7	
South America	241	34
West Indies	17	32

Source: Fay 1917, 11.

breakthroughs were the adaptation of the Bessemer process to copper converting, and the introduction of electrolysis on a commercial scale for the final refining of copper. The dramatic new development of the first decade of the twentieth century was the successful application of the Jackling method of large-scale, nonselective mining, using highly mechanized techniques to remove all material from the mineralized area, waste as well as metal-bearing ore. Complementary to these techniques, indeed essential to their commercial success, was the use of the oil flotation process in concentrating the ore. Oil flotation called for and made possible extremely fine grinding, which reduced milling losses sufficiently to make exploitation of low-grade "porphyry" coppers economically feasible.[11]

Together these techniques made possible a steady reduction in the average

11. This account draws primarily upon Parsons (1933) and Schmitz (1986, 403–5).

Table 8.3   **Average Yields of Copper Ore (percentage)**

1800	English	9.27
1850	English	7.84
1870–85	English	6.56
1880	United States	3.00
1889	United States	3.32
1902	United States	2.73
1906	United States	2.50
1907	United States	2.11
1908	United States	2.07
1909	United States	1.98
1910	United States	1.88
1911–20	United States	1.66
1921–30	United States	1.53

Sources: Elliott et al. 1937, 374; Leong et al. 1940.

grade of American copper ore, as shown in table 8.3. By contrast, in copper-rich Chile—where output was stagnant—yields averaged 10–13 percent between 1880 and 1910 (Przeworski 1980, 26, 183, 197). From these facts alone, one might infer that the United States had simply pressed its internal margin of extraction further than Chile, into higher-cost ores. But figure 8.3 makes it evident that the real price of copper was *declining* during this very period, confirming that the fall in yields was an indication of technological progress. Indeed, there is an exponential link between the reduction in yield and the expansion of ore reserves, through a formula known to geologists as Lasky's law, an inverse relationship between the grade of ore and the size of the deposit (Lasky 1950). Capital requirements and long time horizons made copper an industry for corporate giants, enterprises that internalized many of the complementarities and spillovers in copper technology (Schmitz 1986). But these firms also drew extensively upon national infrastructural investments in geological knowledge and in the training of mining engineers.

8.5   The Organization of Knowledge: Chemical Engineering as an American Innovation

Textbooks say that, around the turn of the twentieth century, the technologies of the first industrial revolution (steam, coal, and iron) gave way to the more science-based technologies of the second industrial revolution (electricity, chemicals, and internal combustion). The change in underlying science shifted technology from its nineteenth-century demands for tangible capital and resources toward more intangible forms of capital such as knowledge and advanced education (Abramovitz and David 1996). From this vantage point, the rise of the industrial research laboratories depicted in figure 8.1 may be seen as a response to the opportunities created by these new technologies, and a vehicle for propelling them forward.

This description accounts for one aspect of the change between the centuries, but understates the extent to which the new American industries of the twentieth century drew upon the legacy of the nineteenth-century national technological community. To give a few examples:

1. As in the case of copper, the electrolytic metallurgical revolution of the 1890s was an extension of the long drive to develop and exploit the nation's mineral potential. Charles Martin Hall's electrolytic process of 1886 culminated a decades-long "search for cheap aluminum," and instantly raised the value of bauxite, or aluminum ore.[12] From the "worthless" brine under Midland, Michigan, the Dow chemical company was able to manufacture some 150 profitable electrolytic bromine products (Levenstein 1995).

2. Both electrical and chemical industries depended heavily on the nation's long-standing expertise in metal manufactures and metalworking. Having invented cheap aluminum, the forerunner of Alcoa had to draw upon the metallurgical, ingot-casting, and metalworking expertise of the Pittsburgh area, to perfect its manufacturing methods and develop new uses for the product. To facilitate this process, it followed a strategy of publishing its research results in full (Graham and Pruitt 1990, chap. 1). Alcoa and other electrochemicals firms worked closely with machinists and mechanical engineers, because equipment design was critical to their research. Although the Germans were the undisputed world leaders in chemical science before World War I, an informed observer wrote in 1900: "As far as I have been able to judge from my personal experience, the American Manufacturers [sic] are far ahead of all others, and their success has been entirely due to the apparatus employed" (quoted in Trescott 1982, 12).

3. The institutions of higher education and technical training that grew up originally around civil, mechanical, and mining engineering were well positioned to adapt to the new technological order. Trained chemists were employed in industrial laboratories as early as the 1860s, but before 1900 they chiefly worked on routine materials testing, well within the boundaries of frontier science of that time (Rosenberg 1985). Nonetheless, the pattern of academic adaptation to changing industrial demands was well established, in contrast to the traditions of training state engineers in France and Germany (Lundgreen 1990). Well before World War I, the United States became the world leader in years of higher education per capita, notwithstanding its lag in basic science (Maddison 1987, table A-12). Patterns of training and professional specialization also reflected a distinct American style, as illustrated by the rise of chemical engineering.

The origins of the term "chemical engineer" are shrouded in mystery. Some trace it back to antiquity, but an immediate forerunner to U.S. adoption was a

---

12. Trescott (1981) rejects the oft-heard statement that the methods of Hall and his French counterpart, L. T. Héroult, were virtually identical. Hall's method dissolved bauxite, while European methods focused on obtaining aluminum from its halide salts (p. 60).

series of lectures by George E. Davis of Manchester, England, in 1888. Elaboration of the hybrid as a professional specialty was, according to its historians, an American innovation (Guédon 1980; Trescott 1982). Although the nature of the specialty became clarified only some time after its founding, from the beginning the concept was not the same as applied chemistry. In fact, it grew most directly out of mechanical engineering, with a focus on the design, construction, and maintenance of plant and apparatus to perform chemical operations. MIT established its first course in 1888, and was quickly followed by Pennsylvania (1892), Tulane (1894), Wisconsin (1898), Michigan (1898), and many others. The American Institute of Chemical Engineers, a professional association, was founded in 1908.

What came to distinguish chemical engineering was the concept of "unit operations," a term coined by Arthur D. Little in 1915, to refer to the notion of breaking down chemical processes into elemental components such as evaporation, filtration, grinding, crushing, and so on, which had features common to many different chemical contexts. This increase in the level of abstraction and generality gave the core concept something of the effect of a "general-purpose technology."[13] The contrast was with the tradition of chemical analysis, in which the chemist developed an intimate but particularized knowledge of specific substances. Although Little's concept was not codified in the form of a textbook until the 1920s, the codification reflected the practices of industry-university relationships emerging over a more extended period of time (Soros 1980; Trescott 1982; Misa 1985). Certainly a strong orientation toward practical industrial utility was a feature of chemical engineering from the beginning. Indeed, Arthur D. Little was not a faculty member at the time of his 1915 report to the president of MIT, but his consulting firm was an active employer of MIT graduates. Not long after, nearly all the MIT chemical engineering faculty were engaged as consultants or employees in the oil industry (Weber 1980). At MIT and elsewhere, enrollments in the new field grew rapidly (table 8.4).

The most dramatic return to the new professional specialty came with the rise of petrochemicals during the 1920s. Here we truly have a marriage of old and new learning, as the entire technology of petroleum discovery, drilling, refining, and utilization had been an American specialty for nearly a century before. It can also legitimately be considered a return to scale at the national level, because the search for by-products was an outgrowth of the vast American enterprise of petroleum refining. Prior to the 1920s, however, there was little contact between petroleum companies and the chemical industry. With the shift of basic feedstock from coal tar to petroleum, the United States surged into the forefront, building on close university-industry partnerships like that between New Jersey Standard and MIT at the research facility in Baton Rouge, Louisiana (Landau and Rosenberg 1992). As the chemical engineer Peter Spitz

---

13. This analogy is suggested by Rosenberg (1998), with a theoretical citation to Bresnahan and Trajtenberg (1995).

Table 8.4   Baccalaureates Awarded in Chemistry and Chemical Engineering at
                 MIT, 1885–1934

	Chemistry	Chemical Engineering
1885–89	38	—
1890–94	50	31
1895–99	98	49
1900–1904	78	51
1905–19	82	65
1910–14	50	132
1915–19	63	187
1920–24	52	419
1925–29	81	238
1930–34	71	240

Source: Servos 1980, 538.

(1988, xiii) has written: "Regardless of the fact that Europe's chemical industry was for a long time more advanced than that in the United States, the future of organic chemicals was going to be related to petroleum, not coal, as soon as companies such as Union Carbide, Standard Oil (New Jersey), Shell, and Dow turned their attention to the production of petrochemicals." After World War II, the German chemical industry required a substantial institutional and attitudinal readjustment to the petroleum base, which by then had become the world standard (Stokes 1994).

If chemical engineering transformed the configuration by which technological knowledge was accumulated, the discipline itself was transformed by its interactions with institutionalized research programs at major corporations. Du Pont in particular, which launched an ambitious research agenda in basic science beginning in the late 1920s, experienced the inadequacies of the then-current level of rigor in chemical engineering (with the possible exception of MIT). Under the leadership of Allan Colburn and Thomas Chilton, Du Pont contrived to put the discipline on a firmer scientific and mathematical footing. Another Du Pont chemical engineer, John Howard Perry, published the *Chemical Engineer's Handbook* in the 1930s, which sold over 150,000 copies over the next twenty years (Hounshell and Smith 1988, 275–85).

Despite the powerful influence of Du Pont and other large research-oriented companies, scientists maintained an independent professional identity. With academic employment as an option, companies often had to adapt their employment conditions to match the individual freedoms of a university setting (Wise 1980). At Alcoa, researchers were encouraged to "identify closely with their engineering and scientific professions, to attend professional conferences and society meetings, to write papers and generally to keep in touch with things going on in the outside scientific community" (Graham and Pruitt 1990, 203). In his 1926 memo proposing a program of fundamental research at Du

Pont, Charles Stine listed the advantages of recruiting Ph.D.'s as one of the prime reasons, holding out only the *possibility* that the project might lead to practical applications—though in the end it certainly did (Hounshell and Smith 1988, 223). Although company recruiters stressed the advantages of the absence of teaching (!), top research scientists were also eager to publish their findings in professional journals, often a subject of disputes with the company (e.g., p. 238). At Du Pont the most productive research teams did not stay together for more than a few years at a time, because of departures for universities or other employment (pp. 243, 283, 285). Through all its years of success, Du Pont never settled on a lasting institutional solution to these issues (Hounshell 1992).

This is not meant to imply that the entire corporate research enterprise was continually fraught with contradictions and instability. To the contrary, Du Pont's underlying commitment was firm. The point is that the evolution of American technological learning was shaped by the interactions between profit-seeking firms and semi-independent professional scientists, and this fact placed limits on the corporation's ability to appropriate knowledge and channel technologies in their most favored directions. The contrast is with Germany, which resisted chemical engineering as an autonomous discipline until the 1960s, opting instead for a team-based approach to the design of chemical plants and apparatus, combining chemists with mechanical engineers and other specialists (Guédon 1980; Schoenemann 1980). From a technical standpoint this solution may have been just as good. But whether it would have worked in America is doubtful.

What distinguished the U.S. chemical industry internationally was not so much the giant "all around" companies, but the numbers and vitality of smaller, more specialized firms (Arora and Gambardella 1998). The coexistence and complementarity of large and small technology-based firms has been a persistent feature of the United States in major twentieth-century industries.

8.6 Organized Corporate Research and National Learning Networks

If the argument of this paper is correct, it raises the question of what became of American learning networks across the rest of the twentieth century, and specifically what were the implications of organized industrial research for the strong *national* orientation of the networks they inherited. Because these networks were only partly visible and not subject to precise measurement, any proposed account of their changing shape and direction through time must be tentative. But available evidence seems consistent with the view that the first generations of formalized research structures actually intensified the national distinctiveness of American collective learning. Ultimately, however, progress toward increasingly abstract general scientific principles has been a force for the globalization of technological communities.

This conjecture begins with the evident correlation between research laboratories and the rise of large integrated corporations producing primarily for the national market. The essay by Steven Usselman (chap. 2 in this volume) calls attention to the powerful drive toward research coordination in the case of the railroad industry, whose capital stock really did consist of an interconnected national network. But the railroads were an extreme case. Most of the corporate entities that came out of the turn-of-the-century merger wave were oriented toward the national market, and Chandlerian coordination between production and distribution was central to the performance of those that succeeded. The sponsors of early research laboratories were major corporations with market power, such as General Electric, Westinghouse, Du Pont, Eastman Kodak, and AT&T. Indeed, protecting that market power through strategic patent development was in many cases a prime motive for initiating corporate research (Reich 1985).

But when corporate research labs evolved into a more progressive role, as they often did whatever the original intentions, more often than not their success took the form of new product development. The flow of new products often seemed to be driven by the internal logic of a technological trajectory, but their commercial success was unavoidably linked to the tastes and budgets of American households. The era from the 1920s to the 1960s gave rise to the theory of the "product cycle," according to which new products developed first in the United States because they drew upon new scientific knowledge, but also because they tended to be responsive to the wants of high-income American consumers, for telephones, automobiles, refrigerators, cameras, radios, nylons, cellophane, and many other novelties. The observation that some of these demand patterns were cultural idiosyncrasies rather than income effects only underscores the inference that producer-consumer interaction intensified the national distinctiveness of the learning process.

Product-demand channels were reinforced by improved coordination between university training and the specifications of corporate employment. These systems also tended to be national in scope. The establishment of uniform standards for graduate degrees under the American Association of Universities was a self-conscious effort at network creation, as a means of enhancing the reputation and effectiveness of the university system. The institutional arrangements were peculiarly American: mass provision of undergraduate education as a means of financing research and graduate training (Geiger 1986, 17–18, 68). Close linkages between university instruction and industrial demands for trained personnel was an accepted pattern from the late nineteenth century (Rosenberg and Nelson 1994). In the 1920s, the movement for technical standardization to achieve the "elimination of waste in materials" spilled over into formalized systems to define employee qualifications and job specifications, for "the elimination of waste in people" (Noble 1977, 82–83). Both sides of the exchange were nationally defined, often at considerable variance from practice in other countries. For example, curricula came to reflect the expectation that career paths in engineering would ultimately lead to positions in management, and this combination was a peculiar American specialty (Rae 1979).

Critics of American capitalism often interpret these developments as evidence of the excessive influence of large corporations on the direction of technological change and on the research and training decisions of universities. Corporate domination was never complete, however. The article by Lamoreaux and Sokoloff (chap. 1 in this volume) points to the continued vitality of independent inventors well into the twentieth century, as indicated by the registration of patents. Although the importance of in-house corporate research was on the ascendancy during the interwar period, according to David Mowery (1995) these facilities were complementary to externally contracted research services, and often functioned as a way to monitor and evaluate innovations originating elsewhere—mainly, in that era, elsewhere within the United States. At the universities, advice on employment opportunities may have been welcomed by both faculty and students, but the independence of academic research agendas and career paths is just as persistent a feature of the American tradition (Servos 1980). It would be more appropriate to say, therefore, that the interwar period was characterized by the crystallization of an advanced, internally compatible national network of innovation, within which organized corporate research was one major component. This view is quite compatible with that advanced by Leslie Hannah (chap. 7 in this volume), which suggests that the premier American corporations were not endowed with unusually long life, and seen in isolation they were more like than unlike their counterparts in other advanced nations. Much of their distinctive performance derived from their place in the dense networks of the U.S. economy.

But it is difficult to distinguish forces that may have been inherent in the drive for economic and institutional coordination, from the broader trends in the global economy during this era. The interwar years were a time of economic nationalism around the world, of disruption in the international trade and payments system, and of impending military crises that drove many countries toward self-sufficiency in technology as well as resources. Subsequently, the events of World War II pushed the United States into a position of science-based technological leadership far beyond anything that would have been generated by normal economic forces (Nelson and Wright 1992). At that time the American market was highly idiosyncratic, not just because of national tastes but because American incomes were so much higher than those of any other country in the world. With the postwar liberalization of world trade, dispersion of natural-resource supplies around the globe, and economic recovery in countries that had been devastated by the war, the extremes of national differentiation have greatly receded, increasing the degree of "technological congruence" between nations (Abramovitz and David 1996).

A more fundamental force behind the attenuation of national networks is that modern technologies increasingly draw upon science, and scientific networks are inherently international. Although the distinction between "scientific" and "nonscientific" technologies is difficult to define rigorously, the core idea is straightforward: scientific technologies draw upon general, abstract, and universal principles, as opposed to empirical observations and trial and error. Almost by definition, scientific innovations are more readily transferable from one application and one location to another (Arora and Gambardella 1994). It certainly appears that the "technology of technological change" has changed in this way, for reasons broadly associated with the evolution of organized research structures, academic and governmental as well as corporate.

Patent counts are by no means comprehensive measures of technological change, but the geographic origins of patents can give us some information about technological networks, and the evidence seems to support this view in broad terms. Between 1870 and 1930, more than 90 percent of U.S. patents were assigned to U.S. residents, with no apparent trend during this period. Between 1963 and 1968, the figure fell to 80 percent, and by the late 1970s to 60 percent. During the 1980s the share continued to fall, and in the 1990s it has stabilized at just over 50 percent. Of course these aggregate trends obscure significant variation between industries. But the trend toward internationalization seems to be strongest in those fields characterized by existence of a strong science base, and the presence of large managerial companies.[14]

This interpretation does not imply that the countries of the world are converging in every dimension into one homogeneous puree. Bruce Kogut has forcefully argued that many national institutional arrangements are far more persistent historically and less transferable than technological understanding itself. An example is what he refers to as "national organizing principles of work," a category encompassing such features as job tenure, hierarchy, job specifications, and skill acquisition (Kogut 1990, 1992). Features of the American "national innovation system" continue to be distinctive, linked to such enduring national traits and institutions as the antitrust tradition, high labor mobility and weak job attachments, a strong venture-capital sector, and independent universities and professions (Nelson 1993). If such differences are persistent, then we should expect to observe continuing national differences in the types of technologies that are developed and selected for implementation. But these observations do not gainsay the conclusion that technological networks no longer display the tight linkage between learning and national conditions that prevailed a century ago.

---

14. These figures are drawn from Cantwell (1989, 23); Pavitt (1988, 142–43); Thomson and Nelson (1996, table 1); National Science Board (1996, appendix table 6–7). The generalizations in the last sentence come from Thomson and Nelson.

References

Abramovitz, Moses, and Paul A. David. 1973. Reinterpreting Economic Growth: Parables and Realities. *American Economic Review* 63:428–39.

———. 1996. Convergence and Deferred Catch-up. In *The Mosaic of Economic Growth,* ed. Ralph Landau, Timothy Taylor, and Gavin Wright. Stanford, CA: Stanford University Press.

Allen, Robert C. 1983. Collective Invention. *Journal of Economic Behavior and Organization* 4:1–24.

Ames, Edward, and Nathan Rosenberg. 1968. The Enfield Arsenal in Theory and History. *Economic Journal* 78:827–42.

Arora, Ashish, and Alfonso Gambardella. 1994. The Changing Technology of Technological Change. *Research Policy* 23:523–32.

———. 1998. Evolution of Industry Structure in the Chemical Industry. In *Chemicals and Long-Term Economic Growth,* ed. Ashish Arora, Ralph Landau, and Nathan Rosenberg. New York: Wiley & Sons.

Arrow, Kenneth J. 1962. Economic Welfare and the Allocation of Resources for Invention. In Universities–National Bureau of Economic Research, *The Rate and Direction of Inventive Activity.* Princeton: Princeton University Press.

Arthur, W. B. 1989. Competing Technologies, Increasing Returns, and Lock-in by Historical Events. *Economic Journal* 99:116–31.

Blainey, Geoffrey. 1969. *The Rush That Never Ended: A History of Australian Mining.* 2d edition. Carlton, Victoria: Melbourne University Press.

Boot, H. M. 1995. How Skilled Were Lancashire Cotton Factory Workers in 1833? *Economic History Review* 48:283–303.

Bresnahan, Timothy F., and M. Trajtenberg. 1995. General Purpose Technologies: "Engines of Growth"? *Journal of Econometrics* 65:83–108.

Broadberry, Steven N. 1993. Manufacturing and the Convergence Hypothesis. *Journal of Economic History* 53:772–95.

———. 1994a. Comparative Productivity in British and American Manufacturing during the Nineteenth Century. *Explorations in Economic History* 31:521–48.

———. 1994b. Technological Leadership and Productivity Leadership in Manufacturing since the Industrial Revolution. *Economic Journal* 104:291–302.

Bruce, Robert V. 1987. *The Launching of Modern American Science, 1846–1876.* New York: Knopf.

Calvert, Monte. 1967. *The Mechanical Engineer in America, 1830–1910.* Baltimore: Johns Hopkins University Press.

Cantwell, John. 1989. *Technological Innovation and Multinational Corporations.* Oxford: Basil Blackwell.

Catling, Harold. 1970. *The Spinning Mule.* Reprint. Todmorden: Lancashire Library, 1986.

Chandler, Alfred D., Jr. 1977. *The Visible Hand.* Cambridge, MA: Belknap Press.

———. 1994. The Competitive Performance of U.S. Industrial Enterprises since the Second World War. *Business History Review* 68 (spring): 1–72.

Christy, Samuel B. 1893. Growth of American Mining Schools and Their Relation to the Mining Industry. *Transactions of the American Institute of Mining Engineers* 23:444–65.

Clark, Gregory. 1987. Why Isn't the Whole World Developed? *Journal of Economic History* 47:141–73.

Constant, Edward. 1983. Scientific Theory and Technological Testability: Science, Dynamometers, and Water Turbines in the Nineteenth Century. *Technology and Culture* 24:183–98.

Copeland, M. T. 1909–10. Technical Development in Cotton Manufacturing since 1860. *Quarterly Journal of Economics* 24:109–59.

David, Paul A. 1974. *Technical Choice, Innovation, and Economic Growth.* New York: Cambridge University Press.

———. 1985. Clio and the Economics of QWERTY. *American Economic Review* 75:332–36.

David, Paul A., and Gavin Wright. 1997. Increasing Returns and the Genesis of American Resource Abundance. *Industrial and Corporate Change,* 6 (March): 203–45.

De Waal, Enid. 1985. American Technology in South African Gold Mining before 1899. *Optima* 33:81–85.

Elliott, William Yandell, Elizabeth S. May, J. W. F. Rowe, Alex Skelton, and Donald H. Wallace. 1937. *International Control in the Non-Ferrous Metals.* New York: Macmillan.

Fay, Albert H. 1917. Census of Mining Engineers, Metallurgists, and Chemists. United States Bureau of Mines Technical Paper no. 179. Washington, DC: Government Printing Office.

Field, Alexander J. 1983. Land Abundance, Interest/Profit Rates, and Nineteenth-Century American and British Technology. *Journal of Economic History* 43:405–31.

Geiger, Ronald L. 1986. *To Advance Knowledge.* New York: Oxford University Press.

Goldin, Claudia, and Kenneth Sokoloff. 1982. Women, Children, and Industrialization in the Early Republic. *Journal of Economic History* 42:741–74.

Graham, Margaret B. W., and Bettye H. Pruitt. 1990. *R&D for Industry: A Century of Technical Innovation at Alcoa.* Cambridge: Cambridge University Press.

Granovetter, Mark. 1995. Coase Revisited: Business Groups in the Modern Economy. *Industrial and Corporate Change* 4:93–130.

Guédon, Jean-Claude. 1980. Conceptual and Institutional Obstacles to the Emergence of Unit Operations in Europe. In *History of Chemical Engineering,* ed. William F. Furter. Washington, DC: American Chemical Society.

Habakkuk, H. J. 1962. *American and British Technology in the Nineteenth Century.* Cambridge: Cambridge University Press.

Harley, C. K. 1974. Skilled Labor and the Choice of Technique in Edwardian Industry. *Explorations in Economic History* 11:391–414.

———. 1992. International Competitiveness of the Antebellum American Cotton Textile Industry. *Journal of Economic History* 52:559–84.

Hendrickson, Walter B. 1961. Nineteenth-Century State Geological Surveys: Early Government Support for Science. *Isis* 52:357–71.

Hoke, Donald R. 1990. *Imperious Yankees: The Rise of the American System of Manufactures in the Private Sector.* New York: Columbia University Press.

Hoover, Herbert C. 1909. *Principles of Mining.* New York: Hill.

Hounshell, David A. 1984. *From the American System to Mass Production, 1800–1932.* Baltimore: Johns Hopkins University Press.

———. 1992. Continuity and Change in the Management of Industrial Research: The Du Pont Company, 1902–1980. In *Technology and Enterprise in a Historical Perspective,* ed. G. Dosi, R. Giannetti, and Pier Angelo Toninelli. Oxford: Clarendon Press.

Hounshell, David A., and John Kenly Smith, Jr. 1988. *Science and Corporate Strategy: Du Pont R&D, 1902–1980.* Cambridge: Cambridge University Press.

International Federation of Master Cotton Spinners' and Manufacturers' Associations. 1908. *Official Report of the Fifth Annual Congress.* Manchester, England: International Federation of Master Cotton Spinners' and Manufacturers' Associations.

Israel, Paul. 1992. *From Machine Shop to Industrial Laboratory.* Baltimore: Johns Hopkins University Press.

Jaffe, Adam B., Manuel Trajtenberg, and Rebecca Henderson. 1993. Geographic Localization of Knowledge Spillovers as Evidenced by Patent Citations. *Quarterly Journal of Economics* 108:577–98.

Katz, Michael L., and Carl Shapiro. 1994. Systems Competition and Network Effects. *Journal of Economic Perspectives* 8:93–115.

Kennedy, Paul. 1987. *The Rise and Fall of the Great Powers.* New York: Random House.

Kogut, Bruce. 1990. The Permeability of Borders and the Speed of Learning among Countries. In *Globalization of Firms and the Competitiveness of Nations,* ed. John H. Dunning, Bruce Kogut, and Magnus Blomström. Lund, Sweden: Lund University Press.

———. 1992. National Organizing Principles of Work and the Erstwhile Dominance of the American Multinational Corporation. *Industrial and Corporate Change* 1: 285–325.

Landau, Ralph, and Nathan Rosenberg. 1992. Successful Commercialization in the Chemical Process Industries. In *Technology and the Wealth of Nations,* ed. Ralph Landau, David Mowery, and Nathan Rosenberg. Stanford, CA: Stanford University Press.

Lasky, S. G. 1950. How Tonnage and Grade Relations Help Predict Ore Reserves. *Engineering and Mining Journal* 151:81–85.

Layton, Edwin T. 1979. Scientific Technology, 1845–1900: The Hydraulic Turbine and the Origins of American Industrial Research. *Technology and Culture* 20:64–89.

Lazonick, William. 1981. Production Relations, Labor Productivity, and the Choice of Technique: British and US Cotton Spinning. *Journal of Economic History* 41: 491–516.

Leong, Y. S., Emil Erdreich, J. C. Burritt, O. E. Kiessling, C. E. Nighman, and George C. Heikes. 1940. Technology, Employment, and Output per Man in Copper Mining. Works Projects Administration, National Research Project, with Department of the Interior, Bureau of Mines. Report E-12. Philadelphia, February.

Levenstein, Margaret. 1995. Mass Production Conquers the Pool. *Journal of Economic History* 55: 575–611.

Lozier, John William. 1986. *Taunton and Mason: Cotton Machinery and Locomotive Manufacture in Taunton, Massachusetts, 1811–1861.* New York: Garland.

Lundgreen, Peter. 1990. Engineering Education in Europe and the USA, 1750–1930. *Annals of Science* 47:33–75.

Maddison, Angus. 1987. Growth and Slowdown in Advanced Capitalist Economies. *Journal of Economic Literature* 25:649–98.

———. 1991. *Dynamic Forces in Capitalist Development.* Oxford: Oxford University Press.

Manning, Thomas G. 1967. *Government in Science: The U.S. Geological Survey, 1867–1894.* Lexington: University of Kentucky Press.

Marshall, Alfred. 1920. *Industry and Trade.* London: Macmillan.

McMath, Robert C., Jr. 1985. *Engineering the New South: Georgia Tech, 1885–1985.* Athens: University of Georgia Press.

Misa, Thomas J. 1985. The Changing Market for Chemical Knowledge. *History and Technology* 2:245–68.

———. 1995. *A Nation of Steel.* Baltimore: Johns Hopkins University Press.

More, Charles. 1980. *Skill and the English Working Class, 1870–1914.* London: Croom Helm.

Mowery, David C. 1995. The Boundaries of the U.S. Firm in R&D. In *Coordination and Information,* ed. Naomi R. Lamoreaux and Daniel M. G. Raff. Chicago: University of Chicago Press.

Mowery, David C., and Nathan Rosenberg. 1989. *Technology and the Pursuit of Economic Growth.* Cambridge: Cambridge University Press.

National Science Board. 1996. *Science and Engineering Indicators.* Washington, DC: Government Printing Office.

Nelson, Richard R., ed. 1993. *National Innovation Systems: A Comparative Analysis.* New York: Oxford University Press.

Nelson, Richard R., and Gavin Wright. 1992. The Rise and Fall of American Technological Leadership. *Journal of Economic Literature* 30:1931–64.

Nobel Foundation Directory. 1995–96. Stockholm: Nobel Foundation.

Noble, David F. 1977. *America by Design.* New York: Oxford University Press.

Ochs, Kathleen H. 1992. The Rise of the American Mining Engineers: A Case Study of the Colorado School of Mines. *Technology and Culture* 33:278–301.

Olmstead, Alan, and Paul Rhode. 1993. Induced Innovation in American Agriculture: A Reconsideration. *Journal of Political Economy* 101:100–118.

Owen, Edgar Wesley. 1975. *The Trek of the Oil Finders: A History of Exploration for Petroleum.* Tulsa: American Association of Petroleum Geologists.

Parsons, A. B. 1933. *The Porphyry Coppers.* New York: American Institute of Mining and Metallurgical Engineers.

Paul, Rodman Wilson. 1960. Colorado as a Pioneer of Science in the Mining West. *Mississippi Valley Historical Review* 47:34–50.

Pavitt, Keith. 1988. International Patterns of Technological Accumulation. In *Strategies in Global Competition,* ed. Neil Hoad and Jan-Erik Vahlne. London: Croom Helm.

Price, Derek J. De Solla. 1963. *Little Science, Big Science.* New York: Columbia University Press.

Przeworski, Joanne Fox. 1980. *The Decline of the Copper Industry in Chile and the Entrance of North American Capital, 1870–1916.* New York: Arno Press.

Pursell, Carroll. 1972. Science and Industry. In *Nineteenth-Century American Science: A Reappraisal,* ed. George H. Daniels. Evanston: Northwestern University Press.

Rae, John. 1979. The Application of Science to Industry. In *The Organization of Knowledge in Modern America, 1860–1920,* ed. Alexandra Oleson and John Voss. Baltimore: Johns Hopkins University Press.

Read, Thomas Thornton. 1941. *The Development of Mineral Industry Education in the United States.* New York: American Institute of Mining and Metallurgical Engineers.

Reich, Leonard S. 1985. *The Making of American Industrial Research.* Cambridge: Cambridge University Press.

Romer, Paul M. 1986. Increasing Returns and Long-Run Growth. *Journal of Political Economy* 94:1002–37.

———. 1990. Endogenous Technological Change. *Journal of Political Economy* 98: S71–S102.

———. 1996. Why Indeed in America? Theory, History, and the Origins of Modern Economic Growth. *American Economic Review* 86:202–6.

Rosenberg, Nathan. 1963. Technological Change in the Machine Tool Industry, 1840–1910. *Journal of Economic History* 23:414–43.

———. [1981] 1995. Why in America? In *Exploring the Black Box.* Cambridge: Cambridge University Press.

———. 1985. The Commercial Exploitation of Science by American Industry. In *The Uneasy Alliance,* ed. K. B. Clark, R. B. Hayes, and C. Lorenz. Boston: Harvard Business School Press.

———. 1998. Chemical Engineering as a General Purpose Technology. In *General Purpose Technologies and Economic Growth,* ed. Elhanan Helpman. Cambridge: MIT Press.

Rosenberg, Nathan, and Richard R. Nelson. 1994. American Universities and Technical Advance in Industry. *Research Policy* 23:323–48.

Sandberg, Lars. 1974. *Lancashire in Decline.* Columbus: Ohio State University Press.

Saxonhouse, Gary, and Gavin Wright. 1984. Rings and Mules around the World. In *Technique, Spirit, and Form in the Making of the Modern Economies: Essays in Honor of William N. Parker,* ed. Gary Saxonhouse and Gavin Wright. Research in Economic History, Supp. 3. Greenwich, CT: JAI Press.

Schmitz, Christopher J. 1979. *World Non-Ferrous Metal Production and Prices, 1700–1976.* London: Cass.

———. 1986. The Rise of Big Business in the World Copper Industry, 1870–1930. *Economic History Review* 39:392–410.

———. 1995. The World's Largest Industrial Companies of 1912. *Business History* 37:85–96.

Schoenemann, Karl. 1980. Chemical Engineering in Germany. In *History of Chemical Engineering,* ed. William F. Furter. Washington, DC: American Chemical Society.

Servos, John W. 1980. The Industrial Relations of Science: Chemical Engineering at MIT, 1900–1939. *Isis* 71:531–49.

Sokoloff, Kenneth L. 1984. Was the Transition from the Artisanal Shop to the Non-Mechanized Factory Associated with Gains in Efficiency? *Explorations in Entrepreneurial History* 21: 351–82.

———. 1988. Inventive Activity in Early America: Evidence from Patent Records. *Journal of Economic History* 48:813–50.

Soros, John W. 1980. The Industrial Relations of Science: Chemical Engineering at MIT, 1900–1939. *Isis* 71:531–49.

Spence, Clark C. 1970. *Mining Engineers and the American West, 1849–1933.* New Haven: Yale University Press.

Spitz, Peter H. 1988. *Petrochemicals: The Rise of an Industry.* New York: Wiley & Sons.

Stokes, R. G. 1994. *Opting for Oil.* Cambridge: Cambridge University Press.

Teece, David J. 1992. Strategies for Capturing the Financial Benefits from Technological Innovation. In *Technology and the Wealth of Nations,* ed. Nathan Rosenberg, Ralph Landau, and David C. Mowery. Stanford, CA: Stanford University Press.

Temin, Peter. 1966. Labor Scarcity and the Problem of American Industrial Efficiency in the 1850s. *Journal of Economic History* 26:277–98.

———. 1988. Product Quality and Vertical Integration in the Early Cotton Textile Industry. *Journal of Economic History* 48:891–907.

Thomson, Ross. 1989. *The Path to Mechanized Shoe Production in the United States.* Chapel Hill: University of North Carolina Press.

———. 1993. Economic Forms of Technological Change. In *Learning and Technological Change,* ed. Ross Thomson. New York: St. Martin's.

Thomson, Ross, and Richard R. Nelson. 1996. The Internationalization of Technology, 1874–1929. Paper presented to the annual meetings of the Economic History Association.

Trescott, Martha Moore. 1981. *The Rise of the American Electrochemicals Industry, 1880–1910.* Westport, CT: Greenwood Press.

———. 1982. Unit Operations in the Chemical Industry. In *A Century of Chemical Engineering,* ed. William F. Furter. New York: Plenum Press.

Weber, Harold. 1980. The Improbable Achievement: Chemical Engineering at MIT. In *History of Chemical Engineering,* ed. William F. Furter. Washington, DC: American Chemical Society.

Williamson, Harold F., Ralph Andreano, Arnold R. Daum, and Gilbert C. Klose. 1963. *The American Petroleum Industry: The Age of Energy.* Evanston: Northwestern University Press.

Wilson, A. J. 1992. *The Professionals: The Institute of Mining and Metallurgy, 1892–1992.* London: Institute of Mining and Metallurgy.

Wise, George. 1980. A New Role for Professional Scientists in Industry. *Technology and Culture* 21:408–29.
Wright, Gavin. 1986. *Old South, New South.* New York: Basic Books.
———. 1990. The Origins of American Industrial Success, 1879–1940. *American Economic Review* 80:651–68.

Comment   Alexander J. Field

Research in economic history and administrative service in a university motivate both practical and scholarly interest in organizational persistence and dynamics. This conference has reinforced my belief in the value of an evolutionary perspective for understanding these phenomena. Such a perspective draws an analogy between the influence of environmental forces on the survival of organisms in biological populations, and corresponding processes affecting the persistence of organizations. There is one key difference, however, between natural selection as it occurs in the world of plants and animals and its functioning among organizations. This difference concerns the role of mutations, which in the biological context are largely random while in the organizational context are the results of specific human intervention.

In a rapidly changing environment, a new strategic departure may enable a firm to persist or grow. But if the nature of the environmental change is misperceived, or misforecast, or if the costs and benefits of the mutation are improperly estimated, such initiatives can create problems and in the worst case prove disastrous for the firm or organization because they will draw financial resources and administrative attention away from its core activities: those activities that exploit the differential capabilities that have given the firm its competitive advantage.

There has been so much written about the challenges of overcoming inertia that some leaders might be forgiven for thinking that their job was simply to maximize the rate of organizational mutation. This conclusion, of course, makes no more sense than a public-policy recommendation that we should increase the irradiation of the human population on the grounds that some of the resultant genetic changes might be evolutionarily adaptive. The challenge of organizational leadership is to establish a framework in which the ability of an organization to survive and prosper (its evolutionary fitness) and its ability to adapt to changing environmental influences (the two go hand in hand in a dynamic context) can be sustained. David Hounshell's discussion (chap. 5) of a key meeting at the Ford Motor Company in 1949 is a detailed dissection of such a critical meeting. Major strategic departures can save an organization,

Alexander J. Field is the Michel and Mary Orradre Professor of Economics at Santa Clara University.

and we can only marvel at the adroitness with which Microsoft, in a very short time period, reoriented its strategy around the Internet. But bold departures can also come close to destroying an organization, if they do not prove evolutionarily adaptive. A case in point is Sears's entry into the real-estate and stock-brokerage businesses in the early 1980s, discussed in the paper by Daniel Raff and Peter Temin (chap. 6). In retrospect (it is of course easy to be a Monday-morning quarterback), Sears might have been better advised to stick to its retailing knitting, aggressively taking advantage of the new inventory-control, logistical, and point-of-sale opportunities created by advances in information technology, a policy it now appears to be following.

The Sears experience is a reminder that formal planning processes *alone* will not guarantee evolutionarily favorable outcomes. Indeed, in the 1980s, extensive multiparticipant strategic planning exercises appear, ex post, to have resulted in worse decisions than was true of the largely autocratic process of the 1920s, in which General (Robert) Wood, with the approval of only one other individual (the CEO) brilliantly set up retail establishments away from the center city in a manner that built on the organization's success as a mail-order firm and effectively (for a time) met the challenge of the automobile. What counts ultimately is the respective logic and analyses that underlie these decisions.

The evolutionary perspective is useful in helping us understand why organizations persist, and how we can influence the probability that they do. But in this context, it is also worth stepping back and reflecting on why we care. There are usually strong individual incentives for managers to maintain the viability of firms, and bankruptcy and firm shutdown incur clear personal costs. But why, from a social perspective, does it matter? After all, physical capital and personnel don't disappear just because an organization ceases functioning. Evolutionary theory helps us understand why we do and should care. First, when a successful organization emerges, it does so by stitching together resources and people in a manner that gives the entity collective capabilities that exceed the sum of the capabilities of the individuals, even if each of the firm's members were given a per capita share of the resources. These superior collective capabilities are what give the successful firm its evolutionary advantage. Some of this advantage results from indivisibilities in physical capital, giving rise to economies of scale, but much also comes from investment in both processes and knowledge. Some of these investments have limited value outside the organization.

Another way of thinking about investments in firm-specific capital is that they are the embodiment of the firm's particular history and culture. This knowledge, although valuable internally, is largely worthless outside of the firm. Enabling a firm to persist and prosper means that organization-specific resources—knowledge, processes, personnel—can continue to be effectively utilized. There is inevitably value lost—often substantial—when an entity is dismantled and its component parts (those with value outside the dismantling firm) redeployed. In extreme cases this is a necessary, even salutary, development. More often, it is a symptom of managerial failure.

The acquisition of organizational knowledge and capability is important even in a technologically stable environment. In Kazuhiro Mishina's paper (chap. 4 in this volume), for example, a clear argument is made that, in the case of the dramatic reductions in the costs of producing the Boeing B-17 bomber, the most critical learning took place among networks of managers as they discovered how to organize production, both physically and temporally, in the context of a dramatic and mandated increase in the speed of throughput. From the strict standpoint of aeronautical, mechanical, and electrical engineering, the technology underlying the production of the bomber had not altered, although the cost of manufacturing one fell dramatically.

Engineering breakthroughs that enable firms to move rapidly out along supply curves are sources of cost reduction more familiar to economic historians. Gavin Wright's innovation lies in insisting that we expand the scope for discussion of such learning from the individual firm to the nation. Focusing particularly on cotton textiles, mining, and chemical engineering, Wright identifies a number of national characteristics: antitrust, high labor mobility and weak job attachment, a strong venture-capital sector, and independent universities and professions that underlay and, perhaps to an attenuated degree, still underlie American *technological networks*. These networks, consistent with the complementary existence of large and small technology-based companies, provide the institutional underpinnings for talking about national technological styles, and perhaps national competitive advantages. Wright titles his paper "Can a Nation Learn?" but it is also about whether it is meaningful to talk about nations as economic actors, with distinctive technological personalities and capabilities that are more than the sum of the individual capabilities of firms and organizations.

On the general conceptual question, of course Wright is right: at the national level there is knowledge and learning that permits citizens collectively to accomplish more than if they were not stitched together by this specific human capital. An obvious example in many countries consists of language. An enormous amount of effort takes place in our educational systems to teach students spelling, the meaning of words, the rules of grammar, with the objective of turning out individuals who are effective oral and written communicators. That knowledge is of course valuable and enabling to the degree that others share it. It may not be valuable outside of the country or linguistic region, just as firm-specific knowledge may have little value outside of one organization.

In fact Wright elevates language to a more general metaphor describing learning at the national level in chemical engineering, geology, and the sciences of mining and mineral extraction. Through an infrastructure of governmental and educational institutions, the Geological Survey office and schools of mines at Berkeley, Colorado, and Columbia, for example, a language for thinking about mineral exploitation spread across the country in a way that enabled America, far more effectively than other regions similarly endowed with resources, to achieve world leadership. Americans insisted on their own names for geological strata, to the consternation of European scientists, but there is more to this than simple chauvinism. It had the effect of differentiating and protecting a particular style or network of national communication and learning, a network that gave the country differential capabilities. Here are examples in which it is meaningful to speak of collective capabilities that extended beyond the individual firm although not necessarily beyond the regional or national boundary.

Wright suggests toward the end of his paper that the importance of nations as loci for technological learning has diminished with the increasing dominance of science-based technologies, and that such learning at the end of the twentieth century is far more likely to take place on a transnational scale. Certainly the data cited on trends in the share of U.S. patents of domestic origin supports this view. But what of more localized, regionally based learning networks?

It may be useful to consider Alfred Marshall's description of external economies, surely motivated by the economic experience of places such as the Manchester-Liverpool conurbation or the networks of metalworking expertise in the Birmingham area. Small and medium-sized firms clustered together because they benefited from the easy interchange of ideas and personnel. Marshall (1920, 237) believed that the relative importance of external economies was increasing.

> For External economies are constantly growing in importance relatively to Internal in all matters of Trade-knowledge: newspapers, and trade and technical publications of all kinds are perpetually scouting for him and bringing him much of the knowledge he wants—knowledge which a little while ago would have been beyond the reach of anyone who could not afford to have well-paid agents in many distant places. Again, it is to his interest also that the secrecy of business is on the whole diminishing, and that the most important improvements in method seldom remain secret for long after they have passed from the experimental stage. It is to his [the small manufacturer's] advantage that changes in manufacture depend less on mere rules of thumb and more on broad developments of scientific principle: and that many of these are made by students in the pursuit of knowledge for its own sake, and are promptly published in the general interest.

Note that Marshall attributes the growing importance of external economies to the increased dominance of science-based over experiential learning. For Wright, the impact of that trend is less clear, in the late nineteenth century appearing to foster national technological networks, but in the twentieth to coincide with the migration of technological change into the orbits of either in-house R&D labs or more global learning networks. Although the Marshallian mechanisms described are similar to those in Wright's paper, Marshall's insights seem to have been motivated by more regionally localized learning than is the case for Wright. Partly this is because the former's ideas represented to a greater degree a distillation of the history of the more geographically compact British experience, whereas the latter's insights are more directly conditioned by studies of U.S. economic history.

Whether or not "national" learning has been largely supplanted by global networks, the kind of highly localized phenomena that gave rise to Marshall's insights about external economies are alive and well in the late twentieth century in the United States, as is clear to anyone living amid the booming Silicon Valley economy (this is written in spring of 1997). In spite of the great difficulty and high cost of finding commercial real estate, apartments, storage lockers, personnel, and so forth, many companies still desperately want to be close to the action. Marshall's description of external economies was put forth in some sense precisely to account for what Wright describes: an economy or sector marked by the complementary coexistence of large and small firms associated with an industry structure characterized by lack of dominance by large firms, high labor mobility, and weak job attachments. It would be hard to find a better description of the current organization of Silicon Valley software, semiconductor, mass storage, and networking hardware sectors.

Wright, however, describes networks of learning with greater geographic reach. His focus is explicitly on the emerging industries of the late nineteenth century, with their greater reliance on science and research conducted by professionally trained personnel. Thus Wright's emphasis on the role of independent universities and professions. In this context, the much greater geographic dispersion of American universities and in particular their lack of concentration in the national capital may help in understanding differences in national styles of learning, comparing the United States say with British or European counterparts. Most of the comparative references in the current version of the paper apply to Britain: more comparative study of the French and German cases might be useful.

How much of what Wright describes for the late nineteenth century is historically specific, reflecting, perhaps, the golden age of the consulting engineer? To what degree did the increased importance of organized, firm-funded R&D laboratories lead (contrary to Marshall) to a greater emphasis on secrecy, appropriability of investments in R&D, and a restriction on the freer flow of information through professional networks described here? Steven Usselman's paper (chap. 2 in this volume) describes, for example, the way the railroad industry attempted to canalize research effort in areas anticipated to be complementary to the national network being operated, and shut down or discouraged inquiry in areas viewed as likely to be unproductive or even to threaten the established technological paradigm.

Has the integration of research into more formalized R&D labs during the twentieth century meant that the more democratic style of research described by Wright is shut down? Is this trend counterbalanced by the emergence of "global academies" of scientific and professional communities interacting through international conferences, email, and scientific publication? R&D spending today is heavily concentrated in a small number of sectors: aeronautics, chemicals, instrumentation, electrical machinery, and so forth. Has this pattern remained relatively stable over time? Is it the case that, while the importance of professional networks has declined in some sectors, it has increased in others? Do more industries come to resemble what Usselman describes for railroads at the turn of the century? Or is there no real trend? Questions such as these are crucial for further research.

Reference

Marshall, Alfred. 1920. *Principles of economics.* 8th edition. London: Macmillan.

Contributors

Jeremy Atack
Department of Economics
415 Calhoun Hall
Vanderbilt University
Nashville, TN 37235

Alexander J. Field
Department of Economics
Kenna Hall 300-M
Santa Clara University
Santa Clara, CA 95053

David Genesove
Department of Economics
Room E52-380A
Massachusetts Institute of Technology
50 Memorial Drive
Cambridge, MA 02139

Leslie Hannah
City University Business School
Frobisher Crescent
Barbican Center
London EC2Y 8HB England

David A. Hounshell
Department of History
Carnegie Mellon University
Pittsburgh, PA 15213

Adam B. Jaffe
Department of Economics
Brandeis University
Waltham, MA 02254

Bruce Kogut
Department of Management
The Wharton School
University of Pennsylvania
Philadelphia, PA 19104

Naomi R. Lamoreaux
Department of Economics
University of California
405 Hilgard Avenue
Los Angeles, CA 90095

Margaret Levenstein
Department of Economics
Lorch Hall
University of Michigan
Ann Arbor, MI 48109

Thomas J. Misa
Department of Humanities
Illinois Institute of Technology
Chicago, IL 60616

Kazuhiro Mishina
Japan Advanced Institute of Science
    and Technology
15 Asahidai
Tatsunokuchi, Ishikawa
Japan 923-12

Wallace P. Mullin
Department of Economics
101 Marshall Hall
Michigan State University
East Lansing, MI 48824

Daniel M. G. Raff
Department of Management
The Wharton School
University of Pennsylvania
Philadelphia, PA 19104

Kenneth L. Sokoloff
Department of Economics
University of California
405 Hilgard Avenue
Los Angeles, CA 90095

Peter Temin
Department of Economics
Room E52-280A
Massachusetts Institute of Technology
50 Memorial Drive
Cambridge, MA 02139

Ross Thomson
Department of Economics
University of Vermont
479 Main Street
Burlington, VT 05405

Steven W. Usselman
School of History, Technology, and
   Society
Georgia Institute of Technology
Atlanta, GA 30332

Sidney G. Winter
Department of Management
The Wharton School
2000SH-DH
Philadelphia, PA 19104

Gavin Wright
Department of Economics
Stanford University
Stanford, CA 94305

Name Index

Abell, Rollin, 52
Abernathy, Frederick H., 242
Abramovitz, Moses, 4, 14n8, 296, 299, 313, 319
Aero Digest, 160
Air Materiel Command, 149, 160, 165, 167n29, 169n30, 176
Albert, Bill, 114n21
Alchian, Armen A., 145, 151n11, 153, 160nn18, 19
Alexander, Barbara, 131
Alford, B. W. E., 262
Allen, Robert, 304
Allison, Graham T., 209, 211n5
Ames, Edward, 300
Amsden, Alice H., 290
Anderson, P., 200n48
Andress, F., 147
Anthony, Robert, 203
Argote, L., 169, 171, 175
Armour, H. O., 274n36
Arora, Ashish, 317, 320
Arrow, Kenneth J., 20, 170n34, 199, 200, 304
Arthur, W. B., 296n1
Asher, H., 151n11, 173
Ashley, William J., 2
Atack, Jeremy, 93n6, 96t
Avery, Sewell, 250n1
Aviation, 155n13, 166; 165

Bachelder, Asahel, 99–100
Baker, Jonathan B., 132
Baker, William R., 44

Ballou, Judge, 119–20
Baloff, N., 173
Bateman, Fred, 96t
Beall, W. E., 157n15
Beckman, S. L., 169, 171, 175
Berner, Robert, 245n12
Biggs, Lindy, 196n35
Blainey, Geoffrey, 311
Boardman, H. W., and Company, 24n7
Boot, H. M., 302n4
Boston Consulting Group, 147
Bowers, P. M., 157nn15, 17, 159f, 162
Brand, Donald, 131
Breech, Ernest R., 188–89, 193–95, 197, 200, 202, 212, 214
Brennan, Edward, 234
Bresnahan, Timothy, 315n13
Bright, James R., 205n55
Broadberry, S. N., 264, 266, 267n27, 274, 298, 300
Brown, Donaldson, 203
Brown, John K., 68n20
Bruce, Robert V., 306, 308–9
Brueckner, Jan, 93n6
Brush, Thomas, 181
Bucey, B. K., 164, 165
Bugas, John S., 197
Byrne, John A., 202n50, 204n52

Cable, John, 274n36
Calhoun, Daniel H., 83n56
Calvert, Monte, 305n6
Cantwell, John, 320n14

Subject Index